CONNECT FEATURES

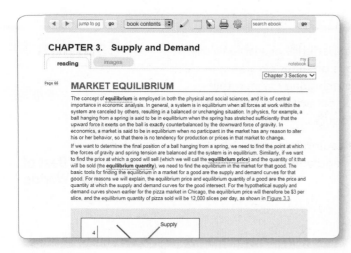

eBook

Connect includes a media-rich eBook that allows you to share your notes with your students. Your students can insert and review their own notes, highlight the text, search for specific information, and interact with media resources. Using an eBook with Connect gives your students a complete digital solution that allows them to access their materials from any computer.

Tegrity

Make your classes available anytime, anywhere. With simple, one-click recording, students can search for a word or phrase and be taken to the exact place in your lecture that they need to review.

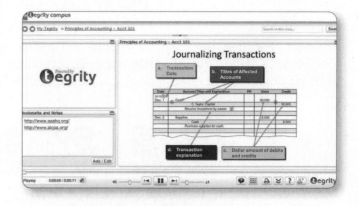

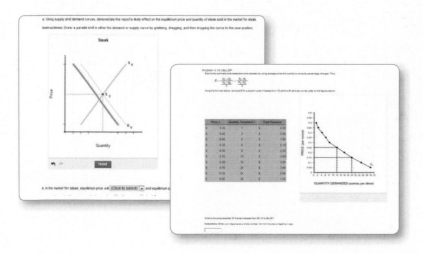

Graphing Tool

The graphing tool within Connect Economics provides opportunities for students to draw, interact with, manipulate, and analyze graphs in their online auto-graded assignments as they would with paper and pencil. The Connect graphs are identical in presentation to the graphs in the book, so students can easily relate their assignments to their reading material.

EASY TO USE

Learning Management System Integration

McGraw-Hill Campus is a one-stop teaching and learning experience available to use with any learning management system. McGraw-Hill Campus provides single sign-on to faculty and students for all McGraw-Hill material and technology from within the school website. McGraw-Hill Campus also allows instructors instant access to all supplements and teaching materials for all McGraw-Hill products.

Blackboard users also benefit from McGraw-Hill's industry-leading integration, providing single sign-on to access all Connect assignments and automatic feeding of assignment results to the Blackboard grade book.

The **Best** of **Both Worlds**

POWERFUL REPORTING

Connect generates comprehensive reports and graphs that provide instructors with an instant view of the performance of individual students, a specific section, or multiple sections. Since all content is mapped to learning objectives, Connect reporting is ideal for accreditation or other administrative documentation.

At a Glance Insights | Assignment Results & Statistics Reports | Student Performance Reports | Item Analysis Reports | Category Analysis Reports | At-Risk Student Reports | LearnSmart Reports

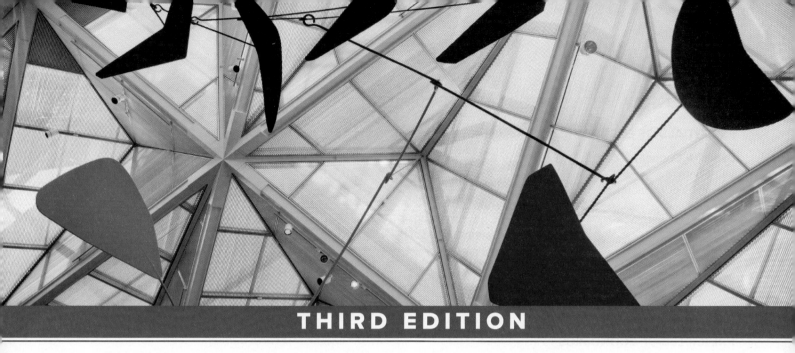

THIRD EDITION

Principles of
MICROECONOMICS
A STREAMLINED APPROACH

THE McGRAW-HILL SERIES IN ECONOMICS

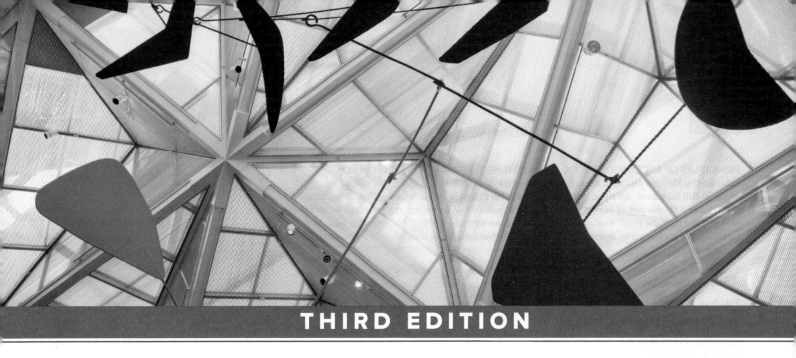

THIRD EDITION

Principles of
MICROECONOMICS
A STREAMLINED APPROACH

ROBERT H. FRANK

Cornell University

BEN S. BERNANKE

Brookings Institution [affiliated]
Former Chairman, Board of Governors of the Federal Reserve System

KATE ANTONOVICS

University of California, San Diego

ORI HEFFETZ

Cornell University

Mc
Graw
Hill
Education

ABOUT THE AUTHORS

ROBERT H. FRANK

Robert H. Frank is the H. J. Louis Professor of Management and Professor of Economics at Cornell's Johnson School of Management, where he has taught since 1972. His "Economic View" column appears regularly in *The New York Times*. He is a Distinguished Senior Fellow at Demos. After receiving his B.S. from Georgia Tech in 1966, he taught math and science for two years as a Peace Corps Volunteer in rural Nepal. He received his M.A. in statistics in 1971 and his Ph.D. in economics in 1972 from The University of California at Berkeley. During leaves of absence from Cornell, he has served as chief economist for the Civil Aeronautics Board (1978–1980), a Fellow at the Center for Advanced Study in the Behavioral Sciences (1992–93), Professor of American Civilization at l'École des Hautes Études en Sciences Sociales in Paris (2000–01), and the Peter and Charlotte Schoenfeld Visiting Faculty Fellow at the NYU Stern School of Business in 2008–09. His papers have appeared in the *American Economic Review, Econometrica,* the *Journal of Political Economy,* and other leading professional journals.

Professor Frank is the author of a best-selling intermediate economics textbook—*Microeconomics and Behavior,* Ninth Edition (Irwin/McGraw-Hill, 2015). His research has focused on rivalry and cooperation in economic and social behavior. His books on these themes include *Choosing the Right Pond* (Oxford, 1995), *Passions Within Reason* (W. W. Norton, 1988), *What Price the Moral High Ground?* (Princeton, 2004), *Falling Behind* (University of California Press, 2007), *The Economic Naturalist* (Basic Books, 2007), *The Economic Naturalist's Field Guide* (Basic Books, 2009), and *The Darwin Economy* (Princeton, 2011), which have been translated into 22 languages. *The Winner-Take-All Society* (The Free Press, 1995), co-authored with Philip Cook, received a Critic's Choice Award, was named a Notable Book of the Year by *The New York Times,* and was included in *BusinessWeek*'s list of the 10 best books of 1995. *Luxury Fever* (The Free Press, 1999) was named to the *Knight-Ridder* Best Books list for 1999.

Professor Frank has been awarded an Andrew W. Mellon Professorship (1987–1990), a Kenan Enterprise Award (1993), and a Merrill Scholars Program Outstanding Educator Citation (1991). He is a co-recipient of the 2004 Leontief Prize for Advancing the Frontiers of Economic Thought. He was awarded the Johnson School's Stephen Russell Distinguished Teaching Award in 2004, 2010, and 2012, and the School's Apple Distinguished Teaching Award in 2005. His introductory microeconomics course has graduated more than 7,000 enthusiastic economic naturalists over the years.

BEN S. BERNANKE

Professor Bernanke received his B.A. in economics from Harvard University in 1975 and his Ph.D. in economics from MIT in 1979. He taught at the Stanford Graduate School of Business from 1979 to 1985 and moved to Princeton University in 1985, where he was named the Howard Harrison and Gabrielle Snyder Beck Professor of Economics and Public Affairs, and where he served as Chairman of the Economics Department.

Professor Bernanke was sworn in on February 1, 2006, as Chairman and a member of the Board of Governors of the Federal Reserve System—his second term expired January 31, 2014. Professor Bernanke also serves as Chairman of the Federal Open Market Committee, the Fed's principal monetary policymaking body. He was appointed as a member of the Board to a full 14-year term, which expires January 31, 2020. Before his appointment as Chairman, Professor Bernanke was Chairman of the President's Council of Economic Advisers, from June 2005 to January 2006.

Professor Bernanke's intermediate textbook, with Andrew Abel and Dean Croushore, *Macroeconomics,* Eighth Edition (Addison-Wesley, 2011), is a best seller in its field. He has authored more than 50 scholarly publications in macroeconomics, macroeconomic history, and finance. He has done significant research on the causes of the Great Depression, the role of financial markets and institutions in the business cycle, and measurement of the effects of monetary policy on the economy.

Professor Bernanke has held a Guggenheim Fellowship and a Sloan Fellowship, and he is a Fellow of the Econometric Society and of the American Academy of Arts and Sciences. He served as the Director of the Monetary Economics Program of the National Bureau of Economic Research (NBER) and as a member of the NBER's Business Cycle Dating Committee. In July 2001, he was appointed editor of the *American Economic Review*. Professor Bernanke's work with civic and professional groups includes having served two terms as a member of the Montgomery Township (N.J.) Board of Education. Visit Professor Bernanke's blog at www.brookings.edu/blogs/ben-bernanke.

KATE ANTONOVICS

Professor Antonovics received her B.A. from Brown University in 1993 and her Ph.D. in economics from the University of Wisconsin in 2000. Shortly thereafter, she joined the faculty in the Economics Department at the University of California, San Diego, where she has been ever since.

Professor Antonovics is known for her superb teaching and her innovative use of technology in the classroom. Her highly popular introductory-level microeconomics course regularly enrolls over 450 students each fall. She also teaches labor economics at both the undergraduate and graduate level. In 2012, she received the UCSD Department of Economics award for best undergraduate teaching.

Professor Antonovics's research has focused on racial discrimination, gender discrimination, affirmative action, intergenerational income mobility, learning, and wage dynamics. Her papers have appeared in the *American Economic Review,* the *Review of Economics and Statistics,* the *Journal of Labor Economics,* and the *Journal of Human Resources.* She is a member of both the American Economic Association and the Society of Labor Economists.

ORI HEFFETZ

Professor Heffetz received his B.A. in physics and philosophy from Tel Aviv University in 1999 and his Ph.D. in economics from Princeton University in 2005. He is an Associate Professor of Economics at the Samuel Curtis Johnson Graduate School of Management at Cornell University, where he has taught since 2005.

Bringing the real world into the classroom, Professor Heffetz has created a unique macroeconomics course that introduces basic concepts and tools from economic theory and applies them to current news and global events. His popular classes are taken by hundreds of students every year, on the Cornell Ithaca campus and, via live videoconferencing, in dozens of cities across the U.S., Canada, and beyond.

Professor Heffetz's research studies the social and cultural aspects of economic behavior, focusing on the mechanisms that drive consumers' choices and on the links between economic choices, individual well-being, and policymaking. He has published scholarly work on household consumption patterns, individual economic decision making, and survey methodology and measurement. He was a visiting researcher at the Bank of Israel during 2011, is currently a Faculty Research Fellow at the National Bureau of Economic Research (NBER), and serves on the editorial board of *Social Choice and Welfare.*

Although many millions of dollars are spent each year on introductory economics instruction in American colleges and universities, the return on this investment has been disturbingly low. Studies have shown, for example, that several months after having taken a principles of economics course, former students are no better able to answer simple economics questions than others who never even took the course. Most students, it seems, leave our introductory courses without having learned even the most important basic economic principles.

The problem, in our view, is that these courses almost always try to teach students far too much. In the process, really important ideas get little more coverage than minor ones, and everything ends up going by in a blur. The human brain tends to ignore new information unless it comes up repeatedly. That's hardly surprising, since only a tiny fraction of the terabytes of information that bombard us each day is likely to be relevant for anything we care about. Only when something comes up a third or fourth time does the brain start laying down new circuits for dealing with it.

Yet when planning their lectures, many instructors ask themselves, "How much can I cover today?" And because modern electronic media enable them to click through upwards of 100 PowerPoint slides in an hour, they feel they've better served their students the more information they've put before them. But that's not the way learning works. Professors should instead be asking, "How much can my students absorb?"

Our approach to this text was inspired by our conviction that students will learn far more if we attempt to cover much less. Our basic premise is that a small number of basic principles do most of the heavy lifting in economics, and that if we focus narrowly and repeatedly on those principles, students can actually master them in just a single semester.

The enthusiastic reactions of users of previous editions of our textbook affirm the validity of this premise. Avoiding excessive reliance on formal mathematical derivations, we present concepts intuitively through examples drawn from familiar contexts.

ADAPTING TO CLASSROOM TRENDS

Baumol's cost disease refers to the tendency for costs to rise more rapidly for goods and services for which growth in labor productivity is either slow or nonexistent. For example, it still takes four musicians to perform Beethoven's String Quartet Number 14 in C-sharp Minor today, just as when the piece debuted in 1826, even though labor productivity has risen hundreds-fold for many other goods

We are very excited to offer for the first time an entire video series based on Economic Naturalist examples not found in this edition. A series of videos covering some of our favorite micro- and macro-focused examples can be used as part of classroom presentations, or assigned for homework within Connect. All of these videos can be shared on social media to encourage students to share these fascinating and thought-provoking applications of economics in everyday life.

Active Learning Stressed

The only way to learn to hit an overhead smash in tennis is through repeated practice. The same is true for learning economics. Accordingly, we consistently introduce new ideas in the context of simple examples and then follow them with applications showing how they work in familiar settings. At frequent intervals, we pose concept checks that both test and reinforce the understanding of these ideas. The end-of-chapter questions and problems are carefully crafted to help students internalize and extend basic concepts, and are available within Connect as assignable content so that instructors can require students to engage with this material. Experience with earlier editions confirms that this approach really does prepare students to apply basic economic principles to solve economic puzzles drawn from the real world.

Modern Microeconomics

- *The cost-benefit principle, which tells us to take only those actions whose benefits exceed their costs, is the core idea behind the economic way of thinking.* Introduced in Chapter 1 and employed repeatedly thereafter, this principle is more fully developed here than in any other text. It underlies the argument for economic efficiency as an important social goal. Rather than speak of trade-offs between efficiency and other goals, we stress that maximizing economic surplus—that is, taking those actions whose benefits exceed their costs—facilitates the achievement of every goal we care about.

- One of the biggest hurdles to the fruitful application of cost-benefit thinking is to recognize and measure the relevant costs and benefits. Common decision pitfalls identified by 2002 Nobel Laureate Daniel Kahneman and others—such as the tendency to ignore implicit costs, the tendency not to ignore sunk costs, and the tendency to confuse average and marginal costs and benefits—are introduced early in Chapter 1 and invoked repeatedly in subsequent chapters.

- There is perhaps no more exciting toolkit for the economic naturalist than a few *principles of elementary game theory.* In Chapter 8, we show how these principles enable students to answer a variety of strategic questions that arise in the marketplace and everyday life. We believe that the insights of the Nobel Laureate Ronald Coase are indispensable for understanding a host of familiar laws, customs, and social norms. In Chapter 9 we show how such devices function to minimize misallocations that result from externalities.

ORGANIZATION OF THE THIRD EDITION

- **More and clearer emphasis on and repetition of basic concepts:** If we asked a thousand economists to provide their own versions of the most important economic principles, we'd get a thousand different lists. Yet to dwell on their differences would be to miss their essential similarities. It is less important to have exactly the best short list of principles than it is to use some well-thought-out list of this sort.

- **An introduction to macroeconomics:** In Chapter 3 we provide a sneak peak into macroeconomics, especially useful for students who won't move on to take this portion of the course. It provides some context around economics concepts that are widely discussed in media today like the causes and aftermath of the Great Recession and actions taken by the Fed.

- **Strong connection drawn between core concepts:** Chapter 6 makes strong connections among market equilibrium and efficiency, the cost of preventing price adjustments, economic profit, and the invisible hand theory.

- **Using economics to help make policy decisions:** Chapter 10 features important policy decisions and uses economics to sort out the best options. Health care, environmental regulation, international trade, and income redistribution are all discussed in this relevant and interesting chapter.

- **Flexible coverage of international economics:** Chapter 11 introduces the concept of comparative advantage as a basis for trade.

CHANGES IN THE THIRD EDITION

Changes Common to All Chapters

In all chapters, the narrative has been tightened and shortened slightly. Many of the examples have been updated, with a focus on examples that connect to current events such as the financial crisis of 2008 and the Great Recession of 2007–2009. The examples and exercises from the previous edition have been redesigned to provide more clarity and ease of use. A majority of the appendixes have been removed. Data have been updated throughout.

Chapter-by-Chapter Changes

- **Chapter 2:** This is Chapter 3 from the previous edition. The comparative advantage material that was in the former Chapter 2 now appears in Chapter 11.

- **Chapter 3:** New to this edition, this chapter serves as an introduction to macroeconomics for those who will not continue to take this course. It provides context around economics concepts that are widely discussed in the media.

- **Chapters 4–10:** Content and data updates have been added as needed.

- **Chapter 11:** International trade material previously in Chapter 10 has been moved here along with the opportunity cost discussion that appeared in the former Chapter 2 on comparative advantage. Production possibilities curve material has been eliminated.

ORGANIZED LEARNING IN THE THIRD EDITION

Chapter Learning Objectives

Students and professors can be confident that the organization of each chapter surrounds common themes outlined by four to seven learning objectives listed on the first page of each chapter. These objectives, along with AACSB and Bloom's Taxonomy Learning Categories,

are connected to all test bank questions and end-of-chapter material to offer a comprehensive, thorough teaching and learning experience. Reports available within Connect allow instructors to easily output data related to student performance across chapter learning objectives, AACSB criteria, and Bloom's Taxonomy Learning Categories.

Assurance of Learning Ready

Many educational institutions today are focused on the notion of assurance of learning, an important element of some accreditation standards. *Principles of Microeconomics, A Streamlined Approach, 3/e,* is designed specifically to support your assurance of learning initiatives with a simple, yet powerful, solution.

Instructors can use Connect to easily query for learning objectives that directly relate to the objectives of the course and then use the reporting features of Connect to aggregate student results in a similar fashion, making the collection and presentation of assurance of learning data simple and easy.

AACSB Statement

The McGraw-Hill Companies is a proud corporate member of AACSB International. Recognizing the importance and value of AACSB accreditation, the authors of *Principles of Microeconomics, A Streamlined Approach, 3/e,* have sought to recognize the curricula guidelines detailed in AACSB standards for business accreditation by connecting questions in the test bank and end-of-chapter material to the general knowledge and skill guidelines found in AACSB standards. It is important to note that the statements contained in *Principles of Microeconomics, A Streamlined Approach, 3/e* are provided only as a guide for the users of this text.

A NOTE ON THE WRITING OF THIS EDITION

Ben Bernanke was sworn in on February 1, 2006, as Chairman and a member of the Board of Governors of the Federal Reserve System, a position to which he was reappointed in January 2010. From June 2005 until January 2006, he served as chairman of the President's Council of Economic Advisers. These positions have allowed him to play an active role in making U.S. economic policy, but the rules of government service have restricted his ability to participate in the preparation of previous editions. Now that his second term as Chairman of the Federal Reserve is complete, we are happy to announce that Ben has been actively involved in the revision of the macro portion of the third edition.

ACKNOWLEDGMENTS

Our thanks first and foremost go to our brand manager, Katie Hoenicke, and our product developer, Christina Kouvelis. Katie encouraged us to think deeply about how to improve the book and helped us transform our ideas into concrete changes. Christina shepherded us through the revision process with intelligence, sound advice, and good humor. We are grateful as well to the production team, whose professionalism (and patience) was outstanding: Harvey Yep, content project manager; Kristin Bradley, assessment project manager; Matt Diamond, lead designer; and all of those who worked on the production team to turn our manuscript into the book you see now. Finally, we also thank Virgil Lloyd, marketing manager, and Dave O'Donnell, marketing specialist, for getting our message into the wider world.

Special thanks to Per Norander, University of North Carolina at Charlotte, for his energy, creativity, and help in refining the assessment material in both the text and Connect; Sukanya Kemp, University of Akron, for her detailed accuracy check of the learning glass videos; Anna Thompson and Eric Schulman, Cornell University, for their efforts in researching and collecting macro data updates; Alvin Angeles and team at the University of California, San Diego, for his efforts in the production and editing of the learning glass videos; and Kevin Bertotti and the team at ITVK for their creativity in transforming Economic Naturalist examples into dynamic and engaging video vignettes.

Finally, our sincere thanks to the following teachers and colleagues, whose thorough reviews and thoughtful suggestions led to innumerable substantive improvements to *Principles of Microeconomics, A Streamlined Approach, 3/e.*

Mark Abajian, *San Diego Mesa College*

Richard Agesa, *Marshall University*

Seemi Ahmad, *Dutchess Community College*

Chris Azevedo, *University of Central Missouri*

Narine Badasyan, *Murray State University*

Sigridur Benediktsdottir, *Yale University*

Brian C. Brush, *Marquette University*

Giuliana Campanelli Andreopoulos, *William Paterson University*

J. Lon Carlson, *Illinois State University*

Joni Charles, *Texas State University*

Anoshua Chaudhuri, *San Francisco State University*

Nan-Ting Chou, *University of Louisville*

Manabendra Dasgupta, *University of Alabama at Birmingham*

Craig Dorsey, *College of DuPage*

Dennis Edwards, *Coastal Carolina University*

Roger Frantz, *San Diego State University*

Mark Frascatore, *Clarkson University*

Greg George, *Macon State College*

Seth Gershenson, *Michigan State University*

Amy D. Gibson, *Christopher Newport University*

Rajeev Goel, *Illinois State University*

Susan He, *Washington State University*

John Hejkal, *University of Iowa*

Kuang-Chung Hsu, *Kishwaukee College*

Greg Hunter, *California State University–Pomona*

Derek Johnson, *University of Connecticut*

Sukanya Kemp, *University of Akron*

Brian Kench, *University of Tampa*

Fredric R. Kolb, *University of Wisconsin–Eau Claire*

Donald J. Liu, *University of Minnesota–Twin Cities*

Ida Mirzaie, *The Ohio State University*

Diego Nocetti, *Clarkson University*

Stephanie Owings, *Fort Lewis College*

Martin Pereyra, *University of Missouri*

Ratha Ramoo, *Diablo Valley College*

Bill Robinson, *University of Nevada–Las Vegas*

Brian Rosario, *University of California–Davis*

Elyce Rotella, *Indiana University*

Jeffrey Rubin, *Rutgers University*

Naveen Sarna, *Northern Virginia Community College*

Sumati Srinivas, *Radford University*

Thomas Stevens, *University of Massachusetts*

Carolyn Fabian Stumph, *Indiana University* and *Purdue University–Fort Wayne*

Markland Tuttle, *Sam Houston State University*

David Vera, *California State University–Fresno*

Nancy Virts, *California State University–Northridge*

Elizabeth Wheaton, *Southern Methodist University*

William C. Wood, *James Madison University*

DISTINGUISHING FEATURES

Economic Naturalist Examples

Each Economic Naturalist example starts with a question to spark interest in learning an answer. These examples fuel interest while teaching students to see economics in the world around them. Videos of select Economic Naturalist examples can be found within Connect.

The Economic Naturalist 1.3

Why do the keypad buttons on drive-up automated teller machines have Braille dots?

Braille dots on elevator buttons and on the keypads of walk-up automated teller machines enable blind people to participate more fully in the normal flow of daily activity. But even though blind people can do many remarkable things, they cannot drive automobiles on public roads. Why, then, do the manufacturers of automated teller machines install Braille dots on the machines at drive-up locations?

The answer to this riddle is that once the keypad molds have been manufactured, the cost of producing buttons with Braille dots is no higher than the cost of producing smooth buttons. Making both would require separate sets of molds and

---

EXAMPLE 1.1   Comparing Costs and Benefits

Should you walk downtown to save $10 on a $25 computer game?

Imagine you are about to buy a $25 computer game at the nearby campus store when a friend tells you that the same game is on sale at a downtown store for only $15. If the downtown store is a 30-minute walk away, where should you buy the game?

The Cost-Benefit Principle tells us that you should buy it downtown if the benefit of doing so exceeds the cost. The benefit of taking any action is the dollar value of everything you gain by taking it. Here, the benefit of buying downtown is exactly $10, since that's the amount you'll save on the price of the game. The cost of taking any action is the dollar value of everything you give up by taking it. Here, the cost of buying downtown is the dollar value you assign to the time and trouble it takes to make the trip. But how do we estimate that value?

Numbered Examples

Throughout the text, numbered and titled examples are referenced and called out to further illustrate concepts. With our use of engaging questions and examples from everyday life to apply economic concepts, the ultimate goal is to see that each human action is a result of an implicit or explicit cost-benefit calculation.

Concept Checks

These self-test questions in the body of the chapter enable students to determine whether the preceding material has been understood and reinforce understanding before reading further. Detailed Answers to Concept Checks are found at the end of each chapter.

CONCEPT CHECK 2.6

What will happen to the equilibrium price and quantity in the corn tortilla chip market if both of the following events occur: (1) researchers discover that a vitamin found in corn helps protect against cancer and heart disease and (2) a swarm of locusts destroys part of the corn crop?

RECAP ↑

MARKET EQUILIBRIUM

Market equilibrium, the situation in which all buyers and sellers are satisfied with their respective quantities at the market price, occurs at the intersection of the supply and demand curves. The corresponding price and quantity are called the *equilibrium price* and the *equilibrium quantity.*

Unless prevented by regulation, prices and quantities are driven toward their equilibrium values by the actions of buyers and sellers. If the price is initially too high, so that there is excess supply, frustrated sellers will cut their price in order to sell more. If the price is initially too low, so that there is excess demand, competition among buyers drives the price upward. This process continues until equilibrium is reached.

Recap

Sprinkled throughout each chapter are Recap boxes that underscore and summarize the importance of the preceding material and key concept takeaways.

SUPPLEMENTS

The following ancillaries are available for quick download and convenient access via the Instructor Resource material available through McGraw-Hill Connect®.

Solutions Manual

Prepared by the authors with assistance from Per Norander, University of North Carolina at Charlotte, this manual provides detailed answers to the end-of-chapter review questions and problems.

Test Bank

The test bank has been carefully revised and reviewed for accuracy. Hundreds of questions have been categorized by chapter learning objectives, AACSB learning categories, Bloom's Taxonomy objectives, and level of difficulty.

Computerized Test Bank

McGraw-Hill's EZ Test is a flexible and easy-to-use electronic testing program that allows you to create tests from book-specific items. It accommodates a wide range of question types and you can add your own questions. Multiple versions of the test can be created and any test can be exported for use with course management systems. EZ Test Online gives you a place to administer your EZ Test–created exams and quizzes online. Additionally, you can access the test bank through McGraw-Hill Connect.

PowerPoints

Presentation slides contain a detailed, chapter-by-chapter review of the important ideas presented in the textbook, accompanied by animated graphs and slide notes. You can edit, print, or rearrange the slides to fit the needs of your course.

Customizable Micro Lecture Notes and PowerPoints

One of the biggest hurdles to an instructor considering changing textbooks is the prospect of having to prepare new lecture notes and slides. For this microeconomics text, this hurdle no longer exists. A full set of lecture notes for *Principles of Microeconomics,* prepared by Bob Frank for his award-winning introductory microeconomics course at Cornell University, is available as Microsoft Word files that instructors are welcome to customize as they see fit. The challenge for any instructor is to reinforce the lessons of the text in lectures without generating student unrest by merely repeating what's in the book. These lecture notes address that challenge by constructing examples that run parallel to those presented in the book, yet are different from them in interesting contextual ways. Also available is a complete set of richly illustrated PowerPoint files to accompany these lecture notes. Instructors are also welcome to customize these files as they wish.

MCGRAW-HILL'S CUSTOMER EXPERIENCE GROUP

We understand that getting the most from your new technology can be challenging. That's why our services don't stop after you purchase our products. You can e-mail our Product Specialists 24 hours a day to get product training online. Or you can search our knowledge bank of Frequently Asked Questions on our support website. For Customer Support, call **800-331-5094**, or visit **www.mhhe.com/support**.

TEGRITY CAMPUS

 Tegrity Campus is a fully automated lecture capture solution used in traditional, hybrid, "flipped classes" and online courses to record lessons, lectures, and skills. Its personalized learning features make study time incredibly efficient and its ability to affordably scale brings this benefit to every student on campus. Patented search technology and real-time LMS integrations make Tegrity the market-leading solution and service.

MCGRAW-HILL CREATE

 McGraw-Hill Create™ is a self-service website that allows you to create customized course materials using McGraw-Hill's comprehensive, cross-disciplinary content and digital products. You can even access third-party content such as readings, articles, cases, videos, and more. Arrange the content you've selected to match the scope and sequence of your course. Personalize your book with a cover design and choose the best format for your students—eBook, color print, or black-and-white print. And, when you are done, you'll receive a PDF review copy in just minutes!

Required=Results

McGraw-Hill Connect®
Learn Without Limits

Connect is a teaching and learning platform that is proven to deliver better results for students and instructors.

Connect empowers students by continually adapting to deliver precisely what they need, when they need it, and how they need it, so your class time is more engaging and effective.

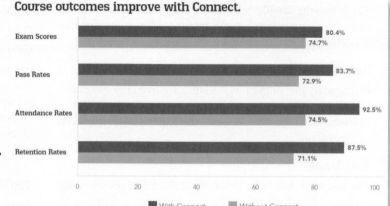

Course outcomes improve with Connect.

	With Connect	Without Connect
Exam Scores	80.4%	74.7%
Pass Rates	83.7%	72.9%
Attendance Rates	92.5%	74.5%
Retention Rates	87.5%	71.1%

■ With Connect   ■ Without Connect

Using **Connect** improves passing rates by **10.8%** and retention by **16.4%**.

88% of instructors who use **Connect** require it; instructor satisfaction **increases** by 38% when **Connect** is required.

Analytics

Connect Insight®

Connect Insight is Connect's new one-of-a-kind visual analytics dashboard—now available for both instructors and students—that provides at-a-glance information regarding student performance, which is immediately actionable. By presenting assignment, assessment, and topical performance results together with a time metric that is easily visible for aggregate or individual results, Connect Insight gives the user the ability to take a just-in-time approach to teaching and learning, which was never before available. Connect Insight presents data that empowers students and helps instructors improve class performance in a way that is efficient and effective.

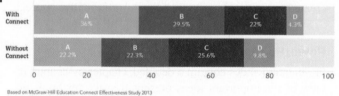

Connect helps students achieve better grades

	A	B	C	D	
With Connect	36%	29.5%	22%	4.3%	
Without Connect	22.2%	22.3%	25.6%	9.8%	

Based on McGraw-Hill Education Connect Effectiveness Study 2013

Students can view their results for any **Connect** course.

Mobile

Connect's new, intuitive mobile interface gives students and instructors flexible and convenient, anytime–anywhere access to all components of the Connect platform.

Adaptive

THE FIRST AND ONLY **ADAPTIVE READING EXPERIENCE** DESIGNED TO TRANSFORM THE WAY STUDENTS READ

More students earn **A's** and **B's** when they use McGraw-Hill Education **Adaptive** products.

SmartBook®

Proven to help students improve grades and study more efficiently, SmartBook contains the same content within the print book, but actively tailors that content to the needs of the individual. SmartBook's adaptive technology provides precise, personalized instruction on what the student should do next, guiding the student to master and remember key concepts, targeting gaps in knowledge and offering customized feedback, and driving the student toward comprehension and retention of the subject matter. Available on smartphones and tablets, SmartBook puts learning at the student's fingertips—anywhere, anytime.

Over **4 billion questions** have been answered, making McGraw-Hill Education products more intelligent, reliable, and precise.

www.learnsmartadvantage.com

STUDENTS WANT

Mc Graw Hill Education SMARTBOOK®

95% of students reported **SmartBook** to be a more effective way of reading material

100% of students want to use the Practice Quiz feature available within **SmartBook** to help them study

100% of students reported having reliable access to off-campus wifi

90% of students say they would purchase **SmartBook** over print alone

95% reported that **SmartBook** would impact their study skills in a positive way

Mc Graw Hill Education

*Findings based on a 2015 focus group survey at Pellissippi State Community College administered by McGraw-Hill Education

BRIEF CONTENTS

CONTENTS

ECONOMIC NATURALIST EXAMPLES

1.1 Why do many hardware manufacturers include more than $1,000 of "free" software with a computer selling for only slightly more than that?

1.2 Why don't auto manufacturers make cars without heaters?

1.3 Why do the keypad buttons on drive-up automatic teller machines have Braille dots?

2.1 When the federal government implements a large pay increase for its employees, why do rents for apartments located near Washington Metro stations go up relative to rents for apartments located far away from Metro stations?

2.2 Why do major term papers go through so many more revisions today than in the 1970s?

2.3 Why do the prices of some goods, like airline tickets to Europe, go up during the months of heaviest consumption, while others, like sweet corn, go down?

3.1 Is the low unemployment rate in Germany, whose government advocates austerity, evidence against Keynes's argument?

4.1 Why does California experience chronic water shortages?

4.2 Why do the wealthy in Manhattan live in smaller houses than the wealthy in Seattle?

4.3 Why did people turn to four-cylinder cars in the 1970s, only to shift back to six- and eight-cylinder cars in the 1990s?

4.4 Why are automobile engines smaller in England than in the United States?

4.5 Why are waiting lines longer in poorer neighborhoods?

4.6 Will a higher tax on cigarettes curb teenage smoking?

4.7 Why was the luxury tax on yachts such a disaster?

5.1 When recycling is left to private market forces, why are many more aluminum beverage containers recycled than glass ones?

5.2 Why are gasoline prices so much more volatile than car prices?

6.1 Why do supermarket checkout lines all tend to be roughly the same length?

6.2 Are there "too many" smart people working as corporate earnings forecasters?

7.1 Why does Intel sell the overwhelming majority of all microprocessors used in personal computers?

7.2 Why do many movie theaters offer discount tickets to students?

7.3 Why might an appliance retailer instruct its clerks to hammer dents into the sides of its stoves and refrigerators?

8.1 Why are cartel agreements notoriously unstable?

8.2 How did Congress unwittingly solve the television advertising dilemma confronting cigarette producers?

8.3 Why do people shout at parties?

8.4 Why do we often see convenience stores located on adjacent street corners?

9.1 What is the purpose of free speech laws?

9.2 Why does the government subsidize private property owners to plant trees on their hillsides?

9.3 Why do blackberries in public parks get picked too soon?

9.4 Why are shared milkshakes consumed too quickly?

9.5 Why do football players take anabolic steroids?

10.1 Why is a patient with a sore knee more likely to receive an MRI exam if he has conventional health insurance than if he belongs to a health maintenance organization?

11.1 Who benefited from and who was hurt by voluntary export restraints on Japanese automobiles in the 1980s?

11.2 What is fast track authority?

Thinking Like an Economist

LEARNING OBJECTIVES

After reading this chapter, you should be able to:

LO1 Explain why having more of any good thing almost always requires making do with less of something else.

LO2 Explain and apply the Cost-Benefit Principle, which says that an action should be taken if, but only if, its benefit is at least as great as its cost.

LO3 Discuss three important pitfalls that occur when applying the Cost-Benefit Principle inconsistently.

LO4 Explain why, if you want to predict people's behavior, a good place to start is by examining their incentives.

How many students are in your introductory economics class? Some classes have just 20 or so. Others average 35, 100, or 200 students. At some schools, introductory economics classes may have as many as 2,000 students. What size is best?

If cost were no object, the best size might be a single student. Think about it: the whole course, all term long, with just you and your professor! Everything could be custom-tailored to your own background and ability. You could cover the material at just the right pace. The tutorial format also would promote close communication and personal trust between you and your professor. And your grade would depend more heavily on what you actually learned than on your luck when taking multiple-choice exams. Let's suppose, for the sake of discussion, that students have been shown to learn best in the tutorial format.

Why, then, do so many introductory classes still have hundreds of students? The simple reason is that costs *do* matter. They matter not just to the university administrators who must build classrooms and pay faculty salaries, but also to *you*. The direct cost of providing you with your own personal introductory economics course might easily top $50,000. *Someone* has to pay these costs. In private universities, a large share of the cost would be recovered directly from higher tuition payments. In state universities, the burden would be split between higher tuition payments and higher tax payments. But, in either case, the course would be unaffordable for most students.

With larger classes, of course, the cost per student goes down. For example, an introductory economics course with 300 students might cost as little as $200 per student. But a class that large would surely compromise the quality of the learning environment. Compared to the custom tutorial format, however, it would be dramatically more affordable.

In choosing what size introductory economics course to offer, then, university administrators confront a classic economic trade-off. In making the class larger, they lower the quality of instruction—a bad thing. At the same time, they reduce costs and hence the tuition students must pay—a good thing.

In this chapter, we'll introduce some simple ideas that will help you understand and explain patterns of behavior you observe in the world around you. These principles also will help you avoid three pitfalls that plague decision makers in everyday life.

ECONOMICS: STUDYING CHOICE IN A WORLD OF SCARCITY

Even in rich societies like the United States, *scarcity* is a fundamental fact of life. There is never enough time, money, or energy to do everything we want to do or have everything we'd like to have. **Economics** is the study of how people make choices under conditions of scarcity and of the results of those choices for society.

In the class-size example just discussed, a motivated economics student might definitely prefer to be in a class of 20 rather than a class of 100, everything else being equal. But other things, of course, are not equal. Students can enjoy the benefits of having smaller classes, but only at the price of having less money for other activities. The student's choice inevitably will come down to the relative importance of competing activities.

That such trade-offs are widespread and relevant is one of the most important ideas of economics. Although we have boundless needs and wants, the resources available to us are limited. So having more of one good thing usually means having less of another.

Inherent in the idea of a trade-off is the fact that choice involves compromise between competing interests. Economists resolve such trade-offs by using cost-benefit analysis, which is based on the disarmingly simple principle that an action should be taken if, and only if, its benefits exceed its costs. We call this statement the *Cost-Benefit Principle.*

With this principle in mind, let's think about our class-size question again. Imagine that classrooms come in only two sizes—100-seat lecture halls and 20-seat classrooms—and that your university currently offers introductory economics courses to classes of 100 students. Question: Should administrators reduce the class size to 20 students? Answer: Reduce if, and only if, the value of the improvement in instruction outweighs its additional cost.

This rule sounds simple. But to apply it we need some way to measure the relevant costs and benefits, a task that's often difficult in practice. If we make a few simplifying assumptions, however, we can see how the analysis might work. On the cost side, the primary expense of reducing class size from 100 to 20 is that we'll now need five professors instead of just one. We'll also need five smaller classrooms rather than a single big one, and this too may add slightly to the expense of the move. Let's suppose that classes with 20 cost $1,000 per student more than those with 100. Should administrators switch to the smaller class size? If they apply the Cost-Benefit Principle, they will realize that *doing so makes sense only if the value of attending the smaller class is at least $1,000 per student greater than the value of attending the larger class.*

Would you (or your family) be willing to pay an extra $1,000 for a smaller class? If not, and if other students feel the same way, then sticking with the larger class size makes sense. But if you and others would be willing to pay the extra tuition, then reducing the class size makes good economic sense.

Notice that the "best" class size, from an economic point of view, will generally not be the same as the "best" size from the point of view of an educational psychologist. That's because the economic definition of "best" takes into account both the benefits *and* the costs of different class sizes. The psychologist ignores costs and looks only at the learning benefits of different class sizes.

In practice, of course, different people feel differently about the value of smaller classes. People with high incomes, for example, tend to be willing to pay more for the advantage. That helps to explain why average class size is smaller, and tuition higher, at private schools whose students come predominantly from high-income families.

The cost-benefit framework for thinking about the class-size problem also suggests a possible reason for the gradual increase in average class size that has been taking place in American colleges and universities. During the last 30 years, professors' salaries have risen sharply, making smaller classes more costly. During the same period, median family income—and hence the willingness to pay for smaller classes—has remained roughly constant. When the cost of offering smaller classes goes up but willingness to pay for smaller classes does not, universities shift to larger class sizes.

Are small classes "better" than large ones?

economics the study of how people make choices under conditions of scarcity and of the results of those choices for society

Scarcity and the trade-offs that result also apply to resources other than money. Bill Gates is one of the richest men on Earth. His wealth was once estimated at over $100 billion. That's more than the combined wealth of the poorest 40 percent of Americans. Gates could buy more houses, cars, vacations, and other consumer goods than he could possibly use. Yet he, like the rest of us, has only 24 hours each day and a limited amount of energy. So even he confronts trade-offs. Any activity he pursues—whether it be building his business empire or redecorating his mansion or tending to his charitable foundation— uses up time and energy that he could otherwise spend on other things. Indeed, someone once calculated that the value of Gates's time is so great that pausing to pick up a $100 bill from the sidewalk simply wouldn't be worth his while.

If Bill Gates saw a $100 bill lying on the sidewalk, would it be worth his time to pick it up?

rational person someone with well-defined goals who tries to fulfill those goals as best he or she can

APPLYING THE COST-BENEFIT PRINCIPLE

In studying choice under scarcity, we'll usually begin with the premise that people are **rational**, which means they have well-defined goals and try to fulfill them as best they can. The Cost-Benefit Principle is a fundamental tool for the study of how rational people make choices.

As in the class-size example, often the only real difficulty in applying the cost-benefit rule is to come up with reasonable measures of the relevant benefits and costs. Only in rare instances will exact dollar measures be conveniently available. But the cost-benefit framework can lend structure to your thinking even when no relevant market data are available.

To illustrate how we proceed in such cases, the following example asks you to decide whether to perform an action whose cost is described only in vague, qualitative terms.

EXAMPLE 1.1   Comparing Costs and Benefits

Should you walk downtown to save $10 on a $25 computer game?

Imagine you are about to buy a $25 computer game at the nearby campus store when a friend tells you that the same game is on sale at a downtown store for only $15. If the downtown store is a 30-minute walk away, where should you buy the game?

The Cost-Benefit Principle tells us that you should buy it downtown if the benefit of doing so exceeds the cost. The benefit of taking any action is the dollar value of everything you gain by taking it. Here, the benefit of buying downtown is exactly $10, since that's the amount you'll save on the price of the game. The cost of taking any action is the dollar value of everything you give up by taking it. Here, the cost of buying downtown is the dollar value you assign to the time and trouble it takes to make the trip. But how do we estimate that value?

One way is to perform the following hypothetical auction. Imagine that a stranger has offered to pay you to do an errand that involves the same walk downtown (perhaps to drop off a letter for her at the post office). If she offered you a payment of, say, $1,000, would you accept? If so, we know that your cost of walking downtown and back must be less than $1,000. Now imagine her offer being reduced in small increments until you finally refuse the last offer. For example, if you'd agree to walk downtown and back for $9.00 but not for $8.99, then your cost of making the trip is $9.00. In this case, you should buy the game downtown because the $10 you'll save (your benefit) is greater than your $9.00 cost of making the trip.

But suppose your cost of making the trip had been greater than $10. In that case, your best bet would have been to buy the game from the nearby campus store. Confronted with this choice, different people may choose differently, depending on how costly they think it is to make the trip downtown. But although there is no uniquely correct choice, most people who are asked what they would do in this situation say they would buy the game downtown.

Economic Surplus

economic surplus the benefit of taking an action minus its cost

Suppose that in Example 1.1 your "cost" of making the trip downtown was $9. Compared to the alternative of buying the game at the campus store, buying it downtown resulted in an **economic surplus** of $1, the difference between the benefit of making the trip and its cost. In general, your goal as an economic decision maker is to choose those actions that generate the largest possible economic surplus. This means taking all actions that yield a positive total economic surplus, which is just another way of restating the Cost-Benefit Principle.

Note that the fact that your best choice was to buy the game downtown doesn't imply that you *enjoy* making the trip, any more than choosing a large class means that you prefer large classes to small ones. It simply means that the trip is less unpleasant than the prospect of paying $10 extra for the game. Once again, you've faced a trade-off. In this case, the choice was between a cheaper game and the free time gained by avoiding the trip.

Opportunity Cost

opportunity cost the value of what must be forgone to undertake an activity

Of course, your mental auction could have produced a different outcome. Suppose, for example, that the time required for the trip is the only time you have left to study for a difficult test the next day. Or suppose you are watching one of your favorite movies on cable, or that you are tired and would love a short nap. In such cases, we say that the **opportunity cost** of making the trip—that is, the value of what you must sacrifice to walk downtown and back—is high and you are more likely to decide against making the trip.

Strictly speaking, your opportunity cost of engaging in an activity is the value of everything you must sacrifice to engage in it. For instance, if seeing a movie requires not only that you buy a $10 ticket but also that you give up a $20 babysitting job that you would have been willing to do for free, then the opportunity cost of seeing the film is $30.

Under this definition, *all* costs—both implicit and explicit—are opportunity costs. Unless otherwise stated, we will adhere to this strict definition.

We must warn you, however, that some economists use the term *opportunity cost* to refer only to the implicit value of opportunities forgone. Thus, in the example just discussed, these economists wouldn't include the $10 ticket price when calculating the opportunity cost of seeing the film. But virtually all economists would agree that your opportunity cost of not doing the babysitting job is $20.

In the previous example, if watching the last hour of the cable TV movie is the most valuable opportunity that conflicts with the trip downtown, the opportunity cost of making the trip is the dollar value you place on pursuing that opportunity. It is the largest amount you'd be willing to pay to avoid missing the end of the movie. Note that the opportunity cost of making the trip is not the combined value of *all* possible activities you could have pursued, but only the value of your *best* alternative—the one you would have chosen had you not made the trip.

Throughout the text we'll pose concept checks like the one that follows. You'll find that pausing to answer them will help you to master key concepts in economics. Because doing these concept checks isn't very costly (indeed, many students report that they're actually fun), the Cost-Benefit Principle indicates that it's well worth your while to do them.

CONCEPT CHECK 1.1

Refer to Example 1.1. You would again save $10 by buying the game downtown rather than at the campus store, but your cost of making the trip is now $12, not $9. By how much would your economic surplus be smaller if you bought the game downtown rather than at the campus store?

The Role of Economic Models

Economists use the Cost-Benefit Principle as an abstract model of how an idealized rational individual would choose among competing alternatives. (By "abstract model" we mean a simplified description that captures the essential elements of a situation and allows us to analyze them in a logical way.) A computer model of a complex phenomenon like climate change, which must ignore many details and includes only the major forces at work, is an example of an abstract model.

Noneconomists are sometimes harshly critical of the economist's cost-benefit model on the grounds that people in the real world never conduct hypothetical mental auctions before deciding whether to make trips downtown. But this criticism betrays a fundamental misunderstanding of how abstract models can help to explain and predict human behavior. Economists know perfectly well that people don't conduct hypothetical mental auctions when they make simple decisions. All the Cost-Benefit Principle really says is that a rational decision is one that is explicitly or implicitly based on a weighing of costs and benefits.

Most of us make sensible decisions most of the time, without being consciously aware that we are weighing costs and benefits, just as most people ride a bike without being consciously aware of what keeps them from falling. Through trial and error, we gradually learn what kinds of choices tend to work best in different contexts, just as bicycle riders internalize the relevant laws of physics, usually without being conscious of them.

Even so, learning the explicit principles of cost-benefit analysis can help us make better decisions, just as knowing about physics can help in learning to ride a bicycle. For instance, when a young economist was teaching his oldest son to ride a bike, he followed the time-honored tradition of running alongside the bike and holding onto his son, then giving him a push and hoping for the best. After several hours and painfully skinned elbows and knees, his son finally got it. A year later, someone pointed out that the trick to riding a bike is to turn slightly in whichever direction the bike is leaning. Of course! The economist passed this information along to his second son, who learned to ride almost instantly. Just as knowing a little physics can help you learn to ride a bike, knowing a little economics can help you make better decisions.

RECAP ↑

COST-BENEFIT ANALYSIS

Scarcity is a basic fact of economic life. Because of it, having more of one good thing almost always means having less of another. The Cost-Benefit Principle holds that an individual (or a firm or a society) should take an action if, and only if, the extra benefit from taking the action is at least as great as the extra cost. The benefit of taking any action minus the cost of taking the action is called the *economic surplus* from that action. Hence, the Cost-Benefit Principle suggests that we take only those actions that create additional economic surplus.

THREE IMPORTANT DECISION PITFALLS*

Rational people will apply the Cost-Benefit Principle most of the time, although probably in an intuitive and approximate way, rather than through explicit and precise calculation. Knowing that rational people tend to compare costs and benefits enables economists to predict their likely behavior. As noted earlier, for example, we can predict that students from wealthy families are more likely than others to attend colleges that offer small classes. (Again, while the cost of small classes is the same for all families, their benefit, as measured by what people are willing to pay for them, tends to be higher for wealthier families.)

Yet researchers have identified situations in which people tend to apply the Cost-Benefit Principle inconsistently. In these situations, the Cost-Benefit Principle may not predict behavior accurately. But it proves helpful in another way, by identifying specific strategies for avoiding bad decisions.

---

*The examples in this section are inspired by the pioneering research of Daniel Kahneman and the late Amos Tversky. Kahneman was awarded the 2002 Nobel Prize in economics for his efforts to integrate insights from psychology into economics. You can read more about this work in Kahneman's brilliant 2011 book, *Thinking Fast and Slow* (New York: Macmillan).

Pitfall 1: Measuring Costs and Benefits as Proportions Rather than Absolute Dollar Amounts

As the next example makes clear, even people who seem to know they should weigh the pros and cons of the actions they are contemplating sometimes don't have a clear sense of how to measure the relevant costs and benefits.

EXAMPLE 1.2 | **Comparing Costs and Benefits**

Should you walk downtown to save $10 on a $2,020 laptop computer?

You are about to buy a $2,020 laptop computer at the nearby campus store when a friend tells you that the same computer is on sale at a downtown store for only $2,010. If the downtown store is half an hour's walk away, where should you buy the computer?

Assuming that the laptop is light enough to carry without effort, the structure of this example is exactly the same as that of Example 1.1. The only difference is that the price of the laptop is dramatically higher than the price of the computer game. As before, the benefit of buying downtown is the dollar amount you'll save, namely, $10. And since it's exactly the same trip, its cost also must be the same as before. So if you are perfectly rational, you should make the same decision in both cases. Yet when people are asked what they would do in these situations, the overwhelming majority say they'd walk downtown to buy the game but would buy the laptop at the campus store. When asked to explain, most of them say something like "The trip was worth it for the game because you save 40 percent, but not worth it for the laptop because you save only $10 out of $2,020."

This is faulty reasoning. The benefit of the trip downtown is not the *proportion* you save on the original price. Rather, it is the *absolute dollar amount* you save. The benefit of walking downtown to buy the laptop is $10, exactly the same as for the computer game. And since the cost of the trip must also be the same in both cases, the economic surplus from making both trips must be exactly the same. That means that a rational decision maker would make the same decision in both cases. Yet, as noted, most people choose differently.

Implicit costs are like dogs that fail to bark in the night.

The pattern of faulty reasoning in the decision just discussed is one of several decision pitfalls to which people are often prone. In the discussion that follows, we will identify two additional decision pitfalls. In some cases, people ignore costs or benefits that they ought to take into account. On other occasions they are influenced by costs or benefits that are irrelevant.

CONCEPT CHECK 1.2

Which is more valuable: saving $100 on a $2,000 plane ticket to Tokyo or saving $90 on a $200 plane ticket to Chicago?

Pitfall 2: Ignoring Implicit Costs

Sherlock Holmes, Arthur Conan Doyle's legendary detective, was successful because he saw details that most others overlooked. In *Silver Blaze,* Holmes is called on to investigate the theft of an expensive racehorse from its stable. A Scotland Yard inspector assigned to the case asks Holmes whether some particular aspect of the crime requires further study. "Yes," Holmes replies, and describes "the curious incident of the dog in the nighttime." "The dog did nothing in the nighttime," responds the puzzled inspector. But, as Holmes realized, that was precisely the problem! The watchdog's failure to bark when

Silver Blaze was stolen meant that the watchdog knew the thief. This clue ultimately proved the key to unraveling the mystery.

Just as we often don't notice when a dog fails to bark, many of us tend to overlook the implicit value of activities that fail to happen. As discussed earlier, however, intelligent decisions require taking the value of forgone opportunities properly into account.

The opportunity cost of an activity, once again, is the value of all that must be forgone in order to engage in that activity. If buying a computer game downtown means not watching the last hour of a movie, then the value to you of watching the end of that movie is an implicit cost of the trip. Many people make bad decisions because they tend to ignore the value of such forgone opportunities. To avoid overlooking implicit costs, economists often translate questions like "Should I walk downtown?" into ones like "Should I walk downtown or watch the end of the movie?"

EXAMPLE 1.3   Implicit Cost

Should you use your frequent-flyer coupon to fly to Fort Lauderdale for spring break?

With spring break only a week away, you are still undecided about whether to go to Fort Lauderdale with a group of classmates at the University of Iowa. The round-trip airfare from Cedar Rapids is $500, but you have a frequent-flyer coupon you could use for the trip. All other relevant costs for the vacation week at the beach total exactly $1,000. The most you would be willing to pay for the Fort Lauderdale vacation is $1,350. That amount is your benefit of taking the vacation. Your only alternative use for your frequent-flyer coupon is for your trip to Boston the weekend after spring break to attend your brother's wedding. (Your coupon expires shortly thereafter.) If the Cedar Rapids–Boston round-trip airfare is $400, should you use your frequent-flyer coupon to fly to Fort Lauderdale for spring break?

The Cost-Benefit Principle tells us that you should go to Fort Lauderdale if the benefits of the trip exceed its costs. If not for the complication of the frequent-flyer coupon, solving this problem would be a straightforward matter of comparing your benefit from the week at the beach to the sum of all relevant costs. And since your airfare and other costs would add up to $1,500, or $150 more than your benefit from the trip, you would not go to Fort Lauderdale.

But what about the possibility of using your frequent-flyer coupon to make the trip? Using it for that purpose might make the flight to Fort Lauderdale seem free, suggesting you'd reap an economic surplus of $350 by making the trip. But doing so also would mean you'd have to fork over $400 for your airfare to Boston. So the implicit cost of using your coupon to go to Fort Lauderdale is really $400. If you use it for that purpose, the trip still ends up being a loser because the cost of the vacation, $1,400, exceeds the benefit by $50. In cases like these, you're much more likely to decide sensibly if you ask yourself, "Should I use my frequent-flyer coupon for this trip or save it for an upcoming trip?"

Is your flight to Fort Lauderdale "free" if you travel on a frequent-flyer coupon?

©The McGraw-Hill Companies, Inc./ Barry Barker, photographer

We cannot emphasize strongly enough that the key to using the Cost-Benefit Principle correctly lies in recognizing precisely what taking a given action prevents us from doing. Concept Check 1.3 illustrates this point by modifying the details of Example 1.3 slightly.

CONCEPT CHECK 1.3

Refer to the given information in Example 1.3, but this time your frequent-flyer coupon expires in a week, so your only chance to use it will be for the Fort Lauderdale trip. Should you use your coupon?

Pitfall 3: Failure to Think at the Margin

When deciding whether to take an action, the only relevant costs and benefits are those that would occur as a result of taking the action. Sometimes people are influenced by costs they ought to ignore. Other times they compare the wrong costs and benefits. *The only costs that should influence a decision about whether to take an action are those we can avoid by not taking the action. Similarly, the only benefits we should consider are those that would not occur unless the action were taken.* As a practical matter, however, many decision makers appear to be influenced by costs or benefits that would have occurred no matter what. Thus, people are often influenced by **sunk costs**—costs that are beyond recovery at the moment a decision is made. For example, money spent on a nontransferable, nonrefundable airline ticket is a sunk cost.

sunk cost a cost that is beyond recovery at the moment a decision must be made

As the following example illustrates, sunk costs must be borne *whether or not an action is taken,* so they are irrelevant to the decision of whether to take the action.

EXAMPLE 1.4	Sunk Cost

How much should you eat at an all-you-can-eat restaurant?

Sangam, an Indian restaurant in Philadelphia, offers an all-you-can-eat lunch buffet for $10. Customers pay $10 at the door, and no matter how many times they refill their plates, there is no additional charge. One day, as a goodwill gesture, the owner of the restaurant tells 20 randomly selected guests that their lunch is on the house. The remaining guests pay the usual price. If all diners are rational, will there be any difference in the average quantity of food consumed by people in these two groups?

Having eaten their first helping, diners in each group confront the following question: "Should I go back for another helping?" For rational diners, if the benefit of doing so exceeds the cost, the answer is yes; otherwise it is no. Note that at the moment of decision, the $10 charge for the lunch is a sunk cost. Those who paid it have no way to recover it. Thus, for both groups, the (extra) cost of another helping is exactly zero. And since the people who received the free lunch were chosen at random, there's no reason their appetites or incomes should be any different from those of other diners. The benefit of another helping thus should be the same, on average, for people in both groups. And since their respective costs and benefits are the same, the two groups should eat the same number of helpings, on average.

Psychologists and economists have experimental evidence, however, that people in such groups do *not* eat similar amounts.[1] In particular, those for whom the luncheon charge is not waived tend to eat substantially more than those for whom the charge is waived. People in the former group seem somehow determined to "get their money's worth." Their implicit goal is apparently to minimize the average cost per bite of the food they eat. Yet minimizing average cost is not a particularly sensible objective. It brings to mind the man who drove his car on the highway at night, even though he had nowhere to go, because he wanted to boost his average fuel economy. The irony is that diners who are determined to get their money's worth usually end up eating too much.

The fact that the cost-benefit criterion failed the test of prediction in Example 1.4 does nothing to invalidate its advice about what people *should* do. If you are letting sunk costs influence your decisions, you can do better by changing your behavior.

In addition to paying attention to costs and benefits that should be ignored, people often use incorrect measures of the relevant costs and benefits. This error often occurs when we must choose the *extent* to which an activity should be pursued (as opposed to

[1]See, for example, Richard Thaler, "Toward a Positive Theory of Consumer Choice," *Journal of Economic Behavior and Organization* 1, no. 1 (1980).

choosing whether to pursue it at all). We can apply the Cost-Benefit Principle in such situations by repeatedly asking the question "Should I increase the level at which I am currently pursuing the activity?"

In attempting to answer this question, the focus should always be on the benefit and cost of an *additional* unit of activity. To emphasize this focus, economists refer to the cost of an additional unit of activity as its **marginal cost**. Similarly, the benefit of an additional unit of the activity is its **marginal benefit**.

When the problem is to discover the proper level for an activity, the cost-benefit rule is to keep increasing the level as long as the marginal benefit of the activity exceeds its marginal cost. As the following example illustrates, however, people often fail to apply this rule correctly.

marginal cost the increase in total cost that results from carrying out one additional unit of an activity

marginal benefit the increase in total benefit that results from carrying out one additional unit of an activity

EXAMPLE 1.5   Focusing on Marginal Costs and Benefits

Should NASA expand the space shuttle program from four launches per year to five?

Professor Kösten Banifoot, a prominent supporter of the National Aeronautics and Space Administration's (NASA) space shuttle program, estimated that the gains from the program are currently $24 billion per year (an average of $6 billion per launch) and that its costs are currently $20 billion per year (an average of $5 billion per launch). On the basis of these estimates, Professor Banifoot testified before Congress that NASA should definitely expand the space shuttle program. Should Congress follow his advice?

To discover whether the advice makes economic sense, we must compare the marginal cost of a launch to its marginal benefit. The professor's estimates, however, tell us only the **average cost** and **average benefit** of the program. These are, respectively, the total cost of the program divided by the number of launches and the total benefit divided by the number of launches. Knowing the average benefit and average cost per launch for all shuttles launched thus far is simply not useful for deciding whether to expand the program. Of course, the average cost of the launches undertaken so far *might* be the same as the cost of adding another launch. But it also might be either higher or lower than the marginal cost of a launch. The same holds true regarding average and marginal benefits.

Suppose, for the sake of discussion, that the benefit of an additional launch is in fact the same as the average benefit per launch thus far, $6 billion. Should NASA add another launch? Not if the cost of adding the fifth launch would be more than $6 billion. And the fact that the average cost per launch is only $5 billion simply does not tell us anything about the marginal cost of the fifth launch.

Suppose, for example, that the relationship between the number of shuttles launched and the total cost of the program is as described in Table 1.1. The average

average cost the total cost of undertaking *n* units of an activity divided by *n*

average benefit the total benefit of undertaking *n* units of an activity divided by *n*

TABLE 1.1
How Total Cost Varies with the Number of Launches

Number of launches	Total cost ($ billions)	Average cost ($ billions/launch)
0	0	0
1	3	3
2	7	3.5
3	12	4
4	20	5
5	32	6.4

cost per launch (third column) when there are four launches would then be $20 billion/4 = $5 billion per launch, just as Professor Banifoot testified. But note in the second column of the table that adding a fifth launch would raise costs from $20 billion to $32 billion, making the marginal cost of the fifth launch $12 billion. So if the benefit of an additional launch is $6 billion, increasing the number of launches from four to five would make absolutely no economic sense.

The following example illustrates how to apply the Cost-Benefit Principle correctly in this case.

EXAMPLE 1.6   **Focusing on Marginal Costs and Benefits**

How many space shuttles should NASA launch?

NASA must decide how many space shuttles to launch. The benefit of each launch is estimated to be $6 billion and the total cost of the program again depends on the number of launches as shown in Table 1.1. How many shuttles should NASA launch?

NASA should continue to launch shuttles as long as the marginal benefit of the program exceeds its marginal cost. In this example, the marginal benefit is constant at $6 billion per launch, regardless of the number of shuttles launched. NASA should thus keep launching shuttles as long as the marginal cost per launch is less than or equal to $6 billion.

Applying the definition of marginal cost to the total cost entries in the second column of Table 1.1 yields the marginal cost values in the third column of Table 1.2. (Because marginal cost is the change in total cost that results when we change the number of launches by one, we place each marginal cost entry midway between the rows showing the corresponding total cost entries.) Thus, for example, the marginal cost of increasing the number of launches from one to two is $4 billion, the difference between the $7 billion total cost of two launches and the $3 billion total cost of one launch.

TABLE 1.2
How Marginal Cost Varies with the Number of Launches

Number of launches	Total cost ($ billions)	Marginal cost ($ billions/launch)
0	0	
		3
1	3	
		4
2	7	
		5
3	12	
		8
4	20	
		12
5	32	

As we see from a comparison of the $6 billion marginal benefit per launch with the marginal cost entries in the third column of Table 1.2, the first three launches satisfy the cost-benefit test, but the fourth and fifth launches do not. NASA should thus launch three space shuttles.

CONCEPT CHECK 1.4

If the marginal benefit of each launch, as shown in Example 1.6, had been not $6 billion but $9 billion, how many shuttles should NASA have launched?

The cost-benefit framework emphasizes that the only relevant costs and benefits in deciding whether to pursue an activity further are *marginal* costs and benefits—measures that correspond to the *increment* of activity under consideration. In many contexts, however, people seem more inclined to compare the *average* cost and benefit of the activity. As Example 1.5 made clear, increasing the level of an activity may not be justified, even though its average benefit at the current level is significantly greater than its average cost.

CONCEPT CHECK 1.5

Should a basketball team's best player take all the team's shots?

A professional basketball team has a new assistant coach. The assistant notices that one player scores on a higher percentage of his shots than other players. Based on this information, the assistant suggests to the head coach that the star player should take *all* the shots. That way, the assistant reasons, the team will score more points and win more games.

On hearing this suggestion, the head coach fires his assistant for incompetence. What was wrong with the assistant's idea?

RECAP ↑

THREE IMPORTANT DECISION PITFALLS

1. **The pitfall of measuring costs or benefits proportionally.** Many decision makers treat a change in cost or benefit as insignificant if it constitutes only a small proportion of the original amount. Absolute dollar amounts, not proportions, should be employed to measure costs and benefits.

2. **The pitfall of ignoring implicit costs.** When performing a cost-benefit analysis of an action, it is important to account for all relevant costs, including the implicit value of alternatives that must be forgone in order to carry out the action. A resource (such as a frequent-flyer coupon) may have a high implicit cost, even if you originally got it "for free," if its best alternative use has high value. The identical resource may have a low implicit cost, however, if it has no good alternative uses.

3. **The pitfall of failing to think at the margin.** When deciding whether to perform an action, the only costs and benefits that are relevant are those that would result from taking the action. It is important to ignore sunk costs—those costs that cannot be avoided even if the action isn't taken. Even though a ticket to a concert may have cost you $100, if you've already bought it and cannot sell it to anyone else, the $100 is a sunk cost and shouldn't influence your decision about whether to go to the concert. It's also important not to confuse average costs and benefits with marginal costs and benefits. Decision makers often have ready information about the total cost and benefit of an activity, and from these it's simple to compute the activity's average cost and benefit. A common mistake is to conclude that an activity should be increased if its average benefit exceeds its average cost. The Cost-Benefit Principle tells us that the level of an activity should be increased if, and only if, its *marginal* benefit exceeds its *marginal* cost.

Some costs and benefits, especially marginal costs and benefits and implicit costs, are important for decision making, while others, like sunk costs and average costs and benefits, are essentially irrelevant. This conclusion is implicit in our original statement of the Cost-Benefit Principle (an action should be taken if, and only if, the extra benefits of taking it exceed the extra costs).

NORMATIVE ECONOMICS VERSUS POSITIVE ECONOMICS

The examples discussed in the preceding section make the point that people *sometimes* choose irrationally. We must stress that our purpose in discussing these examples was not to suggest that people *generally* make irrational choices. On the contrary, most people appear to choose sensibly most of the time, especially when their decisions are important or familiar ones. The economist's focus on rational choice thus offers not only useful advice about making better decisions, but also a basis for predicting and explaining human behavior. We used the cost-benefit approach in this way when discussing how rising faculty salaries have led to larger class sizes. And as we will see, similar reasoning helps to explain human behavior in virtually every other domain.

The Cost-Benefit Principle is an example of a **normative economic principle**, one that provides guidance about how we *should* behave. For example, according to the Cost-Benefit Principle, we should ignore sunk costs when making decisions about the future. As our discussion of the various decision pitfalls makes clear, however, the Cost-Benefit Principle is not always a **positive**, or descriptive, **economic principle**, one that describes how we actually *will* behave. As we saw, the Cost-Benefit Principle can be tricky to implement, and people sometimes fail to heed its prescriptions.

That said, we stress that knowing the relevant costs and benefits surely does enable us to predict how people will behave much of the time. If the benefit of an action goes up, it is generally reasonable to predict that people will be more likely to take that action. And conversely, if the cost of an action goes up, the safest prediction will be that people will be less likely to take that action.

When the Cost-Benefit Principle helps us predict people's behavior, it also acts as a positive economic principle. The principle stresses that the relevant costs and benefits usually help us predict behavior, but at the same time does not insist that people behave rationally in each instance. For example, if the price of heating oil were to rise sharply, we would invoke the Cost-Benefit Principle to say that people *should* turn their thermostats down. And although some may not follow that advice, the Cost-Benefit Principle would also predict that average thermostat settings *will* in fact go down.

ECONOMICS: MICRO AND MACRO

By convention, we use the term **microeconomics** to describe the study of individual choices and of group behavior in individual markets. **Macroeconomics**, by contrast, is the study of the performance of national economies and of the policies that governments use to try to improve that performance. Macroeconomics tries to understand the determinants of such things as the national unemployment rate, the overall price level, and the total value of national output.

Our focus in this chapter is on issues that confront the individual decision maker, whether that individual confronts a personal decision, a family decision, a business decision, a government policy decision, or indeed any other type of decision. Further on, we'll consider economic models of groups of individuals such as all buyers or all sellers in a specific market. Later still we'll turn to broader economic issues and measures.

No matter which of these levels is our focus, however, our thinking will be shaped by the fact that, although economic needs and wants are effectively unlimited, the material and human resources that can be used to satisfy them are finite. Clear thinking about

normative economic principle one that says how people should behave

positive economic principle one that predicts how people will behave

microeconomics the study of individual choice under scarcity and its implications for the behavior of prices and quantities in individual markets

macroeconomics the study of the performance of national economies and the policies that governments use to try to improve that performance

economic problems must therefore always take into account the idea of trade-offs—the idea that having more of one good thing usually means having less of another. Our economy and our society are shaped to a substantial degree by the choices people have made when faced with trade-offs.

THE APPROACH OF THIS TEXT

Choosing the number of students to register in each class is just one of many important decisions in planning an introductory economics course. Another concerns which topics to include on the course syllabus. There's a virtually inexhaustible set of issues that might be covered in an introductory course, but only limited time in which to cover them. There's no free lunch. Covering some inevitably means omitting others.

All textbook authors are forced to pick and choose. A textbook that covered *all* the issues would take up more than a whole floor of your campus library. It is our firm view that most introductory textbooks try to cover far too much. One reason that each of us was drawn to the study of economics is that a relatively short list of the discipline's core ideas can explain a great deal of the behavior and events we see in the world around us. So rather than cover a large number of ideas at a superficial level, our strategy is to focus on this short list of core ideas, returning to each entry again and again, in many different contexts. This strategy will enable you to internalize these ideas remarkably well in the brief span of a single course. And the benefit of learning a small number of important ideas well will far outweigh the cost of having to ignore a host of other, less important ones.

A second important element in our philosophy is a belief in the importance of active learning. In the same way that you can learn Spanish only by speaking and writing it, or tennis only by playing the game, you can learn economics only by *doing* economics. And because we want you to learn how to do economics, rather than just to read or listen passively as the authors or your instructor does economics, we'll make every effort to encourage you to stay actively involved.

For example, instead of just telling you about an idea, we'll usually first motivate the idea by showing you how it works in the context of a specific example. Often, these examples will be followed by concept checks for you to try, as well as applications that show the relevance of the idea to real life. Try working the concept checks *before* looking up the answers (which are at the end of each corresponding chapter).

Think critically about the applications: Do you see how they illustrate the point being made? Do they give you new insight into the issue? Work the problems at the end of the chapters and take extra care with those relating to points that you don't fully understand. Apply economic principles to the world around you. (We'll say more about this when we discuss economic naturalism below.) Finally, when you come across an idea or example that you find interesting, tell a friend about it. You'll be surprised to discover how much the mere act of explaining it helps you understand and remember the underlying principle. The more actively you can become engaged in the learning process, the more effective your learning will be.

ECONOMIC NATURALISM

With the rudiments of the cost-benefit framework under your belt, you are now in a position to become an "economic naturalist," someone who uses insights from economics to help make sense of observations from everyday life. People who have studied biology are able to observe and marvel at many details of nature that would otherwise have escaped their notice. For example, on a walk in the woods in early April, the novice may see only trees. In contrast, the biology student notices many different species of trees and understands why some are already in leaf while others still lie dormant. Likewise, the novice may notice that in some animal species males are much larger than females, but the biology student knows that pattern occurs only in species in which males take several mates. Natural selection favors larger males in those species because their greater size helps them prevail in the often bloody contests among males for access to females. In contrast, males tend to be roughly the same size as females in monogamous species, in which there is much less fighting for mates.

Learning a few simple economic principles broadens our vision in a similar way. It enables us to see the mundane details of ordinary human existence in a new light. Whereas the uninitiated often fail even to notice these details, the economic naturalist not only sees them, but becomes actively engaged in the attempt to understand them. Let's consider a few examples of questions economic naturalists might pose for themselves.

The Economic Naturalist 1.1

Why do many hardware manufacturers include more than $1,000 worth of "free" software with a computer selling for only slightly more than that?

The software industry is different from many others in the sense that its customers care a great deal about product compatibility. When you and your classmates are working on a project together, for example, your task will be much simpler if you all use the same word-processing program. Likewise, an executive's life will be easier at tax time if her financial software is the same as her accountant's.

The implication is that the benefit of owning and using any given software program increases with the number of other people who use that same product. This unusual relationship gives the producers of the most popular programs an enormous advantage and often makes it hard for new programs to break into the market.

Recognizing this pattern, Intuit Corp. offered computer makers free copies of *Quicken,* its personal financial-management software. Computer makers, for their part, were only too happy to include the program, since it made their new computers more attractive to buyers. *Quicken* soon became the standard for personal financial-management programs. By giving away free copies of the program, Intuit "primed the pump," creating an enormous demand for upgrades of *Quicken* and for more advanced versions of related software. Thus, *TurboTax,* Intuit's personal income-tax software, has become the standard for tax-preparation programs.

Inspired by this success story, other software developers have jumped onto the bandwagon. Most hardware now comes bundled with a host of free software programs. Some software developers are even rumored to *pay* computer makers to include their programs!

The Economic Naturalist 1.1 illustrates a case in which the *benefit* of a product depends on the number of other people who own that product. As the next Economic Naturalist demonstrates, the *cost* of a product may also depend on the number of others who own it.

The Economic Naturalist 1.2

Why don't auto manufacturers make cars without heaters?

Virtually every new car sold in the United States today has a heater. But not every car has a satellite navigation system. Why this difference?

One might be tempted to answer that, although everyone *needs* a heater, people can get along without navigation systems. Yet heaters are of little use in places like Hawaii and southern California. What is more, cars produced as recently as the 1950s did *not* all have heaters. (The classified ad that led one young economic naturalist to his first car, a 1955 Pontiac, boasted that the vehicle had a radio, heater, and whitewall tires.)

Although heaters cost extra money to manufacture and are not useful in all parts of the country, they do not cost *much* money and are useful on at least a few days each year in most parts of the country. As time passed and people's incomes grew, manufacturers found that people were ordering fewer and fewer cars without heaters. At some point it actually became cheaper to put heaters in *all* cars, rather than bear the administrative expense of making some cars with heaters and others without. No doubt a few buyers would still order a car without a heater if they could save some money in the process, but catering to these customers is just no longer worth it.

Similar reasoning explains why certain cars today cannot be purchased without a satellite navigation system. Buyers of the 2015 BMW 750i, for example, got one whether they wanted it or not. Most buyers of this car, which sells for more than $75,000, have high incomes, so the overwhelming majority of them would have chosen to order a navigation system had it been sold as an option. Because of the savings made possible when all cars are produced with the same equipment, it would have actually cost BMW more to supply cars for the few who would want them without navigation systems.

Buyers of the least-expensive makes of car have much lower incomes on average than BMW 750i buyers. Accordingly, most of them have more pressing alternative uses for their money than to buy navigation systems for their cars, and this explains why some inexpensive makes continue to offer navigation systems only as options. But as incomes continue to grow, new cars without navigation systems will eventually disappear.

The insights afforded by The Economic Naturalist 1.2 suggest an answer to the following strange question:

The Economic Naturalist 1.3

Why do the keypad buttons on drive-up automated teller machines have Braille dots?

Braille dots on elevator buttons and on the keypads of walk-up automated teller machines enable blind people to participate more fully in the normal flow of daily activity. But even though blind people can do many remarkable things, they cannot drive automobiles on public roads. Why, then, do the manufacturers of automated teller machines install Braille dots on the machines at drive-up locations?

The answer to this riddle is that once the keypad molds have been manufactured, the cost of producing buttons with Braille dots is no higher than the cost of producing smooth buttons. Making both would require separate sets of molds and

Why do the keypad buttons on drive-up automated teller machines have Braille dots?

two different types of inventory. If the patrons of drive-up machines found buttons with Braille dots harder to use, there might be a reason to incur these extra costs. But since the dots pose no difficulty for sighted users, the best and cheapest solution is to produce only keypads with dots.

The preceding Economic Naturalist example was suggested by Cornell student Bill Tjoa, in response to the following assignment:

CONCEPT CHECK 1.6

In 500 words or less, use cost-benefit analysis to explain some pattern of events or behavior you have observed in your own environment.

There is probably no more useful step you can take in your study of economics than to perform several versions of the assignment in Concept Check 1.6. Students who do so almost invariably become lifelong economic naturalists. Mastery of economic concepts does not decay with the passage of time, but actually grows stronger. We urge you, in the strongest possible terms, to make this investment!

SUMMARY

- Economics is the study of how people make choices under conditions of scarcity and of the results of those choices for society. Economic analysis of human behavior begins with the assumption that people are rational—that they have well-defined goals and try to achieve them as best they can. In trying to achieve their goals, people normally face trade-offs: Because material and human resources are limited, having more of one good thing means making do with less of some other good thing. *(LO1)*

- Our focus in this chapter has been on how rational people make choices among alternative courses of action. Our basic tool for analyzing these decisions is cost-benefit analysis. The Cost-Benefit Principle says that a person should take an action if, and only if, the benefit of that action is at least as great as its cost. The benefit of an action is defined as the largest dollar amount the person would be willing to pay in order to take the action. The cost of an action is defined as the dollar value of everything the person must give up in order to take the action. *(LO2)*

- In using the cost-benefit framework, we need not presume that people choose rationally all the time. Indeed, we identified three common pitfalls that plague decision makers in all walks of life: a tendency to treat small proportional changes as insignificant, a tendency to ignore implicit costs, and a tendency to fail to think at the margin—for example, by failing to ignore sunk costs or by failing to compare marginal costs and benefits. *(LO3)*

- Often the question is not whether to pursue an activity but rather how many units of it to pursue. In these cases, the rational person pursues additional units as long as the marginal benefit of the activity (the benefit from pursuing an additional unit of it) exceeds its marginal cost (the cost of pursuing an additional unit of it). *(LO4)*

- Microeconomics is the study of individual choices and of group behavior in individual markets, while macroeconomics is the study of the performance of national economics and of the policies that governments use to try to improve economic performance.

KEY TERMS

average benefit
average cost
economic surplus
economics
macroeconomics

marginal benefit
marginal cost
microeconomics
normative economic principle
opportunity cost

positive economic principle
rational person
sunk cost

REVIEW QUESTIONS

1. A friend of yours on the tennis team says, "Private tennis lessons are definitely better than group lessons." Explain what you think he means by this statement. Then use the Cost-Benefit Principle to explain why private lessons are not necessarily the best choice for everyone. *(LO2)*

2. True or false: Your willingness to drive downtown to save $30 on a new appliance should depend on what fraction of the total selling price $30 is. Explain. *(LO3)*

3. Why might someone who is trying to decide whether to see a movie be more likely to focus on the $10 ticket price than on the $20 she would fail to earn by not babysitting? *(LO3)*

4. Many people think of their air travel as being free when they use frequent-flyer coupons. Explain why these people are likely to make wasteful travel decisions. *(LO3)*

5. Is the nonrefundable tuition payment you made to your university this semester a sunk cost? How would your answer differ if your university were to offer a full tuition refund to any student who dropped out of school during the first two months of the semester? *(LO3)*

PROBLEMS

1. Suppose the most you would be willing to pay to have a freshly washed car before going out on a date is $6. The smallest amount for which you would be willing to wash someone else's car is $3.50. You are going out this evening and your car is dirty. How much economic surplus would you receive from washing it? *(LO2)*

2. To earn extra money in the summer, you grow tomatoes and sell them at a local farmers' market for $0.30 per pound. By adding compost to your garden, you can increase your yield as shown in the table below. If compost costs $0.50 per pound and your goal is to make as much profit as possible, how many pounds of compost should you add? *(LO2)*

Pounds of compost	Pounds of tomatoes
	100
1	120
2	125
3	128
4	130
5	131
6	131.5

3.* You and your friend Joe have identical tastes. At 2 p.m., you go to the local Ticketmaster outlet and buy a $30 ticket to a basketball game to be played that night in Syracuse, 50 miles north of your home in Ithaca. Joe plans to attend the same game, but because he cannot get to the Ticketmaster outlet, he plans to buy his ticket at the game. Tickets sold at the game cost only $25 because they carry no Ticketmaster surcharge. (Many people nonetheless pay the higher price at Ticketmaster, to be sure of getting good seats.) At 4 p.m., an unexpected snowstorm begins, making the prospect of the drive to Syracuse much less attractive than before (but ensuring the availability of good seats). If both you and Joe are rational, is one of you more likely to attend the game than the other? *(LO2)*

4. Tom is a mushroom farmer. He invests all his spare cash in additional mushrooms, which grow on otherwise useless land behind his barn. The mushrooms double in weight during their first year, after which time they are harvested and sold at a constant price per pound. Tom's friend Dick asks Tom for a loan of $200, which he promises to repay after one year. How much interest will Dick have to pay Tom in order for Tom to recover his opportunity cost of making the loan? Explain briefly. *(LO3)*

5. Suppose that in the last few seconds you devoted to question 1 on your physics exam you earned 4 extra points, while in the last few seconds you devoted to question 2 you earned 10 extra points. You earned a total of 48 and 12 points, respectively, on the two questions and the total time you spent on each was the same. If you could take the exam again, how—if at all—should you reallocate your time between these questions? *(LO3)*

6. Martha and Sarah have the same preferences and incomes. Just as Martha arrived at the theater to see a play, she discovered that she had lost the $10 ticket she had purchased earlier. Sarah also just arrived at the theater planning to buy a ticket to see the same play when she discovered that she had lost a $10 bill from her wallet. If both Martha and Sarah are rational and both still have enough money to pay for a ticket, is one of them more likely than the other to go ahead and see the play anyway? *(LO3)*

7. Residents of your city are charged a fixed weekly fee of $6 for garbage collection. They are allowed to put out as many cans as they wish. The average household disposes

*Denotes more difficult problem.

of three cans of garbage per week under this plan. Now suppose that your city changes to a "tag" system. Each can of garbage to be collected must have a tag affixed to it. The tags cost $2 each and are not reusable. What effect do you think the introduction of the tag system will have on the total quantity of garbage collected in your city? Explain briefly. *(LO4)*

8. Once a week, Smith purchases a six-pack of cola and puts it in his refrigerator for his two children. He invariably discovers that all six cans are gone on the first day. Jones also purchases a six-pack of cola once a week for his two children, but unlike Smith, he tells them that each may drink no more than three cans per week. If the children use cost-benefit analysis each time they decide whether to drink a can of cola, explain why the cola lasts much longer at Jones's house than at Smith's. *(LO4)*

9.* For each long-distance call anywhere in the continental United States, a new phone service will charge users $0.30 per minute for the first 2 minutes and $0.02 per minute for additional minutes in each call. Tom's current phone service charges $0.10 per minute for all calls, and his calls are never shorter than 7 minutes. If Tom's dorm switches to the new phone service, what will happen to the average length of his calls? *(LO4)*

10.* The meal plan at university A lets students eat as much as they like for a fixed fee of $500 per semester. The average student there eats 250 pounds of food per semester. University B charges $500 for a book of meal tickets that entitles the student to eat 250 pounds of food per semester. If the student eats more than 250 pounds, he or she pays $2 for each additional pound; if the student eats less, he or she gets a $2 per pound refund. If students are rational, at which university will average food consumption be higher? Explain briefly. *(LO4)*

ANSWERS TO CONCEPT CHECKS

1.1 The benefit of buying the game downtown is again $10 but the cost is now $12, so your economic surplus would be $2 smaller than if you'd bought it at the campus store. *(LO2)*

1.2 Saving $100 is $10 more valuable than saving $90, even though the percentage saved is much greater in the case of the Chicago ticket. *(LO3)*

1.3 Since you now have no alternative use for your coupon, the opportunity cost of using it to pay for the Fort Lauderdale trip is zero. That means your economic surplus from the trip will be $1,350 − $1,000 = $350 > 0, so you should use your coupon and go to Fort Lauderdale. *(LO3)*

1.4 The marginal benefit of the fourth launch is $9 billion, which exceeds its marginal cost of $8 billion, so the fourth launch should be added. But the fifth launch should not, since its marginal cost ($12 billion) exceeds its marginal benefit ($9 billion). *(LO3)*

1.5 If the star player takes one more shot, some other player must take one less. The fact that the star player's *average* success rate is higher than the other players' does not mean that the probability of making his *next* shot (the marginal benefit of having him shoot once more) is higher than the probability of another player making his next shot. Indeed, if the best player took all his team's shots, the other team would focus its defensive effort entirely on him, in which case letting others shoot would definitely pay. *(LO3)*

*Denotes more difficult problem.

Working with Equations, Graphs, and Tables

Although many of the examples and most of the end-of-chapter problems in this book are quantitative, none requires mathematical skills beyond rudimentary high school algebra and geometry. In this brief appendix, we review some of the skills you'll need for dealing with these examples and problems.

One important skill is to be able to read simple verbal descriptions and translate the information they provide into the relevant equations or graphs. You'll also need to be able to translate information given in tabular form into an equation or graph, and sometimes you'll need to translate graphical information into a table or equation. Finally, you'll need to be able to solve simple systems with two equations and two unknowns. The following examples illustrate all the tools you'll need.

USING A VERBAL DESCRIPTION TO CONSTRUCT AN EQUATION

We begin with an example that shows how to construct a long-distance telephone billing equation from a verbal description of the billing plan.

EXAMPLE 1A.1   A Verbal Description

Your long-distance telephone plan charges you $5 per month plus $0.10 per minute for long-distance calls. Write an equation that describes your monthly telephone bill.

An **equation** is a simple mathematical expression that describes the relationship between two or more **variables**, or quantities that are free to assume different values in some range. The most common type of equation we'll work with contains two types of variables: **dependent variables** and **independent variables**. In this example, the dependent variable is the dollar amount of your monthly telephone bill and the independent variable is the variable on which your bill depends, namely, the volume of long-distance calls you make during the month. Your bill also depends on the $5 monthly fee and the $0.10 per minute charge. But, in this example, those amounts are **constants**, not variables. A constant, also called a **parameter**, is a quantity in an equation that is fixed in value, not free to vary. As the terms suggest, the dependent variable describes an outcome that depends on the value taken by the independent variable.

Once you've identified the dependent variable and the independent variable, choose simple symbols to represent them. In algebra courses, X is typically used to represent the independent variable and Y the dependent variable. Many people find it easier to remember what the variables stand for, however, if they choose symbols that are linked in some straightforward way to the quantities that the variables represent. Thus, in this example, we might use B to represent your monthly *bill* in dollars and T to represent the total *time* in minutes you spent during the month on long-distance calls.

equation a mathematical expression that describes the relationship between two or more variables

variable a quantity that is free to take a range of different values

dependent variable a variable in an equation whose value is determined by the value taken by another variable in the equation

independent variable a variable in an equation whose value determines the value taken by another variable in the equation

constant (or **parameter**) a quantity that is fixed in value

Having identified the relevant variables and chosen symbols to represent them, you are now in a position to write the equation that links them:

$$B = 5 + 0.10T, \qquad (1A.1)$$

where B is your monthly long-distance bill in dollars and T is your monthly total long-distance calling time in minutes. The fixed monthly fee (5) and the charge per minute (0.10) are parameters in this equation. Note the importance of being clear about the units of measure. Because B represents the monthly bill in dollars, we must also express the fixed monthly fee and the per-minute charge in dollars, which is why the latter number appears in Equation 1A.1 as 0.10 rather than 10. Equation 1A.1 follows the normal convention in which the dependent variable appears by itself on the left-hand side while the independent variable or variables and constants appear on the right-hand side.

Once we have the equation for the monthly bill, we can use it to calculate how much you'll owe as a function of your monthly volume of long-distance calls. For example, if you make 32 minutes of calls, you can calculate your monthly bill by simply substituting 32 minutes for T in Equation 1A.1:

$$B = 5 + 0.10(32) = 8.20. \qquad (1A.2)$$

Your monthly bill when you make 32 minutes of calls is thus equal to $8.20.

CONCEPT CHECK 1A.1

Under the monthly billing plan described in Example 1A.1, how much would you owe for a month during which you made 45 minutes of long-distance calls?

GRAPHING THE EQUATION OF A STRAIGHT LINE

The next example shows how to portray the billing plan described in Example 1A.1 as a graph.

EXAMPLE 1A.2   Graphing an Equation

Construct a graph that portrays the monthly long-distance telephone billing plan described in Example 1A.1, putting your telephone charges, in dollars per month, on the vertical axis and your total volume of calls, in minutes per month, on the horizontal axis.

The first step in responding to this instruction is the one we just took, namely, to translate the verbal description of the billing plan into an equation. When graphing an equation, the normal convention is to use the vertical axis to represent the dependent variable and the horizontal axis to represent the independent variable. In Figure 1A.1, we therefore put B on the vertical axis and T on the horizontal axis. One way to construct the graph shown in the figure is to begin by plotting the monthly bill values that correspond to several different total amounts of long-distance calls. For example, someone who makes 10 minutes of calls during the month would have a bill of $B = 5 + 0.10(10) = \$6$. Thus, in Figure 1A.1 the value of 10 minutes per month on the horizontal axis corresponds to a bill of $6 per month on the vertical axis (point A). Someone who makes 30 minutes of long-distance calls during the month will have a monthly bill of $B = 5 + 0.10(30) = \$8$, so the value of 30 minutes per month on the horizontal axis corresponds to $8 per month on the vertical axis (point C). Similarly, someone who makes 70 minutes of long-distance calls during the month will have a monthly bill of $B = 5 + 0.10(70) = \$12$, so the value of

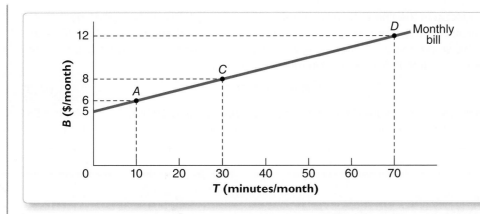

FIGURE 1A.1

The Monthly Telephone Bill in Example 1A.1.

The graph of the equation $B = 5 + 0.10T$ is the straight line shown. Its vertical intercept is 5 and its slope is 0.10.

70 minutes on the horizontal axis corresponds to $12 on the vertical axis (point *D*). The line joining these points is the graph of the monthly billing Equation 1A.1.

As shown in Figure 1A.1, the graph of the equation $B = 5 + 0.10T$ is a straight line. The parameter 5 is the **vertical intercept** of the line—the value of *B* when $T = 0$, or the point at which the line intersects the vertical axis. The parameter 0.10 is the **slope** of the line, which is the ratio of the **rise** of the line to the corresponding **run**. The ratio rise/run is simply the vertical distance between any two points on the line divided by the horizontal distance between those points. For example, if we choose points *A* and *C* in Figure 1A.1, the rise is $8 - 6 = 2$ and the corresponding run is $30 - 10 = 20$, so rise/run $= 2/20 = 0.10$. More generally, for the graph of any equation $Y = a + bX$, the parameter *a* is the vertical intercept and the parameter *b* is the slope.

vertical intercept in a straight line, the value taken by the dependent variable when the independent variable equals zero

slope in a straight line, the ratio of the vertical distance the straight line travels between any two points *(rise)* to the corresponding horizontal distance *(run)*

DERIVING THE EQUATION OF A STRAIGHT LINE FROM ITS GRAPH

The next example shows how to derive the equation for a straight line from a graph of the line.

EXAMPLE 1A.3   Deriving an Equation from a Graph

Figure 1A.2 shows the graph of the monthly billing plan for a new long-distance plan. What is the equation for this graph? How much is the fixed monthly fee under this plan? How much is the charge per minute?

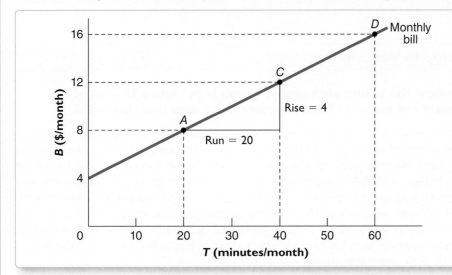

FIGURE 1A.2

Another Monthly Long-Distance Plan.

The vertical distance between points *A* and *C* is $12 - 8 = 4$ units, and the horizontal distance between points *A* and *C* is $40 - 20 = 20$, so the slope of the line is $4/20 = 1/5 = 0.20$. The vertical intercept (the value of *B* when $T = 0$) is 4. So the equation for the billing plan shown is $B = 4 + 0.20T$.

The slope of the line shown is the rise between any two points divided by the corresponding run. For points A and C, rise $= 12 - 8 = 4$ and run $= 40 - 20 = 20$, so the slope equals rise/run $= 4/20 = 1/5 = 0.20$. And since the horizontal intercept of the line is 4, its equation must be given by

$$B = 4 + 0.20T. \tag{1A.3}$$

Under this plan, the fixed monthly fee is the value of the bill when $T = 0$, which is \$4. The charge per minute is the slope of the billing line, 0.20, or 20 cents per minute.

CONCEPT CHECK 1A.2

Write the equation for the billing plan shown in the accompanying graph. How much is its fixed monthly fee? Its charge per minute?

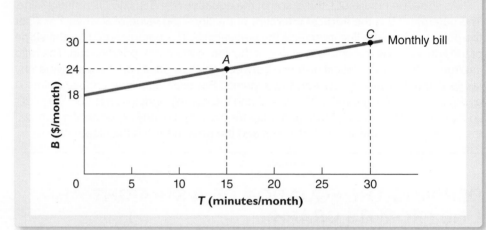

CHANGES IN THE VERTICAL INTERCEPT AND SLOPE

The next two examples and concept checks provide practice in seeing how a line shifts with a change in its vertical intercept or slope.

| EXAMPLE 1A.4 | Change in Vertical Intercept |

Show how the billing plan whose graph is in Figure 1A.2 would change if the monthly fixed fee were increased from \$4 to \$8.

An increase in the monthly fixed fee from \$4 to \$8 would increase the vertical intercept of the billing plan by \$4 but would leave its slope unchanged. An increase in the fixed fee thus leads to a parallel upward shift in the billing plan by \$4, as shown in Figure 1A.3. For any given number of minutes of long-distance calls, the monthly charge on the new bill will be \$4 higher than on the old bill. Thus 20 minutes of calls per month cost \$8 under the original plan (point A) but \$12 under the new plan (point A'). And 40 minutes cost \$12 under the original plan (point C), \$16 under the new plan (point C'); and 60 minutes cost \$16 under the original plan (point D), \$20 under the new plan (point D').

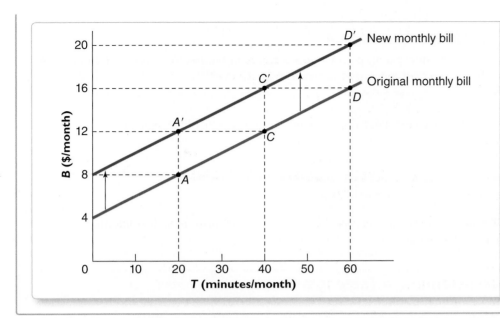

FIGURE 1A.3

The Effect of an Increase in the Vertical Intercept.

An increase in the vertical intercept of a straight line produces an upward parallel shift in the line.

CONCEPT CHECK 1A.3

Show how the billing plan whose graph is in Figure 1A.2 would change if the monthly fixed fee were reduced from $4 to $2.

EXAMPLE 1A.5   Change in Slope

Show how the billing plan whose graph is in Figure 1A.2 would change if the charge per minute were increased from $0.20 to $0.40.

Because the monthly fixed fee is unchanged, the vertical intercept of the new billing plan continues to be 4. But the slope of the new plan, shown in Figure 1A.4, is 0.40, or twice the slope of the original plan. More generally, in the equation $Y = a + bX$, an increase in b makes the slope of the graph of the equation steeper.

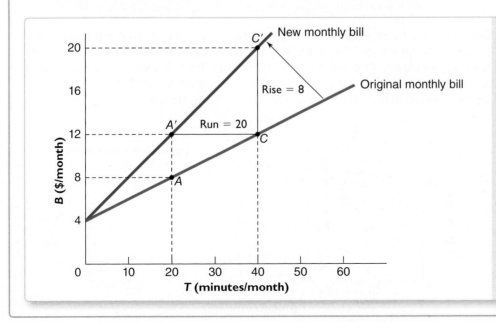

FIGURE 1A.4

The Effect of an Increase in the Charge per Minute.

Because the fixed monthly fee continues to be $4, the vertical intercept of the new plan is the same as that of the original plan. With the new charge per minute of $0.40, the slope of the billing plan rises from 0.20 to 0.40.

CONCEPT CHECK 1A.4

Show how the billing plan whose graph is in Figure 1A.2 would change if the charge per minute were reduced from $0.20 to $0.10.

Concept Check 1A.4 illustrates the general rule that in an equation $Y = a + bX$, a reduction in b makes the slope of the graph of the equation less steep.

CONSTRUCTING EQUATIONS AND GRAPHS FROM TABLES

The next example and concept check show how to transform tabular information into an equation or graph.

EXAMPLE 1A.6	Transforming a Table to a Graph

Table 1A.1 shows four points from a monthly long-distance telephone billing equation. If all points on this billing equation lie on a straight line, find the vertical intercept of the equation and graph it. What is the monthly fixed fee? What is the charge per minute? Calculate the total bill for a month with 1 hour of long-distance calls.

TABLE 1A.1
Points on a Long-Distance Billing Plan

Long-distance bill ($/month)	Total long-distance calls (minutes/month)
10.50	10
11.00	20
11.50	30
12.00	40

One approach to this problem is simply to plot any two points from the table on a graph. Since we are told that the billing equation is a straight line, that line must be the one that passes through any two of its points. Thus, in Figure 1A.5 we use A to denote the point from Table 1A.1 for which a monthly bill of $11 corresponds to 20 minutes per month of calls (second row) and C to denote the point for which a

FIGURE 1A.5

Plotting the Monthly Billing Equation from a Sample of Points.

Point A is taken from row 2, Table 1A.1, and point C from row 4. The monthly billing plan is the straight line that passes through these points.

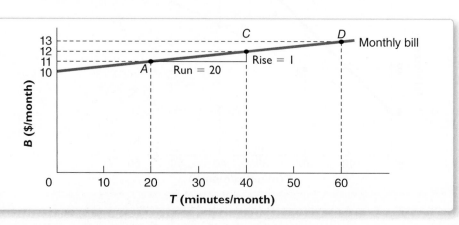

monthly bill of $12 corresponds to 40 minutes per month of calls (fourth row). The straight line passing through these points is the graph of the billing equation.

Unless you have a steady hand, however, or use extremely large graph paper, the method of extending a line between two points on the billing plan is unlikely to be very accurate. An alternative approach is to calculate the equation for the billing plan directly. Since the equation is a straight line, we know that it takes the general form $B = f + sT$, where f is the fixed monthly fee and s is the slope. Our goal is to calculate the vertical intercept f and the slope s. From the same two points we plotted earlier, A and C, we can calculate the slope of the billing plan as s = rise/run = $1/20 = 0.05$.

So all that remains is to calculate f, the fixed monthly fee. At point C on the billing plan, the total monthly bill is $12 for 40 minutes, so we can substitute $B = 12$, $s = 0.05$, and $T = 40$ into the general equation $B = f + sT$ to obtain

$$12 = f + 0.05(40), \tag{1A.4}$$

or

$$12 = f + 2, \tag{1A.5}$$

which solves for $f = 10$. So the monthly billing equation must be

$$B = 10 + 0.05T. \tag{1A.6}$$

For this billing equation, the fixed fee is $10 per month, the calling charge is 5 cents per minute ($0.05/minute), and the total bill for a month with 1 hour of long-distance calls is $B = 10 + 0.05(60) = \$13$, just as shown in Figure 1A.5.

CONCEPT CHECK 1A.5

The following table shows four points from a monthly long-distance telephone billing plan.

Long-distance bill ($/month)	Total long-distance calls (minutes/month)
20.00	10
30.00	20
40.00	30
50.00	40

If all points on this billing plan lie on a straight line, find the vertical intercept of the corresponding equation without graphing it. What is the monthly fixed fee? What is the charge per minute? How much would the charges be for 1 hour of long-distance calls per month?

SOLVING SIMULTANEOUS EQUATIONS

The next example and concept check demonstrate how to proceed when you need to solve two equations with two unknowns.

EXAMPLE 1A.7   Solving Simultaneous Equations

Suppose you are trying to choose between two rate plans for your long-distance telephone service. If you choose Plan 1, your charges will be computed according to the equation

$$B = 10 + 0.04T, \tag{1A.7}$$

where **B** is again your monthly bill in dollars and **T** is your monthly volume of long-distance calls in minutes. If you choose Plan 2, your monthly bill will be computed according to the equation

$$B = 20 + 0.02T. \tag{1A.8}$$

How many minutes of long-distance calls would you have to make each month, on average, to make Plan 2 cheaper?

Plan 1 has the attractive feature of a relatively low monthly fixed fee, but also the unattractive feature of a relatively high rate per minute. In contrast, Plan 2 has a relatively high fixed fee but a relatively low rate per minute. Someone who made an extremely low volume of calls (for example, 10 minutes per month) would do better under Plan 1 (monthly bill = $10.40) than under Plan 2 (monthly bill = $20.20) because the low fixed fee of Plan 1 would more than compensate for its higher rate per minute. Conversely, someone who made an extremely high volume of calls (say, 10,000 minutes per month) would do better under Plan 2 (monthly bill = $220) than under Plan 1 (monthly bill = $410) because Plan 2's lower rate per minute would more than compensate for its higher fixed fee.

Our task here is to find the *break-even calling volume,* which is the monthly calling volume for which the monthly bill is the same under the two plans. One way to answer this question is to graph the two billing plans and see where they cross. At that crossing point, the two equations are satisfied simultaneously, which means that the monthly call volumes will be the same under both plans, as will the monthly bills.

In Figure 1A.6, we see that the graphs of the two plans cross at *A,* where both yield a monthly bill of $30 for 500 minutes of calls per month. The break-even calling volume for these plans is thus 500 minutes per month. If your calling volume is higher than that, on average, you will save money by choosing Plan 2. For example, if you average 700 minutes, your monthly bill under Plan 2 ($34) will be $4 cheaper than under Plan 1 ($38). Conversely, if you average fewer than 500 minutes each month, you will do better under Plan 1. For example, if you average only 200 minutes, your monthly bill under Plan 1 ($18) will be $6 cheaper than under Plan 2 ($24). At 500 minutes per month, the two plans cost exactly the same ($30).

The question posed here also may be answered algebraically. As in the graphical approach just discussed, our goal is to find the point (*T, B*) that satisfies both billing equations simultaneously. As a first step, we rewrite the two billing equations, one on top of the other, as follows:

$$B = 10 + 0.04T. \quad \text{(Plan 1)}$$
$$B = 20 + 0.02T. \quad \text{(Plan 2)}$$

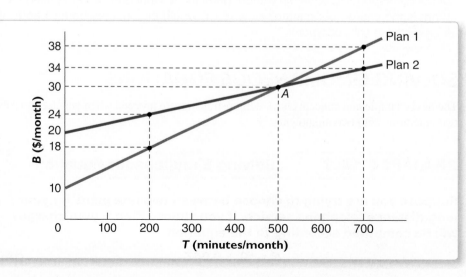

FIGURE 1A.6

The Break-Even Volume of Long-Distance Calls.

When your volume of long-distance calls is 500 minutes per month, your monthly bill will be the same under both plans. For higher calling volumes, Plan 2 is cheaper; Plan 1 is cheaper for lower volumes.

As you'll recall from high school algebra, if we subtract the terms from each side of one equation from the corresponding terms of the other equation, the resulting differences must be equal. So if we subtract the terms on each side of the Plan 2 equation from the corresponding terms in the Plan 1 equation, we get

$$B = 10 + 0.04T \qquad \text{(Plan 1)}$$
$$-B = -20 - 0.02T \qquad \text{(−Plan 2)}$$
$$0 = -10 + 0.02T \qquad \text{(Plan 1 − Plan 2)}.$$

Finally, we solve the last equation (Plan 1 − Plan 2) to get $T = 500$.

Plugging $T = 500$ into either plan's equation, we then find $B = 30$. For example, Plan 1's equation yields $10 + 0.04(500) = 30$, as does Plan 2's: $20 + 0.2(500) = 30$.

Because the point $(T, B) = (500, 30)$ lies on the equations for both plans simultaneously, the algebraic approach just described is often called *the method of simultaneous equations*.

CONCEPT CHECK 1A.6

Suppose you are trying to choose between two rate plans for your long-distance telephone service. If you choose Plan 1, your monthly bill will be computed according to the equation

$$B = 10 + 0.10T \qquad \text{(Plan 1)},$$

where B is again your monthly bill in dollars and T is your monthly volume of long-distance calls in minutes. If you choose Plan 2, your monthly bill will be computed according to the equation

$$B = 100 + 0.01T \qquad \text{(Plan 2)}.$$

Use the algebraic approach described in the preceding example to find the break-even level of monthly call volume for these plans.

KEY TERMS

constant	parameter	variable
dependent variable	rise	vertical intercept
equation	run	
independent variable	slope	

ANSWERS TO APPENDIX CONCEPT CHECKS

1A.1 To calculate your monthly bill for 45 minutes of calls, substitute 45 minutes for T in Equation 1A.1 to get $B = 5 + 0.10(45) = \$9.50$.

1A.2 Calculating the slope using points A and C, we have rise $= 30 - 24 = 6$ and run $= 30 - 15 = 15$, so rise/run $= 6/15 = 2/5 = 0.40$. And since the horizontal intercept of the line is 18, its equation is $B = 18 + 0.40T$. Under this plan, the fixed monthly fee is \$18 and the charge per minute is the slope of the billing line, 0.40, or \$0.40 per minute.

1A.3 A \$2 reduction in the monthly fixed fee would produce a downward parallel shift in the billing plan by \$2.

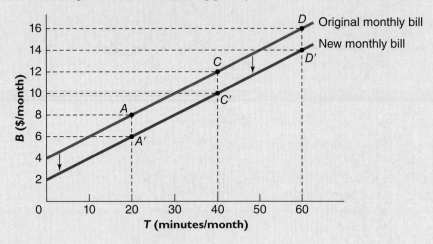

1A.4 With an unchanged monthly fixed fee, the vertical intercept of the new billing plan continues to be 4. The slope of the new plan is 0.10, half the slope of the original plan.

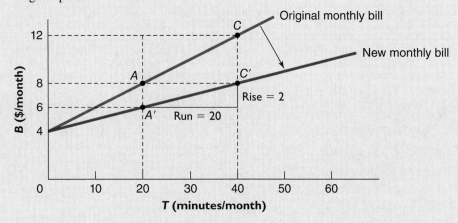

1A.5 Let the billing equation be $B = f + sT$, where f is the fixed monthly fee and s is the slope. From the first two points in the table, calculate the slope $s =$ rise/run $= 10/10 = 1.0$. To calculate f, we can use the information in row 1 of the table to write the billing equation as $20 = f + 1.0(10)$ and solve for $f = 10$. So the monthly billing equation must be $B = 10 + 1.0T$. For this billing equation, the fixed fee is \$10 per month, the calling charge is \$1 per minute, and the total bill for a month with 1 hour of long-distance calls is $B = 10 + 1.0(60) = \$70$.

1A.6 Subtracting the Plan 2 equation from the Plan 1 equation yields the equation

$$0 = -90 + 0.09T \qquad \text{(Plan 1 − Plan 2)},$$

which solves for $T = 1,000$. So if you average more than 1,000 minutes of long-distance calls each month, you'll do better on Plan 2.

Supply and Demand

LEARNING OBJECTIVES

After reading this chapter, you should be able to:

LO1 Describe how the demand and supply curves summarize the behavior of buyers and sellers in the marketplace.

LO2 Discuss how the supply and demand curves interact to determine equilibrium price and quantity.

LO3 Illustrate how shifts in supply and demand curves cause prices and quantities to change.

LO4 Explain why markets in equilibrium tend to leave no unexploited opportunities available to individuals.

2

The stock of foodstuffs on hand at any moment in New York City's grocery stores, restaurants, and private kitchens is sufficient to feed the area's 10 million residents for at most a week or so. Since most of these residents have nutritionally adequate and highly varied diets, and since almost no food is produced within the city proper, provisioning New York requires that millions of pounds of food and drink be delivered to locations throughout the city each day.

No doubt many New Yorkers, buying groceries at their favorite local markets or eating at their favorite Italian restaurants, give little or no thought to the nearly miraculous coordination of people and resources required to feed city residents on a daily basis. But near-miraculous it is, nevertheless. Even if the supplying of New York City consisted only of transporting a fixed collection of foods to a given list of destinations each day, it would be quite an impressive operation, requiring at least a small (and well-managed) army to carry out.

Yet the entire process is astonishingly more complex than that. For example, the system must somehow ensure that not only *enough* food is delivered to satisfy New Yorkers' discriminating palates, but also the *right kinds* of food. There can't be too much pheasant and not enough smoked eel; or too much bacon and not enough eggs; or too much caviar and not enough canned tuna; and so on. Similar judgments must be made *within* each category of food and drink: There must be the right amount of Swiss cheese and the right amounts of provolone, gorgonzola, and feta.

But even this doesn't begin to describe the complexity of the decisions and actions required to provide our nation's largest city with its daily bread. Someone has to decide where each particular type of food gets produced, and how, and by whom. Someone must decide how much of each type of food gets delivered to *each* of the tens of thousands of restaurants and grocery stores in the city. Someone must determine whether the deliveries should be made in big trucks or small ones, arrange that the trucks be in the right place at the right time, and ensure that gasoline and qualified drivers be available.

Thousands of individuals must decide what role, if any, they will play in this collective effort. Some people—just the right number—must choose to drive food delivery trucks rather than trucks that deliver lumber. Others—again, just the right number—must become the mechanics who fix these trucks rather than carpenters who build houses. Others must become farmers rather than architects or bricklayers. Still others must become chefs in upscale restaurants, or flip burgers at McDonald's, instead of becoming plumbers or electricians.

Yet despite the almost incomprehensible number and complexity of the tasks involved, somehow the supplying of New York City manages to get done remarkably smoothly. Oh, a grocery store will occasionally run out of flank steak or a diner will sometimes be told that someone else has just ordered the last serving of roast duck. But if episodes like these stick in memory, it is only because they are rare. For the most part, New York's food delivery system—like that of every other city in the country—functions so seamlessly that it attracts virtually no notice.

The situation is strikingly different in New York City's rental housing market. According to one estimate, the city needs between 20,000 and 40,000 new housing units each year merely to keep up with population growth and to replace existing housing that is deteriorated beyond repair. The actual rate of new construction in the city, however, is only 6,000 units per year. As a result, America's most densely populated city has been experiencing a protracted housing shortage. Yet, paradoxically, in the midst of this shortage, apartment houses are being demolished; and in the vacant lots left behind, people from the neighborhoods are planting flower gardens!

New York City is experiencing not only a growing shortage of rental housing, but also chronically strained relations between landlords and tenants. In one all-too-typical case, for example, a photographer living in a loft on the Lower East Side waged an eight-year court battle with his landlord that generated literally thousands of pages of

legal documents. "Once we put up a doorbell for ourselves," the photographer recalled, "and [the landlord] pulled it out, so we pulled out the wires to his doorbell."[1] The landlord, for his part, accused the photographer of obstructing his efforts to renovate the apartment. According to the landlord, the tenant preferred for the apartment to remain in substandard condition since that gave him an excuse to withhold rent payments.

Same city, two strikingly different patterns: In the food industry, goods and services are available in wide variety and people (at least those with adequate income) are generally satisfied with what they receive and the choices available to them. In contrast, in the rental housing industry, chronic shortages and chronic dissatisfaction are rife among both buyers and sellers. Why this difference?

The brief answer is that New York City relies on a complex system of administrative rent regulations to allocate housing units but leaves the allocation of food essentially in the hands of market forces—the forces of supply and demand. Although intuition might suggest otherwise, both theory and experience suggest that the seemingly chaotic and unplanned outcomes of market forces, in most cases, can do a better job of allocating economic resources than can (for example) a government agency, even if the agency has the best of intentions.

In this chapter we'll explore how markets allocate food, housing, and other goods and services, usually with remarkable efficiency despite the complexity of the tasks. To be sure, markets are by no means perfect, and our stress on their virtues is to some extent an attempt to counteract what most economists view as an underappreciation by the general public of their remarkable strengths. But, in the course of our discussion, we'll see why markets function so smoothly most of the time and why bureaucratic rules and regulations rarely work as well in solving complex economic problems.

Why does New York City's food distribution system work so much better than its housing market?

[1] Quoted by John Tierney, "The Rentocracy: At the Intersection of Supply and Demand," *New York Times Magazine,* May 4, 1997, p. 39.

To convey an understanding of how markets work is a major goal of this course, and in this chapter we provide only a brief introduction and overview. As the course proceeds, we'll discuss the economic role of markets in considerably more detail, paying attention to some of the problems of markets as well as their strengths.

WHAT, HOW, AND FOR WHOM? CENTRAL PLANNING VERSUS THE MARKET

No city, state, or society—regardless of how it is organized—can escape the need to answer certain basic economic questions. For example, how much of our limited time and other resources should we devote to building housing, how much to the production of food, and how much to providing other goods and services? What techniques should we use to produce each good? Who should be assigned to each specific task? And how should the resulting goods and services be distributed among people?

In the thousands of different societies for which records are available, issues like these have been decided in essentially one of two ways. One approach is for all economic decisions to be made centrally, by an individual or small number of individuals on behalf of a larger group. For example, in many agrarian societies throughout history, families or other small groups consumed only those goods and services that they produced for themselves, and a single clan or family leader made most important production and distribution decisions. On an immensely larger scale, the economic organization of the former Soviet Union (and other communist countries) was also largely centralized. In so-called centrally planned communist nations, a central bureaucratic committee established production targets for the country's farms and factories, developed a master plan for how to achieve the targets (including detailed instructions concerning who was to produce what), and set up guidelines for the distribution and use of the goods and services produced.

Neither form of centralized economic organization is much in evidence today. When implemented on a small scale, as in a self-sufficient family enterprise, centralized decision making is certainly feasible. However, the jack-of-all-trades approach was doomed once it became clear how dramatically people could improve their living standards by specialization—that is, by having each individual focus his or her efforts on a relatively narrow range of tasks. And with the fall of the Soviet Union and its satellite nations in the late 1980s, there are now only three communist economies left in the world: Cuba, North Korea, and China. The first two of these appear to be on their last legs, economically speaking, and China has largely abandoned any attempt to control production and distribution decisions from the center. The major remaining examples of centralized allocation and control now reside in the bureaucratic agencies that administer programs like New York City's rent controls—programs that are themselves becoming increasingly rare.

At the beginning of the twenty-first century, we are therefore left, for the most part, with the second major form of economic system, one in which production and distribution decisions are left to individuals interacting in private markets. In the so-called capitalist, or free-market, economies, people decide for themselves which careers to pursue and which products to produce or buy. In fact, there are no *pure* free-market economies today. Modern industrial countries are more properly described as "mixed economies." Their goods and services are allocated by a combination of free markets, regulation, and other forms of collective control. Still, it makes sense to refer to such systems as free-market economies because people are for the most part free to start businesses, shut them down, or sell them. And within broad limits, the distribution of goods and services is determined by individual preferences backed by individual purchasing power, which in most cases comes from the income people earn in the labor market.

In country after country, markets have replaced centralized control for the simple reason that they tend to assign production tasks and consumption benefits much more effectively. The popular press and conventional wisdom often assert that economists disagree about important issues. (As someone once quipped, "If you lay all the economists in the world end to end, they still wouldn't reach a conclusion.") The fact is, however, that there is overwhelming agreement among economists about a broad range of issues. A substantial majority believes that markets are the most effective means for allocating society's scarce resources. For example, a recent survey found that more than 90 percent of American professional economists believe that rent regulations like the ones implemented by New York City do more harm than good. That the stated aim of these regulations—to make rental housing more affordable for middle- and low-income families—is clearly benign was not enough to prevent them from wreaking havoc on New York City's housing market. To see why, we must explore how goods and services are allocated in private markets, and why nonmarket means of allocating goods and services often do not produce the expected results.

BUYERS AND SELLERS IN MARKETS

market the market for any good consists of all buyers and sellers of that good

Beginning with some simple concepts and definitions, we will explore how the interactions among buyers and sellers in markets determine the prices and quantities of the various goods and services traded. We begin by defining a market: The **market** for any good consists of all the buyers and sellers of that good. So, for example, the market for pizza on a given day in a given place is just the set of people (or other economic actors such as firms) potentially able to buy or sell pizza at that time and location.

In the market for pizza, sellers comprise the individuals and companies that either do sell—or might, under the right circumstances, sell—pizza. Similarly, buyers in this market include all individuals who buy—or might buy—pizza.

In most parts of the country, a decent pizza can still be had for less than $12. Where does the market price of pizza come from? Looking beyond pizza to the vast array of other goods that are bought and sold every day, we may ask, "Why are some goods cheap and others expensive?" Aristotle had no idea. Nor did Plato, or Copernicus, or Newton. On reflection, it is astonishing that, for almost the entire span of human history, not even the most intelligent and creative minds on Earth had any real inkling of how to answer that seemingly simple question. Even Adam Smith, the Scottish moral philosopher whose *Wealth of Nations* launched the discipline of economics in 1776, suffered confusion on this issue.

Smith and other early economists (including Karl Marx) thought that the market price of a good was determined by its cost of production. But although costs surely do affect prices, they cannot explain why one of Pablo Picasso's paintings sells for so much more than one of Jackson Pollock's.

Stanley Jevons and other nineteenth-century economists tried to explain price by focusing on the value people derived from consuming different goods and services. It certainly seems plausible that people will pay a lot for a good they value highly. Yet willingness to pay cannot be the whole story, either. Deprive a person in the desert of water, for example, and he will be dead in a matter of hours, and yet water sells for less than a penny a gallon. By contrast, human beings can get along perfectly well without gold, and yet gold sells for more than $1,000 an ounce.

Cost of production? Value to the user? Which is it? The answer, which seems obvious to today's economists, is that both matter. Writing in the late nineteenth century, the British economist Alfred Marshall was among the first to show clearly how costs and value interact to determine both the prevailing market price for a good and the amount of it that is bought and sold. Our task in the pages ahead will be to explore Marshall's insights and gain some practice in applying them. As a first step, we

Why do Pablo Picasso's paintings sell for so much more than Jackson Pollock's?

© Wu Ching-teng/Xinhua Press/Corbis Wire/Corbis

A Jackson Pollock painting.

© Peter Horree/Alamy

introduce the two main components of Marshall's pathbreaking analysis: the demand curve and the supply curve.

The Demand Curve

In the market for pizza, the **demand curve** for pizza is a simple schedule or graph that tells us how many slices people would be willing to buy at different prices. By convention, economists usually put price on the vertical axis of the demand curve and quantity on the horizontal axis.

A fundamental property of the demand curve is that it is downward-sloping with respect to price. For example, the demand curve for pizza tells us that as the price of pizza falls, buyers will buy more slices. Thus, the daily demand curve for pizza in Chicago on a given day might look like the curve seen in Figure 2.1. (Although economists usually refer to demand and supply "curves," we often draw them as straight lines in examples.)

The demand curve in Figure 2.1 tells us that when the price of pizza is low—say $2 per slice—buyers will want to buy 16,000 slices per day, whereas they will want to buy only 12,000 slices at a price of $3 and only 8,000 at a price of $4. The demand curve for pizza—as for any other good—slopes downward for multiple reasons. Some have to do with the individual consumer's reactions to price changes. Thus, as pizza becomes more expensive, a consumer may switch to chicken sandwiches, hamburgers, or other foods that substitute for pizza. This is called the **substitution effect** of a price change. In addition, a price increase reduces the quantity demanded because it reduces purchasing power: A consumer simply can't afford to buy as many slices of pizza at higher prices as at lower prices. This is called the **income effect** of a price change.

Another reason the demand curve slopes downward is that consumers differ in terms of how much they're willing to pay for the good. The Cost-Benefit Principle tells us that a given person will buy the good if the benefit he expects to receive from it exceeds its cost. The benefit is the **buyer's reservation price**, the highest dollar amount he'd be willing to pay for the good. The cost of the good is the actual amount that the buyer actually must pay for it, which is the market price of the good. In most markets, different buyers have different reservation prices. So, when the good sells for a high price, it will satisfy the cost-benefit test for fewer buyers than when it sells for a lower price.

To put this same point another way, the fact that the demand curve for a good is downward-sloping reflects the fact that the reservation price of the marginal buyer declines as the quantity of the good bought increases. Here the marginal buyer is the person who purchases the last unit of the good sold. If buyers are currently purchasing 12,000 slices of pizza a day in Figure 2.1, for example, the reservation price for the buyer of the 12,000th slice must be $3. (If someone had been willing to pay more than that, the quantity demanded at a price of $3 would have been more than 12,000 to begin with.) By

demand curve a schedule or graph showing the quantity of a good that buyers wish to buy at each price

substitution effect the change in the quantity demanded of a good that results because buyers switch to or from substitutes when the price of the good changes

income effect the change in the quantity demanded of a good that results because a change in the price of a good changes the buyer's purchasing power

buyer's reservation price the largest dollar amount the buyer would be willing to pay for a good

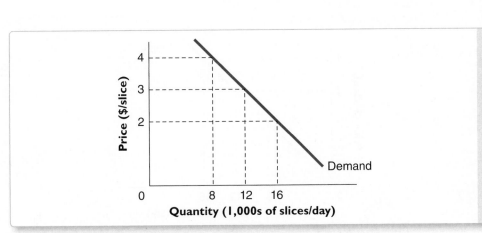

FIGURE 2.1

The Daily Demand Curve for Pizza in Chicago.

The demand curve for any good is a downward-sloping function of its price.

similar reasoning, when the quantity sold is 16,000 slices per day, the marginal buyer's reservation price must be only $2.

We defined the demand curve for any good as a schedule telling how much of it consumers wish to purchase at various prices. This is called the *horizontal interpretation* of the demand curve. Using the horizontal interpretation, we start with price on the vertical axis and read the corresponding quantity demanded on the horizontal axis. Thus, at a price of $4 per slice, the demand curve in Figure 2.1 tells us that the quantity of pizza demanded will be 8,000 slices per day.

The demand curve also can be interpreted in a second way, which is to start with quantity on the horizontal axis and then read the marginal buyer's reservation price on the vertical axis. Thus, when the quantity of pizza sold is 8,000 slices per day, the demand curve in Figure 2.1 tells us that the marginal buyer's reservation price is $4 per slice. This second way of reading the demand curve is called the *vertical interpretation*.

CONCEPT CHECK 2.1

In Figure 2.1, what is the marginal buyer's reservation price when the quantity of pizza sold is 10,000 slices per day? For the same demand curve, what will be the quantity of pizza demanded at a price of $2.50 per slice?

The Supply Curve

supply curve a graph or schedule showing the quantity of a good that sellers wish to sell at each price

In the market for pizza, the **supply curve** is a simple schedule or graph that tells us, for each possible price, the total number of slices that all pizza vendors would be willing to sell at that price. What does the supply curve of pizza look like? The answer to this question is based on the logical assumption that suppliers should be willing to sell additional slices as long as the price they receive is sufficient to cover their opportunity cost of supplying them. Thus, if what someone could earn by selling a slice of pizza is insufficient to compensate her for what she could have earned if she had spent her time and invested her money in some other way, she will not sell that slice. Otherwise, she will.

Just as buyers differ with respect to the amounts they are willing to pay for pizza, sellers also differ with respect to their opportunity cost of supplying pizza. For those with limited education and work experience, the opportunity cost of selling pizza is relatively low (because such individuals typically do not have a lot of high-paying alternatives). For others, the opportunity cost of selling pizza is of moderate value, and for still others—like rock stars and professional athletes—it is prohibitively high. In part because of these differences in opportunity cost among people, the daily supply curve of pizza will be *upward-sloping* with respect to price. As an illustration, see Figure 2.2, which shows a hypothetical supply curve for pizza in the Chicago market on a given day.

FIGURE 2.2

The Daily Supply Curve of Pizza in Chicago.

At higher prices, sellers generally offer more units for sale.

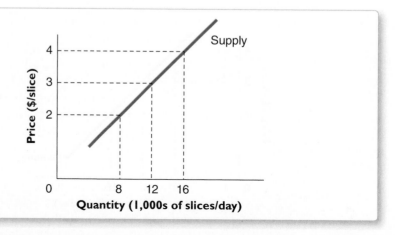

The reason the supply curve slopes upward may be seen as a consequence of the fact that as we expand the production of pizza, we turn first to those whose opportunity cost of producing pizza is lowest, and only then to others with a higher opportunity cost.

Like the demand curve, the supply curve can be interpreted either horizontally or vertically. Under the horizontal interpretation, we begin with a price and then go over to the supply curve to read the quantity that sellers wish to sell at that price on the horizontal axis. For instance, at a price of $2 per slice, sellers in Figure 2.2 wish to sell 8,000 slices per day.

Under the vertical interpretation, we begin with a quantity and then go up to the supply curve to read the corresponding marginal cost on the vertical axis. Thus, if sellers in Figure 2.2 are currently supplying 12,000 slices per day, the opportunity cost of the marginal seller is $3 per slice. In other words, the supply curve tells us that the marginal cost of producing the 12,000th slice of pizza is $3. (If someone could produce a 12,001st slice for less than $3, she would have an incentive to supply it, so the quantity of pizza supplied at $3 per slice would not have been 12,000 slices per day to begin with.) By similar reasoning, when the quantity of pizza supplied is 16,000 slices per day, the marginal cost of producing another slice must be $4. The **seller's reservation price** for selling an additional unit of a good is her marginal cost of producing that good. It is the smallest dollar amount for which she would not be worse off if she sold an additional unit.

seller's reservation price the smallest dollar amount for which a seller would be willing to sell an additional unit, generally equal to marginal cost

CONCEPT CHECK 2.2

In Figure 2.2, what is the marginal cost of a slice of pizza when the quantity of pizza sold is 10,000 slices per day? For the same supply curve, what will be the quantity of pizza supplied at a price of $3.50 per slice?

RECAP ↑

DEMAND AND SUPPLY CURVES

The *market* for a good consists of the actual and potential buyers and sellers of that good. For any given price, the *demand curve* shows the quantity that demanders would be willing to buy and the *supply curve* shows the quantity that suppliers of the good would be willing to sell. Suppliers are willing to sell more at higher prices (supply curves slope upward) and demanders are willing to buy less at higher prices (demand curves slope downward).

MARKET EQUILIBRIUM

The concept of **equilibrium** is employed in both the physical and social sciences, and it is of central importance in economic analysis. In general, a system is in equilibrium when all forces at work within the system are canceled by others, resulting in a balanced or unchanging situation. In physics, for example, a ball hanging from a spring is said to be in equilibrium when the spring has stretched sufficiently that the upward force it exerts on the ball is exactly counterbalanced by the downward force of gravity. In economics, a market is said to be in equilibrium when no participant in the market has any reason to alter his or her behavior, so that there is no tendency for production or prices in that market to change.

If we want to determine the final position of a ball hanging from a spring, we need to find the point at which the forces of gravity and spring tension are balanced and the system is in equilibrium. Similarly, if we want to find the price at which a good will sell

equilibrium a balanced or unchanging situation in which all forces at work within a system are canceled by others

FIGURE 2.3

The Equilibrium Price and Quantity of Pizza in Chicago.

The equilibrium quantity and price of a product are the values that correspond to the intersection of the supply and demand curves for that product.

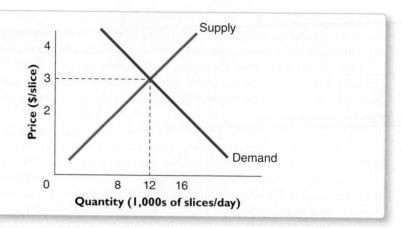

equilibrium price and **equilibrium quantity** the price and quantity at the intersection of the supply and demand curves for the good

(which we will call the **equilibrium price**) and the quantity of it that will be sold (the **equilibrium quantity**), we need to find the equilibrium in the market for that good. The basic tools for finding the equilibrium in a market for a good are the supply and demand curves for that good. For reasons we will explain, the equilibrium price and equilibrium quantity of a good are the price and quantity at which the supply and demand curves for the good intersect. For the hypothetical supply and demand curves shown earlier for the pizza market in Chicago, the equilibrium price will therefore be $3 per slice, and the equilibrium quantity of pizza sold will be 12,000 slices per day, as shown in Figure 2.3.

Note that at the equilibrium price of $3 per slice, both sellers and buyers are "satisfied" in the following sense: Buyers are buying exactly the quantity of pizza they wish to buy at that price (12,000 slices per day) and sellers are selling exactly the quantity of pizza they wish to sell (also 12,000 slices per day). And since they are satisfied in this sense, neither buyers nor sellers face any incentives to change their behavior.

market equilibrium occurs in a market when all buyers and sellers are satisfied with their respective quantities at the market price

Note the limited sense of the term "satisfied" in the definition of **market equilibrium**. It doesn't mean that sellers wouldn't be pleased to receive a price higher than the equilibrium price. Rather, it means only that they're able to sell all they wish to sell at that price. Similarly, to say that buyers are satisfied at the equilibrium price doesn't mean that they wouldn't be happy to pay less than that price. Rather, it means only that they're able to buy exactly as many units of the good as they wish to at the equilibrium price.

Note also that if the price of pizza in our Chicago market were anything other than $3 per slice, either buyers or sellers would be frustrated. Suppose, for example, that the price of pizza were $4 per slice, as shown in Figure 2.4. At that price, buyers wish to buy

FIGURE 2.4

Excess Supply.

When price exceeds equilibrium price, there is excess supply, or surplus, the difference between quantity supplied and quantity demanded.

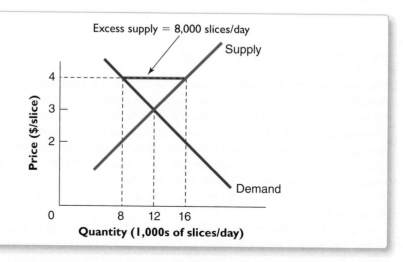

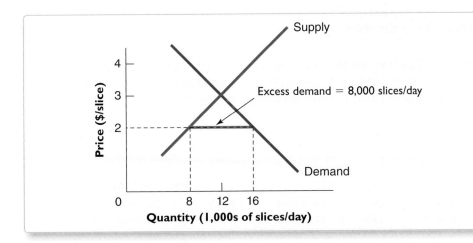

FIGURE 2.5

Excess Demand.

When price lies below equilibrium price, there is excess demand, the difference between quantity demanded and quantity supplied.

only 8,000 slices per day, but sellers wish to sell 16,000. And since no one can force someone to buy a slice of pizza against her wishes, this means that buyers will buy only the 8,000 slices they wish to buy. So when price exceeds the equilibrium price, it is sellers who end up being frustrated. At a price of $4 in this example, they are left with an **excess supply** of 8,000 slices per day.

Conversely, suppose that the price of pizza in our Chicago market were less than the equilibrium price—say, $2 per slice. As shown in Figure 2.5, buyers want to buy 16,000 slices per day at that price, whereas sellers want to sell only 8,000. And since sellers cannot be forced to sell pizza against their wishes, this time it is the buyers who end up being frustrated. At a price of $2 per slice in this example, they experience an **excess demand** of 8,000 slices per day.

An extraordinary feature of private markets for goods and services is their automatic tendency to gravitate toward their respective equilibrium prices and quantities. The mechanisms by which the adjustment happens are implicit in our definitions of excess supply and excess demand. Suppose, for example, that the price of pizza in our hypothetical market was $4 per slice, leading to excess supply as shown in Figure 2.4. Because sellers are frustrated in the sense of wanting to sell more pizza than buyers wish to buy, sellers have an incentive to take whatever steps they can to increase their sales. The simplest strategy available to them is to cut their price slightly. Thus, if one seller reduced his price from $4 to, say, $3.95 per slice, he would attract many of the buyers who had been paying $4 per slice for pizza supplied by other sellers. Those sellers, in order to recover their lost business, would then have an incentive to match the price cut. But notice that if all sellers lowered their prices to $3.95 per slice, there would still be considerable excess supply. So sellers would face continuing incentives to cut their prices. This pressure to cut prices won't go away until prices fall all the way to $3 per slice.

Conversely, suppose that price starts out less than the equilibrium price—say, $2 per slice. This time it is buyers who are frustrated. A person who can't get all the pizza he wants at a price of $2 per slice has an incentive to offer a higher price, hoping to obtain pizza that would otherwise have been sold to other buyers. And sellers, for their part, will be only too happy to post higher prices as long as queues of frustrated buyers remain.

The upshot is that price has a tendency to gravitate to its equilibrium level under conditions of either excess supply or excess demand. And when price reaches its equilibrium level, both buyers and sellers are satisfied in the technical sense of being able to buy or sell precisely the amounts of their choosing.

excess supply the amount by which quantity supplied exceeds quantity demanded when the price of a good exceeds the equilibrium price

excess demand the amount by which quantity demanded exceeds quantity supplied when the price of a good lies below the equilibrium price

EXAMPLE 2.1   Market Equilibrium

Samples of points on the demand and supply curves of a pizza market are provided in Table 2.1. Graph the demand and supply curves for this market and find its equilibrium price and quantity.

TABLE 2.1
Points along the Demand and Supply Curves of a Pizza Market

Demand for Pizza		Supply of Pizza	
Price ($/slice)	Quantity demanded (1,000s of slices/day)	Price ($/slice)	Quantity supplied (1,000s of slices/day)
1	8	1	2
2	6	2	4
3	4	3	6
4	2	4	8

The points in the table are plotted in Figure 2.6 and then joined to indicate the supply and demand curves for this market. These curves intersect to yield an equilibrium price of $2.50 per slice and an equilibrium quantity of 5,000 slices per day.

FIGURE 2.6

Graphing Supply and Demand and Finding Equilibrium Price and Quantity.

To graph the demand and supply curves, plot the relevant points given in the table and then join them with a line. Equilibrium price and quantity occur at the intersection of these curves.

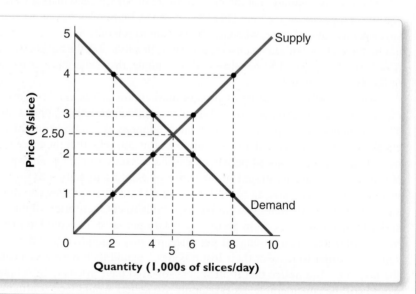

We emphasize that market equilibrium doesn't necessarily produce an ideal outcome for all market participants. Thus, in Example 2.1, market participants are satisfied with the amount of pizza they buy and sell at a price of $2.50 per slice, but for a poor buyer this may signify little more than that he *can't* buy additional pizza without sacrificing other more highly valued purchases.

Indeed, buyers with extremely low incomes often have difficulty purchasing even basic goods and services, which has prompted governments in almost every society to attempt to ease the burdens of the poor. Yet the laws of supply and demand cannot simply be repealed by an act of the legislature. In the next section, we'll see that when legislators attempt to prevent markets from reaching their equilibrium prices and quantities, they often do more harm than good. Fortunately, there are other, more effective, ways of providing assistance to needy families.

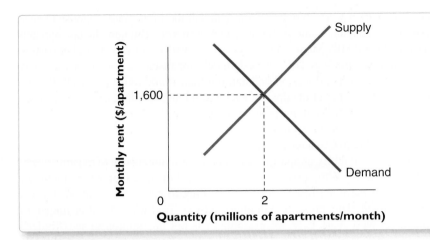

FIGURE 2.7

An Unregulated Housing Market.

For the supply and demand curves shown, the equilibrium monthly rent is $1,600 and 2 million apartments will be rented at that price.

Rent Controls Reconsidered

Consider again the market for rental housing units in New York City and suppose that the demand and supply curves for one-bedroom apartments are as shown in Figure 2.7. This market, left alone, would reach an equilibrium monthly rent of $1,600, at which 2 million one-bedroom apartments would be rented. Both landlords and tenants would be satisfied, in the sense that they would not wish to rent either more or fewer units at that price.

This wouldn't necessarily mean, of course, that all is well and good. Many potential tenants, for example, might simply be unable to afford a rent of $1,600 per month and thus be forced to remain homeless (or to move out of the city to a cheaper location). Suppose that, acting purely out of benign motives, legislators made it unlawful for landlords to charge more than $800 per month for one-bedroom apartments. Their stated aim in enacting this law was that no person should have to remain homeless because decent housing was unaffordable.

But note in Figure 2.8 that when rents for one-bedroom apartments are prevented from rising above $800 per month, landlords are willing to supply only 1 million apartments per month, 1 million fewer than at the equilibrium monthly rent of $1,600. Note also that at the controlled rent of $800 per month, tenants want to rent 3 million one-bedroom apartments per month. (For example, many people who would have decided to live in New Jersey rather than pay $1,600 a month in New York will now choose to live in the city.) So when rents are prevented from rising above $800 per month, we see an excess demand for one-bedroom apartments of 2 million units each month. Put another way, the rent controls result in a housing shortage of 2 million units each month. What is more, the number of apartments actually available *declines* by 1 million units per month.

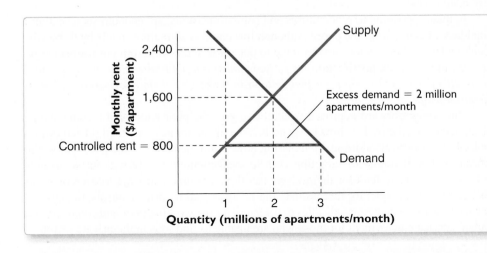

FIGURE 2.8

Rent Controls.

When rents are prohibited from rising to the equilibrium level, the result is excess demand in the housing market.

If the housing market were completely unregulated, the immediate response to such a high level of excess demand would be for rents to rise sharply. But here the law prevents them from rising above $800. Many other ways exist, however, in which market participants can respond to the pressures of excess demand. For instance, owners will quickly learn that they are free to spend less on maintaining their rental units. After all, if there are scores of renters knocking at the door of each vacant apartment, a landlord has considerable room to maneuver. Leaking pipes, peeling paint, broken furnaces, and other problems are less likely to receive prompt attention—or, indeed, any attention at all—when rents are set well below market-clearing levels.

Nor are reduced availability of apartments and poorer maintenance of existing apartments the only difficulties. With an offering of only 1 million apartments per month, we see in Figure 2.8 that there are renters who'd be willing to pay as much as $2,400 per month for an apartment. This pressure will almost always find ways, legal or illegal, of expressing itself. In New York City, for example, it is not uncommon to see "finder's fees" or "key deposits" as high as several thousand dollars. Owners who cannot charge a market-clearing rent for their apartments also have the option of converting them to condominiums or co-ops, which enables them to sell their assets for prices much closer to their true economic value.

Even when rent-controlled apartment owners don't hike their prices in these various ways, serious misallocations result. For instance, ill-suited roommates often remain together despite their constant bickering because each is reluctant to reenter the housing market. Or a widow might steadfastly remain in her seven-room apartment even after her children have left home because it is much cheaper than alternative dwellings not covered by rent control. It would be much better for all concerned if she relinquished that space to a larger family that valued it more highly. But under rent controls, she has no economic incentive to do so.

There's also another more insidious cost of rent controls. In markets without rent controls, landlords cannot discriminate against potential tenants on the basis of race, religion, sexual orientation, physical disability, or national origin without suffering an economic penalty. Refusal to rent to members of specific groups would reduce the demand for their apartments, which would mean having to accept lower rents. When rents are artificially pegged below their equilibrium level, however, the resulting excess demand for apartments enables landlords to engage in discrimination with no further economic penalty.

Rent controls are not the only instance in which governments have attempted to repeal the law of supply and demand in the interest of helping the poor. During the late 1970s, for example, the federal government tried to hold the price of gasoline below its equilibrium level out of concern that high gasoline prices imposed unacceptable hardships on low-income drivers. As with controls in the rental housing market, unintended consequences of price controls in the gasoline market made the policy an extremely costly way of trying to aid the poor. For example, gasoline shortages resulted in long lines at the pumps, a waste not only of valuable time, but also of gasoline as cars sat idling for extended periods.

In their opposition to rent controls and similar measures, are economists revealing a total lack of concern for the poor? Although this claim is sometimes made by those who don't understand the issues, or who stand to benefit in some way from government regulations, there is little justification for it. *Economists simply realize that there are much more effective ways to help poor people than to try to give them apartments and other goods at artificially low prices.*

One straightforward approach would be to give the poor additional income and let them decide for themselves how to spend it. True, there are also practical difficulties involved in transferring additional purchasing power into the hands of the poor—most importantly, the difficulty of targeting cash to the genuinely needy without weakening others' incentives to fend for themselves. But there are practical ways to overcome this difficulty. For example, for far less than the waste caused by price controls, the government could afford generous subsidies to the wages of the working poor and could sponsor public-service employment for those who are unable to find jobs in the private sector.

Regulations that peg prices below equilibrium levels have far-reaching effects on market outcomes. The following concept check asks you to consider what happens when a price control is established at a level above the equilibrium price.

CONCEPT CHECK 2.3

In the rental housing market whose demand and supply curves are shown below, what will be the effect of a law that prevents rents from rising above $1,200 per month?

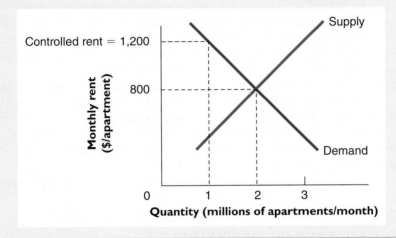

Pizza Price Controls?

The sources of the contrast between the rent-controlled housing market and the largely unregulated food markets in New York City can be seen more vividly by trying to imagine what would happen if concern for the poor led the city's leaders to implement price controls on pizza. Suppose, for example, that the supply and demand curves for pizza are as shown in Figure 2.9 and that the city imposes a **price ceiling** of $2 per slice, making it unlawful to charge more than that amount. At $2 per slice, buyers want to buy 16,000 slices per day, but sellers want to sell only 8,000.

price ceiling a maximum allowable price, specified by law

At a price of $2 per slice, every pizza restaurant in the city will have long queues of buyers trying unsuccessfully to purchase pizza. Frustrated buyers will behave rudely to clerks, who will respond in kind. Friends of restaurant managers will begin to get preferential treatment. Devious pricing strategies will begin to emerge (such as the $2 slice of pizza sold in combination with a $5 cup of Coke). Pizza will be made from poorer-quality ingredients. Rumors will begin to circulate about sources of black-market pizza. And so on.

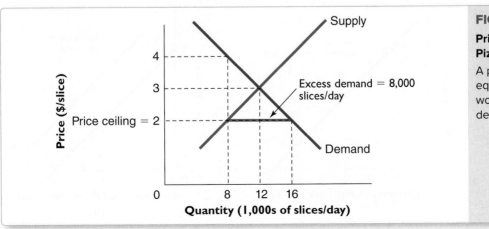

FIGURE 2.9

Price Controls in the Pizza Market.

A price ceiling below the equilibrium price of pizza would result in excess demand for pizza.

The very idea of not being able to buy a pizza seems absurd, yet precisely such things happen routinely in markets in which prices are held below the equilibrium levels. For example, prior to the collapse of communist governments, it was considered normal in those countries for people to stand in line for hours to buy bread and other basic goods, while the politically connected had first choice of those goods that were available.

RECAP ↑

MARKET EQUILIBRIUM

Market equilibrium, the situation in which all buyers and sellers are satisfied with their respective quantities at the market price, occurs at the intersection of the supply and demand curves. The corresponding price and quantity are called the *equilibrium price* and the *equilibrium quantity.*

Unless prevented by regulation, prices and quantities are driven toward their equilibrium values by the actions of buyers and sellers. If the price is initially too high, so that there is excess supply, frustrated sellers will cut their price in order to sell more. If the price is initially too low, so that there is excess demand, competition among buyers drives the price upward. This process continues until equilibrium is reached.

PREDICTING AND EXPLAINING CHANGES IN PRICES AND QUANTITIES

change in the quantity demanded a movement along the demand curve that occurs in response to a change in price

change in demand a shift of the entire demand curve

If we know how the factors that govern supply and demand curves are changing, we can make informed predictions about how prices and the corresponding quantities will change. But when describing changing circumstances in the marketplace, we must take care to recognize some important terminological distinctions. For example, we must distinguish between the meanings of the seemingly similar expressions **change in the quantity demanded** and **change in demand**. When we speak of a "change in the quantity demanded," this means the change in the quantity that people wish to buy that occurs in response to a change in price. For instance, Figure 2.10(a) depicts an increase in the quantity demanded that occurs in response to a reduction in the price of tuna. When the price falls from $2 to $1 per can, the quantity demanded rises from 8,000 to 10,000 cans per day. By contrast, when we speak of a "change in demand," this means a *shift in the entire demand curve.* For example, Figure 2.10(b) depicts an increase in demand, meaning that at every price the quantity demanded is higher than before. In summary, a "change in the quantity demanded" refers to a movement *along* the demand curve and a "change in demand" means a *shift* of the entire curve.

FIGURE 2.10

An Increase in the Quantity Demanded versus an Increase in Demand.

(a) An increase in quantity demanded describes a downward movement along the demand curve as price falls.
(b) An increase in demand describes an outward shift of the demand curve.

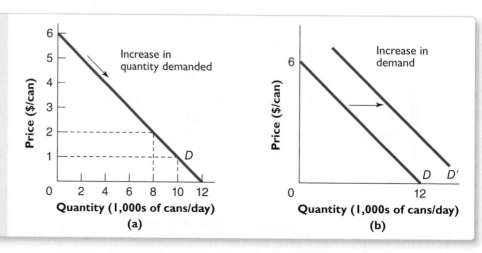

A similar terminological distinction applies on the supply side of the market. A **change in supply** means a shift in the entire supply curve, whereas a **change in the quantity supplied** refers to a movement along the supply curve.

Alfred Marshall's supply and demand model is one of the most useful tools of the economic naturalist. Once we understand the forces that govern the placements of supply and demand curves, we're suddenly in a position to make sense of a host of interesting observations in the world around us.

change in supply a shift of the entire supply curve

change in the quantity supplied a movement along the supply curve that occurs in response to a change in price

Shifts in Demand

To get a better feel for how the supply and demand model enables us to predict and explain price and quantity movements, it's helpful to begin with a few simple examples. The first one illustrates a shift in demand that results from events outside the particular market itself.

EXAMPLE 2.2   **Complements**

What will happen to the equilibrium price and quantity of tennis balls if court rental fees decline?

Let the initial supply and demand curves for tennis balls be as shown by the curves S and D in Figure 2.11, where the resulting equilibrium price and quantity are $1 per ball and 40 million balls per month, respectively. Tennis courts and tennis balls are what economists call **complements**, goods that are more valuable when used in combination than when used alone. Tennis balls, for example, would be of little value if there were no tennis courts on which to play. (Tennis balls would still have *some* value even without courts—for example, to the parents who pitch them to their children for batting practice.) As tennis courts become cheaper to use, people will respond by playing more tennis, and this will increase their demand for tennis balls. A decline in court-rental fees will thus shift the demand curve for tennis balls rightward to D'. (A "rightward shift" of a demand curve also can be described as an "upward shift." These distinctions correspond, respectively, to the horizontal and vertical interpretations of the demand curve.)

complements two goods are complements in consumption if an increase in the price of one causes a leftward shift in the demand curve for the other (or if a decrease causes a rightward shift)

Note in Figure 2.11 that, for the illustrative demand shift shown, the new equilibrium price of tennis balls, $1.40, is higher than the original price and the new equilibrium quantity, 58 million balls per month, is higher than the original quantity.

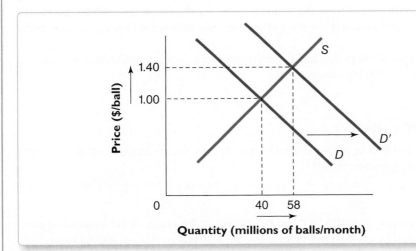

FIGURE 2.11

The Effect on the Market for Tennis Balls of a Decline in Court-Rental Fees.

When the price of a complement falls, demand shifts right, causing equilibrium price and quantity to rise.

EXAMPLE 2.3   **Substitutes**

What will happen to the equilibrium price and quantity of overnight letter delivery service as the price of Internet access falls?

substitutes two goods are substitutes in consumption if an increase in the price of one causes a rightward shift in the demand curve for the other (or if a decrease causes a leftward shift)

Suppose the initial supply and demand curves for overnight letter deliveries are as shown by the curves *S* and *D* in Figure 2.12 and that the resulting equilibrium price and quantity are denoted *P* and *Q*. E-mail messages and overnight letters are examples of what economists call **substitutes**, meaning that, in many applications at least, the two serve similar functions for people. (Many noneconomists would call them substitutes, too. Economists don't *always* choose obscure terms for important concepts!) When two goods or services are substitutes, a decrease in the price of one will cause a leftward shift in the demand curve for the other. (A "leftward shift" in a demand curve can also be described as a "downward shift.") Diagrammatically, the demand curve for overnight delivery service shifts from *D* to *D'* in Figure 2.12.

As the figure shows, both the new equilibrium price, *P'*, and the new equilibrium quantity, *Q'*, are lower than the initial values, *P* and *Q*. Cheaper Internet access probably won't put Federal Express and UPS out of business, but it will definitely cost them many customers.

FIGURE 2.12

The Effect on the Market for Overnight Letter Delivery of a Decline in the Price of Internet Access.

When the price of a substitute falls, demand shifts left, causing equilibrium price and quantity to fall.

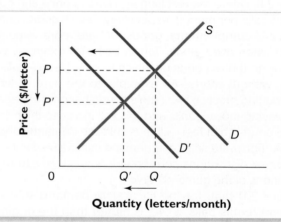

To summarize, economists define goods as substitutes if an increase in the price of one causes a rightward shift in the demand curve for the other. By contrast, goods are complements if an increase in the price of one causes a leftward shift in the demand curve for the other.

The concepts of substitutes and complements enable you to answer questions like the one posed in the following concept check.

CONCEPT CHECK 2.4

How will a decline in airfares affect intercity bus fares and the price of hotel rooms in resort communities?

Demand curves are shifted not just by changes in the prices of substitutes and complements but also by other factors that change the amounts people are willing to pay for a given good or service. One of the most important such factors is income.

The Economic Naturalist 2.1

When the federal government implements a large pay increase for its employees, why do rents for apartments located near Washington Metro stations go up relative to rents for apartments located far away from Metro stations?

For the citizens of Washington, D.C., a substantial proportion of whom are government employees, it's more convenient to live in an apartment located one block from the nearest subway station than to live in one that is 20 blocks away. Conveniently located apartments thus command relatively high rents. Suppose the initial demand and supply curves for such apartments are as shown in Figure 2.13. Following a federal pay raise, some government employees who live in less convenient apartments will be willing and able to use part of their extra income to bid for more conveniently located apartments, and those who already live in such apartments will be willing and able to pay more to keep them. The effect of the pay raise is thus to shift the demand curve for conveniently located apartments to the right, as indicated by the demand curve labeled D'. As a result, both the equilibrium price and quantity of such apartments, P' and Q', will be higher than before.

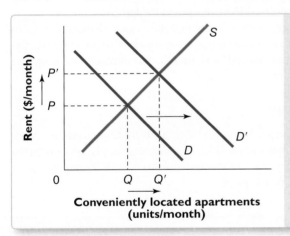

FIGURE 2.13

The Effect of a Federal Pay Raise on the Rent for Conveniently Located Apartments in Washington, D.C.

An increase in income shifts demand for a normal good to the right, causing equilibrium price and quantity to rise.

Who gets to live in the most conveniently located apartments?

It might seem natural to ask how there could be an increase in the number of conveniently located apartments, which might appear to be fixed by the constraints of geography. But we must never underestimate the ingenuity of sellers when they confront an opportunity to make money by supplying more of something that people want. For example, if rents rose sufficiently, some landlords might respond by converting warehouse space to residential use. Or perhaps people with cars who do not place high value on living near a subway station might sell their apartments to landlords, thereby freeing them for people eager to rent them. (Note that these responses constitute movements along the supply curve of conveniently located apartments, as opposed to shifts in that supply curve.)

When incomes increase, the demand curves for most goods will behave like the demand curve for conveniently located apartments, and in recognition of that fact, economists have chosen to call such goods **normal goods**.

Not all goods are normal goods, however. In fact, the demand curves for some goods actually shift leftward when income goes up. Such goods are called **inferior goods**.

When would having more money tend to make you want to buy less of something? In general, this happens with goods for which there exist attractive substitutes that sell for only slightly higher prices. Apartments in unsafe, inconveniently located neighborhoods

normal good a good whose demand curve shifts rightward when the incomes of buyers increase and leftward when the incomes of buyers decrease

inferior good a good whose demand curve shifts leftward when the incomes of buyers increase and rightward when the incomes of buyers decrease

are an example. Most residents would choose to move out of such neighborhoods as soon as they could afford to, which means that an increase in income would cause the demand for such apartments to shift leftward.

> ### CONCEPT CHECK 2.5
> How will a large pay increase for federal employees affect the rents for apartments located far away from Washington Metro stations?

Ground beef with high fat content is another example of an inferior good. For health reasons, most people prefer grades of meat with low fat content, and when they do buy high-fat meats it's usually a sign of budgetary pressure. When people in this situation receive higher incomes, they usually switch quickly to leaner grades of meat.

Preferences, or tastes, are another important factor that determines whether the purchase of a given good will satisfy the Cost-Benefit Principle. Steven Spielberg's film *Jurassic Park* appeared to kindle a powerful, if previously latent, preference among children for toy dinosaurs. When this film was first released, the demand for such toys shifted sharply to the right. And the same children who couldn't find enough dinosaur toys suddenly seemed to lose interest in toy designs involving horses and other present-day animals, whose respective demand curves shifted sharply to the left.

Expectations about the future are another factor that may cause demand curves to shift. If Apple Macintosh users hear a credible rumor, for example, that a cheaper or significantly upgraded model will be introduced next month, the demand curve for the current model is likely to shift leftward.

Shifts in the Supply Curve

The preceding examples involved changes that gave rise to shifts in demand curves. Next, we'll look at what happens when supply curves shift. Because the supply curve is based on costs of production, anything that changes production costs will shift the supply curve, resulting in a new equilibrium quantity and price.

EXAMPLE 2.4   **Increasing Opportunity Cost**

What will happen to the equilibrium price and quantity of skateboards if the price of fiberglass, a substance used for making skateboards, rises?

Suppose the initial supply and demand curves for skateboards are as shown by the curves S and D in Figure 2.14, resulting in an equilibrium price and quantity of

FIGURE 2.14

The Effect on the Skateboard Market of an Increase in the Price of Fiberglass.

When input prices rise, supply shifts left, causing equilibrium price to rise and equilibrium quantity to fall.

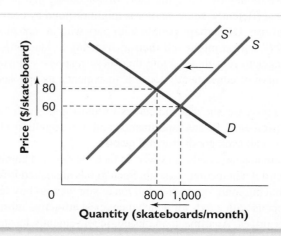

$60 per skateboard and 1,000 skateboards per month, respectively. Since fiber-glass is one of the materials used to produce skateboards, the effect of an increase in its price is to raise the marginal cost of producing skateboards. How will this affect the supply curve of skateboards? Recall that the supply curve is upward-sloping because when the price of skateboards is low, only those potential sellers whose marginal cost of making skateboards is low can sell boards profitably, whereas at higher prices, those with higher marginal costs also can enter the market profitably. So if the cost of one of the materials used to produce skateboards rises, the number of potential sellers who can profitably sell skateboards at any given price will fall. And this, in turn, implies a leftward shift in the supply curve for skateboards. Note that a "leftward shift" in a supply curve also can be viewed as an "upward shift" in the same curve. The first corresponds to the horizontal interpretation of the supply curve, while the second corresponds to the vertical interpretation. We will use these expressions to mean exactly the same thing. The new supply curve (after the price of fiberglass rises) is the curve labeled S' in Figure 2.14.

Does an increase in the cost of fiberglass have any effect on the demand curve for skateboards? The demand curve tells us how many skateboards buyers wish to purchase at each price. Any given buyer is willing to purchase a skateboard if his reservation price for it exceeds its market price. And since each buyer's reservation price, which is based on the benefits of owning a skateboard, does not depend on the price of fiberglass, there should be no shift in the demand curve for skateboards.

In Figure 2.14, we can now see what happens when the supply curve shifts left-ward and the demand curve remains unchanged. For the illustrative supply curve shown, the new equilibrium price of skateboards, $80, is higher than the original price, and the new equilibrium quantity, 800 per month, is lower than the original quantity. (These new equilibrium values are merely illustrative. There is insufficient information provided in the example to determine their exact values.) People who don't place a value of at least $80 on owning a skateboard will choose to spend their money on something else.

The effects on equilibrium price and quantity run in the opposite direction whenever marginal costs of production decline, as illustrated in the next example.

EXAMPLE 2.5   Reduction of Marginal Cost

What will happen to the equilibrium price and quantity of new houses if the wage rate of carpenters falls?

Suppose the initial supply and demand curves for new houses are as shown by the curves S and D in Figure 2.15, resulting in an equilibrium price of $120,000 per

FIGURE 2.15

The Effect on the Market for New Houses of a Decline in Carpenters' Wage Rates.

When input prices fall, supply shifts right, causing equilibrium price to fall and equilibrium quantity to rise.

house and an equilibrium quantity of 40 houses per month, respectively. A decline in the wage rate of carpenters reduces the marginal cost of making new houses, and this means that, for any given price of houses, more builders can profitably serve the market than before. Diagrammatically, this means a rightward shift in the supply curve of houses, from S to S'. (A "rightward shift" in the supply curve also can be described as a "downward shift.")

Does a decrease in the wage rate of carpenters have any effect on the demand curve for houses? The demand curve tells us how many houses buyers wish to purchase at each price. Because carpenters are now earning less than before, the maximum amount that they are willing to pay for houses may fall, which would imply a leftward shift in the demand curve for houses. But because carpenters make up only a tiny fraction of all potential home buyers, we may assume that this shift is negligible. Thus, a reduction in carpenters' wages produces a significant rightward shift in the supply curve of houses, but no appreciable shift in the demand curve.

We see from Figure 2.15 that the new equilibrium price, $90,000 per house, is lower than the original price and the new equilibrium quantity, 50 houses per month, is higher than the original quantity.

Examples 2.4 and 2.5 involved changes in the cost of a material, or input, in the production of the good in question—fiberglass in the production of skateboards and carpenters' labor in the production of houses. As the following example illustrates, supply curves also shift when technology changes.

The Economic Naturalist 2.2

Why do major term papers go through so many more revisions today than in the 1970s?

Students in the dark days before word processors were in widespread use could not make even minor revisions in their term papers without having to retype their entire manuscript from scratch. The availability of word-processing technology has, of course, radically changed the picture. Instead of having to retype the entire draft, now only the changes need be entered.

In Figure 2.16, the curves labeled S and D depict the supply and demand curves for revisions in the days before word processing, and the curve S' depicts the supply curve for revisions today. As the diagram shows, the result is not only a sharp decline in the price per revision, but also a corresponding increase in the equilibrium number of revisions.

Why does written work go through so many more revisions now than in the 1970s?

FIGURE 2.16

The Effect of Technical Change on the Market for Term-Paper Revisions.

When a new technology reduces the cost of production, supply shifts right, causing equilibrium price to fall and equilibrium quantity to rise.

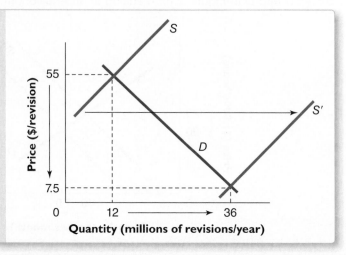

Note that in The Economic Naturalist 2.2 we implicitly assumed that students purchased typing services in a market. In fact, however, many students type their own term papers. Does that make a difference? Even if no money actually changes hands, students pay a price when they revise their term papers—namely, the opportunity cost of the time it takes to perform that task. Because technology has radically reduced that cost, we would expect to see a large increase in the number of term-paper revisions even if most students type their own work.

Changes in input prices and technology are two of the most important factors that give rise to shifts in supply curves. In the case of agricultural commodities, weather may be another important factor, with favorable conditions shifting the supply curves of such products to the right and unfavorable conditions shifting them to the left. (Weather also may affect the supply curves of nonagricultural products through its effects on the national transportation system.) Expectations of future price changes also may shift current supply curves, as when the expectation of poor crops from a current drought causes suppliers to withhold supplies from existing stocks in the hope of selling at higher prices in the future. Changes in the number of sellers in the market also can cause supply curves to shift.

Four Simple Rules

For supply and demand curves that have the conventional slopes (upward-sloping for supply curves, downward-sloping for demand curves), the preceding examples illustrate the four basic rules that govern how shifts in supply and demand affect equilibrium prices and quantities. These rules are summarized in Figure 2.17.

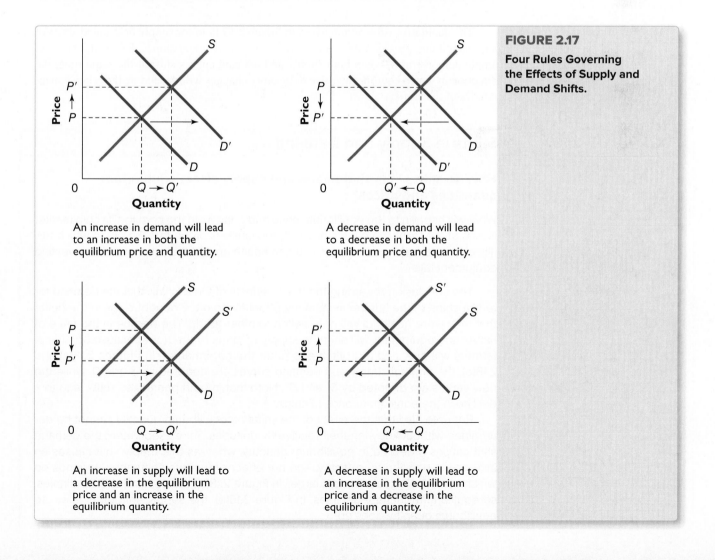

FIGURE 2.17

Four Rules Governing the Effects of Supply and Demand Shifts.

An increase in demand will lead to an increase in both the equilibrium price and quantity.

A decrease in demand will lead to a decrease in both the equilibrium price and quantity.

An increase in supply will lead to a decrease in the equilibrium price and an increase in the equilibrium quantity.

A decrease in supply will lead to an increase in the equilibrium price and a decrease in the equilibrium quantity.

FACTORS THAT SHIFT SUPPLY AND DEMAND

Factors that cause an increase (rightward or upward shift) in demand:

1. A decrease in the price of complements to the good or service.
2. An increase in the price of substitutes for the good or service.
3. An increase in income (for a normal good).
4. An increased preference by demanders for the good or service.
5. An increase in the population of potential buyers.
6. An expectation of higher prices in the future.

When these factors move in the opposite direction, demand will shift left.

Factors that cause an increase (rightward or downward shift) in supply:

1. A decrease in the cost of materials, labor, or other inputs used in the production of the good or service.
2. An improvement in technology that reduces the cost of producing the good or service.
3. An improvement in the weather (especially for agricultural products).
4. An increase in the number of suppliers.
5. An expectation of lower prices in the future.

When these factors move in the opposite direction, supply will shift left.

The qualitative rules summarized in Figure 2.17 hold for supply or demand shifts of any magnitude, provided the curves have their conventional slopes. But as the next example demonstrates, when both supply and demand curves shift at the same time, the direction in which equilibrium price or quantity changes will depend on the relative magnitudes of the shifts.

EXAMPLE 2.6   **Shifts in Supply and Demand**

How do shifts in both demand and supply affect equilibrium quantities and prices?

What will happen to the equilibrium price and quantity in the corn tortilla chip market if both of the following events occur: (1) researchers prove that the oils in which tortilla chips are fried are harmful to human health and (2) the price of corn harvesting equipment falls?

The conclusion regarding the health effects of the oils will shift the demand for tortilla chips to the left because many people who once bought chips in the belief that they were healthful will now switch to other foods. The decline in the price of harvesting equipment will shift the supply of chips to the right because additional farmers will now find it profitable to enter the corn market. In Figures 2.18(a) and 2.18(b), the original supply and demand curves are denoted by S and D, while the new curves are denoted by S' and D'. Note that in both panels the shifts lead to a decline in the equilibrium price of chips.

But note also that the effect of the shifts on equilibrium quantity cannot be determined without knowing their relative magnitudes. Taken separately, the demand shift causes a decline in equilibrium quantity, whereas the supply shift causes an increase in equilibrium quantity. The net effect of the two shifts thus depends on which of the individual effects is larger. In Figure 2.18(a), the demand shift dominates, so equilibrium quantity declines. In Figure 2.18(b), the supply shift dominates, so equilibrium quantity goes up.

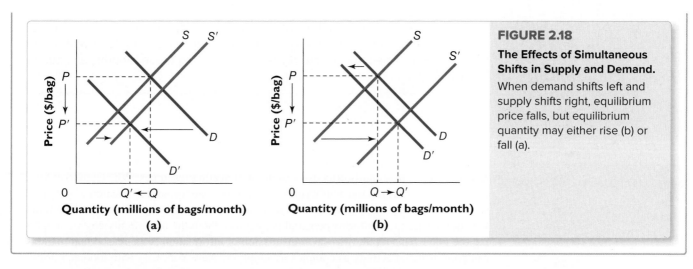

FIGURE 2.18

The Effects of Simultaneous Shifts in Supply and Demand.

When demand shifts left and supply shifts right, equilibrium price falls, but equilibrium quantity may either rise (b) or fall (a).

The following concept check asks you to consider a simple variation on the problem posed in the previous example.

CONCEPT CHECK 2.6

What will happen to the equilibrium price and quantity in the corn tortilla chip market if both of the following events occur: (1) researchers discover that a vitamin found in corn helps protect against cancer and heart disease and (2) a swarm of locusts destroys part of the corn crop?

The Economic Naturalist 2.3

Why do the prices of some goods, like airline tickets to Europe, go up during the months of heaviest consumption, while others, like sweet corn, go down?

Seasonal price movements for airline tickets are primarily the result of seasonal variations in demand. Thus, ticket prices to Europe are highest during the summer months because the demand for tickets is highest during those months, as shown in Figure 2.19(a), where the w and s subscripts denote winter and summer values, respectively.

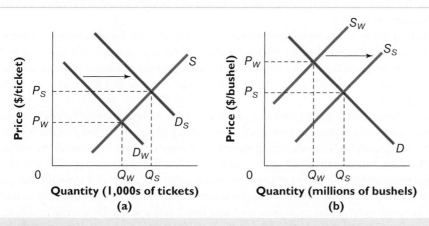

FIGURE 2.19

Seasonal Variation in the Air Travel and Corn Markets.

(a) Prices are highest during the period of heaviest consumption when heavy consumption is the result of high demand. (b) Prices are lowest during the period of heaviest consumption when heavy consumption is the result of high supply.

Why are some goods cheapest during the months of heaviest consumption, while others are most expensive during those months?

By contrast, seasonal price movements for sweet corn are primarily the result of seasonal variations in supply. The price of sweet corn is lowest in the summer months because its supply is highest during those months, as seen in Figure 2.19(b).

EFFICIENCY AND EQUILIBRIUM

Markets represent a highly effective system of allocating resources. When a market for a good is in equilibrium, the equilibrium price conveys important information to potential suppliers about the value that potential demanders place on that good. At the same time, the equilibrium price informs potential demanders about the opportunity cost of supplying the good. This rapid, two-way transmission of information is the reason that markets can coordinate an activity as complex as supplying New York City with food and drink, even though no one person or organization oversees the process.

But are the prices and quantities determined in market equilibrium socially optimal, in the sense of maximizing total economic surplus? That is, does equilibrium in unregulated markets always maximize the difference between the total benefits and total costs experienced by market participants? As we'll see, the answer is "it depends": A market that is out of equilibrium, such as the rent-controlled New York housing market, always creates opportunities for individuals to arrange transactions that will increase their individual economic surplus. As we'll also see, however, a market for a good that is in equilibrium makes the largest possible contribution to total economic surplus only when its supply and demand curves fully reflect all costs and benefits associated with the production and consumption of that good.

Cash on the Table

In economics we assume that all exchange is purely voluntary. This means that a transaction cannot take place unless the buyer's reservation price for the good exceeds the seller's reservation price. When that condition is met and a transaction takes place, both parties receive an economic surplus. The **buyer's surplus** from the transaction is the difference between his reservation price and the price he actually pays. The **seller's surplus** is the difference between the price she receives and her reservation price. The **total surplus** from the transaction is the sum of the buyer's surplus and the seller's surplus. It is also equal to the difference between the buyer's reservation price and the seller's reservation price.

Suppose there is a potential buyer whose reservation price for an additional slice of pizza is $4 and a potential seller whose reservation price is only $2. If this buyer purchases a slice of pizza from this seller for $3, the total surplus generated by this exchange is $4 − $2 = $2, of which $4 − $3 = $1 is the buyer's surplus and $3 − $2 = $1 is the seller's surplus.

A regulation that prevents the price of a good from reaching its equilibrium level unnecessarily prevents exchanges of this sort from taking place, and in the process reduces total economic surplus. Consider again the effect of price controls imposed in the market for pizza. The demand curve in Figure 2.20 tells us that if a price ceiling of $2 per slice were imposed, only 8,000 slices of pizza per day would be sold. At that quantity, the vertical interpretations of the supply and demand curves tell us that a buyer would be willing to pay as much as $4 for an additional slice and that a seller would be willing to sell one for as little as $2. The difference—$2 per slice—is the additional economic surplus that would result if an additional slice were produced and sold. As noted earlier, an extra slice sold at a price of $3 would result in an additional $1 of economic surplus for both buyer and seller.

When a market is out of equilibrium, it's always possible to identify mutually beneficial exchanges of this sort. When people have failed to take advantage of all mutually

buyer's surplus the difference between the buyer's reservation price and the price he or she actually pays

seller's surplus the difference between the price received by the seller and his or her reservation price

total surplus the difference between the buyer's reservation price and the seller's reservation price

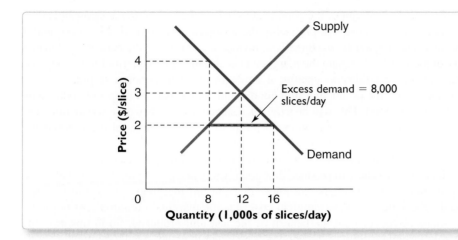

FIGURE 2.20

Price Controls in the Pizza Market.

A price ceiling below the equilibrium price of pizza would result in excess demand for pizza.

beneficial exchanges, we often say that there's "**cash on the table**"— the economist's metaphor for unexploited opportunities. When the price in a market is below the equilibrium price, there's cash on the table because the reservation price of sellers (marginal cost) will always be lower than the reservation price of buyers. In the absence of a law preventing buyers from paying more than $2 per slice, restaurant owners would quickly raise their prices and expand their production until the equilibrium price of $3 per slice were reached. At that price, buyers would be able to get precisely the 12,000 slices of pizza they want to buy each day. All mutually beneficial opportunities for exchange would have been exploited, leaving no more cash on the table.

It should be no surprise that buyers and sellers in the marketplace have an uncanny ability to detect the presence of cash on the table. It is almost as if unexploited opportunities give off some exotic scent triggering neurochemical explosions in the olfactory centers of their brains. The desire to scrape cash off the table and into their pockets is what drives sellers in each of New York City's thousands of individual food markets to work diligently to meet their customers' demands. That they succeed to a far higher degree than participants in the city's rent-controlled housing market is plainly evident. Whatever flaws it might have, the market system moves with considerably greater speed and agility than any centralized allocation mechanisms yet devised. But as we emphasize in the following section, this does not mean that markets *always* lead to the greatest good for all.

cash on the table an economic metaphor for unexploited gains from exchange

Smart for One, Dumb for All

The **socially optimal quantity** of any good is the quantity that maximizes the total economic surplus that results from producing and consuming the good. From the Cost-Benefit Principle, we know that we should keep expanding production of the good as long as its marginal benefit is at least as great as its marginal cost. This means that the socially optimal quantity is that level for which the marginal cost and marginal benefit of the good are the same.

When the quantity of a good is less than the socially optimal quantity, boosting its production will increase total economic surplus. By the same token, when the quantity of a good exceeds the socially optimal quantity, reducing its production will increase total economic surplus. **Economic efficiency**, or **efficiency**, occurs when all goods and services in the economy are produced and consumed at their respective socially optimal levels.

Efficiency is an important social goal. Failure to achieve efficiency means that total economic surplus is smaller than it could have been. Movements toward efficiency make the total economic pie larger, making it possible for everyone to have a larger slice.

Is the market equilibrium quantity of a good efficient? That is, does it maximize the total economic surplus received by participants in the market for that good? When the private market for a given good is in equilibrium, we can say that the cost *to the seller* of

socially optimal quantity the quantity of a good that results in the maximum possible economic surplus from producing and consuming the good

efficiency (or **economic efficiency)** a condition that occurs when all goods and services are produced and consumed at their respective socially optimal levels

producing an additional unit of the good is the same as the benefit *to the buyer* of having an additional unit. If all costs of producing the good are borne directly by sellers, and if all benefits from the good accrue directly to buyers, it follows that the market equilibrium quantity of the good will equate the marginal cost and marginal benefit of the good. And this means that the equilibrium quantity also maximizes total economic surplus.

But sometimes the production of a good entails costs that fall on people other than those who sell the good. This will be true, for instance, for goods whose production generates significant levels of environmental pollution. As extra units of these goods are produced, the extra pollution harms other people besides sellers. In the market equilibrium for such goods, the benefit *to buyers* of the last good produced is, as before, equal to the cost incurred by sellers to produce that good. But since producing that good also imposes pollution costs on others, we know that the *full* marginal cost of the last unit produced—the seller's private marginal cost plus the marginal pollution cost borne by others—must be higher than the benefit of the last unit produced. So in this case the market equilibrium quantity of the good will be larger than the socially optimal quantity. Total economic surplus would be higher if output of the good were lower. Yet neither sellers nor buyers have any incentive to alter their behavior.

Another possibility is that people other than those who buy a good may receive significant benefits from it. For instance, when someone purchases a vaccination against measles from her doctor, she not only protects herself, but also makes it less likely that others will catch this disease. From the perspective of society as a whole, we should keep increasing the number of vaccinations until their marginal cost equals their marginal benefit. The marginal benefit of a vaccination is the value of the protection it provides the person vaccinated *plus* the value of the protection it provides all others. Private consumers, however, will choose to be vaccinated only if the marginal benefit *to them* exceeds the price of the vaccination. In this case, then, the market equilibrium quantity of vaccinations will be smaller than the quantity that maximizes total economic surplus. Again, however, individuals would have no incentive to alter their behavior.

Situations like the ones just discussed provide examples of behaviors that we may call "smart for one but dumb for all." In each case, the individual actors are behaving rationally. They are pursuing their goals as best they can, and yet there remain unexploited opportunities for gain from the point of view of the whole society. The difficulty is that these opportunities cannot be exploited by individuals acting alone. In subsequent chapters, we will see how people can often organize collectively to exploit such opportunities.

> **RECAP ↑**
>
> **MARKETS AND SOCIAL WELFARE**
>
> When the supply and demand curves for a good reflect all significant costs and benefits associated with the production and consumption of that good, the market equilibrium will result in the largest possible economic surplus. But if people other than buyers benefit from the good, or if people other than sellers bear costs because of it, market equilibrium need not result in the largest possible economic surplus.

SUMMARY

- The demand curve is a downward-sloping line that tells what quantity buyers will demand at any given price. The supply curve is an upward-sloping line that tells what quantity sellers will offer at any given price. *(LO1)*

- Alfred Marshall's model of supply and demand explains why neither cost of production nor value to the purchaser

(as measured by willingness to pay) is, by itself, sufficient to explain why some goods are cheap and others are expensive. To explain variations in price, we must examine the interaction of cost and willingness to pay. As we've seen in this chapter, goods differ in price because of differences in their respective supply and demand curves. *(LO2)*

- Market equilibrium occurs when the quantity buyers demand at the market price is exactly the same as the quantity that sellers offer. The equilibrium price–quantity pair is the one at which the demand and supply curves intersect. In equilibrium, market price measures both the value of the last unit sold to buyers and the cost of the resources required to produce it. *(LO2)*

- When the price of a good lies above its equilibrium value, there is an excess supply of that good. Excess supply motivates sellers to cut their prices and price continues to fall until equilibrium price is reached. When price lies below its equilibrium value, there is excess demand. With excess demand, frustrated buyers are motivated to offer higher prices and the upward pressure on prices persists until equilibrium is reached. A remarkable feature of the market system is that, relying only on the tendency of people to respond in self-interested ways to market price signals, it somehow manages to coordinate the actions of literally billions of buyers and sellers worldwide. When excess demand or excess supply occurs, it tends to be small and brief, except in markets where regulations prevent full adjustment of prices. *(LO2)*

- The basic supply and demand model is a primary tool of the economic naturalist. Changes in the equilibrium price of a good, and in the amount of it traded in the marketplace, can be predicted on the basis of shifts in its supply or demand curves. The following four rules hold for any good with a downward-sloping demand curve and an upward-sloping supply curve:
  1. An increase in demand will lead to an increase in equilibrium price and quantity.
  2. A reduction in demand will lead to a reduction in equilibrium price and quantity.
  3. An increase in supply will lead to a reduction in equilibrium price and an increase in equilibrium quantity.
  4. A decrease in supply will lead to an increase in equilibrium price and a reduction in equilibrium quantity. *(LO3)*

- Incomes, tastes, population, expectations, and the prices of substitutes and complements are among the factors that shift demand schedules. Supply schedules, in turn, are primarily governed by such factors as technology, input prices, expectations, the number of sellers, and, especially for agricultural products, the weather. *(LO3)*

- The efficiency of markets in allocating resources does not eliminate social concerns about how goods and services are distributed among different people. For example, we often lament the fact many buyers enter the market with too little income to buy even the most basic goods and services. Concern for the well-being of the poor has motivated many governments to intervene in a variety of ways to alter the outcomes of market forces. Sometimes these interventions take the form of laws that peg prices below their equilibrium levels. Such laws almost invariably generate harmful, if unintended, consequences. Programs like rent-control laws, for example, lead to severe housing shortages, black marketeering, and a rapid deterioration of the relationship between landlords and tenants. *(LO4)*

- If the difficulty is that the poor have too little money, the best solution is to discover ways of boosting their incomes directly. The law of supply and demand cannot be repealed by the legislature. But legislatures do have the capacity to alter the underlying forces that govern the shape and position of supply and demand schedules. *(LO4)*

- When the supply and demand curves for a good reflect all significant costs and benefits associated with the production and consumption of that good, the market equilibrium price will guide people to produce and consume the quantity of the good that results in the largest possible economic surplus. This conclusion, however, does not apply if others, besides buyers, benefit from the good (as when someone benefits from his neighbor's purchase of a vaccination against measles) or if others besides sellers bear costs because of the good (as when its production generates pollution). In such cases, market equilibrium does not result in the greatest gain for all. *(LO4)*

KEY TERMS

buyer's reservation price	efficiency	normal good
buyer's surplus	equilibrium	price ceiling
cash on the table	equilibrium price	seller's reservation price
change in demand	equilibrium quantity	seller's surplus
change in the quantity demanded	excess demand	socially optimal quantity
change in the quantity supplied	excess supply	substitutes
change in supply	income effect	substitution effect
complements	inferior good	supply curve
demand curve	market	total surplus
economic efficiency	market equilibrium	

REVIEW QUESTIONS

1. Explain the distinction between the horizontal and vertical interpretations of the demand curve. *(LO1)*

2. Why isn't knowing the cost of producing a good sufficient to predict its market price? *(LO2)*

3. In recent years, a government official proposed that gasoline price controls be imposed to protect the poor from rising gasoline prices. What evidence could you consult to discover whether this proposal was enacted? *(LO2)*

4. Distinguish between the meanings of the expressions "change in demand" and "change in the quantity demanded." *(LO3)*

5. Give an example of behavior you have observed that could be described as "smart for one but dumb for all." *(LO4)*

PROBLEMS

connect

1. How would each of the following affect the U.S. market supply curve for corn? *(LO1)*
   a. A new and improved crop rotation technique is discovered.
   b. The price of fertilizer falls.
   c. The government offers new tax breaks to farmers.
   d. A tornado sweeps through Iowa.

2. Indicate how you think each of the following would shift demand in the indicated market: *(LO1)*
   a. The incomes of buyers in the market for Adirondack vacations increases.
   b. Buyers in the market for pizza read a study linking pepperoni consumption to heart disease.
   c. Buyers in the market for CDs learn of an increase in the price of downloadable MP3s (a substitute for CDs).
   d. Buyers in the market for CDs learn of an increase in the price of CDs.

3. An Arizona student claims to have spotted a UFO over the desert outside of Tucson. How will his claim affect the *supply* (not the quantity supplied) of binoculars in Tucson stores? *(LO1)*

4. State whether the following pairs of goods are complements, or substitutes, or both. *(LO3)*
   a. Washing machines and dryers.
   b. Tennis rackets and tennis balls.
   c. Ice cream and chocolate.
   d. Cloth diapers and disposable diapers.

5. How will an increase in the birth rate affect the equilibrium price of land? *(LO3)*

6. What will happen to the equilibrium price and quantity of beef if the price of chickenfeed increases? (assume that chicken and beef are substitutes) *(LO3)*

7. How will a new law mandating an increase in required levels of automobile insurance affect the equilibrium price and quantity in the market for new automobiles? *(LO3)*

8. Predict what will happen to the equilibrium price and quantity of oranges if the following events take place. *(LO3)*
   a. A study finds that a daily glass of orange juice reduces the risk of heart disease.
   b. The price of grapefruit falls drastically.
   c. The wage paid to orange pickers rises.
   d. Exceptionally good weather provides a much greater than expected harvest.

9. Suppose the current issue of *The New York Times* reports an outbreak of mad cow disease in Nebraska, as well as the discovery of a new breed of chicken that gains more weight than existing breeds that consume the same amount of food. How will these developments affect the equilibrium price and quantity of chickens sold in the United States? *(LO3)*

10. Twenty-five years ago, tofu was available only from small businesses operating in predominantly Asian sections of large cities. Today tofu has become popular as a high-protein health food and is widely available in supermarkets throughout the United States. At the same time, tofu production has evolved to become factory-based using modern food-processing technologies. Draw a diagram with demand and supply curves depicting the market for tofu 25 years ago and the market for tofu today. Given the information above, what does the demand–supply model predict about changes in the volume of tofu sold in the United States between then and now? What does it predict about changes in the price of tofu? *(LO3)*

ANSWERS TO CONCEPT CHECKS

2.1 At a quantity of 10,000 slices per day, the marginal buyer's reservation price is $3.50 per slice. At a price of $2.50 per slice, the quantity demanded will be 14,000 slices per day. *(LO1)*

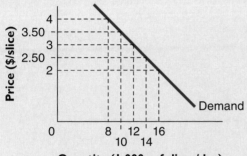

2.2 At a quantity of 10,000 slices per day, the marginal cost of pizza is $2.50 per slice. At a price of $3.50 per slice, the quantity supplied will be 14,000 slices per day. *(LO1)*

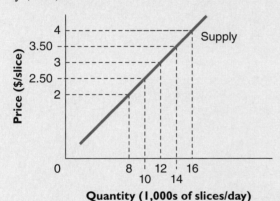

2.3 Since landlords are permitted to charge less than the maximum rent established by rent-control laws, a law that sets the maximum rent at $1,200 will have no effect on the rents actually charged in this market, which will settle at the equilibrium value of $800 per month. *(LO2)*

2.4 Travel by air and travel by intercity bus are substitutes, so a decline in airfares will shift the demand for bus travel to the left, resulting in lower bus fares and fewer bus trips taken. Travel by air and the use of resort hotels are complements, so a decline in airfares will shift the demand for resort hotel rooms to the right, resulting in higher hotel rates and an increase in the number of rooms rented. *(LO3)*

2.5 Apartments located far from Washington Metro stations are an inferior good. A pay increase for federal workers will thus shift the demand curve for such apartments downward, which will lead to a reduction in their equilibrium rent. *(LO3)*

2.6 The vitamin discovery shifts the demand for chips to the right and the crop losses shift the supply of chips to the left. Both shifts result in an increase in the equilibrium price of chips. But depending on the relative magnitude of the shifts, the equilibrium quantity of chips may either rise (top figure) or fall (bottom figure). *(LO3)*

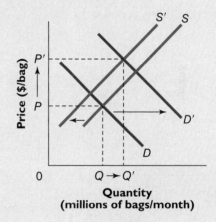

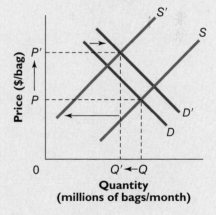

The Algebra of Supply and Demand

In the text of this chapter, we developed supply and demand analysis in a geometric framework. The advantage of this framework is that many find it an easier one within which to visualize how shifts in either curve affect equilibrium price and quantity.

It is a straightforward extension to translate supply and demand analysis into algebraic terms. In this brief appendix, we show how this is done. The advantage of the algebraic framework is that it greatly simplifies computing the numerical values of equilibrium prices and quantities.

Consider, for example, the supply and demand curves in Figure 2A.1, where P denotes the price of the good and Q denotes its quantity. What are the equations of these curves?

Recall from the appendix *Working with Equations, Graphs, and Tables* that the equation of a straight-line demand curve must take the general form $P = a + bQ^d$, where P is the price of the product (as measured on the vertical axis), Q^d is the quantity demanded at that price (as measured on the horizontal axis), a is the vertical intercept of the demand curve, and b is its slope. For the demand curve shown in Figure 2A.1, the vertical intercept is 16 and the slope is -2. So the equation for this demand curve is

$$P = 16 - 2Q^d. \tag{2A.1}$$

Similarly, the equation of a straight-line supply curve must take the general form $P = c + dQ^s$, where P is again the price of the product, Q^s is the quantity supplied at that price, c is the vertical intercept of the supply curve, and d is its slope. For the supply curve shown in Figure 2A.1, the vertical intercept is 4 and the slope is also 4. So the equation for this supply curve is

$$P = 4 + 4Q^s. \tag{2A.2}$$

If we know the equations for the supply and demand curves in any market, it is a simple matter to solve them for the equilibrium price and quantity using the method of

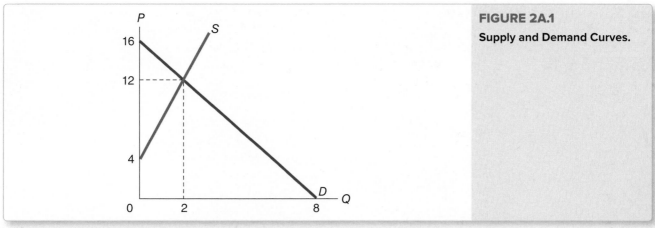

FIGURE 2A.1

Supply and Demand Curves.

simultaneous equations described in the appendix *Working with Equations, Graphs, and Tables*. The following example illustrates how to apply this method.

EXAMPLE 2A.1 | **Simultaneous Equations**

If the supply and demand curves for a market are given by $P = 4 + 4Q^s$ and $P = 16 - 2Q^d$, respectively, find the equilibrium price and quantity for this market.

In equilibrium, we know that $Q^s = Q^d$. Denoting this common value as Q^*, we may then equate the right-hand sides of Equations 2A.1 and 2A.2 and solve

$$4 + 4Q^* = 16 - 2Q^*, \tag{2A.3}$$

which yields $Q^* = 2$. Substituting $Q^* = 2$ back into either the supply or demand equation gives the equilibrium price $P^* = 12$.

Of course, having already begun with the graphs of Equations 2A.1 and 2A.2 in hand, we could have identified the equilibrium price and quantity by a simple glance at Figure 2A.1. (That is why it seems natural to say that the graphical approach helps us visualize the equilibrium outcome.) As the following concept check illustrates, the advantage of the algebraic approach to finding the equilibrium price and quantity is that it is much less painstaking than having to produce accurate drawings of the supply and demand schedules.

CONCEPT CHECK 2A.1

Find the equilibrium price and quantity in a market whose supply and demand curves are given by $P = 2Q^s$ and $P = 8 - 2Q^d$, respectively.

ANSWER TO APPENDIX CONCEPT CHECK

2A.1 Let Q^* denote the equilibrium quantity. Since the equilibrium price and quantity lie on both the supply and demand curves, we equate the right-hand sides of the supply and demand equations to obtain

$$2Q^* = 8 - 2Q^*,$$

which solves for $Q^* = 2$. Substituting $Q^* = 2$ back into either the supply or demand equation gives the equilibrium price $P^* = 4$.

3

LEARNING OBJECTIVES

After reading this chapter, you should be able to:

LO1 Describe the similarities between the Dutch tulip bubble of the seventeenth century and the American housing bubble of the early 2000s and explain how each precipitated a major economic downturn.

LO2 Explain why classical macroeconomic theorists thought that economic downturns would be both brief and self-correcting.

LO3 Explain why Keynes believed that downturns would last a long time in the absence of government stimulus.

LO4 Explain how evidence from the aftermath of the 2008 financial crisis bears on the debate between Keynes and the classical macroeconomists.

LO5 Critically analyze the claim that because a family must cut its spending when its income declines, a government should also cut its spending during a downturn.

LO6 Describe strategies that promise to help avoid protracted future downturns.

A Brief Look at Macroeconomics

George Bernard Shaw once said that even if all the economists in the world were laid end to end, they still wouldn't reach a conclusion. Economists do of course disagree with one another about some issues. But far more remarkable is the strong consensus among them about most important policy questions.

In recent years, the public perception that economists can't agree has stemmed largely from prominent coverage given to a dispute about the answer to what sounds like a simple question: When the economy is in a slump, as it has been in many countries since the worldwide financial crisis of 2008, should governments increase their spending? And should governments take steps to make it easier for businesses and consumers to borrow money? Disagreement about the answer to these questions came to be known as the great austerity debate.

On one side was a group of economists who insisted that the best response to the economic downturn was for governments to cut spending sharply. Spending less on public services, roads, bridges, and other programs, and keeping public debt from increasing in the process, they argued, would help restore public confidence, which they thought would lead consumers and businesses to increase their spending.

A second group of economists—far larger than the first and the one with which we identify—argued the reverse. Unemployment was much higher than normal, we explained, simply because total spending was insufficient to employ everyone who wanted to work. In our view, the government should spend more heavily and make borrowing easier, both with the aim of putting people back to work more quickly.

In this chapter, we'll consider the great austerity debate in some detail. One reason for giving it prominent early coverage is that it provides a good framework for previewing some of the most important ideas in macroeconomics. But far more important, we want to expose you to these ideas early in the book because the failure of politicians and the broader public to understand them resulted in economic waste on a grand scale. That many of the world's economies were operating well below full strength in the wake of the financial crisis could have been prevented. Because we failed to adopt the best policy response to the crisis, the total value of goods and services produced worldwide was literally many trillions of dollars smaller than it could have been.

We'll begin with a brief review of the events that led up to the 2008 financial crisis and explain how it precipitated the deepest economic downturn since the Great Depression of the 1930s. Next we'll discuss what classical macroeconomic theory, which was developed prior to the Great Depression, had to say about how government should respond to economic downturns. Then we'll review the challenge to classical macroeconomics posed by the great British economist John Maynard Keynes. Next, we'll note why our limited experience with severely depressed economies makes it difficult to resolve disputes about the proper role of macroeconomic policy conclusively. And finally, we'll discuss strategies for responding to economic downturns that do not require resolution of the great austerity debate.

THE FINANCIAL CRISIS OF 2008

financial crisis a sharp decline in the prices of financial or other assets that forces borrowers to offer additional assets for sale, further depressing prices

Financial crises have been occurring periodically ever since market systems enabled people to invest with borrowed money. One of the earliest recorded instances was the Dutch tulip bubble of the seventeenth century. Tulip plants affected by a virus produce flowers whose petals display spectacularly beautiful colored striations. These became status symbols in the gardens of the wealthy. Since the virus limited the plants' ability to reproduce, these favored varieties remained relatively scarce. And because incomes in the Netherlands were rising rapidly during that period, the prices of the rarest, most sought-after plants rose in tandem.

Before long, speculators were buying tulips not for their intrinsic beauty but in the expectation of selling them later at even higher prices. At the peak of what came to be called tulip mania, in March of 1637, certain bulbs were selling for roughly ten times the annual income of a skilled craftsman.

That sounds preposterous, and it was. But it's not difficult to see how otherwise sensible investors might have been drawn in by tulip mania. When prices were rising rapidly, it was common knowledge that people with no special skill or willingness to work hard were buying tulips and seeing their investments double in the span of just weeks or even days. For many, it was hard to remain on the sidelines while their friends and neighbors were enjoying such windfalls. And as more people began investing in tulips, the result was further upward pressure on prices.

Rare tulips: Worth ten times a skilled craftsman's annual salary?

Statens Museum for Kunst/National Gallery of Denmark

A key point to remember is that jumping into this market wasn't necessarily a bad idea: You could make a lot of money if you didn't stay too long. Those who bought tulips, held them for a spell, and then sold while prices were still rising were often huge winners.

The late Herb Stein, an economic adviser to President Richard Nixon, once famously said, "If something cannot go on forever, it will stop." And so it was with tulip price growth. People began to ask, how could a single tulip be worth more than ten times a skilled worker's annual income? There's no good answer to that question. Once people began losing confidence that tulip prices would continue rising, the game was essentially over. Prices began falling sharply, which led investors to sell their stocks as quickly as possible, in the hope of avoiding further losses. The resulting increase in supply, of course, put further downward pressure on prices. In a matter of months, large numbers of tulip speculators were bankrupt.

If those who were buying tulips were purchasing them with only their own money, a tulip bubble would be less likely to spiral out of control and put the broader economy at risk. But because many tulip speculators were investing with borrowed money, the sharp decline in tulip prices created a financial panic that spread far beyond the tulip market. When tulip speculators went bankrupt, they couldn't repay their loans to banks, leaving lenders dangerously short of funds. Once citizens began to fear that their bank deposits weren't secure, their first impulse was to withdraw their funds immediately. And when that happened, the pressure on banks increased sharply. Large numbers of people, most of whom had never purchased even a single tulip, suddenly found their bank accounts wiped out.

speculative bubble rapid growth in asset prices, usually caused by unrealistic expectations of further price growth

A similar **speculative bubble** in the American housing market spawned the financial crisis of 2008. Note in Figure 3.1, for example, the steep increase in the rate of growth of American house prices that began during the late 1990s. Prices were rising so rapidly during that period that the housing market began to attract speculators, just as the

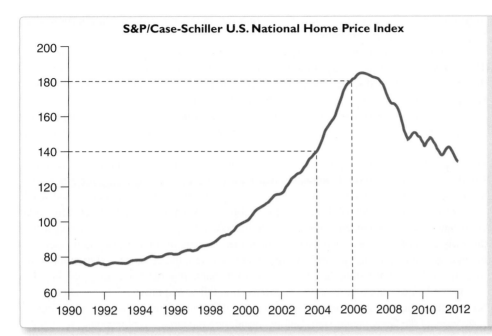

FIGURE 3.1

The American Housing Bubble.

Between 2000 and 2007, many people were buying houses only because they hoped to be able to sell them later at a profit. This caused a sharp run-up in prices prior to 2007, followed by an equally sharp decline after 2007.

Source: S&P Dow Jones Indices LLC. The launch date of the S&P/Case-Shiller U.S. National Home Price Index was May 18, 2006.

seventeenth-century Dutch tulip market had. To make a lot of money, you didn't need to be smart or hardworking. All you had to do was take out a loan, buy a house for a small down payment, then sell it a few years later for a handsome profit. The more expensive the house you bought, the more money you made.

CONCEPT CHECK 3.1

Suppose you bought a house for $100,000 in 2004 with money borrowed at an annual interest rate of 5 percent. If you sold the house two years later, approximately how much money would you have made net of your interest costs?

As the decade wore on, however, evidence began accumulating that housing prices were becoming divorced from the underlying services that houses provide. One measure of that gap was that the monthly cost of owning a house had become much larger than the monthly cost of renting the same house. Some economists had been warning for years that houses were becoming overpriced, and by 2006 average house prices stopped growing.

Many people had been buying houses that were well beyond their means, expecting to meet their mortgage payments by taking out periodic loans against the rising values of those houses. With house prices no longer rising, however, they could no longer obtain such loans, and many were forced to put their houses on the market. The increased supply of houses for sale caused prices to fall, which in turn caused still more people to put their houses on the market. The result was the dramatic downward spiral in post-2007 house prices clearly visible in Figure 3.1. The side effects of that plunge in prices delivered a devastating blow to the broader economy.

From our discussion of supply and demand, recall that income and wealth are important determinants of the demand for products. Because a major share of the wealth of a typical household consists of the value of its house, most consumers experienced big reductions in their wealth when housing prices fell sharply, and that caused them to spend less.

While house prices had been rising sharply, banks had been making trillions of dollars of mortgage loans. The fact that many borrowers could no longer meet their monthly payments put a large proportion of these loans in jeopardy, which in turn put the entire banking system at risk of failure. Companies that relied on short-term loans to conduct their business could no longer get them. Consumers who relied on loans to buy cars and other durable goods were also denied credit. As sales contracted, a sense of alarm began to spread. By the summer of 2008, broad indexes of stock prices had fallen more than 50 percent from their 2007 peaks.

Facing reduced demand for their products, businesses began to lay off workers. Those who lost their jobs were forced to curtail their spending further, which reinforced the growing downward spiral. Even those who remained employed began spending less, because of the rational fear that they might lose their jobs.

With consumer spending much reduced, businesses not only could get by with fewer workers, but also could reduce their investment spending. Since they already had more capacity than necessary to meet current demand for their products, they had no reason to buy more equipment or build bigger factories. This reduction in business spending further intensified the downward spiral. Companies that built factories and machinery for other businesses began to lay off workers, causing those newly jobless people to spend less, and so on.

The cumulative result of these downward forces was that in 2008, the total value of all goods and services produced in the United States was falling even faster than it was during the early days of the Great Depression. The same was true of total employment. Because the international banking system is highly interconnected, the crisis spread to other countries. It was hard to overstate the sense of economic panic that pervaded the globe in 2008.

In the United States, at least, the economic free fall would prove relatively short-lived, because the American government responded very differently from the way it had during the early years of the Great Depression. Before considering the more recent response, it's helpful to review the earlier episode. Herbert Hoover was the American president then, and his policy recommendations were heavily influenced by the thinking of classical macroeconomic theory.

CLASSICAL MACROECONOMIC THEORY

classical macroeconomic theorists early economic theorists who believed that economic downturns would generally reverse themselves quickly without policy intervention

Classical macroeconomic theorists believed that since the economy as a whole was just a collection of many individual markets, patterns of macroeconomic activity should closely resemble the patterns we observe in individual markets. In particular, they believed that the broader economy would be self-regulating in much the same way that individual markets are.

In our discussion of supply and demand theory, we saw that individual markets have a powerful tendency to reach equilibrium on their own. If the price of a good is above equilibrium, for example, there will be excess supply, giving sellers powerful incentives to cut their prices. Conversely, when price is below equilibrium, there will be excess demand, in which case sellers are generally quick to seize the opportunity to raise prices. In short, the price of a good in any individual market seldom departs from its equilibrium level for extended periods.

Classical macroeconomic theorists believed that the economy as a whole should exhibit similar autonomous tendencies to return quickly to any departure from equilibrium. They didn't deny that financial crises could occur. (How could they? Such crises had occurred many times in the past, and a particularly bad one had just been sparked by the collapse of American stock prices in October of 1929.) Rather, they argued that labor markets in the aggregate behave much like individual markets for any other good or service. If there's substantial excess supply in the labor market as a whole (that is, if many more people want to work than firms want to hire at current wages), that imbalance should quickly right itself. Wages would fall, they argued, which would reduce the cost of producing goods and services, which in turn would reduce prices generally. And with the fall in wages and prices, the money held by consumers would become more valuable in real terms. Feeling richer, they would buy more goods and services, which, in turn, would cause firms to hire more workers to produce them.

Their advice to Herbert Hoover? Just go about the government's business as usual, with no backing away from the commitment to maintain a balanced budget. But since millions of people had lost their jobs in 1929 and 1930, income tax revenue had fallen sharply. Balancing the budget would thus require steep cuts in government spending. Hoover failed to balance the government's budget, however, and as history would demonstrate, that was actually a good thing—for had he done so, job losses during the early years of the Great Depression would have been even greater. But things weren't getting better, either, and would not begin to improve until a new president took office in 1933 on the promise to execute a different strategy.

THE KEYNESIAN REVOLUTION AND THE NEW DEAL

The British economist John Maynard Keynes didn't publish *The General Theory of Employment, Interest, and Money* until 1936, some seven years after the onset of the Great Depression. But he had been discussing his ideas with world leaders long before the book appeared, urging them to depart from the prescriptions of classical macroeconomic theory.

Keynes argued that when an event like a financial crisis throws an economy into a deep downturn, there is no tendency for it to recover quickly. To the classical theorists who insisted that unemployment would be cured by spontaneously falling wages, Keynes responded that wages are "**sticky downwards**"—by which he meant that although wages rise quickly when there is excess demand for labor, they stubbornly resist falling when there is excess supply. Economists continue to debate why there might be such an asymmetry. But whatever its cause might be, the empirical evidence overwhelmingly confirms its existence. In industry after industry, country after country, significant downward movements in wages are exceedingly rare.

Absent the **economic stimulus** the classical theorists expected from falling wages, Keynes argued that an economy in a depressed state would tend to remain that way for an extended period. The classical economists were wrong, he felt, to conclude that the national labor market would adjust to a demand shortfall as quickly as individual labor markets do. If the demand for workers declines in a single labor market, unemployed workers can seek employment in other markets where demand remains strong. This exodus of workers can restore equilibrium in the original labor market even if the wage in that market doesn't fall. But it's a different story if *all* labor markets suffer from insufficient demand. If wages are slow to fall everywhere, there are no safe havens for unemployed workers to seek new employment.

The basic problem, as Keynes saw it, was that there was too little spending to justify hiring all the people who wanted to work, and no private actors on the scene had any incentive to increase their spending levels. Consumers wouldn't spend more, he argued, because they were busy paying down debt and fearful of losing their jobs, if they hadn't already lost them. Nor would businesses spend more, since they already had sufficient capacity to produce more than people wanted to buy.

Keynes also emphasized that the behavior of market participants was influenced not just by the usual calculations of costs and benefits, but also by psychological factors, which he called "**animal spirits**." If people's mood turned suddenly pessimistic, for example, spending could fall sharply even in the absence of other influences. Pessimism was clearly widespread during the early days of the Great Depression, and the resulting declines in spending did nothing to relieve that mood. In short, Keynes argued, two of the main components of total spending in the economy—consumption by households, and investment by businesses—were likely to remain depressed indefinitely.

At that time, trade with other nations accounted for only a tiny portion of economic activity in the United States, which meant that there was only one other category of significant spending—namely, spending by government. The key to getting the economy back on its feet, Keynes argued, was for government to increase its own spending dramatically. And since tax revenue was depressed by the low level of private economic activity, the only way government could spend more was by borrowing. Government could also help promote increased spending by taking action to prevent bank failures, which, as noted earlier, contributed to the aggregate shortfall in total spending.[1]

John Maynard Keynes, 1883–1946.

sticky downwards the tendency of prices and wages to resist downward movements

economic stimulus increased government spending or interest rate reductions undertaken to stimulate spending during economic downturns

animal spirits emotions that shift supply and demand curves in ways that cause prices to depart from levels expected to prevail in the long run

---

[1] We do not discuss monetary policy—in practice, the setting of short-term interest rates by a government agency called the central bank—in this chapter. We just note here that Keynesians see monetary policy as a useful tool complementing government spending during periods of high unemployment. By keeping interest rates low in times when the economy is performing below its potential, the central bank encourages consumers to borrow and spend and firms to invest in new capital. Like government spending, this additional spending by households and firms adds to the demand for goods and services, helping to put the unemployed back to work.

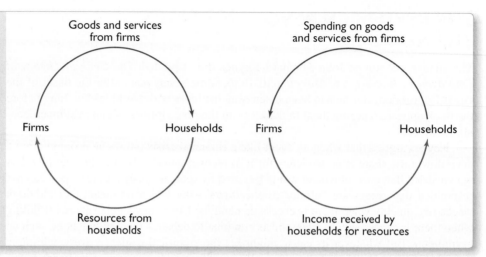

FIGURE 3.2

Two Circular Flow Diagrams.
The left panel shows that households supply labor and capital to firms, which use those resources to produce goods and services for households. The right panel shows that households receive income from firms for the resources they supply, which they then spend on goods and services from firms.

To many, that advice seemed heretical. When a family fell on hard times, critics asked, didn't it have to tighten its belt? Why should government be any different? But while that objection may sound compelling, Keynes understood that the analogy between governments and families was misleading. Yes, a family must consume less when it falls on hard times. But the same rule doesn't apply to government during a deep economic downturn, he argued, because additional government spending is often the only way to bring the downturn quickly to an end.

The so-called circular flow diagrams in Figure 3.2 help illuminate the simple logic behind Keynes's argument. The left panel depicts resource flows in the macroeconomy, showing how households provide productive resources to firms (their own labor, for example, and money to buy machines), which then use those resources to produce goods and services for households. The right panel shows how the income received by households from firms (most of it in the form of wages and salaries) is then spent to buy the very same goods from firms that household members were hired to produce.

As these diagrams help to illustrate, there is a fundamental disconnect between what any individual family could hope to achieve by tightening its budget, on the one hand, and what the economy as a whole could hope to achieve by spending less. Note in the right panel, for example, that if everyone spends less, firms will produce less, which in turn creates a negative feedback effect. Because firms are producing less, they purchase fewer resources from households. And that means households receive less income, which in turn means that they'll need to reduce their spending still further, and so on.

Classical macroeconomic theorists were of course well aware of circular flows in the economy. Such flows underlie a famous relationship known as **Say's Law**, after the French economist Jean Baptiste Say (1737–1832). The total value of all goods and services produced in a country is called its gross domestic product, or GDP. Say's Law states that GDP, which is exactly equal to the sum of all incomes generated by the production of all products and services, must be exactly sufficient to purchase those same products and services. Some economists have shortened Say's Law to "Supply creates its own demand."

Say was correct that the incomes generated when the economy is at full employment are always sufficient to pay for all that is produced. But what if people want to save part of their incomes? Classical economists responded that when people deposited money in their savings accounts, banks would respond by lending that money to businesses, which would then invest it, thereby effectively purchasing additional goods and services to compensate for those that the saving households did not purchase. If necessary, banks would reduce the interest rate on loans in order to induce businesses to invest the available funds. And this is in fact what happens when the economy is operating normally.

But Say's Law does not imply that the economy will automatically tend toward full employment. Suppose, for example, that some event (a financial crisis, for example)

Say's Law the claim, attributed to the French classical macroeconomist Jean Baptiste Say, that any aggregate value of goods produced necessarily creates an equal value of aggregate demand for those goods

causes people to become pessimistic about the future and that, to safeguard against hard times ahead, they decide to spend a smaller proportion of their incomes. Keynes argued that when the economy is operating well below full employment, nothing guarantees that the extra dollars saved will be invested.

He acknowledged that banks would reduce the interest rates on loans in the hope of stimulating additional borrowing. But interest rates can fall only so far, and businesses may find it unattractive to take out additional loans even when interest rates fall all the way to zero. After all, why should a business borrow money to build a bigger factory when its existing factory is already big enough to produce more than its customers want to buy?

If the economy remained in a slump for a sufficiently long time, Keynes recognized, spending would eventually begin to recover. Prices and wages would finally begin to fall, and as factories and equipment began to wear out, businesses would begin to invest. But as Keynes also famously wrote, "In the long run, we are all dead. Economists set themselves too easy, too useless a task if in tempestuous seasons they can only tell us that when the storm is past the ocean is flat again."[2] Keynes asked, in effect, why wait years or even decades for the economy to right itself when increased government spending could get the job done so much more quickly?

Franklin Delano Roosevelt, who was sworn in as the 32nd president of the United States in early 1933, met with Keynes in 1934. But even after that meeting, Roosevelt was reluctant to embrace Keynes's unbalanced budget recommendations publicly. An examination of Roosevelt's actual policies, however, suggests that he took much of Keynes's message to heart. Hoover had praised balanced budgets publicly but failed to achieve them, and the same was true of Roosevelt. But unlike Hoover, Roosevelt actually took vigorous steps to expand employment through public spending.

One of the sources of budget shortfalls during Roosevelt's early years was the major new spending he initiated for public projects. These included the Civilian Conservation Corps, which built many public parks and upgraded many others; the Works Progress Administration, which built numerous roads and public structures; the Tennessee Valley Authority, which provided electric power to a large swath of the southeastern United States; and the Social Security Administration, which boosted the incomes of millions of retirees.

Roosevelt also took action to discourage bank failures, by initiating government guarantees that citizens' deposits would be redeemed even if banks were to fail. This step freed depositors from the fear that if they didn't withdraw their money right away, it might not be available to them in the future.

FDR's approach was thus to pay lip service to the goal of balanced budgets, while at the same time, characterizing his programs for putting people back to work as emergency measures whose cost should not be included in the normal budget process. When critics denounced him for failing to balance the budget, he was unapologetic:

Franklin Delano Roosevelt: "To balance our budget in 1933 or 1934 or 1935 would have been a crime against the American people."

Library of Congress Prints and Photographs Division [LC-USZ62-90270]

> To balance our budget in 1933 or 1934 or 1935 would have been a crime against the American people. To do so we should either have had to make a capital levy that would have been confiscatory, or we should have had to set our face against human suffering with callous indifference. When Americans suffered, we refused to pass by on the other side. Humanity came first.
>
> No one lightly lays a burden on the income of a Nation. But this vicious tightening circle of our declining national income simply had to be broken. The bankers and the industrialists of the Nation cried aloud that private business was powerless to break it. They turned, as they had a right to turn, to the Government. We accepted the final responsibility of Government, after all else had failed, to spend money when no one else had money left to spend.[3]

[2]John Maynard Keynes, "The Theory of Money and the Foreign Exchanges," *A Tract on Monetary Reform* (1924).
[3]www.fdrlibrary.marist.edu.

The unemployment rate declined significantly in the wake of Roosevelt's programs to stimulate the economy, but even by 1937, it remained significantly above where it had been before the stock market crash of 1929. Facing increasing political pressure to balance the federal budget, the president agreed to cut back on the various stimulus programs in 1937, whereupon the country quickly slid into another deep recession. Despite FDR's implicit defense of Keynesian stimulus measures, some economists have argued that, in light of the magnitude of the spending shortfall, his federal budgets did not supply nearly enough net stimulus to the American economy during most of the 1930s. As the economist E. Cary Brown put it in an influential paper, for example, "Fiscal policy did not work [during the depression] because it was not tried."[4]

The country rebounded to full employment only after the massive increase in government expenditures associated with the country's entry into World War II.

THE LESSONS OF POST-CRISIS EXPERIENCE

American Recovery and Reinvestment Act a combination of increased government spending and tax cuts introduced in 2009 in the hope of shortening the Great Recession

Troubled Asset Relief Program (TARP) U.S. government purchase of assets and equity from financial institutions to strengthen its financial sector and to prevent large financial institutions from collapse

In 2009, the United States Congress passed the **American Recovery and Reinvestment Act**, a program that called for roughly $800 billion of additional budgetary stimulus—including infrastructure spending, tax cuts, energy investments, and grants to states to retain teachers and first responders.[5] The U.S. government's response to the financial crisis also included the **Troubled Asset Relief Program (TARP)**, whose purpose was to prevent large financial institutions from collapsing. The latter steps were taken because the guarantees on cash deposits in banks enacted during the 1930s did not cover funds deposited in a growing number of large financial institutions that operated outside the formal banking industry and were hence not subject to standard banking regulations.

At the time, many economists warned that the Recovery Act was far too small to remedy a total spending shortfall estimated at roughly $2 trillion.

Another concern was that much of the act's additional spending was being offset by large reductions in state and local government spending. Unlike the federal government, which is constitutionally permitted to run budget deficits, lower-level governments generally operate under legal charters that require balanced budgets (although they often fail to achieve them). In the face of sharply reduced tax revenues, many state and local governments had no choice but to reduce spending.

Unemployment in the United States has declined substantially since its 2009 peak but only frustratingly slowly. This has led many critics of the Recovery Act to charge that economic stimulus didn't work. Most economists, however, reject that view. For example, economists at the nonpartisan Congressional Budget Office estimated that between 1.3 million and 3.5 million employed Americans would not have had jobs in late 2010 in the absence of the stimulus program.[6] Most experienced policy economists from both sides of the political aisle now agree that additional government stimulus not only helps a depressed economy recover more quickly, but also results in smaller budget deficits in the long run. Yet a relatively small group of economists continues to argue that public austerity is the proper response to persistently high unemployment.

austerity any combination of government spending reductions and tax increases implemented with the intention of reducing government budget deficits

Austerity advocates not only insisted that stimulus measures paid for with borrowed money would not hasten economic recovery; they also predicted that such measures would have two additional specific effects: They would produce substantial inflation (widespread increases in the prices of goods and services) and would also lead to sharply higher interest rates. Neither prediction has come to pass. Interest rates have remained

[4]E. Cary Brown, "Fiscal Policy in the 'Thirties Reappraised,'" *American Economic Review*, 46, no. 5 (December 1956), pp. 857–859.
[5]The U.S. government's response to the financial crisis also included the Troubled Asset Relief Program (TARP), whose purpose was to prevent large financial institutions from collapsing, and extended insurance covering large deposits in money market funds.
[6]Congressional Budget Office, "Estimated Impact of the American Recovery and Reinvestment Act on Employment and Economic Output from October 2010 to December 2010," February 2011, www.cbo.gov/sites/default/files/cbofiles/ftpdocs/120xx/doc12074/02-23-arra.pdf.

near record low levels since the crisis began, a period during which the prices of goods and services have also been rising at lower-than-normal rates.

The predictions advanced by austerity advocates actually make perfect sense in the context of an economy that is operating at full capacity. Suppose, for example, that government borrows money to pay workers to build additional roads. If the economy is already at full employment, every dollar of private savings is already being channeled into investment spending. If government wants to borrow more of the existing pool of savings, there will be excess demand for that money and its price—the interest rate—will be bid up. And if the economy is already at full employment, government can build new roads only by bidding workers away from existing projects, which will require paying them a higher wage. Higher wages, in turn, translate into higher prices. In short, deficit spending in an economy at full employment crowds out private spending, causing increases in both interest rates and the average price level.

But that's not at all what supply and demand analysis predicts will happen when the economy is in a downturn like the one precipitated by the 2008 financial crisis. People are trying to save more, but businesses have no reason to channel the additional savings into investment. Since there was already an excess supply of savings, government can borrow more without bidding up interest rates. And they can build new roads by hiring unemployed workers, so there is also no reason to expect higher wages and prices. In short, Keynes's predictions about how prices and interest rates would respond to economic stimulus in a downturn were completely consistent with what actually happened.

WHY DOES THE DISPUTE LINGER?

As noted, a majority of economists now accept the Keynesian prescriptions for how best to proceed when the economy is in a deep downturn caused by a financial crisis. Yet austerity proponents continue to advocate forcefully for their position. And because many of Keynes's arguments run counter to popular economic intuitions, the urgings of austerity advocates have considerable rhetorical force. As noted earlier, for example, everyday experience teaches that families must spend less when their incomes decline, so it's totally natural that many people think the same must be true for governments.

Austerity advocates also insist that unless governments borrow less, we will consign our offspring to lives of poverty. This claim also resonates, because people know that when families recklessly run up big debts, they often compromise the economic opportunities of their children.

Keynes's choice of one particular illustration of the logic of deficit-financed government spending during a downturn surely bears at least some responsibility for lingering opposition to his proposals. As he wrote in *The General Theory*, for example,

> If the Treasury were to fill old bottles with banknotes, bury them at suitable depths in disused coalmines which are then filled up to the surface with town rubbish, and leave it to private enterprise on well-tried principles of laissez-faire to dig the notes up again . . . , there need be no more unemployment and, with the help of the repercussions, the real income of the community, and its capital wealth also, would probably become a good deal greater than it actually is.[7]

Although Keynes quickly added that it would of course be better if the government were to spend more on activities that were actually useful, the damage was done. His vivid example helped his opponents create the impression that government stimulus meant wasteful government spending, and *nobody* favors that.

Opposition to Keynesian remedies is also likely to stem in part from legitimate differences in people's views about the proper scope of government. It is no surprise, for example, that anti-Keynesian views are far more likely to be held by those who strongly believe that government's role in economic life should be as small as possible.

[7]Keynes, *The General Theory*, chap. 8, https://ebooks.adelaide.edu.au/k/keynes/john_maynard/k44g/chapter8.html.

There are reasonable rejoinders to each of these objections. Keynes explained, for example, that the analogy between governments and families breaks down when the economy is deeply depressed. And as we'll see, it often makes sense for even an indebted family to engage in further borrowing. As Keynes also explained, the best government stimulus is for things people find genuinely useful, and there is no shortage of options in that regard. Nor would there be any inconsistency in someone's believing that government's scope should be limited during normal times, yet simultaneously believing that government could intervene productively during occasional deep economic downturns.

CONCEPT CHECK 3.2

Explain how the right-hand circular flow diagram in Figure 3.2 can be used to explain Keynes's "Paradox of Thrift," which states that if all households attempt to increase their savings, the result may be a reduction in aggregate savings.

What is clear, in any event, is that when the next deep downturn inevitably occurs, arguments will resume about whether deficit spending will help speed recovery. And if recent experience is any guide, the likely result will again be partial political paralysis or at best half measures that needlessly prolong the human suffering that depressions always inflict.

The fact that severe financial crises occur only infrequently means that we're unlikely to have the detailed statistical evidence that would be required to resolve all disagreements about their causes and potential remedies. But uncertainty is not a prescription for inaction. No one would claim, for example, that a nation should disband its military forces simply because it is uncertain that a rival will invade. By the same token, it may often be prudent to employ plausible depression countermeasures even in the absence of complete consensus about whether they will work.

AVOIDING PROTRACTED DOWNTURNS IN THE FUTURE

Merely repeating Keynes's arguments, however, is unlikely to change the political debate about government economic policy. We must look for ways to reframe the conversation. A first step is to recognize the human cost imposed by extended economic downturns. Long-term unemployment, for example, often results in hunger and depression, and is a leading cause of suicide. In the current downturn, long-term unemployment has been at record levels. Recent graduates have had to begin their careers in the most difficult labor market since the Great Depression. Their slow start will mean lower incomes for a lifetime.

Because businesses are not investing at normal levels—again, why build new factories if you can already produce more than consumers want to buy?—the nation's future stock of productive equipment will be permanently smaller. And that means slower growth in productivity and wages. Widespread unemployment and lagging wages have also meant higher poverty rates and more children with inadequate nutrition. In each case, the effect is to reduce future tax receipts, pushing government budgets further into the red.

In the light of such costs, no one denies that it would be good if the economy could *somehow* be coaxed back to full employment more quickly. Reaching agreement on how to promote that goal becomes easier once we recognize that virtually everyone views certain specific increases in government spending as useful. So it should be relatively easy to reach agreement on those increases, independent of one's views about the efficacy of Keynesian stimulus policy more generally.

For example, the Nevada Department of Transportation describes a 10-mile stretch of Interstate 80 that is badly in need of repair. If the job were done today, they report, it could be accomplished for $6 million. But if it's delayed for just two years, weather and traffic will eat more deeply into the roadbed, boosting the job's cost to $30 million. According to the American Association of State Highway and Transportation Officials, substandard roads also cause $335 in annual damage per vehicle on the road. Still more troubling, those roads cause many easily preventable deaths and injuries. Those costs also mount with delay.

It's of course true that in the midst of a deep economic downturn, many workers capable of doing the work are unemployed. Waiting until the economy recovered would mean having to bid many of them away from other productive tasks. In a depressed economy, much of the equipment required for the job is also sitting idle, the required materials are extremely cheap on world markets, and the interest rates to finance the work are at record lows. So being in the midst of an economic downturn definitely reinforces the case for doing this work as quickly as possible. But the case for tackling such jobs right away is compelling even apart from any need to stimulate employment.

Or consider another example, this one involving two major bottlenecks on the Northeast rail corridor. Because of low clearances in two locations, double-decker freight containers cannot travel along that corridor. Instead they're carried by truck, mostly along I-95, which is now clogged with freight traffic at almost every hour. The bottlenecks could be cleared at a cost of $6 billion, which would result in direct savings of $12 billion, not counting the implicit value of reduced noise and environmental damage from the extra truck traffic. The case for making this investment right away would be decisive even in an economy at full employment. In a depressed economy it is even more compelling.

Some people object to the additional government debt that such projects would require. Thus, as austerity proponents like to say, governments can't spend beyond their means indefinitely, any more than businesses or families can. It's a fair statement if we're talking about the long run. But in the short run, it's simply false. When prudent investment opportunities arise, families, businesses, and governments can and should spend more than they take in.

Consider an indebted family that must decide whether to borrow $5,000 to install additional insulation in its attic, a project that would reduce its utility bills by an average of $100 a month and require loan payments of $50 a month. In the short run, obviously, the project would increase the family's indebtedness. But can there be any doubt that the family would be better off, in both the short and the long run, by going ahead with it? Even while making payments on the loan, it would have $50 more each month. And once the loan was paid off, it would have $100 a month more. What possible argument could be offered against this project?

The same logic applies to virtually every overdue infrastructure investment. A recent report by the American Society of Civil Engineers has identified an inventory of some $3.6 trillion in such overdue investments.[8] Paying for them would require more government debt, of course. But while austerity advocates fret that such projects would impoverish our grandchildren, they concede that the investments can't be postponed indefinitely, and that they'll become much more expensive the longer we wait. So it's actually *failure* to undertake these projects that would saddle our grandchildren with larger debt.

Since the case for accelerating infrastructure repairs would be compelling even if the economy were at full employment, an agreement to spend more money on infrastructure refurbishment during economic downturns would not require austerity proponents to concede the merits of traditional Keynesian stimulus policy. Nor would it require them to abandon their concerns about the national debt. In short, the philosophical foundation for an agreement is already firmly in place.

---

[8]American Society of Civil Engineers, *2013 Report Card for American Infrastructure*, www.infrastructurereportcard.org.

The Economic Naturalist 3.1

Is the low unemployment rate in Germany, whose government advocates austerity, evidence against Keynes's argument?

Although the German government was one of the most outspoken defenders of fiscal austerity, the unemployment rate in Germany in the wake of the financial crisis has actually been significantly lower than in most other industrial countries. Isn't that evidence against Keynes's claim that increased government spending helps speed economic recovery in depressed economies?

The usefulness of refocusing the great austerity debate on infrastructure quickly becomes evident upon a visit to Berlin, Germany, where the entire city seems under construction. In every direction, cranes and other heavy equipment dominate the landscape. Many projects are in the private sector, but innumerable others—including bridge and highway repairs, new subway stations, and other infrastructure work—are financed by taxpayers.

Since the German government has been one of the most outspoken advocates of fiscal austerity in the aftermath of the financial crisis, that might seem to be a contradiction. But it is not. Fiscally responsible businesses routinely borrow to invest, and so do most governments.

The American infrastructure backlog owes in part to fears about growing public debt that have caused wholesale cutbacks in American public investment. The Germans of course yield to no one in their distaste for indebtedness. But they also understand the distinction between consumption and investment. By borrowing, they've made investments whose future benefits will far outweigh repayment costs. There's nothing foolhardy about that.

Although a preponderance of evidence suggests that Keynes was right about stimulus policy, the German experience illustrates that progress is possible without settling that question. The Germans are investing in infrastructure not to provide short-term economic stimulus but because those investments promise high returns. Yet their undeniable side effect has been to boost employment substantially in the short run.

Needless to say, not all German public investments have met expectations. Berlin's future airport, for example, has suffered multiple delays and cost overruns, and parts of the city's recently constructed central rail station had to be closed for several months for major repairs. But private investment projects suffer occasional setbacks, too, and no one argues that businesses should stop investing on that account.

Although the Germans did not get bogged down in debate over stimulus policy, their high level of infrastructure spending has been no less effective at putting people to work for lack of being called stimulus explicitly. The German economy's relatively strong post-crisis performance is of course not solely a consequence of robust infrastructure spending. The country's exports were relatively cheap in the wake of the crisis, for example, enabling export growth to offset some reductions in domestic demand caused by the crisis.

Berlin, Germany: Praise for austerity amidst heavy spending on infrastructure.

© Yulia Reznikov/Moment Open/Getty Images

CONCLUDING REMARKS

Although we began this chapter with the observation that economists are in broad agreement about most important policy questions, agreement is clearly far from unanimous when it comes to Keynesian stimulus measures. Vocal opposition to such measures, albeit from a small proportion of professional economists, is likely to continue to handicap efforts to speed recovery from deep economic downturns.

Fortunately, there is almost no disagreement among economists about the desirability of keeping our national infrastructure in good working order. Evidence for that claim comes from the responses of a panel of economic experts assembled by the University of Chicago Booth School of Business. Those experts, who represent diverse ideological viewpoints, were asked to react to a variety of statements, including the following:

"Because the U.S. has underspent on new projects, maintenance, or both, the federal government has an opportunity to increase average incomes by spending more on roads, railways, bridges, and airports." More than 96 percent of respondents who expressed an opinion about this statement either agreed or agreed strongly with it.[9] Not all of the economists in the Booth survey are enthusiastic supporters of Keynesian stimulus measures during downturns. But that highlights the advantage of focusing on infrastructure spending, which makes compelling sense even when the economy is at full employment.

We should also expect most voters to respond positively to proposals to accelerate infrastructure maintenance during economic downturns, since doing so reduces costs while visibly increasing employment. So even in the face of continued disagreement about the efficacy of Keynesian stimulus measures, we are not necessarily condemned to endure the protracted economic downturns that typically follow severe financial crises.

[9]"Infrastructure," Chicago Booth IGM Forum, May 23, 2013, www.igmchicago.org/igm-economic-experts-panel/poll-results?SurveyID=SV_1ZmH6tDwTR0BRu5.

SUMMARY

- Financial crises have been occurring periodically ever since market systems enabled people to invest with borrowed money. One of the earliest recorded instances was the Dutch tulip bubble of the seventeenth century. Once the price of an asset begins rising rapidly, many people start buying it in the expectation of reselling it later at a profit. Once speculators bid the asset's price up to unrealistically high levels, people start to sell, and prices often decline precipitously. The American housing bubble of the early 2000s followed this pattern, precipitating a major economic downturn. *(LO1)*

- Classical macroeconomic theorists believed that since the economy as a whole was just a collection of many individual markets, the broader economy would be self-regulating in much the same way that individual markets are. They argued that unemployment would lead to falling wages, which in turn would cause employers to hire more workers. They also believed that excess savings would lead to lower interest rates, causing businesses to increase investment. *(LO2)*

- Keynes argued that there is no tendency for an economy to recover quickly in the wake of a financial crisis, in part because wages stubbornly resist falling even when unemployment is high. The problem, as he saw it, was a persistent shortfall of total spending. Consumers wouldn't spend more because they were busy paying down debt and fearful of losing their jobs. And even if interest rates fell all the way to zero, businesses wouldn't spend more because they already had sufficient capacity to produce more than people wanted to buy. Increased government spending, he concluded, was the most effective way to eliminate the spending shortfall quickly. *(LO3)*

- Although most economists now accept Keynes's policy recommendations for how to boost spending during economic downturns, a vocal minority continues to endorse the classical macroeconomists' view that governments should balance their budgets by cutting public spending. Such disputes are inherently difficult to resolve on the basis of hard empirical evidence because deep economic downturns are such rare events. We simply don't have enough experience with them to have gained a detailed understanding of their causes and potential remedies. *(LO4)*

- A minority of economists continue to support economic austerity as the best response to a downturn. The staying power of that view may stem in part from the apparent analogy to the imperatives facing an individual family in financial difficulty. When an individual family suffers a big income decline, it must reduce its spending. But the analogy breaks down at the macro level. When government reduces its spending during an economic downturn, an immediate consequence is that total income in the economy declines still further. *(LO5)*

- One strategy for strengthening support for government stimulus during economic downturns is to focus on public infrastructure spending. There is broad agreement that the nation's roads, bridges, and other infrastructure must be maintained, and that postponing maintenance raises total costs and public debt levels in the long run. Quite apart from its effect as economic stimulus, increased spending on infrastructure repairs during downturns thus makes economic sense because much of the machinery and labor needed for these projects would otherwise sit idle. *(LO6)*

KEY TERMS

American Recovery and Reinvestment Act
animal spirits
austerity

classical macroeconomic theorists
economic stimulus
financial crisis
Say's Law

speculative bubble
sticky downwards
Troubled Asset Relief Program (TARP)

REVIEW QUESTIONS

1. According to the economist Herb Stein, if something cannot go on forever, what will happen? *(LO1)*

2. Explain why it might be rational for someone to have bought a house in 2004, even in the face of evidence that houses had become significantly overpriced by then. *(LO1)*

3. In the wake of the 2008 financial crisis, why were American businesses with lots of cash in their accounts spending so much less than they normally do on new factories and equipment? *(LO3)*

4. During the aftermath of the 2008 financial crisis, why were consumers spending so much less than they normally do? *(LO3)*

5. What happened to state and local government spending levels in the aftermath of the 2008 financial crisis? *(LO4)*

PROBLEMS

1. Suppose you bought a house for $200,000 in 2004 and sold it in 2006. Approximately how much money would you have made? (*Hint*: See Figure 3.1.) How does your answer bear on your answer to Review Question 2? *(LO1)*

2. Classical macroeconomic theorists recommended that governments maintain balanced budgets even during deep economic downturns. If governments followed that recommendation, what would happen to government spending? *(LO2)*

3. Classical macroeconomic theorists said that unemployment couldn't remain abnormally high for long because falling wages would be an incentive for employers to hire more workers. How did Keynes respond to that claim? *(LO2, LO3)*

4. Keynes wrote, in an often-quoted passage, "In the long run, we are all dead." What was his point? *(LO3)*

5. Classical macroeconomic theorists predicted that additional government spending tends to displace spending by consumers and firms. How does the accuracy of this prediction depend on whether the economy is at full employment? *(LO3)*

6. In the wake of the 2008 financial crisis, 20 U.S. states saw reductions in government spending at the state level, while the remaining 30 states saw continued increases. How did the pace of economic recovery differ in the two groups of states? *(LO4)*

7. Austerity advocates predicted that economic stimulus measures would lead to large and rapid increases in both interest rates and inflation. Were those predictions borne out? *(LO4)*

8. Some have compared unemployed workers to unfilled seats on passenger jets. What do the two have in common? *(LO4)*

9. When a family experiences a reduction in income, it generally must reduce the amount it spends. Does the same rule apply to governments? Explain. *(LO5)*

10. Explain why proposals for accelerated expenditures on infrastructure maintenance help sidestep lingering disagreements about how governments might best respond to deep economic downturns. *(LO6)*

ANSWERS TO CONCEPT CHECKS

3.1 According to Figure 3.1, house prices, adjusted for inflation, appreciated by approximately 35 percent between 2004 and 2006. So someone who bought a house in 2004 for $100,000 could have sold it in 2006 for almost $135,000. After deducting the roughly $10,000 in interest costs for those two years, net profit would have been approximately $25,000. *(LO1)*

3.2 A family's income does not depend in any significant way on the total amount spent by its members. So if any single family saves a larger proportion of its income, its total savings will increase. But if all families try to save more at once during a deep economic downturn, their reduced consumption may not be offset by increased business investment. Businesses already have more capacity than they need, so will see no advantage in borrowing those savings to build bigger factories. And in that case total spending would fall, causing total incomes and total savings to fall as well. *(LO5)*

4

LEARNING OBJECTIVES

After reading this chapter, you should be able to:

LO1 Relate the law of demand to the Cost-Benefit Principle.

LO2 Apply the law of demand to consumer decision making to show how it is related to substitution and income effects.

LO3 Discuss the relationship between the individual demand curve and the market demand curve.

LO4 Define the price elasticity of demand and explain what determines whether demand is elastic or inelastic.

LO5 Calculate the price elasticity of demand using information from a demand curve.

LO6 Describe how changes in the price of a good affect total revenue and total expenditure depending on the price elasticity of demand for the good.

LO7 Define the cross-price elasticity of demand and the income elasticity of demand.

Demand and Elasticity

On the northern border of a large university in the East, a creek widens to form a picturesque lake, fondly remembered by generations of alumni as a popular recreation spot. Over the years, the lake had gradually silted in, and by the late 1980s, even paddling a canoe across it had become impossible. A generous alumnus then sponsored an effort to restore the lake. Heavy dredging equipment hauled out load after load of mud, and months later the lake was silt-free.

To mark the occasion, the university held a ceremony. Bands played, the president spoke, a chorus sang, and distinguished visitors applauded the donor's generosity. Hundreds of faculty and students turned out for the festivities. Spotting a good opportunity to promote their product, the proprietors of a local ice cream store set up a temporary stand at the water's edge, with a large sign: "Free Ice Cream."

Word spread. Soon scores of people were lined up waiting to try Vanilla Almond Delight, Hazelnut Cream, and Fudge Faire. The ice cream was plentiful, and because it was free, everyone could obviously afford it—or so it seemed. In fact, many people who wanted ice cream that day never got any. The reason, of course, was that they found waiting in a long line too steep a price to pay for ice cream.

When a good or service is scarce, it must somehow be rationed among competing users. In most markets, monetary prices perform that task. But in the case of a stand offering free ice cream, waiting time becomes the effective rationing device. Having to stand in line is a cost, no less so than having to part with some money.

This example drives home the point that although the demand curve is usually described as a relationship between the quantity demanded of a good and its monetary price, the relationship is really a much more general one. At bottom, the demand curve is a relationship between the quantity demanded and *all* costs—monetary and nonmonetary—associated with acquiring a good.

Our task in this chapter will be to explore the demand side of the market in greater depth than was possible in the *Supply and Demand* chapter, where we introduced the intuitively plausible claim that the quantity demanded of a good or service declines as its price rises. This relationship is known as the *law of demand,* and here we will explore more fully the dual roles of income and substitution. Next, we will see how to generate market demand curves by adding the demand curves for individual buyers horizontally.

Following that, we will introduce the concept of elasticity, a measure of the extent to which quantity demanded and quantity supplied respond to variations in price, income, and other factors. In the chapter *Supply and Demand*, we saw how shifts in supply and demand curves enabled us to predict the direction of change in the equilibrium values of price and quantity. An understanding of price elasticity will enable us to make even more precise statements about the effects of such changes. Finally, we will explore why some goods have higher price elasticity of demand than others and the implications of that fact for how total spending responds to changes in prices.

THE LAW OF DEMAND

With our discussion of the free ice cream offer in mind, let us restate the law of demand as follows:

Law of Demand: People do less of what they want to do as the cost of doing it rises.

By stating the law of demand this way, we can see it as a direct consequence of the Cost-Benefit Principle, which says that an activity should be pursued if (and only if) its benefits are at least as great as its costs. Recall that we measure the benefit of an activity by the highest price we'd be willing to pay to pursue it—namely, our reservation price for the activity. When the cost of an activity rises, it is more likely to exceed our reservation price, and we are therefore less likely to pursue that activity.

The law of demand applies to BMWs, cheap key rings, and "free" ice cream, not to mention compact discs, manicures, medical care, and acid-free rain. It stresses that a "cost" is the sum of *all* the sacrifices—monetary and nonmonetary, implicit and explicit—we must make to engage in an activity.

The Origins of Demand

How much are you willing to pay for the latest Beyoncé release? The answer will clearly depend on how you feel about her music. To her diehard fans, buying the new release might seem absolutely essential; they'd pay a steep price indeed. But those who don't like her music may be unwilling to buy it at any price.

Wants (also called "preferences" or "tastes") are clearly an important determinant of a consumer's reservation price for a good. But that begs the question of where wants come from. Many tastes—such as the taste for water on a hot day or for a comfortable place to sleep at night—are largely biological in origin. But many others are heavily shaped by culture, and even basic cravings may be socially molded. For example, people raised in southern India develop a taste for hot curry dishes, while those raised in England generally prefer milder foods.

Tastes for some items may remain stable for many years, but tastes for others may be highly volatile. Although books about the *Titanic* disaster have been continuously available since the vessel sank in the spring of 1912, not until the appearance of James Cameron's blockbuster film did these books begin to sell in large quantities. In the spring of 1998, five of the 15 books on *The New York Times* paperback bestseller list were about the *Titanic* itself or one of the actors in the film. Yet none of these books, or any other book about the *Titanic*, made the bestseller list in the years since then. Still, echoes of the film continued to reverberate in the marketplace. In the years since its release, for example, demand for ocean cruises has grown sharply and several television networks have introduced shows set on cruise ships.

Peer influence provides another example of how social forces often influence demand. Indeed, it is often the most important single determinant of demand. For instance, if our goal is to predict whether a young man will purchase an illegal recreational drug, knowing how much income he has is not very helpful. Knowing the prices of whiskey and other legal substitutes for illicit drugs also tells us little. Although these factors do influence purchase decisions, by themselves they are weak predictors. But if we know that most of the young man's best friends are heavy drug users, there is a reasonably good chance that he will use drugs as well.

Another important way in which social forces shape demand is in the relatively common desire to consume goods and services that are recognized as the best of their kind. For instance, many people want to hear Placido Domingo sing, not just because of the quality of his voice, but because he is widely regarded as the world's best—or at least the world's best known—living tenor.

Consider, too, the decision of how much to spend on an interview suit. Employment counselors never tire of reminding us that making a good first impression is extremely important when you go for a job interview. At the very least, that means showing up in a suit that looks good. But looking good is a relative concept. If everyone else shows up in a $200 suit, you'll look good if you show up in a $300 suit. But you won't look as good in that same $300 suit if everyone else shows up in suits costing $1,000. The amount you'll choose to spend on an interview suit, then, clearly depends on how much others in your circle are spending.

Needs versus Wants

In everyday language, we distinguish between goods and services people need and those they merely want. For example, we might say that someone wants a ski vacation in Utah, but what he really needs is a few days off from his daily routine; or that someone wants a house with a view, but what she really needs is shelter from the elements. Likewise, since people need protein to survive, we might say that a severely malnourished person needs more protein. But it would strike us as odd to say that anyone—even a malnourished person—needs more prime filet of beef, since health can be restored by consuming far less expensive sources of protein.

Economists like to emphasize that once we have achieved bare subsistence levels of consumption—the amount of food, shelter, and clothing required to maintain our health—we can abandon all reference to needs and speak only in terms of wants. This linguistic distinction helps us to think more clearly about the true nature of our choices.

For instance, someone who says, "Californians don't have nearly as much water as they need" will tend to think differently about water shortages than someone who says, "Californians don't have nearly as much water as they want when the price of water is low." The first person is likely to focus on regulations to prevent people from watering their lawns, or on projects to capture additional runoff from the Sierra Nevada mountains. The second person is more likely to focus on the artificially low price of water in California. Whereas remedies of the first sort are often costly and extremely difficult to implement, raising the price of water is both simple and effective.

The Economic Naturalist 4.1

Why does California experience chronic water shortages?

Some might respond that the state must serve the needs of a large population with a relatively low average annual rainfall. Yet other states, like New Mexico, have even less rainfall per person and do not experience water shortages nearly as often as California. California's problem exists because local governments sell water at extremely low prices, which encourages Californians to use water in ways that make no sense for a state with low rainfall. For instance, rice, which is well suited for conditions in high-rainfall states like South Carolina, requires extensive irrigation in California. But because California farmers can obtain water so cheaply, they plant and flood hundreds of thousands of acres of rice paddies each spring in the Central Valley. Two thousand tons of water are needed to produce one ton of rice, but many other grains can be produced with only half that amount. If the price of California water were higher, farmers would simply switch to other grains.

FIGURE 4.4

Elastic and Inelastic Demand.
Demand for a good is called elastic, unit elastic, or inelastic with respect to price if the price elasticity is greater than 1, equal to 1, or less than 1, respectively.

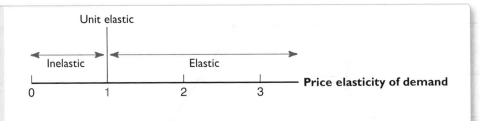

EXAMPLE 4.1   Elasticity of Demand

What is the elasticity of demand for pizza?

When the price of pizza is $1 per slice, buyers wish to purchase 400 slices per day, but when price falls to $0.97 per slice, the quantity demanded rises to 404 slices per day. At the original price, what is the price elasticity of demand for pizza? Is the demand for pizza elastic with respect to price?

The fall in price from $1 to $0.97 is a decrease of 3 percent. The rise in quantity demanded from 400 slices to 404 slices is an increase of 1 percent. The price elasticity of demand for pizza is thus (1 percent)/(3 percent) = 1/3. So when the initial price of pizza is $1, the demand for pizza is not elastic with respect to price; it is inelastic.

CONCEPT CHECK 4.2

What is the elasticity of demand for season ski passes?
    When the price of a season ski pass is $400, buyers, whose demand curve for passes is linear, wish to purchase 10,000 passes per year, but when price falls to $380, the quantity demanded rises to 12,000 passes per year. At the original price, what is the price elasticity of demand for ski passes? Is the demand for ski passes elastic with respect to price?

Determinants of Price Elasticity of Demand

What factors determine the price elasticity of demand for a good or service? To answer this question, recall that, before a rational consumer buys any product, the purchase decision must first satisfy the Cost-Benefit Principle. For instance, consider a good (such as a dorm refrigerator) that you buy only one unit of (if you buy it at all). Suppose that, at the current price, you have decided to buy it. Now imagine that the price goes up by 10 percent. Will a price increase of this magnitude be likely to make you change your mind? The answer will depend on factors like the following.

Substitution Possibilities

When the price of a product you want to buy goes up significantly, you are likely to ask yourself, "Is there some other good that can do roughly the same job, but for less money?" If the answer is yes, then you can escape the effect of the price increase by simply switching to the substitute product. But if the answer is no, you are more likely to stick with your current purchase.

    These observations suggest that demand will tend to be more elastic with respect to price for products for which close substitutes are readily available. Salt, for example, has no close substitutes, which is one reason that the demand for it is highly inelastic. Note,

If the price of salt were to double, would you use less of it?

however, that while the quantity of salt people demand is highly insensitive to price, the same cannot be said of the demand for any *specific brand* of salt. After all, despite what salt manufacturers say about the special advantages of their own labels, consumers tend to regard one brand of salt as a virtually perfect substitute for another. Thus, if Morton were to raise the price of its salt significantly, many people would simply switch to some other brand.

The vaccine against rabies is another product for which there are essentially no attractive substitutes. A person who is bitten by a rabid animal and does not take the vaccine faces a certain and painful death. Most people in that position would pay any price they could afford rather than do without the vaccine.

Budget Share

Suppose the price of key rings suddenly were to double. How would that affect the number of key rings you buy? If you're like most people, it would have no effect at all. Think about it—a doubling of the price of a $1 item that you buy only every few years is simply nothing to worry about. By contrast, if the price of the new car you were about to buy suddenly doubled, you would definitely want to check out possible substitutes such as a used car or a smaller new model. You also might consider holding on to your current car a little longer. The larger the share of your budget an item accounts for, the greater your incentive to look for substitutes when the price of the item rises. Big-ticket items, therefore, tend to have higher price elasticities of demand.

Time

Home appliances come in a variety of models, some more energy-efficient than others. As a general rule, the more efficient an appliance is, the higher its price. Suppose that you were about to buy a new air conditioner and electric rates suddenly rose sharply. It would probably be in your interest to buy a more efficient machine than you had originally planned. However, what if you had already bought a new air conditioner before you learned of the rate increase? You would not think it worthwhile to discard the machine right away and replace it with a more efficient model. Rather, you would wait until the machine wore out, or until you moved, before making the switch.

As this example illustrates, substitution of one product or service for another takes time. Some substitutions occur in the immediate aftermath of a price increase, but many others take place years or even decades later. For this reason, the price elasticity of demand for any good or service will be higher in the long run than in the short run.

> **RECAP** ↑
>
> **FACTORS THAT INFLUENCE PRICE ELASTICITY**
>
> The price elasticity of demand for a good or service tends to be larger when substitutes for the good are more readily available, when the good's share in the consumer's budget is larger, and when consumers have more time to adjust to a change in price.

Some Representative Elasticity Estimates

The entries in Table 4.1 show that the price elasticities of demand for different products often differ substantially—in this sample, ranging from a high of 3.5 for public transportation to a low of 0.1 for food. This variability is explained in part by the determinants of elasticity just discussed. Note, for example, that the price elasticity of demand for green peas is more than nine times that for coffee, reflecting the fact that there are many more close substitutes for green peas than for coffee. Note also the contrast between the low price elasticity of demand for food itself as a category and the high price elasticity of demand for green peas specifically. Unlike green peas, food occupies a substantial share of most family budgets and there are few substitutes for broad spending categories like food.

TABLE 4.1
Historical Price Elasticity of Demand Estimates for Selected Products

Product or Service	Estimated Price Elasticity
Food	0.1
Coffee	0.3
Magazines and newspapers	0.3
Housing	0.6
Tobacco	0.6
Clothing	0.6
Medical care	0.8
Oil	0.9
Motor vehicles	1.1
Beer	1.2
Furniture	1.3
Restaurant meals	1.6
Household electricity	1.9
Boats, pleasure aircraft	2.4
Green peas	2.8
Public transportation	3.5

Sources: K. Elzinga, "The Beer Industry," in *The Structure of American Industry,* ed. Walter Adams (New York: Macmillan, 1977); Ronald Fisher, *State and Local Public Finance* (Chicago: Irwin, 1996); H. S. Houthakker and Lester Taylor, *Consumer Demand in the United States: Analyses and Projections,* 2nd ed. (Cambridge, MA: Harvard University Press, 1970); Ashan Mansur and John Whalley, "Numerical Specification of Applied General Equilibrium Models: Estimation, Calibration, and Data," in *Applied General Equilibrium Analysis,* eds. Herbert Scarf and John Shoven (New York: Cambridge University Press, 1984); Joachim Möller, "Income and Price Elasticities in Different Sectors of the Economy—An Analysis of Structural Change for Germany, the U.K., and the U.S.A." (University of Regensburg, 1998); L. Taylor, "The Demand for Electricity: A Survey," *Bell Journal of Economics* (Spring 1975); and Henri Theil, Ching-Fan Chung, and James Seale, "Advances in Econometrics," Supplement I, 1989, *International Evidence on Consumption Patterns* (Greenwich, CT: JAI Press, 1989).

Using Price Elasticity of Demand

An understanding of the factors that govern price elasticity of demand is necessary not only to make sense of consumer behavior, but also to design effective public policy. Consider, for example, the debate about how taxes affect smoking among teenagers.

The Economic Naturalist 4.6

Will a higher tax on cigarettes curb teenage smoking?

Consultants hired by the tobacco industry have testified in Congress against higher cigarette taxes aimed at curbing teenage smoking. The main reason teenagers smoke is that their friends smoke, these consultants testified, and they concluded that higher taxes would have little effect. Does the consultants' testimony make economic sense?

The consultants are almost certainly right that peer influence is the most important determinant of teen smoking. But that does not imply that a higher tax on cigarettes would have little impact on adolescent smoking rates. Because most teenagers have little money to spend at their own discretion, cigarettes constitute a significant share of a typical teenage smoker's budget. The price elasticity of demand is thus likely to be far from negligible. For at least some teenage smokers, a higher tax would make smoking unafford-able. And even among those who could afford the higher prices, at least some others would choose to spend their money on other things rather than pay the higher prices.

Given that the tax would affect at least *some* teenage smokers, the consultants' argument begins to unravel. If the tax deters even a small number of smokers directly through its effect on the price of cigarettes, it will also deter others indirectly, by reducing the number of peer role models who smoke. And those who refrain because of these indirect effects will in turn no longer influence others to smoke, and so on. So even if the direct effect of higher cigarette taxes on teen smoking is small, the cumulative effects may be extremely large. The mere fact that peer pressure may be the primary determinant of teen smoking therefore does not imply that higher cigarette taxes will have no significant impact on the number of teens who smoke.

Do high cigarette prices discourage teen smoking?

The Economic Naturalist 4.7

Why was the luxury tax on yachts such a disaster?

In 1990, Congress imposed a luxury tax on yachts costing more than $100,000, along with similar taxes on a handful of other luxury goods. Before these taxes were imposed, the Joint Committee on Taxation estimated that they would yield more than $31 million in revenue in 1991. However, the tax actually generated only

Why did the luxury tax on yachts backfire?

a bit more than half that amount, $16.6 million.[1] Several years later, the Joint Economic Committee estimated that the tax on yachts had led to a loss of 7,600 jobs in the U.S. boating industry. Taking account of lost income taxes and increased unemployment benefits, the U.S. government actually came out $7.6 million behind in fiscal 1991 as a result of its luxury taxes—almost $39 million worse than the initial projection. What went wrong?

The 1990 law imposed no luxury taxes on yachts built and purchased outside the United States. What Congress failed to consider was that foreign-built yachts are almost perfect substitutes for yachts built and purchased in the United States. And, no surprise, when prices on domestic yachts went up because of the tax, yacht buyers switched in droves to foreign models. A tax imposed on a good with a high price elasticity of demand stimulates large rearrangements of consumption but yields little revenue. Had Congress done the economic analysis properly, it would have predicted that this particular tax would be a big loser. Facing angry protests from unemployed New England shipbuilders, Congress repealed the luxury tax on yachts in 1993.

A GRAPHICAL INTERPRETATION OF PRICE ELASTICITY

For small changes in price, price elasticity of demand is the proportion by which quantity demanded changes divided by the corresponding proportion by which price changes. This formulation enables us to construct a simple expression for the price elasticity of demand for a good using only minimal information about its demand curve.

Look at Figure 4.5. P represents the current price of a good and Q the quantity demanded at that price. ΔP represents a small change in the current price and the resulting change in quantity demanded is given by ΔQ. The expression $\Delta P/P$ will then stand for the proportion by which price changes and $\Delta Q/Q$ will stand for the corresponding proportion by which quantity changes. These two expressions, along with our definition of the price elasticity of demand (Equation 4.1), give us the formula for price elasticity:

$$\text{Price elasticity} = \epsilon = \frac{\Delta Q/Q}{\Delta P/P}. \tag{4.2}$$

Suppose, for example, that 20 units were sold at the original price of 100 and that, when price rose to 105, quantity demanded fell to 15 units. Neglecting the negative sign

FIGURE 4.5

A Graphical Interpretation of Price Elasticity of Demand.

Price elasticity of demand at any point along a straight-line demand curve is the ratio of price to quantity at that point times the reciprocal of the slope of the demand curve.

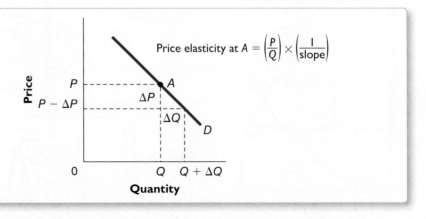

$$\text{Price elasticity at } A = \left(\frac{P}{Q}\right) \times \left(\frac{1}{\text{slope}}\right)$$

[1]For an alternative view, see Dennis Zimmerman, "The Effect of the Luxury Excise Tax on the Sale of Luxury Boats," Congressional Research Service, February 10, 1992.

of the quantity change, we would then have $\Delta Q/Q = 5/20$ and $\Delta P/P = 5/100$, which yields $\epsilon = (5/20)/(5/100) = 5$.

One attractive feature of this formula is that it has a straightforward graphical interpretation. Thus, if we want to calculate the price elasticity of demand at point A on the demand curve shown in Figure 4.5, we can begin by rewriting the right-hand side of Equation 4.2 as $(P/Q) \times (\Delta Q/\Delta P)$. And since the slope of the demand curve is equal to $\Delta P/\Delta Q$, $\Delta Q/\Delta P$ is the reciprocal of that slope: $\Delta Q/\Delta P = 1/\text{slope}$. The price elasticity of demand at point A, denoted ϵ_A, therefore has the following simple formula:

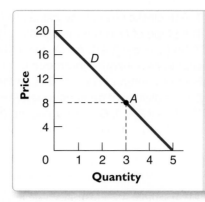

FIGURE 4.6

Calculating Price Elasticity of Demand.

The price elasticity of demand at A is given by $(P/Q) + (1/\text{slope}) = (8/3) \times (1/4) = 2/3$.

$$\epsilon_A = \frac{P}{Q} \times \frac{1}{\text{slope}}. \tag{4.3}$$

To demonstrate how convenient this graphical interpretation of elasticity can be, suppose we want to find the price elasticity of demand at point A on the demand curve in Figure 4.6. The slope of this demand curve is the ratio of its vertical intercept to its horizontal intercept: $20/5 = 4$. So $1/\text{slope} = 1/4$. (Actually, the slope is -4, but we again ignore the minus sign for convenience, since price elasticity of demand always has the same sign.) The ratio P/Q at point A is $8/3$, so the price elasticity at point A is equal to $(P/Q) \times (1/\text{slope}) = (8/3) \times (1/4) = 2/3$. This means that when the price of the good is 8, a 3 percent reduction in price will lead to a 2 percent increase in quantity demanded.

CONCEPT CHECK 4.3

What is the price elasticity of demand when $P = 4$ on the demand curve in Figure 4.6?

EXAMPLE 4.2   **Price Elasticity of Demand**

For the demand curves D_1 and D_2 shown in Figure 4.7, calculate the price elasticity of demand when $P = 4$. What is the price elasticity of demand on D_2 when $P = 1$?

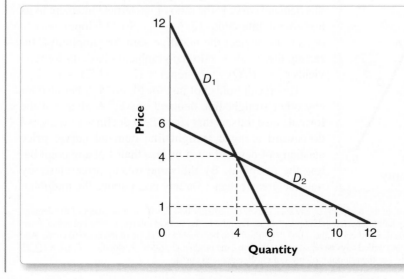

FIGURE 4.7

Price Elasticity and the Steepness of the Demand Curve.

When price and quantity are the same, price elasticity of demand is always greater for the less steep of two demand curves.

These elasticities can be calculated easily using the formula $\epsilon = (P/Q) \times (1/\text{slope})$. The slope of D_1 is the ratio of its vertical intercept to its horizontal intercept: $12/6 = 2$. So $(1/\text{slope})$ is $1/2$ for D_1. Similarly, the slope of D_2 is the ratio of its vertical intercept to its horizontal intercept: $6/12 = 1/2$. So the reciprocal of the slope of D_2 is 2. For both demand curves, $Q = 4$ when $P = 4$, so $(P/Q) = 4/4 = 1$ for each. Thus the price elasticity of demand when $P = 4$ is $(1) \times (1/2) = 1/2$ for D_1 and $(1) \times (2) = 2$ for D_2. When $P = 1$, $Q = 10$ on D_2, so $(P/Q) = 1/10$. Thus price elasticity of demand $= (1/10) \times (2) = 1/5$ when $P = 1$ on D_2.

Example 4.2 illustrates a general rule: If two demand curves have a point in common, the steeper curve must be the less price elastic of the two with respect to price at that point. However, this does not mean that the steeper curve is less elastic at *every* point. Thus, we saw that at $P = 1$, price elasticity of demand on D_2 was only $1/5$, or less than half the corresponding elasticity on the steeper D_1 at $P = 4$.

Price Elasticity Changes along a Straight-Line Demand Curve

As a glance at our elasticity formula makes clear, price elasticity has a different value at every point along a straight-line demand curve. The slope of a straight-line demand curve is constant, which means that $1/\text{slope}$ is also constant. But the price–quantity ratio P/Q declines as we move down the demand curve. The elasticity of demand thus declines steadily as we move downward along a straight-line demand curve.

Since price elasticity is the percentage change in quantity demanded divided by the corresponding percentage change in price, this pattern makes sense. After all, a price movement of a given absolute size is small in percentage terms when it occurs near the top of the demand curve, where price is high, but large in percentage terms when it occurs near the bottom of the demand curve, where price is low. Likewise, a quantity movement of a given absolute value is large in percentage terms when it occurs near the top of the demand curve, where quantity is low, and small in percentage terms when it occurs near the bottom of the curve, where quantity is high.

The graphical interpretation of elasticity also makes it easy to see why the price elasticity of demand at the midpoint of any straight-line demand curve must always be 1. Consider, for example, the price elasticity of demand at point A on the demand curve D shown in Figure 4.8. At that point, the ratio P/Q is equal to $6/3 = 2$. The slope of this demand curve is the ratio of its vertical intercept to its horizontal intercept, $12/6 = 2$. So $(1/\text{slope}) = 1/2$ (again, we neglect the negative sign for simplicity). Inserting these values into the graphical elasticity formula yields $\epsilon_A = (P/Q) \times (1/\text{slope}) = (2) \times (1/2) = 1$.

This result holds not just for Figure 4.8, but also for any other straight-line demand curve.[2] A glance at the formula also tells us that since P/Q declines as we move downward along a straight-line demand curve, price elasticity of demand must be less than 1 at any point below the midpoint. By the same token, price elasticity must be greater than 1 for any point above the midpoint.

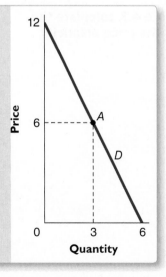

FIGURE 4.8

Elasticity at the Midpoint of a Straight-Line Demand Curve.

The price elasticity of demand at the midpoint of any straight-line demand curve always takes the value 1.

[2]To see why, note that, at the midpoint of any such curve, P is exactly half the vertical intercept of the demand curve and Q is exactly half the horizontal intercept. Since the ratio of the vertical intercept to the horizontal intercept is the slope of the demand curve, the ratio (P/Q) must also be equal to the slope of the demand curve. And this means that $(1/\text{slope})$ will always be equal to (Q/P). Thus, the product $(P/Q) \times (1/\text{slope}) = (P/Q) \times (Q/P)$ will always be exactly 1 at the midpoint of any straight-line demand curve.

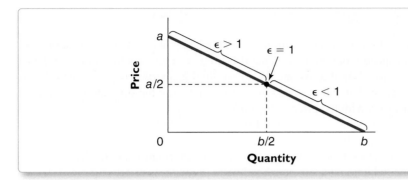

Price Elasticity Regions along a Straight-Line Demand Curve.

Demand is elastic on the top half, unit elastic at the midpoint, and inelastic on the bottom half of a straight-line demand curve.

Figure 4.9 summarizes these findings by denoting the elastic, inelastic, and unit elastic portions of any straight-line demand curve.

Two Special Cases

There are two important exceptions to the general rule that elasticity declines along straight-line demand curves. First, the horizontal demand curve in Figure 4.10(a) has a slope of zero, which means that the reciprocal of its slope is infinite. Price elasticity of demand is thus infinite at every point along a horizontal demand curve. Such demand curves are said to be **perfectly elastic**.

Second, the demand curve in Figure 4.10(b) is vertical, which means that its slope is infinite. The reciprocal of its slope is thus equal to zero. Price elasticity of demand is thus exactly zero at every point along the curve. For this reason, vertical demand curves are said to be **perfectly inelastic**.

perfectly elastic demand
the demand for a good is perfectly elastic with respect to price if its price elasticity of demand is infinite

perfectly inelastic demand
the demand for a good is perfectly inelastic with respect to price if its price elasticity of demand is zero

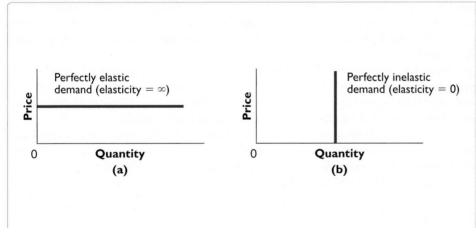

FIGURE 4.10

Perfectly Elastic and Perfectly Inelastic Demand Curves.

The horizontal demand curve (a) is perfectly elastic, or infinitely elastic, at every point. Even the slightest increase in price leads consumers to desert the product in favor of substitutes. The vertical demand curve (b) is perfectly inelastic at every point. Consumers do not, or cannot, switch to substitutes even in the face of large increases in price.

RECAP ↑

CALCULATING PRICE ELASTICITY OF DEMAND

The price elasticity of demand for a good is the percentage change in the quantity demanded that results from a 1 percent change in its price. Mathematically, the elasticity of demand at a point along a demand curve is equal to $(P/Q) \times (1/\text{slope})$, where P and Q represent price and quantity and $(1/\text{slope})$ is the reciprocal of the slope of the demand curve at that point. Demand is elastic with respect to price if the absolute value of its price elasticity exceeds 1; inelastic if price elasticity is less than 1; and unit elastic if price elasticity is equal to 1.

ELASTICITY AND TOTAL EXPENDITURE

Sellers of goods and services have a strong interest in being able to answer questions like "Will consumers spend more on my product if I sell more units at a lower price or fewer units at a higher price?" As it turns out, the answer to this question depends critically on the price elasticity of demand. To see why, let us first examine how the total amount spent on a good varies with the price of the good.

The total daily expenditure on a good is simply the daily number of units bought times the price for which it sells. The market demand curve for a good tells us the quantity that will be sold at each price. We can thus use the information on the demand curve to show how the total amount spent on a good will vary with its price.

To illustrate, let's calculate how much moviegoers will spend on tickets each day if the demand curve is as shown in Figure 4.11 and the price is $2 per ticket (a). The demand curve tells us that, at a price of $2 per ticket, 500 tickets per day will be sold, so total expenditure at that price will be $1,000 per day. If tickets sell not for $2 but for $4 apiece, 400 tickets will be sold each day (b), so total expenditure at the higher price will be $1,600 per day.

Note that the total amount consumers spend on a product each day must equal the total amount sellers of the product receive. That is to say, the terms **total expenditure** and **total revenue** are simply two sides of the same coin:

total expenditure (total revenue) the dollar amount that consumers spend on a product ($P \times Q$) is equal to the dollar amount that sellers receive

Total Expenditure = Total Revenue: The dollar amount that consumers spend on a product ($P \times Q$) is equal to the dollar amount that sellers receive.

It might seem that an increase in the market price of a product should always result in an increase in the total revenue received by sellers. Although that happened in the case we just saw, it needn't always be so. The law of demand tells us that when the price of a good rises, people will buy less of it. The two factors that govern total revenue—price and quantity—will thus always move in opposite directions as we move along a demand curve. When price goes up and quantity goes down, the product of the two may go either up or down.

Note, for example, that for the demand curve shown in Figure 4.12 (which is the same as the one in Figure 4.11), a rise in price from $8 per ticket (a) to $10 per ticket (b) will cause total expenditure on tickets to go down. Thus people will spend $1,600 per day on tickets at a price of $8, but only $1,000 per day at a price of $10.

The general rule illustrated by Figures 4.11 and 4.12 is that a price increase will produce an increase in total revenue whenever it is greater, in percentage terms, than the corresponding percentage reduction in quantity demanded. Although the two price increases (from $2 to $4 and from $8 to $10) were of the same absolute value—$2 in each

---

FIGURE 4.11

The Demand Curve for Movie Tickets.

An increase in price from $2 to $4 per ticket increases total expenditure on tickets.

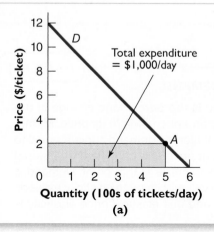

(a)

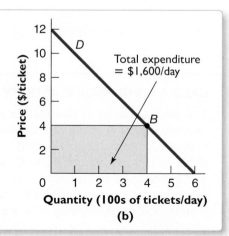

(b)

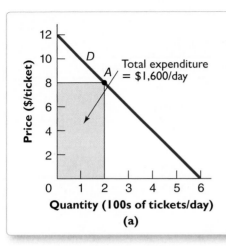 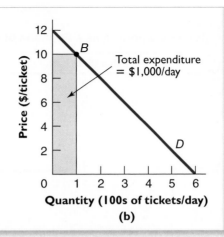

FIGURE 4.12

The Demand Curve for Movie Tickets.

An increase in price from $8 to $10 per ticket results in a fall in total expenditure on tickets.

case—they are much different when expressed as a percentage of the original price. An increase from $2 to $4 represents a 100 percent increase in price, whereas an increase from $8 to $10 represents only a 25 percent increase in price. And although the quantity reductions caused by the two price increases were also equal in absolute terms, they too are very different when expressed as percentages of the quantities originally sold. Thus, although the decline in quantity demanded was 100 tickets per day in each case, it was just a 20 percent reduction in the first case (from 500 units to 400 in Figure 4.11) but a 50 percent reduction in the second (from 200 units to 100 in Figure 4.12). In the second case, the negative effect on total expenditure of the 50 percent quantity reduction outweighed the positive effect of the 25 percent price increase. The reverse happened in the first case: The 100 percent increase in price (from $2 to $4) outweighed the 20 percent reduction in quantity (from 5 units to 4 units).

The following example provides further insight into the relationship between total revenue and price.

EXAMPLE 4.3   Total Revenue and Price

For the demand curve shown in Figure 4.13, draw a separate graph showing how total expenditure varies with the price of movie tickets.

The first step in constructing this graph is to calculate total expenditure for each price shown in the graph and record the results, as in Table 4.2. The next step is to plot total expenditure at each of the price points on a graph, as in Figure 4.14. Finally, sketch the curve by joining these points. (If greater accuracy is required, you can use a larger sample of points than the one shown in Table 4.2.)

Note in Figure 4.14 that as the price per ticket increases from 0 to $6, total expenditure increases. But as the price rises from $6 to $12, total expenditure decreases. Total expenditure reaches a maximum of $1,800 per day at a price of $6.

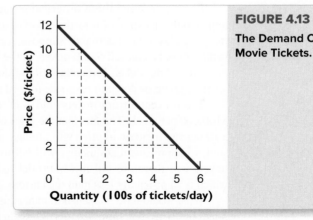

FIGURE 4.13

The Demand Curve for Movie Tickets.

TABLE 4.2
Total Expenditure as a Function of Price

Price ($/ticket)	Total expenditure ($/day)
12	0
10	1,000
8	1,600
6	1,800
4	1,600
2	1,000
0	0

FIGURE 4.14

Total Expenditure as a Function of Price.

For a good whose demand curve is a straight line, total expenditure reaches a maximum at the price corresponding to the midpoint of the demand curve.

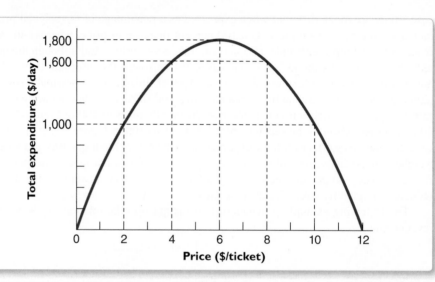

The pattern observed in Example 4.3 holds true in general. For a straight-line demand curve, total expenditure is highest at the price that lies on the midpoint of the demand curve.

Bearing in mind these observations about how expenditure varies with price, let's return to the question of how the effect of a price change on total expenditure depends on the price elasticity of demand. Suppose, for example, that the business manager of a rock band knows he can sell 5,000 tickets to the band's weekly summer concerts if he sets the price at $20 per ticket. If the elasticity of demand for tickets is equal to 3, will total ticket revenue go up or down in response to a 10 percent increase in the price of tickets?

Total revenue from tickets sold is currently ($20/ticket) × (5,000 tickets/week) = $100,000 per week. The fact that the price elasticity of demand for tickets is 3 implies that a 10 percent increase in price will produce a 30 percent reduction in the number of tickets sold, which means that quantity will fall to 3,500 tickets per week. Total expenditure on tickets will therefore fall to (3,500 tickets/week) × ($22/ticket) = $77,000 per week, which is significantly less than the current spending total.

What would have happened to total expenditure if the band manager had *reduced* ticket prices by 10 percent, from $20 to $18? Again assuming a price elasticity of 3, the result would have been a 30 percent increase in tickets sold—from 5,000 per week to 6,500 per week. The resulting total expenditure would have been ($18/ticket) × (6,500 tickets/week) = $117,000 per week, significantly more than the current total.

These examples illustrate the following important rule about how price changes affect total expenditure for an elastically demanded good:

Rule 1. When price elasticity of demand is greater than 1, changes in price and changes in total expenditure always move in opposite directions.

Let's look at the intuition behind this rule. Total expenditure is the product of price and quantity. For an elastically demanded product, the percentage change in quantity will be larger than the corresponding percentage change in price. Thus the change in quantity will more than offset the change in revenue per unit sold.

Now let's see how total spending responds to a price increase when demand is *inelastic* with respect to price. Consider a case like the one just considered except that the elasticity of demand for tickets is not 3 but 0.5. How will total expenditure respond to a 10 percent increase in ticket prices? This time the number of tickets sold will fall by only 5 percent to 4,750 tickets per week, which means that total expenditure on tickets will rise to (4,750 tickets per week) × ($22 per ticket)=$104,500 per week, or $4,500 per week more than the current expenditure level.

In contrast, a 10 percent price reduction (from $20 to $18 per ticket) when price elasticity is 0.5 would cause the number of tickets sold to grow by only 5 percent, from 5,000 per week to 5,250 per week, resulting in total expenditure of ($18 per ticket) × (5,250 tickets per week) = $94,500 per week, significantly less than the current total.

As these examples illustrate, the effect of price changes on total expenditure when demand is inelastic is precisely the opposite of what it was when demand was elastic:

Rule 2. When price elasticity of demand is less than 1, changes in price and changes in total expenditure always move in the same direction.

Again, the intuition behind this rule is straightforward. For a product whose demand is inelastic with respect to price, the percentage change in quantity demanded will be smaller than the corresponding percentage change in price. The change in revenue per unit sold (price) will thus more than offset the change in the number of units sold.

The relationship between elasticity and the effect of a price change on total revenue is summarized in Table 4.3, where the symbol ϵ is used to denote elasticity.

Recall that in the example with which we began our discussion of elasticity, an increase in the price of drugs led to an increase in the total amount spent on drugs. That

TABLE 4.3
Elasticity and the Effect of a Price Change on Total Expenditure

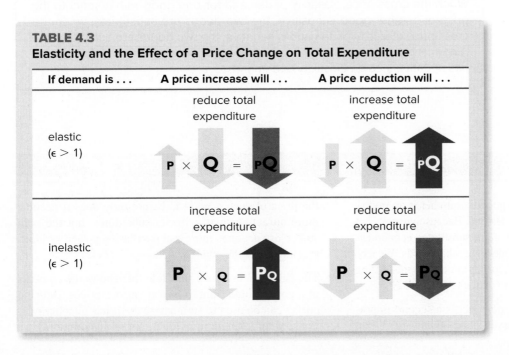

If demand is . . .	A price increase will . . .	A price reduction will . . .
elastic ($\epsilon > 1$)	reduce total expenditure P × Q = PQ	increase total expenditure P × Q = PQ
inelastic ($\epsilon > 1$)	increase total expenditure P × Q = PQ	reduce total expenditure P × Q = PQ

will happen whenever the demand for drugs is inelastic with respect to price, as it was in that example. Had the demand for drugs instead been elastic with respect to price, the drug supply interruption would have led to a reduction in total expenditure on drugs.

INCOME ELASTICITY AND CROSS-PRICE ELASTICITY OF DEMAND

cross-price elasticity of demand the percentage by which the quantity demanded of the first good changes in response to a 1 percent change in the price of the second

income elasticity of demand the percentage by which a good's quantity demanded changes in response to a 1 percent change in income

The elasticity of demand for a good can be defined not only with respect to its own price but also with respect to the prices of substitutes or complements, or even to income. For example, the elasticity of demand for peanuts with respect to the price of cashews—also known as the **cross-price elasticity of demand** for peanuts with respect to cashew prices—is the percentage by which the quantity of peanuts demanded changes in response to a 1 percent change in the price of cashews. The **income elasticity of demand** for peanuts is the percentage by which the quantity demanded of peanuts changes in response to a 1 percent change in income.

Unlike the elasticity of demand for a good with respect to its own price, these other elasticities may be either positive or negative, so it is important to note their algebraic signs carefully. The income elasticity of demand for inferior goods, for example, is negative, whereas the income elasticity of demand for normal goods is positive. When the cross-price elasticity of demand for two goods is positive—as in the peanuts/cashews example—the two goods are substitutes. When it is negative, the two goods are complements. The elasticity of demand for tennis racquets with respect to court rental fees, for example, is less than zero.

CONCEPT CHECK 4.4

If a 10 percent increase in income causes the number of students who choose to attend private universities to go up by 5 percent, what is the income elasticity of demand for private universities?

RECAP ↑

CROSS-PRICE AND INCOME ELASTICITIES

When the cross-price elasticity of demand for one good with respect to the price of another good is positive, the two goods are substitutes; when the cross-price elasticity of demand is negative, the two goods are complements. A normal good has positive income elasticity of demand and an inferior good has negative income elasticity of demand.

SUMMARY

- The ability to substitute one good for another is an important factor behind the law of demand. Because virtually every good or service has at least some substitutes, economists prefer to speak in terms of wants rather than needs. We face choices, and describing our demands as needs is misleading because it suggests we have no options. *(LO1, LO2)*

- For normal goods, the income effect is a second important reason that demand curves slope downward. When

the price of such a good falls, not only does it become more attractive relative to its substitutes, but the consumer also acquires more real purchasing power, and this, too, augments the quantity demanded. *(LO2)*

- The demand curve is a schedule that shows the amounts of a good people want to buy at various prices. Demand curves can be used to summarize the price–quantity relationship for a single individual, but more commonly we employ them to summarize that relationship for an entire market. At any quantity along a demand curve, the corresponding price represents the amount by which the consumer (or consumers) would benefit from having an additional unit of the product. For this reason, the demand curve is sometimes described as a summary of the benefit side of the market. *(LO3)*

- The price elasticity of demand is a measure of how strongly buyers respond to changes in price. It is the percentage change in quantity demanded that occurs in response to a 1 percent change in price. The demand for a good is called elastic with respect to price if the absolute value of its price elasticity is more than 1, inelastic if its price elasticity is less than 1, and unit elastic if its price elasticity is equal to 1 *(LO4)*

- Goods such as salt, which occupy only a small share of the typical consumer's budget and have few or no good substitutes, tend to have low price elasticity of demand. Goods like new cars of a particular make and model, which occupy large budget shares and have many attractive substitutes, tend to have high price elasticity of demand. Price elasticity of demand is higher in the long run than in the short run because people often need time to adjust to price changes. *(LO4)*

- The price elasticity of demand at a point along a demand curve also can be expressed as the formula $\epsilon = (\Delta Q/Q)/(\Delta P/P)$. Here, P and Q represent price and quantity at that point and ΔQ and ΔP represent small changes in price and quantity. For straight-line demand curves, this formula can also be expressed as $\epsilon = (P/Q) \times (1/\text{slope})$. These formulations tell us that price elasticity declines in absolute terms as we move down a straight-line demand curve. *(LO5)*

- A cut in price will increase total spending on a good if demand is elastic but reduce it if demand is inelastic. An increase in price will increase total spending on a good if demand is inelastic but reduce it if demand is elastic. Total expenditure on a good reaches a maximum when price elasticity of demand is equal to 1. *(LO6)*

- Analogous formulas are used to define the elasticity of demand for a good with respect to income and the prices of other goods. In each case, elasticity is the percentage change in quantity demanded divided by the corresponding percentage change in income or price. *(LO7)*

KEY TERMS

cross-price elasticity of demand
elastic
income elasticity of demand
inelastic
law of demand

nominal price
perfectly elastic demand
perfectly inelastic demand
price elasticity of demand
real price

total expenditure
total revenue
unit elastic

REVIEW QUESTIONS

1. Why do economists prefer to speak of demands arising out of "wants" rather than "needs"? *(LO1)*

2. Explain why a good or service that is offered at a monetary price of zero is unlikely to be a truly "free" good from an economic perspective. *(LO2)*

3. Why does a consumer's price elasticity of demand for a good depend on the fraction of the consumer's income spent on that good *(LO4)*

4. Why does the price elasticity of demand for a good decline as we move down along a straight-line demand curve? *(LO5)*

5. Under what conditions will an increase in the price of a product lead to a reduction in total spending for that product? *(LO6)*

6. Why do economists pay little attention to the algebraic sign of the elasticity of demand for a good with respect to its own price, yet pay careful attention to the algebraic sign of the elasticity of demand for a good with respect to another good's price? *(LO7)*

PROBLEMS

connect

1. Which of the following factors would impact a buyer's reservation price for a given good or service: social influence, the price of the good, or the cost of producing the item? *(LO1)*

2. In which type of restaurant do you expect the service to be more prompt and courteous: an expensive gourmet restaurant or an inexpensive diner? Explain. *(LO2)*

3* The buyers' side of the market for amusement park tickets consists of two consumers whose demands are as shown in the diagram below. Graph the market demand curve for this market. *(LO3)*

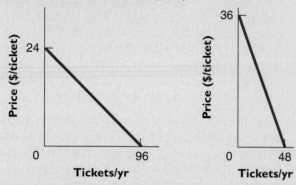

4. Ann lives in Princeton, New Jersey, and commutes by train each day to her job in New York City (20 round trips per month). When the price of a round trip goes up from $10 to $20, she responds by consuming exactly the same number of trips as before, while spending $200 per month less on restaurant meals. *(LO2, LO3)*
   a. Does the fact that her quantity of train travel is completely unresponsive to the price increase imply that Ann is not a rational consumer?
   b. Explain why an increase in train travel might affect the amount she spends on restaurant meals.

5. Is the demand for a particular brand of car, like a Chevrolet, likely to be more or less price elastic than the demand for all cars? Explain. *(LO4)*

6. Calculate the price elasticity of demand (in absolute value) at points *A*, *B*, *C*, *D*, and *E* on the demand curve below. *(LO5)*

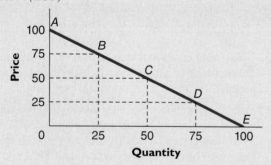

7. The schedule below shows the number of packs of bagels bought in Davis, California, each day at a variety of prices. *(LO5, LO6)*

Price of bagels ($/pack)	Number of packs purchased per day
6	0
5	3,000
4	6,000
3	9,000
2	12,000
1	15,000
0	18,000

a. Graph the daily demand curve for packs of bagels in Davis.
b. Calculate the price elasticity of demand at the point on the demand curve at which the price of bagels is $3 per pack.
c. If all bagel shops increased the price of bagels from $3 per pack to $4 per pack, what would happen to total revenues?
d. Calculate the price elasticity of demand at a point on the demand curve where the price of bagels is $2 per pack.
e. If bagel shops increased the price of bagels from $2 per pack to $3 per pack, what would happen to total revenues?

8. Suppose, while rummaging through your uncle's closet, you found the original painting of *Dogs Playing Poker,* a valuable piece of art. You decide to set up a display in your uncle's garage. The demand curve to see this valuable piece of art is as shown in the diagram. What price should you charge if your goal is to maximize your revenues from tickets sold? On a graph, show the inelastic and elastic regions of the demand curve. *(LO5, LO6)*

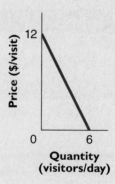

9* Suppose that, in an attempt to induce citizens to conserve energy, the government enacted regulations requiring that all air conditioners be more efficient in their use of electricity. After this regulation was implemented, government officials were then surprised to discover that people used even more electricity than before. Using the concept of price elasticity, explain how this increase might have occurred. *(LO4, LO7)*

10. A 2 percent increase in the price of milk causes a 4 percent reduction in the quantity demanded of chocolate syrup. What is the cross-price elasticity of demand for chocolate syrup with respect to the price of milk? Are the two goods complements or substitutes? *(LO7)*

*Indicates more difficult problems.

ANSWERS TO CONCEPT CHECKS

4.1 Adding the two individual demand curves, (a) and (b), horizontally yields the market demand curve (c): *(LO3)*

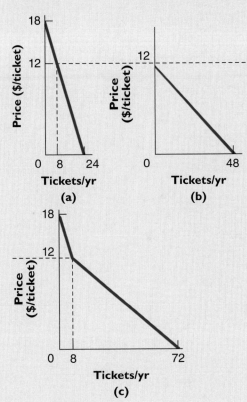

4.2 In response to a 5 percent reduction in the price of ski passes, the quantity demanded increased by 20 percent. The price elasticity of demand for ski passes is thus (20 percent)/(5 percent) = 4, and that means that at the initial price of $400, the demand for ski passes is elastic with respect to price. *(LO4)*

4.3 At point A in the accompanying diagram, $P/Q = 4/4 = 1$. The slope of this demand curve is $20/5 = 4$, so $\epsilon = 1 \times (1/\text{slope}) = 1/4$. *(LO5)*

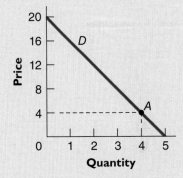

4.4 Income elasticity = percentage change in quantity demanded/percentage change in income = 5 percent/10 percent = 0.5. *(LO7)*

Perfectly Competitive Supply

5

LEARNING OBJECTIVES

After reading this chapter, you should be able to:

LO1 Explain how opportunity cost is related to the supply curve.

LO2 Discuss the relationship between the supply curve for an individual firm and the market supply curve for an industry.

LO3 Determine why price equals marginal cost at the profit-maximizing output level.

LO4 Connect the determinants of supply with the factors that affect individual firms' costs.

LO5 Define and calculate price elasticity of supply.

Cars that took more than 50 hours to assemble in the 1970s are now built in less than 8 hours. Similar productivity growth has occurred in many other manufacturing industries. Yet in many service industries, productivity has grown only slowly, if at all. For example, the London Philharmonic Orchestra performs Beethoven's Fifth Symphony with no fewer musicians today than in 1850. And it still takes a barber about half an hour to cut someone's hair, just as it always has.

Given the spectacular growth in manufacturing workers' productivity, it is no surprise that their real wages have risen more than fivefold during the last century. But why have real wages for service workers risen just as much? If barbers and musicians are no more productive than they were at the turn of the twentieth century, why are they now paid five times as much?

An answer is suggested by the observation that the opportunity cost of pursuing any given occupation is the most one could have earned in some other occupation. Most people who become barbers or musicians could instead have chosen jobs in manufacturing. If workers in service industries were not paid roughly as much as they could have earned in other occupations, many of them would not have been willing to work in service industries in the first place.

The trajectories of wages in manufacturing and service industries illustrate the intimate link between the prices at which goods and services are offered for sale in the market and the opportunity cost of the resources required to produce them.

In the chapter *Demand and Elasticity,* we saw that the demand curve is a schedule that tells how many units buyers wish to purchase at different prices. Our task here is to gain insight into the factors that shape the supply curve, the schedule that tells how many units suppliers wish to sell at different prices.

Although the demand side and the supply side of the market are different in several ways, many of these differences are superficial. Indeed, the behavior of both buyers and sellers is, in an important sense, fundamentally the same. After all, the two groups confront essentially similar questions—in the buyer's case, "Should I buy another unit?" and in the seller's, "Should I sell another unit?" Buyers and sellers use the same criterion for answering these questions. Thus, a rational consumer will buy another unit if its benefit

Why are barbers paid five times as much now as in 1900, even though they can't cut hair any faster than they could then?

exceeds its cost, and a rational seller will sell another unit if the cost of making it is less than the extra revenue he can get from selling it (the familiar Cost-Benefit Principle again).

THINKING ABOUT SUPPLY: THE IMPORTANCE OF OPPORTUNITY COST

Do you live in a state that requires refundable soft drink container deposits? If so, you've probably noticed that some people always redeem their own containers while other people pass up this opportunity, leaving their used containers to be recycled by others. Recycling used containers is a service, and its production obeys the same logic that applies to the production of other goods and services. The following sequence of recycling examples shows how the supply curve for a good or service is rooted in the individual's choice of whether to produce it.

EXAMPLE 5.1   **Cost-Benefit**

How much time should Harry spend recycling soft drink containers?

Harry is trying to decide how to divide his time between his job as a dishwasher in the dining hall, which pays $6 an hour for as many hours as he chooses to work, and gathering soft drink containers to redeem for deposit, in which case his pay depends on both the deposit per container and the number of containers he finds. Earnings aside, Harry is indifferent between the two tasks, and the number of containers he will find depends, as shown in the table below, on the number of hours per day he searches:

Search time (hours/day)	Total number of containers found	Additional number of containers found
0	0	
		600
1	600	
		400
2	1,000	
		300
3	1,300	
		200
4	1,500	
		100
5	1,600	

If the containers may be redeemed for 2 cents each, how many hours should Harry spend searching for containers?

For each additional hour Harry spends searching for soft drink containers, he loses the $6 he could have earned as a dishwasher. This is his hourly opportunity cost of searching for soft drink containers. His benefit from each hour spent searching for containers is the number of additional containers he finds (shown in column 3 of the table) times the deposit he collects per container. Since he can redeem each container for 2 cents, his first hour spent collecting containers will yield earnings of 600($0.02) = $12, or $6 more than he could have earned as a dishwasher.

By the Cost-Benefit Principle, then, Harry should spend his first hour of work each day searching for soft drink containers rather than washing dishes. A second hour searching for containers will yield 400 additional containers, for additional earnings of $8, so it too satisfies the cost-benefit test. A third hour spent searching yields 300 additional containers, for 300($0.02) = $6 of additional earnings. Since this is exactly what Harry could have earned washing dishes, he is indifferent between spending his third hour of work each day on one task or the other. For the sake of discussion, however, we'll assume that he resolves ties in favor of searching for containers, in which case he will spend three hours each day searching for containers.

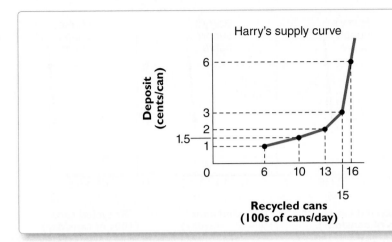

FIGURE 5.1

An Individual Supply Curve for Recycling Services.

When the deposit price increases, it becomes attractive to abandon alternative pursuits to spend more time searching for soft drink containers.

Using the data provided in Example 5.1, what is the lowest redemption price that would tempt Harry to spend at least one hour per day recycling? Since he will find 600 containers in his first hour of search, a 1-cent deposit on each container would enable him to match his $6 per hour opportunity cost. More generally, if the redemption price is p, and the next hour spent searching yields ΔQ additional containers, then Harry's additional earnings from searching the additional hour will be $p(\Delta Q)$. This means that the smallest redemption price that will lead Harry to search another hour must satisfy the equation

$$p(\Delta Q) = \$6. \qquad (5.1)$$

How high would the redemption price of containers have to be to induce Harry to search for a second hour? Since he can find $\Delta Q = 400$ additional containers if he searches for a second hour, the smallest redemption price that will lead him to do so must satisfy $p(400) = \$6$, which solves for $p = 1.5$ cents.

CONCEPT CHECK 5.1

In the example above, calculate the lowest container redemption prices that will lead Harry to search a third, fourth, and fifth hour.

By searching for soft drink containers, Harry becomes, in effect, a supplier of container-recycling services. In Concept Check 5.1, we saw that Harry's reservation prices for his third, fourth, and fifth hours of container search are 2, 3, and 6 cents, respectively. Having calculated these reservation prices, we can now plot his supply curve of container-recycling services. This curve, which plots the redemption price per container on the vertical axis and the number of containers recycled each day on the horizontal axis, is shown in Figure 5.1. Harry's individual supply curve of container-recycling services tells us the number of containers he is willing to recycle at various redemption prices.

The supply curve shown in Figure 5.1 is upward-sloping, just like those we saw in the chapter on supply and demand. There are exceptions to this general rule, but sellers of most goods will offer higher quantities at higher prices.

INDIVIDUAL AND MARKET SUPPLY CURVES

The relationship between the individual and market supply curves for a product is analogous to the relationship between the individual and market demand curves. The quantity that corresponds to a given price on the market demand curve is the sum of the quantities demanded at that price by all individual buyers in the market. Likewise, the quantity that corresponds to any given price on the market supply curve is the sum of the quantities supplied at that price by all individual sellers in the market.

FIGURE 5.2

The Market Supply Curve for Recycling Services.

To generate the market supply curve (c) from the individual supply curves (a) and (b), we add the individual supply curves horizontally.

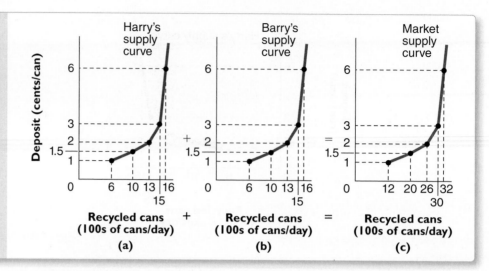

Suppose, for example, that the supply side of the recycling-services market consists only of Harry and his identical twin, Barry, whose individual supply curve is the same as Harry's. To generate the market supply curve, we first put the individual supply curves side by side, as shown in Figure 5.2(a) and (b). We then announce a price, and for that price add the individual quantities supplied to obtain the total quantity supplied in the market. Thus, at a price of 3 cents per container, both Harry and Barry wish to recycle 1,500 cans per day, so the total market supply at that price is 3,000 cans per day. Proceeding in like manner for a sequence of prices, we generate the market supply curve for recycling services shown in Figure 5.2(c). This is the same process of horizontal summation by which we generated market demand curves from individual demand curves in the chapter *Demand and Elasticity*.

Alternatively, if there were many suppliers with individual supply curves identical to Harry's, we could generate the market supply curve by simply multiplying each quantity value on the individual supply curve by the number of suppliers. For instance, Figure 5.3 shows the supply curve for a market in which there are 1,000 suppliers with individual supply curves like Harry's.

Why do individual supply curves tend to be upward-sloping? One explanation is that recyclers will tend to be more productive if they always look first for the containers that are easiest to find—such as those in plain view in readily accessible locations. As the redemption price rises, it will pay to incur the additional cost of searching farther from the beaten path.

If all individuals have identical upward-sloping supply curves, the market supply curve will be upward-sloping as well. But there is an important additional reason for the

FIGURE 5.3

The Market Supply Curve with 1,000 Identical Sellers.

To generate the market supply curve for a market with 1,000 identical sellers, we simply multiply each quantity value on the individual supply curve by 1,000.

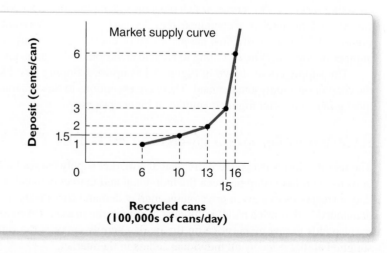

positive slope of market supply curves: Individual suppliers generally differ with respect to their opportunity costs of supplying the product. Thus, whereas people facing unattractive employment opportunities in other occupations may be willing to recycle soft drink containers even when the redemption price is low, those with more attractive options will recycle only if the redemption price is relatively high.

In summary, then, the upward slope of the supply curve reflects the fact that costs tend to rise at the margin when producers expand production, partly because each individual exploits her most attractive opportunities first, but also because different potential sellers face different opportunity costs.

PROFIT-MAXIMIZING FIRMS IN PERFECTLY COMPETITIVE MARKETS

To explore the nature of the supply curve of a product more fully, we must say more about the goals of the organizations that supply the product and the kind of economic environment in which they operate. In virtually every economy, goods and services are produced by a variety of organizations that pursue a host of different motives. The Red Cross supplies blood because its organizers and donors want to help people in need; the local government fixes potholes because the mayor was elected on a promise to do so; karaoke singers perform because they like public attention; and car-wash employees are driven primarily by the hope of making enough money to pay their rent.

Profit Maximization

Notwithstanding this rich variety of motives, *most* goods and services that are offered for sale in a market economy are sold by private firms whose main reason for existing is to earn **profit** for their owners. A firm's profit is the difference between the total revenue it receives from the sale of its product and all costs it incurs in producing it.

A **profit-maximizing firm** is one whose primary goal is to maximize the amount of profit it earns. The supply curves that economists use in standard supply and demand theory are based on the assumption that goods are sold by profit-maximizing firms in **perfectly competitive markets**, which are markets in which individual firms have no influence over the market prices of the products they sell. Because of their inability to influence market price, perfectly competitive firms are often described as **price takers**.

The following four conditions are characteristic of markets that are perfectly competitive:

1. *All firms sell the same standardized product.* Although this condition is almost never literally satisfied, it holds as a rough approximation for many markets. Thus, the markets for concrete building blocks of a given size, or for apples of a given variety, may be described in this way. This condition implies that buyers are willing to switch from one seller to another if by so doing they can obtain a lower price.

2. *The market has many buyers and sellers, each of which buys or sells only a small fraction of the total quantity exchanged.* This condition implies that individual buyers and sellers will be price takers, regarding the market price of the product as a fixed number beyond their control. For example, a single farmer's decision to plant fewer acres of wheat would have no appreciable impact on the market price of wheat, just as an individual consumer's decision to become a vegetarian would have no perceptible effect on the price of beef.

3. *Productive resources are mobile.* This condition implies that if a potential seller identifies a profitable business opportunity in a market, he or she will be able to obtain the labor, capital, and other productive resources necessary to enter that market. By the same token, sellers who are dissatisfied with the opportunities they confront in a given market are free to leave that market and employ their resources elsewhere.

profit the total revenue a firm receives from the sale of its product minus all costs—explicit and implicit—incurred in producing it

profit-maximizing firm a firm whose primary goal is to maximize the difference between its total revenues and total costs

perfectly competitive market a market in which no individual supplier has significant influence on the market price of the product

price taker a firm that has no influence over the price at which it sells its product

4. *Buyers and sellers are well informed.* This condition implies that buyers and sellers are aware of the relevant opportunities available to them. If that were not so, buyers would be unable to seek out sellers who charge the lowest prices, and sellers would have no means of deploying their resources in the markets in which they would earn the most profit.

The market for wheat closely approximates a perfectly competitive market. The market for operating systems for desktop computers, however, does not. More than 90 percent of desktop operating systems are sold by Microsoft, giving the company enough influence in that market to have significant control over the price it charges. For example, if it were to raise the price of its latest edition of Windows by, say, 20 percent, some consumers might switch to Macintosh or Linux, and others might postpone their next upgrade; but many—perhaps even most—would continue with their plans to buy Windows. That pattern, however, appears to be changing with the growing importance of mobile computing.

By contrast, if an individual wheat farmer were to charge even a few cents more than the current market price for a bushel of wheat, he wouldn't be able to sell any of his wheat at all. And since he can sell as much wheat as he wishes at the market price, he has no motive to charge less.

The Demand Curve Facing a Perfectly Competitive Firm

From the perspective of an individual firm in a perfectly competitive market, what does the demand curve for its product look like? Since it can sell as much or as little as it wishes at the prevailing market price, the demand curve for its product is perfectly elastic at the market price. Figure 5.4(a) shows the market demand and supply curves intersecting to determine a market price of P_0. Figure 5.4(b) shows the product demand curve, D_i, as seen by any individual firm in this market, a horizontal line at the market price level P_0.

Many of the conclusions of the standard supply and demand model also hold for **imperfectly competitive firms**—those firms, like Microsoft, that have at least some ability to vary their own prices. But certain other conclusions do not, as we shall see when we examine the behavior of such firms more closely in later chapters.

Since a perfectly competitive firm has no control over the market price of its product, it needn't worry about choosing the level at which to set that price. As we've seen, the equilibrium market price in a competitive market comes from the intersection of the industry supply and demand curves. The challenge confronting the perfectly competitive firm is to choose its output level so that it makes as much profit as it can at that price. As we investigate how the competitive firm responds to this challenge, we'll see that some costs are more important than others.

imperfectly competitive firm a firm that has at least some control over the market price of its product

Production in the Short Run

To gain a deeper understanding of the origins of the supply curve, it is helpful to consider a perfectly competitive firm confronting the decision of how much to produce.

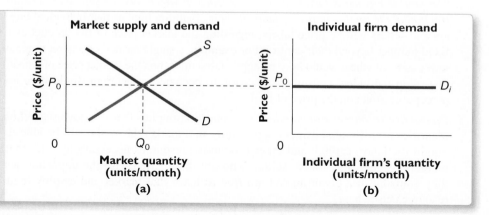

FIGURE 5.4

The Demand Curve Facing a Perfectly Competitive Firm.

The market demand and supply curves intersect to determine the market price of the product (a). The individual firm's demand curve, D_i (b), is a horizontal line at the market price.

TABLE 5.1
Employment and Output for a Glass Bottle Maker

Number of bottles per day	Number of employee-hours per day
0	0
100	1
200	2
300	4
400	7
500	11
600	16
700	22

The firm in question is a small company that makes glass bottles. To keep things simple, suppose that the silica required for making bottles is available free of charge from a nearby desert, and that the only costs incurred by the firm are the wages it pays its employees and the lease payment on its bottle-making machine. The employees and the machine are the firm's only two **factors of production**—inputs used to produce goods and services. In more complex examples, factors of production also might include land, structures, entrepreneurship, and possibly others, but for the moment we consider only labor and capital.

When we refer to the **short run**, we mean a period of time during which at least some of the firm's factors of production cannot be varied. (For our bottle maker, the short run is that period of time during which the firm cannot alter the capacity of its bottle-making machines.) By contrast, when we speak of the **long run**, we refer to a time period of sufficient length that all the firm's factors of production are variable.

Table 5.1 shows how the company's bottle production depends on the number of hours its employees spend on the job each day.

The output-employment relationship described in Table 5.1 exhibits a pattern that is common to many such relationships. Each time we move down one row in the table, output grows by 100 bottles per day, but note in the right column that it takes larger and larger increases in the amount of labor to achieve this increase. Economists refer to this pattern as the **law of diminishing returns**, and it always refers to situations in which at least some factors of production are held fixed, which can be stated as follows:

Law of Diminishing Returns: When some factors of production are held fixed, increased production of the good eventually requires ever larger increases in the variable factor.

In the current example, the **fixed factor** is the bottle-making machine, and the **variable factor** is labor. In the context of this example, the law of diminishing returns says simply that successive increases in bottle output require ever larger increases in labor input. The reason for this pattern often entails some form of congestion. For instance, in an office with three secretaries and only a single computer, we would not expect to get three times as many letters typed per hour as in an office with only one secretary, because only one person can use a computer at a time.

Choosing Output to Maximize Profit

Suppose the lease payment for the company's bottle-making machine and the building that houses it is $40 per day and must be paid whether the company makes any bottles or

factor of production an input used in the production of a good or service

short run a period of time sufficiently short that at least some of the firm's factors of production are fixed

long run a period of time of sufficient length that all the firm's factors of production are variable

law of diminishing returns a property of the relationship between the amount of a good or service produced and the amount of a variable factor required to produce it. The law says that when some factors of production are fixed, increased production of the good eventually requires ever larger increases in the variable factor

fixed factor of production an input whose quantity cannot be altered in the short run

variable factor of production an input whose quantity can be altered in the short run

fixed cost the sum of all payments made to the firm's fixed factors of production

not. This payment is both a **fixed cost** (since it does not depend on the number of bottles per day the firm makes) and, for the duration of the lease, a sunk cost. For short, we'll refer to this cost as the company's *capital cost*. In the following examples, we'll explore how the company's decision about how many bottles to make depends on the price of bottles, the wage, and the cost of capital.

EXAMPLE 5.2   Maximizing Profit

If bottles sell for $35 per hundred, and if the employee's wage is $10 per hour, how many bottles should the company described above produce each day?

The company's goal is to maximize its profit, which is the difference between the revenue it collects from the sale of bottles and the cost of its labor and capital. Table 5.2 shows how the daily number of bottles produced (denoted Q) is related to the company's revenue, employment, costs, and profit.

TABLE 5.2
Output, Revenue, Costs, and Profit

Q (bottles/day)	Total revenue ($/day)	Total labor cost ($/day)	Total cost ($/day)	Profit ($/day)
0	0	0	40	−40
100	35	10	50	−15
200	70	20	60	10
300	105	40	80	25
400	140	70	110	30
500	175	110	150	25
600	210	160	200	10
700	245	220	260	−15

total cost the sum of all payments made to the firm's fixed and variable factors of production

To see how the entries in the table are constructed, let's examine the revenue, wage, cost, and profit values that correspond to 200 units of output (row 3 of Table 5.2). Total revenue is $70, the company's receipts from selling 200 bottles at $35 per hundred. To make 200 bottles, the firm's employee had to work 2 hours (see Table 5.1), and at a wage of $10 per hour that translates into $20 of total labor cost. When the firm's fixed capital cost of $40 per day is added to its total labor cost, we get the **total cost** entry of $60 per day in column 4. The firm's daily profit, finally, is total revenue − total cost = $70 − $60 = $10, the entry in column 5.

From a glance at the final column of Table 5.2, we see that the company's maximum profit, $30 per day, occurs when it produces 400 bottles per day.

EXAMPLE 5.3   Maximizing Profit: A Change in Price

If bottles sell for $45 per hundred, and if the employee's wage is again $10 per hour, how many bottles should the company described above produce each day?

As we see in the entries of Table 5.3, the only consequence of the change in selling price is that total revenue, and hence profit, is now higher than before at every output level. As indicated by the entries of the final column of the table, the company now does best to produce 500 bottles per day, 100 more than when the price was only $35 per hundred.

TABLE 5.3
Output, Revenue, Costs, and Profit

Q (bottles/day)	Total revenue ($/day)	Total labor cost ($/day)	Total cost ($/day)	Profit ($/day)
0	0	0	40	−40
100	45	10	50	−5
200	90	20	60	30
300	135	40	80	55
400	180	70	110	70
500	225	110	150	75
600	270	160	200	70
700	315	220	260	55

EXAMPLE 5.4   Maximizing Profit: A Change in Hourly Wages

If bottles sell for $35 per hundred, and if the employee's wage is now $12 per hour, how many bottles should the company described above produce each day?

With a higher wage rate, labor costs are higher at every level of output, as shown in the third column of Table 5.4, and maximum profit now occurs when the firm produces 300 bottles per day, or 100 fewer than when the wage rate was $10 per hour.

TABLE 5.4
Output, Revenue, Costs, and Profit

Q (bottles/day)	Total revenue ($/day)	Total labor cost ($/day)	Total cost ($/day)	Profit ($/day)
0	0	0	40	−40
100	35	12	52	−17
200	70	24	64	6
300	105	48	88	17
400	140	84	124	16
500	175	132	172	3
600	210	192	232	−22
700	245	264	304	−59

Consider one final variation in the example that follows:

EXAMPLE 5.5   Maximizing Profit: A Change in Capital Cost

If bottles sell for $35 per hundred, and if the employee's wage is $10 per hour, how many bottles should the company produce each day if its capital cost is now $70 instead of $40?

The entries in Table 5.5 are just like those in Table 5.2 except that each entry in the total cost column is $30 higher than before, with the result that each entry in the profit column is $30 lower. Note, however, that the profit-maximizing number of bottles to produce is again 400 per day, precisely the same as when capital cost was only $40 per day. When the company produces 400 bottles daily, its daily profit is 0, but at any other output level its profit would have been negative—that is, it would have been incurring a loss.

TABLE 5.5
Output, Revenue, Costs, and Profit

Q (bottles/day)	Total revenue ($/day)	Total labor cost ($/day)	Total cost ($/day)	Profit ($/day)
0	0	0	70	−70
100	35	10	80	−45
200	70	20	90	−20
300	105	40	110	−5
400	140	70	140	0
500	175	110	180	−5
600	210	160	230	−20
700	245	220	290	−45

Price Equals Marginal Cost: The Seller's Supply Rule

The observation that the profit-maximizing quantity for a firm to supply does not depend on its fixed costs is not an idiosyncrasy of this example. That it holds true in general is an immediate consequence of the Cost-Benefit Principle, which says that a firm should increase its output if, and only if, the *extra* benefit exceeds the *extra* cost. If the firm expands production by 100 bottles per day, its benefit is the extra revenue it gets, which in this case is simply the price of 100 bottles. The cost of expanding production by 100 bottles is by definition the marginal cost of producing 100 bottles—the amount by which total cost increases when bottle production rises by 100 per day. The Cost-Benefit Principle thus tells us that the perfectly competitive firm should keep expanding production as long as the price of the product is greater than marginal cost.

When the law of diminishing returns applies (that is, when some factors of production are fixed), marginal cost goes up as the firm expands production. Under these circumstances, the firm's best option is to supply that level of output for which price and marginal cost are exactly equal.

Note in Example 5.5 that if the company's capital cost had been any more than $70 per day, it would have made a loss at *every* possible level of output. As long as it still had to pay its capital cost, however, its best bet would have been to continue producing

400 bottles per day. It is better, after all, to experience a smaller loss than a larger one. If a firm in that situation expected conditions to remain the same, though, it would want to get out of the bottle business as soon as its equipment lease expired.

A Note on the Firm's Shut-Down Condition

It might seem that a firm that can sell as much output as it wishes at a constant market price would *always* do best in the short run by producing and selling the output level for which price equals marginal cost. But there are exceptions to this rule. Suppose, for example, that the market price of the firm's product falls so low that its revenue from sales is smaller than its **variable cost** when price equals marginal cost. The firm should then cease production for the time being. By shutting down, it will suffer a loss equal to its fixed costs. But by remaining open, it would suffer an even larger loss.

variable cost the sum of all payments made to the firm's variable factors of production

---

CONCEPT CHECK 5.2

In Example 5.5, suppose bottles sold not for $35 per hundred but only $5. Calculate the profit corresponding to each level of output, and verify that the firm's best option is to cease operations in the short run.

Graphing Marginal Cost

To plot the marginal cost curve for a specific company, we would need to know how total cost changes for every possible change in output. In the preceding examples, however, we know the firm's cost for only a small sample of production values. Even with this limited information, though, we can construct a reasonable approximation of the firm's marginal cost curve. Suppose again that the wage is $35 per hour and that capital costs are again $40 per day, so that we again have the production and cost relationships shown in Table 5.2, reproduced below as Table 5.6.

Note that, when the firm expands production from 100 to 200 bottles per day, its increase in cost is $10. When we graph the marginal cost curve, what output level should this $10 marginal cost correspond to? Strictly speaking, it corresponds to neither 100 nor 200, but to the movement between the two. On the graph we thus show the $10 marginal cost value corresponding to an output level midway between 100 and 200 bottles per day—namely, 150 bottles per day, as in Figure 5.5. Similarly, when the firm expands from 200 to 300 bottles per day, its costs go up by $20, so we plot a marginal cost of

TABLE 5.6
Output, Revenue, Costs, and Profit

Q (bottles/day)	Total revenue ($/day)	Total labor cost ($/day)	Total cost ($/day)	Profit ($/day)
0	0	0	40	−40
100	35	10	50	−15
200	70	20	60	10
300	105	40	80	25
400	140	70	110	30
500	175	110	150	25
600	210	160	200	10
700	245	220	260	−15

FIGURE 5.5

The Firm's Marginal Cost of Production.

The firm's cost goes up by $10 when it expands production from 100 bottles per day to 200 bottles per day. The marginal cost of the increased output is thus $10, and by convention we plot that value at a point midway between 100 and 200 bottles per day.

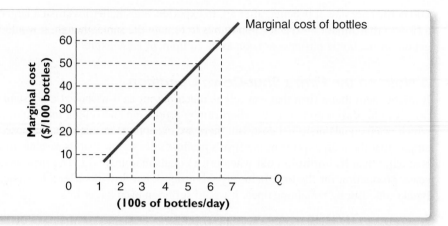

$20 with the output level 250 in Figure 5.5. Proceeding in this fashion, we generate the marginal cost curve shown in the diagram.

Suppose the market price facing the seller whose marginal cost curve is shown in Figure 5.5 is $25 per hundred. If the firm's goal is to make as much profit as possible, how many bottles should it sell? It should sell the quantity for which marginal cost is equal to $25 per hundred, and as we see in Figure 5.6, that quantity is 300 bottles per week.

To gain further confidence that 300 must be the profit-maximizing quantity when the price is $25 per hundred, first suppose that the firm had sold some amount less than that—say, only 200 bottles per day. Its benefit from expanding output by one bottle would then be the bottle's market price, here 25 cents (since bottles sell for $25 per hundred, each individual bottle sells for 25 cents). The cost of expanding output by one bottle is equal (by definition) to the firm's marginal cost, which at 200 bottles per day is only $15/100 = 15 cents (see Figure 5.6). So by selling the 201st bottle for 25 cents and producing it for an extra cost of only 15 cents, the firm will increase its profit by 25 − 15 = 10 cents/day. In a similar way, we can show that for *any* quantity less than the level at which price equals marginal cost, the seller can boost profit by expanding production.

Conversely, suppose that the firm is currently selling more than 300 bottles per day—say, 400—at a price of $25 per hundred. From Figure 5.6 we see that marginal cost at an output of 400 is $35/100 = 35 cents per bottle. If the firm then contracts its output by one bottle per day, it would cut its costs by 35 cents while losing only 25 cents in revenue. As before, its profit would grow by 10 cents per day. The same argument can be made regarding any quantity larger than 300, so if the firm is currently selling an output at which price is less than marginal cost, it can always do better by producing and selling fewer bottles.

We have thus established that if the firm were selling fewer than 300 bottles per day, it could earn more profit by expanding. If it were selling more than 300, it could earn more by

FIGURE 5.6

Price = Marginal Cost: The Perfectly Competitive Firm's Profit-Maximizing Supply Rule.

If price is greater than marginal cost, the firm can increase its profit by expanding production and sales. If price is less than marginal cost, the firm can increase its profit by producing and selling less output.

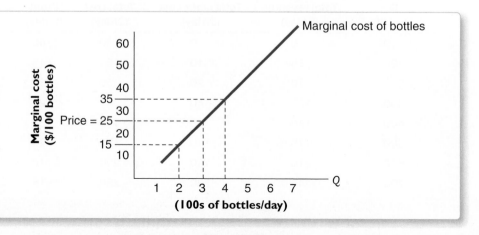

contracting. It follows that at a market price of $25 per hundred, the seller does best by selling 300 units per week, the quantity for which price and marginal cost are exactly the same.

CONCEPT CHECK 5.3

For a bottle price of $25 per hundred, calculate the profit corresponding to each level of output, as in Table 5.6, and verify that the profit-maximizing output is 300 bottles per day.

As further confirmation of the claim that the perfectly competitive firm maximizes profit by setting price equal to marginal cost, note in Figure 5.6 that, when marginal cost is equal to a price of $35 per hundred bottles, the corresponding quantity is 400 bottles per day. This is the same as the profit-maximizing quantity we identified for that price in Table 5.6.

The "Law" of Supply

The law of demand tells us that consumers buy less of a product when its price rises. If there were an analogous law of supply, it would say that producers offer more of a product for sale when its price rises. Is there such a law? We know that supply curves are essentially marginal cost curves and that because of the law of diminishing returns, marginal cost curves are upward-sloping in the short run. And so there is indeed a law of supply that applies as stated in the short run.

In the long run, however, the law of diminishing returns does not apply. (Recall that it holds only if at least some factors of production are fixed.) Because firms can vary the amounts of *all* factors of production they use in the long run, they can often double their production by simply doubling the amount of each input they use. In such cases, costs would be exactly proportional to output and the firm's marginal cost curve in the long run would be horizontal, not upward-sloping. So for now we'll say only that the "law" of supply holds as stated in the short run but not necessarily in the long run. For both the long run and the short run, however, *the perfectly competitive firm's supply curve is its marginal cost curve.*[1]

Every quantity of output along the market supply curve represents the summation of all the quantities individual sellers offer at the corresponding price. So the correspondence between price and marginal cost exists for the market supply curve as well as for the individual supply curves that lie behind it. That is, *for every price–quantity pair along the market supply curve, price will be equal to each seller's marginal cost of production.*

This is why we sometimes say that the supply curve represents the cost side of the market, whereas the demand curve represents the benefit side of the market. At every point along a market demand curve, price represents what buyers would be willing to pay for an additional unit of the product—and this, in turn, is how we measure the amount by which they would benefit by having an additional unit of the product. Likewise, at every point along a market supply curve, price measures what it would cost producers to expand production by one unit.

Applying the Theory of Supply

Whether the activity is producing new soft drink containers or recycling used ones, or indeed any other production activity at all, the same logic governs all supply decisions in perfectly competitive markets (and in any other setting in which sellers can sell as much as they wish to at a constant price): Keep expanding output until marginal cost is equal to the price of the product. This logic helps us understand why recycling efforts are more intensive for some products than others.

---

[1]Again, this rule holds subject to the provision that total revenue exceed variable production cost at the output level for which price equals marginal cost.

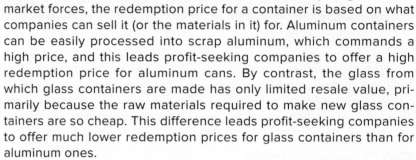

The Economic Naturalist 5.1

When recycling is left to private market forces, why are many more aluminum beverage containers recycled than glass ones?

In both cases, recyclers gather containers until their marginal costs are equal to the containers' respective redemption prices. When recycling is left to market forces, the redemption price for a container is based on what companies can sell it (or the materials in it) for. Aluminum containers can be easily processed into scrap aluminum, which commands a high price, and this leads profit-seeking companies to offer a high redemption price for aluminum cans. By contrast, the glass from which glass containers are made has only limited resale value, primarily because the raw materials required to make new glass containers are so cheap. This difference leads profit-seeking companies to offer much lower redemption prices for glass containers than for aluminum ones.

The high redemption prices for aluminum cans induce many people to track these cans down, whereas the low redemption prices for glass containers lead most people to ignore them. If recycling is left completely to market forces, then, we would expect to see aluminum soft drink containers quickly recycled, whereas glass containers would increasingly litter the landscape. This is in fact the pattern we do see in states without recycling laws. (More on how these laws work in a moment.) This pattern is a simple consequence of the fact that the supply curves of container-recycling services are upward-sloping.

In states that don't have beverage container deposit laws, why are aluminum cans more likely to be recycled than glass bottles?

The acquisition of valuable raw materials is only one of two important benefits from recycling. The second is that, by removing litter, recycling makes the environment more pleasant for everyone. As the next example suggests, this second benefit might easily justify the cost of recycling substantial numbers of glass containers.

EXAMPLE 5.6   Socially Optimal Amount

What is the socially optimal amount of recycling of glass containers?

Suppose that the 60,000 citizens of Burlington, Vermont, would collectively be willing to pay 6 cents for each glass container removed from their local environment. If the local market supply curve of glass container recycling services is as shown in Figure 5.7, what is the socially optimal level of glass container recycling?

Suppose the citizens of Burlington authorize their city government to collect tax money to finance litter removal. If the benefit of each glass container removed, as measured by what residents are collectively willing to pay, is 6 cents, the government should offer to pay 6 cents for each glass container recycled. To maximize the total economic surplus from recycling, we should recycle that number of containers for which the marginal cost of recycling is equal to the 6-cent marginal benefit. Given the market supply curve shown, the optimal quantity is 16,000 containers per day, and that is how many will be redeemed when the government offers 6 cents per container.

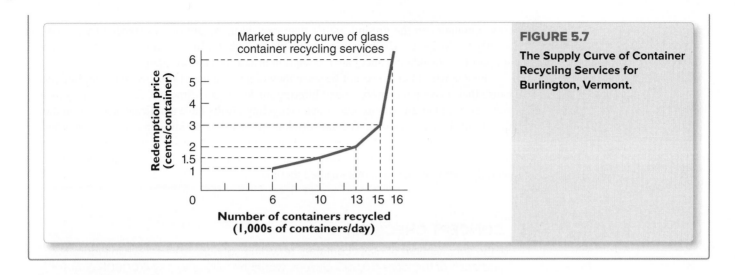

FIGURE 5.7

The Supply Curve of Container Recycling Services for Burlington, Vermont.

Market supply curve of glass container recycling services

Redemption price (cents/container)

Number of containers recycled (1,000s of containers/day)

Although 16,000 containers per day will be removed from the environment in Example 5.6, others will remain. After all, some are discarded in remote locations, and a redemption price of 6 cents per container is simply not high enough to induce people to track them all down.

So why not offer an even higher price and get rid of *all* glass container litter? For Example 5.6, the reason is that the marginal cost of removing the 16,001st glass container each day is greater than the benefit of removing it. Total economic surplus is largest when we remove litter only up to the point that the marginal benefit of litter removal is equal to its marginal cost, which occurs when 16,000 containers per day are recycled. To proceed past that point is actually wasteful.

Many people become upset when they hear economists say that the socially optimal amount of litter is greater than zero. In the minds of these people, the optimal amount of litter is *exactly* zero. But this position completely ignores the Cost-Benefit Principle. Granted, there would be benefits from reducing litter further, but there also would be costs. Spending more on litter removal therefore means spending less on other useful things. No one would insist that the optimal amount of dirt in his own home is zero. (If someone does make this claim, ask him why he doesn't stay home all day vacuuming the dust that is accumulating in his absence.) If it doesn't pay to remove all the dust from your house, it doesn't pay to remove all the bottles from the environment. Precisely the same logic applies in each case.

If 16,000 containers per day is the optimal amount of litter removal, can we expect the individual spending decisions of private citizens to result in that amount of litter removal? Unfortunately we cannot. The problem is that anyone who paid for litter removal individually would bear the full cost of those services while reaping only a tiny fraction of the benefit. In Example 5.6, the 60,000 citizens of Burlington reaped a total benefit of 6 cents per container removed, which means a benefit of only $(6/60,000) = 0.0001$ cent per person! Someone who paid 6 cents for someone else to remove a container would thus be incurring a cost 60,000 times greater than his share of the resulting benefit.

Note that the incentive problem here is similar to the one discussed in the chapter covering supply and demand for the person deciding whether to be vaccinated against an illness. The problem was that the incentive to be vaccinated was too weak because, even though the patient bears the full cost of the vaccination, many of the resulting benefits accrue to others. Thus, an important part of the extra benefit from any one person being vaccinated is that others also become less likely to contract the illness.

The case of glass container litter is an example in which private market forces do not produce the best attainable outcome for society as a whole. Even people who carelessly

© PhotoAlto

Is the socially optimal quantity of litter zero?

toss containers on the ground, rather than recycle them, are often offended by the unsightly landscape to which their own actions contribute. Indeed, this is why they often support laws mandating adequate redemption prices for glass containers.

People who litter do so not because they don't care about the environment, but because their private incentives make littering misleadingly attractive. Recycling requires some effort, after all, yet no individual's recycling efforts have a noticeable effect on the quality of the environment. The soft drink container deposit laws enacted by numerous states were a simple way to bring individual interests more closely into balance with the interests of society as a whole. The vast majority of container litter disappeared almost literally overnight in states that enacted these laws.

CONCEPT CHECK 5.4

If the supply curve of glass container recycling services is as shown in Figure 5.7, and each of the city's 60,000 citizens would be willing to pay 0.00005 cent for each glass container removed from the landscape, at what level should the city government set the redemption price for glass containers, and how many will be recycled each day?

As previously discussed, the supply curve for a good can be interpreted either horizontally or vertically. The horizontal interpretation tells us, for each price, the total quantity that producers wish to sell at that price. The vertical interpretation tells us, for each quantity, the smallest amount a seller would be willing to accept for the good. For the purpose of computing producer surplus, we rely on the vertical interpretation of the supply curve. The value on the vertical axis that corresponds to each point along the supply curve corresponds to the marginal seller's reservation price for the good, which is the marginal cost of producing it. Producer surplus is the cumulative sum of the differences between the market price and these reservation prices. It is the area bounded above by market price and bounded below by the supply curve.

RECAP ↑

PROFIT-MAXIMIZING FIRMS IN PERFECTLY COMPETITIVE MARKETS

The perfectly competitive firm faces a horizontal demand curve for its product, meaning that it can sell any quantity it wishes at the market price. In the short run, the firm's goal is to choose the level of output that maximizes its profits. It will accomplish this by choosing the output level for which its marginal cost is equal to the market price of its product.

DETERMINANTS OF SUPPLY REVISITED

What factors give rise to changes in supply? (Again, remember that a "change in supply" refers to a shift in the entire supply curve, as opposed to a movement along the curve, which we call a "change in the quantity supplied.") A seller will offer more units if the benefit of selling extra output goes up relative to the cost of producing it. And since the benefit of selling output in a perfectly competitive market is a fixed market price that is beyond the seller's control, our search for factors that influence supply naturally focuses on the cost side of the calculation. The preceding examples suggest why the following factors, among others, will affect the likelihood that a product will satisfy the cost-benefit test for a given supplier.

Technology

Perhaps the most important determinant of production cost is technology. Improvements in technology make it possible to produce additional units of output at lower cost. This shifts each individual supply curve downward (or, equivalently, to the right) and hence shifts the market supply curve downward as well. Over time, the introduction of more sophisticated machinery has resulted in dramatic increases in the number of goods produced per hour of effort expended. Every such development gives rise to a rightward shift in the market supply curve.

But how do we know technological change will reduce the cost of producing goods and services? Might not new equipment be so expensive that producers who used it would have higher costs than those who relied on earlier designs? If so, then rational producers simply would not use the new equipment. The only technological changes that rational producers will adopt are those that will reduce their cost of production.

Input Prices

Whereas technological change generally (although not always) leads to gradual shifts in supply, changes in the prices of important inputs can give rise to large supply shifts literally overnight. As we'll see in the upcoming Economic Naturalist 5.2, for example, the price of crude oil, which is the most important input in the production of gasoline, often fluctuates sharply, and the resulting shifts in supply cause gasoline prices to exhibit corresponding fluctuations.

Similarly, when wage rates rise, the marginal cost of any business that employs labor also rises, shifting supply curves to the left (or, equivalently, upward). When interest rates fall, the opportunity cost of capital equipment also falls, causing supply to shift to the right.

The Number of Suppliers

Just as demand curves shift to the right when population grows, supply curves also shift to the right as the number of individual suppliers grows. For example, if container recyclers die or retire at a higher rate than new recyclers enter the industry, the supply curve for recycling services will shift to the left. Conversely, if a rise in the unemployment rate leads more people to recycle soft drink containers (by reducing the opportunity cost of time spent recycling), the supply curve of recycling services will shift to the right.

Expectations

Expectations about future price movements can affect how much sellers choose to offer in the current market. Suppose, for example, that recyclers expect the future price of aluminum to be much higher than the current price because of growing use of aluminum components in cars. The rational recycler would then have an incentive to withhold aluminum from the market at today's lower price, thereby to have more available to sell at the higher future price. Conversely, if recyclers expected next year's price of aluminum to be lower than this year's, their incentive would be to offer more aluminum for sale in today's market.

Changes in Prices of Other Products

Apart from technological change, perhaps the most important determinant of supply is variation in the prices of other goods and services that sellers might produce. Prospectors, for example, search for those precious metals for which the surplus of benefits over costs is greatest. When the price of silver rises, many stop looking for gold and start looking for silver. Conversely, when the price of platinum falls, many platinum prospectors shift their attention to gold.

THE DETERMINANTS OF SUPPLY

Among the relevant factors causing supply curves to shift are new technologies, changes in input prices, changes in the number of sellers, expectations of future price changes, and changes in the prices of other products that firms might produce.

THE PRICE ELASTICITY OF SUPPLY

On the buyer's side of the market, we use price elasticity of demand to measure the responsiveness of quantity demanded to changes in price. On the seller's side of the market, the analogous measure is **price elasticity of supply**. It is defined as the percentage change in quantity supplied that occurs in response to a 1 percent change in price. For example, if a 1 percent increase in the price of peanuts leads to a 2 percent increase in the quantity supplied, the price elasticity of supply of peanuts would be 2.

The mathematical formula for price elasticity of supply at any point is the same as the corresponding expression for price elasticity of demand:

$$\text{Price elasticity of supply} = \frac{\Delta Q/Q}{\Delta P/P}, \tag{5.2}$$

where P and Q are the price and quantity at that point, ΔP is a small change in the initial price, and ΔQ the resulting change in quantity.

As with the corresponding expression for price elasticity of demand, Equation 5.2 can be rewritten as $(P/Q) \times (\Delta Q/\Delta P)$. And since $(\Delta Q/\Delta P)$ is the reciprocal of the slope of the supply curve, the right-hand side of Equation 5.2 is equal to $(P/Q) \times (1/\text{slope})$—the same expression we saw for price elasticity of demand. Price and quantity are always positive, as is the slope of the typical supply curve, which implies that price elasticity of supply will be a positive number at every point.

Consider the supply curve shown in Figure 5.8. The slope of this supply curve is 1/3, so the reciprocal of this slope is 3. Using the formula, this means that the price elasticity of supply at A is $(4/12) \times (3) = 1$. The corresponding expression at B, $(5/15) \times (3)$, yields exactly the same value. Because the ratio P/Q is the same at every point along this supply curve, price elasticity of supply will be exactly 1 at every point along this curve. Note the contrast between this result and our earlier finding that price elasticity of demand declines as we move downward along any straight-line demand curve.

The special property that explains why price elasticity equals 1 at every point in this illustration is the fact that the supply curve was a straight line through the origin. For movements along any such line, both price and quantity always change in exactly the same proportion.

price elasticity of supply the percentage change in the quantity supplied that occurs in response to a 1 percent change in the price of a good or service

FIGURE 5.8

Calculating the Price Elasticity of Supply Graphically.

Price elasticity of supply is $(P/Q) \times (1/\text{slope})$, which at A is $(4/12) \times (12/4) = 1$, exactly the same as at B. The price elasticity of supply is equal to 1 at any point along a straight-line supply curve that passes through the origin.

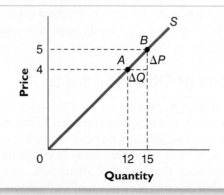

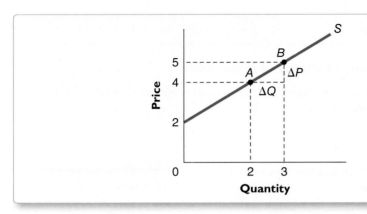

FIGURE 5.9

A Supply Curve for Which Price Elasticity Declines as Quantity Rises.

For the supply curve shown, (1/slope) is the same at every point, but the ratio P/Q declines as Q increases. So elasticity = $(P/Q) \times (1/\text{slope})$ declines as quantity increases.

Elasticity is not constant, however, along straight-line supply curves like the one in Figure 5.9, which does not pass through the origin. Although the slope of this supply curve is equal to 1 at every point, the ratio P/Q declines as we move to the right along the curve. Elasticity at A is equal to $(4/2) \times (1) = 2$, and declines to $(5/3) \times (1) = 5/3$ at B.

CONCEPT CHECK 5.5

For the supply curve shown in Figure 5.9, calculate the elasticity of supply when $P = 3$.

On the buyer's side of the market, two important polar cases were demand curves with infinite price elasticity and zero price elasticity. As the next two examples illustrate, analogous polar cases exist on the seller's side of the market.

EXAMPLE 5.7   Perfectly Inelastic

What is the elasticity of supply of land within the borough limits of Manhattan?

Land in Manhattan sells in the market for a price, just like aluminum or corn or automobiles or any other product. And the demand for land in Manhattan is a downward-sloping function of its price. For all practical purposes, however, its supply is completely fixed. No matter whether its price is high or low, the same amount of it is available in the market. The supply curve of such a good is vertical, and its price elasticity is zero at every price. Supply curves like the one shown in Figure 5.10 are said to be **perfectly inelastic**.

perfectly inelastic supply supply is perfectly inelastic with respect to price if elasticity is zero

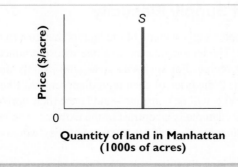

FIGURE 5.10

A Perfectly Inelastic Supply Curve.

Price elasticity of supply is zero at every point along a vertical supply curve.

EXAMPLE 5.8	Perfectly Elastic

What is the elasticity of supply of lemonade?

Suppose that the ingredients required to bring a cup of lemonade to market and their respective costs are as follows:

Paper cup	2.0 cents
Lemon	3.8 cents
Sugar	2.0 cents
Water	0.2 cent
Ice	1.0 cent
Labor (30 seconds @ $6/hour)	5.0 cents

If these proportions remain the same no matter how many cups of lemonade are made, and the inputs can be purchased in any quantities at the stated prices, draw the supply curve of lemonade and compute its price elasticity.

Since each cup of lemonade costs exactly 14 cents to make, no matter how many cups are made, the marginal cost of lemonade is constant at 14 cents per cup. And since each point on a supply curve is equal to marginal cost, this means that the supply curve of lemonade is not upward-sloping but is instead a horizontal line at 14 cents per cup (Figure 5.11). The price elasticity of supply of lemonade is infinite.

FIGURE 5.11

A Perfectly Elastic Supply Curve.

The elasticity of supply is infinite at every point along a horizontal supply curve.

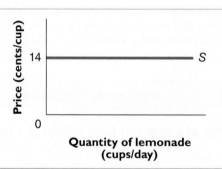

perfectly elastic supply
supply is perfectly elastic with respect to price if elasticity of supply is infinite

Whenever additional units of a good can be produced by using the same combination of inputs, purchased at the same prices, as have been used so far, the supply curve of that good will be horizontal. Such supply curves are said to be **perfectly elastic**.

Determinants of Supply Elasticity

The two preceding examples suggest some of the factors that govern the elasticity of supply of a good or service. The lemonade case was one whose production process was essentially like a cooking recipe. For such cases, we can exactly double our output by doubling each ingredient. If the price of each ingredient remains fixed, the marginal cost of production for such goods will be constant—and hence their horizontal supply curves.

The Manhattan land example is a contrast in the extreme. The inputs that were used to produce land in Manhattan—even if we knew what they were—could not be duplicated at any price.

The key to predicting how elastic the supply of a good will be with respect to price is to know the terms on which additional units of the inputs involved in producing that good can be acquired. In general, the more easily additional units of these inputs can be acquired, the higher price elasticity of supply will be. The following factors (among others) govern the ease with which additional inputs can be acquired by a producer.

Flexibility of Inputs

To the extent that production of a good requires inputs that are also useful for the production of other goods, it is relatively easy to lure additional inputs away from their current uses, making supply of that good relatively elastic with respect to price. Thus the fact that lemonade production requires labor with only minimal skills means that a large pool of workers could shift from other activities to lemonade production if a profitable opportunity arose. Brain surgery, by contrast, requires elaborately trained and specialized labor, which means that even a large price increase would not increase available supplies, except in the very long run.

Mobility of Inputs

If inputs can be easily transported from one site to another, an increase in the price of a product in one market will enable a producer in that market to summon inputs from other markets. For example, the supply of agricultural products is made more elastic with respect to price by the fact that thousands of farm workers are willing to migrate northward during the growing season. The supply of entertainment is similarly made more elastic by the willingness of entertainers to hit the road. Circus performers, lounge singers, comedians, and even exotic dancers often spend a substantial fraction of their time away from home. For instance, according to a 1996 *New York Times* article, the top exotic dancers "basically follow the action, so the same entertainers who worked the Indianapolis 500 now head to Atlanta for the Olympics."

For most goods, the price elasticity of supply increases each time a new highway is built, or when the telecommunications network improves, or indeed when any other development makes it easier to find and transport inputs from one place to another.

Ability to Produce Substitute Inputs

The inputs required to produce finished diamond gemstones include raw diamond crystals, skilled labor, and elaborate cutting and polishing machinery. In time, the number of people with the requisite skills can be increased, as can the amount of specialized machinery. The number of raw diamond crystals buried in the earth is probably fixed in the same way that Manhattan land is fixed, but unlike Manhattan land, rising prices will encourage miners to spend the effort required to find a larger proportion of those crystals. Still, the supply of natural gemstone diamonds tends to be relatively inelastic because of the difficulty of augmenting the number of diamond crystals.

The day is close at hand, however, when gemstone makers will be able to produce synthetic diamond crystals that are indistinguishable from real ones. Indeed, there are already synthetic crystals that fool even highly experienced jewelers. The introduction of a perfect synthetic substitute for natural diamond crystals would increase the price elasticity of supply of diamonds (or, at any rate, the price elasticity of supply of gemstones that look and feel just like diamonds).

Time

Because it takes time for producers to switch from one activity to another, and because it takes time to build new machines and factories and train additional skilled workers, the price elasticity of supply will be higher for most goods in the long run than in the short run. In the short run, a manufacturer's inability to augment existing stocks of equipment and skilled labor may make it impossible to expand output beyond a certain limit. But if a shortage of managers was the bottleneck, new MBAs can be trained in only two years. Or if a shortage of legal staff is the problem, new lawyers can be trained in three years. In the long run, firms can always buy new equipment, build new factories, and hire additional skilled workers.

"In six more weeks, these MBAs will be ready for market."

The conditions that gave rise to the perfectly elastic supply curve for lemonade in the example we discussed earlier are satisfied for many other products in the long run. If a product can be copied (in the sense that any company can acquire the design and other technological information required to produce it), and if the inputs needed for its production are used in roughly fixed proportions and are available at fixed market prices, then the long-run supply curve for that product will be horizontal. But many products do not satisfy these conditions, and their supply curves remain steeply upward-sloping, even in the very long run.

The Economic Naturalist 5.2

Why are gasoline prices so much more volatile than car prices?

Automobile price changes in the United States usually occur just once a year, when manufacturers announce an increase of only a few percentage points. In contrast, gasoline prices often fluctuate wildly from day to day. As shown in Figure 5.12, for example, the highest daily gasoline prices in California's two largest cities were three times higher than the lowest daily prices during a recent year. Why this enormous difference in volatility?

With respect to price volatility, at least two important features distinguish the gasoline market from the market for cars. One is that the short-run price elasticity of demand for gasoline is much smaller than the corresponding elasticity for cars. The other is that supply shifts are much more pronounced and frequent in the gasoline market than in the car market. (See Figure 5.13.)

Why are the two markets different in these ways? Consider first the difference in price elasticities of demand. The quantity of gasoline we demand depends largely on the kinds of cars we own and the amounts we drive them. In the short run, car ownership and commuting patterns are almost completely fixed, so even if the price of gasoline were to change sharply, the quantity we demand would not change by much. In contrast, if there were a sudden dramatic change in the price of cars, we could always postpone or accelerate our next car purchases.

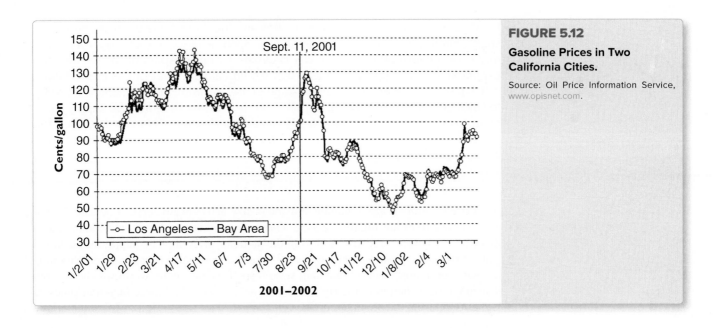

FIGURE 5.12

Gasoline Prices in Two California Cities.

Source: Oil Price Information Service, www.opisnet.com.

To see why the supply curve in the gasoline market experiences larger and more frequent shifts than the supply curve in the car market, we need only examine the relative stability of the inputs employed by sellers in these two markets. Most of the inputs used in producing cars—steel, glass, rubber, plastics, electronic components, labor, and others—are reliably available to carmakers. In contrast, the key input used in making gasoline—crude oil—is subject to profound and unpredictable supply interruptions.

This is so in part because much of the world's supply of crude oil is controlled by OPEC, a group of oil-exporting countries that has sharply curtailed its oil shipments to the United States on several previous occasions. Even in the absence of formal OPEC action, however, large supply curtailments often occur in the oil market—for example, whenever producers fear that political instability might engulf the major oil-producing countries of the Middle East, or as happened in the wake of Hurricane Katrina in 2005.

Note in Figure 5.12 the sharp spike in gasoline prices that occurred just after the terrorist attacks on the World Trade Center and Pentagon on September 11, 2001. Because many believed that the aim of these attacks was to provoke

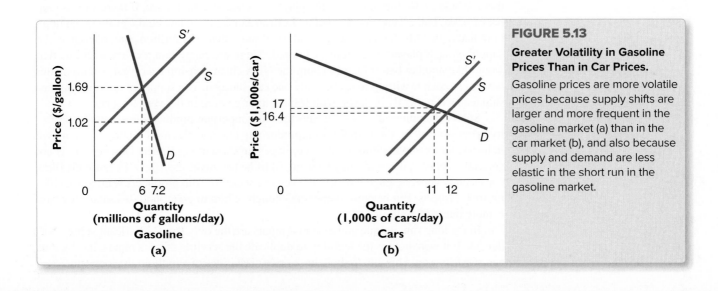

FIGURE 5.13

Greater Volatility in Gasoline Prices Than in Car Prices.

Gasoline prices are more volatile prices because supply shifts are larger and more frequent in the gasoline market (a) than in the car market (b), and also because supply and demand are less elastic in the short run in the gasoline market.

large-scale war between Muslim societies and the West, fears of an impending oil supply interruption were perfectly rational. Such fears alone can trigger a temporary supply interruption, even if war is avoided. The prospect of war creates the expectation of oil supply cutbacks that would cause higher prices in the future, which leads producers to withdraw some of their oil from current markets (in order to sell it at higher prices later). But once the fear of war recedes, the supply curve of gasoline reverts with equal speed to its earlier position. Given the low short-run price elasticity of demand for gasoline, that's all it takes to generate the considerable price volatility we see in this market.

Price volatility is also common in markets in which demand curves fluctuate sharply and supply curves are highly inelastic. One such market was California's unregulated market for wholesale electricity during the summer of 2000. The supply of electrical generating capacity was essentially fixed in the short run. And because air conditioning accounts for a large share of demand, several spells of unusually warm weather caused demand to shift sharply to the right. Price at one point reached more than four times its highest level from the previous summer.

Unique and Essential Inputs: The Ultimate Supply Bottleneck

Fans of professional basketball are an enthusiastic bunch. Directly through their purchases of tickets and indirectly through their support of television advertisers, they spend literally billions of dollars each year on the sport. But these dollars are not distributed evenly across all teams. A disproportionate share of all revenues and product endorsement fees accrue to the people associated with consistently winning teams, and at the top of this pyramid generally stands the National Basketball Association's championship team.

Consider the task of trying to produce a championship team in the NBA. What are the inputs you would need? Talented players, a shrewd and dedicated coach and assistants, trainers, physicians, an arena, practice facilities, means for transporting players to away games, a marketing staff, and so on. And whereas some of these inputs can be acquired at reasonable prices in the marketplace, many others cannot. Indeed, the most important input of all—highly talented players—is in extremely limited supply. *This is so because the very definition of talented player is inescapably relative—simply put, such a player is one who is better than most others.*

Given the huge payoff that accrues to the NBA championship team, it is no surprise that the bidding for the most talented players has become so intense. If there were a long list of basketball players as talented as LeBron James, the Cleveland Cavaliers wouldn't have had to pay Mr. James an annual salary of more than $21 million. But, of course, the supply of such players is extremely limited. There are many hungry organizations that would like nothing better than to claim the NBA championship each year, yet no matter how much each is willing to spend, only one can succeed. The supply of NBA championship teams is perfectly inelastic with respect to price even in the very long run.

Sports champions are by no means the only important product whose supply elasticity is constrained by the inability to reproduce unique and essential inputs. In the movie industry, for example, although the supply of movies starring Robert Downey, Jr., is not perfectly inelastic, there are only so many films he can make each year. Because his films consistently generate huge box office revenues, scores of film producers want to sign him for their projects. But because there isn't enough of him to go around, his salary per film is more than $50 million.

In the long run, unique and essential inputs are the only truly significant supply bottleneck. If it were not for the inability to duplicate the services of such inputs, most goods and services would have extremely high price elasticities of supply in the long run.

SUMMARY

- The supply curve for a good or service is a schedule that, for any price, tells us the quantity that sellers wish to supply at that price. The prices at which goods and services are offered for sale in the market depend, in turn, on the opportunity cost of the resources required to produce them. *(LO1)*

- The demand curve facing a perfectly competitive firm is a horizontal line at the price for which industry supply and demand intersect. *(LO2)*

- Supply curves tend to be upward-sloping, at least in the short run. In general, rational producers will always take advantage of their best opportunities first, moving on to more difficult or costly opportunities only after their best ones have been exhausted. Reinforcing this tendency is the law of diminishing returns, which says that, when some factors of production are held fixed, the amount of additional variable factors required to produce successive increments in output grows larger. *(LO2, LO3)*

- In a typical production process, firms combine inputs, such as capital and labor, to produce output. The amount of a variable input can be altered in the short run, but the amount of a fixed input can be altered only in the long run. *(LO3)*

- For perfectly competitive markets—or, more generally, for markets in which individual sellers can sell whatever quantity they wish at constant price—the seller's best option is to sell that quantity of output for which price equals marginal cost, provided price exceeds the minimum value of average variable cost. The supply curve for the seller thus coincides with the portion of his marginal cost curve, the curve that measures the cost of producing additional units of output. This is why we sometimes say

the supply curve represents the cost side of the market (in contrast to the demand curve, which represents the benefit side of the market). *(LO3)*

- The industry supply curve is the horizontal summation of the supply curves of individual firms in the industry. *(LO3)*

- Among the relevant factors causing the supply curves to shift are new technologies, changes in input prices, changes in the number of sellers, expectations of future price changes, and changes in the prices of other products that firms might produce. *(LO4)*

- Price elasticity of supply is defined as the percentage change in quantity supplied that occurs in response to a 1 percent change in price. The mathematical formula for the price elasticity of supply at any point is $(\Delta Q/Q)/(\Delta P/P)$, where P and Q are the price and quantity at that point, ΔP is a small change in the initial price, and ΔQ is the resulting change in quantity. This formula also can be expressed as $(P/Q) \times (1/\text{slope})$ where $(1/\text{slope})$ is the reciprocal of the slope of the supply curve. *(LO5)*

- The price elasticity of supply of a good depends on how difficult or costly it is to acquire additional units of the inputs involved in producing that good. In general, the more easily additional units of these inputs can be acquired, the higher price elasticity of supply will be. It is easier to expand production of a product if the inputs used to produce that product are similar to inputs used to produce other products, if inputs are relatively mobile, or if an acceptable substitute for existing inputs can be developed. And like the price elasticity of demand, the price elasticity of supply is greater in the long run than in the short run. *(LO5)*

KEY TERMS

factor of production
fixed cost
fixed factor of production
imperfectly competitive firm
law of diminishing returns
long run

perfectly competitive market
perfectly elastic supply
perfectly inelastic supply
price elasticity of supply
price taker
profit

profit-maximizing firm
short run
total cost
variable cost
variable factor of production

REVIEW QUESTIONS

1. Explain why you would expect supply curves to slope upward based on increasing opportunity cost. *(LO1)*

2. Explain why a perfectly competitive firm's demand curve is horizontal. *(LO2)*

3. Which do you think is more likely to be a fixed factor of production for an ice cream producer during the next

two months: its factory building or its workers who operate the machines? Explain. *(LO3)*

4. True or false: The perfectly competitive firm should *always* produce the output level for which price equals marginal cost. *(LO3)*

5. Economists often stress that congestion helps account for the law of diminishing returns. With this in mind, explain why it would be impossible to feed all the people on Earth with food grown in a single flowerpot, even if unlimited water, labor, seed, fertilizer, sunlight, and other inputs were available. *(LO3, LO4)*

6. Why is supply elasticity higher in the long run than in the short run? *(LO5)*

PROBLEMS   connect

1. Zoe is trying to decide how to divide her time between her job as a wedding photographer, which pays $27 per hour for as many hours as she chooses to work, and as a fossil collector, in which her pay depends on both the price of fossils and the number of them she finds. Earnings aside, Zoe is indifferent between the two tasks, and the number of fossils she can find depends on the number of hours a day she searches, as shown in the table below: *(LO1)*

Hours per day	Total fossils per day
1	5
2	9
3	12
4	14
5	15

a. Derive a table with price in dollar increments from $0 to $30 in the first column and the quantity of fossils Zoe is willing to supply per day at that price in the second.

b. Plot these points in a graph with price on the vertical axis and quantity per day on the horizontal. What is this curve called?

2. The supply curves for the only two firms in a competitive industry are given by $P = 2Q_1$ and $P = 2 + Q_2$, where Q_1 is the output of firm 1 and Q_2 is the output of firm 2. What is the market supply curve for this industry? *(Hint:* Graph the two curves side by side; then add their respective quantities at a sample of different prices.) *(LO2)*

3. A price-taking firm makes air conditioners. The market price of one of its new air conditioners is $120. Its total cost information is given in the table below:

Air conditioners per day	Total cost ($ per day)
1	100
2	150
3	220
4	310
5	405
6	510
7	650
8	800

How many air conditioners should the firm produce per day if its goal is to maximize its profit? *(LO3)*

4. Paducah Slugger Company makes baseball bats out of lumber supplied to it by Acme Sporting Goods, which pays Paducah $10 for each finished bat. Paducah's only factors of production are lathe operators and a small building with a lathe. The number of bats per day it produces depends on the number of employee-hours per day, as shown in the table below. *(LO3, LO4)*

Number of bats per day	Number of employee-hours per day
0	0
5	1
10	2
15	4
20	7
25	11
30	16
35	22

a. If the wage is $15 per hour and Paducah's daily fixed cost for the lathe and building is $60, what is the profit-maximizing quantity of bats?

b. What would be the profit-maximizing number of bats if the firm's fixed cost were not $60 per day but only $30?

5. In Problem 4, how would Paducah's profit-maximizing level of output be affected if the government imposed a tax of $10 per day on the company? *(Hint:* Think of this tax as equivalent to a $10 increase in fixed cost.) What would be Paducah's profit-maximizing level of output be if the government imposed a tax of $2 per bat? *(Hint:* Think of this tax as a $2-per-bat increase in the firm's marginal cost.) Why do these two taxes have such different effects? *(LO3, LO4)*

6. How would each of the following affect the U.S. market supply curve for corn? *(LO3, LO4)*

a. The government taxes sodas sweetened with high-fructose corn syrup.

b. The opportunity cost of farmer's time increases.

c. Scientists discover that corn consumption improves performance on standardized tests.

7. The price elasticity of supply for basmati rice (an aromatic strain of rice) is likely to be which of the following? *(LO5)*
   a. Higher in the long run than the short run, because farmers cannot easily change their decisions about how much basmati rice to plant once the current crop has been planted.
   b. High, because consumers have a lot of other kinds of rice and other staple foods to choose from.
   c. Low in both the long and short runs, because rice farming requires only unskilled labor.
   d. High in both the long run and the short run because the inputs required to produce basmati rice can easily be duplicated.

8.* What are the respective price elasticities of supply at A and B on the supply curve shown in the accompanying figure? *(LO5)*

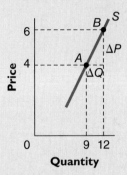

*Indicates more difficult problem.

ANSWERS TO CONCEPT CHECKS

5.1 Since Harry will find 300 containers if he searches a third hour, we find his reservation price for searching a third hour by solving $p(300) = \$6$ for $p = 2$ cents. His reservation prices for additional hours of search are calculated in an analogous way. *(LO1)*

Fourth hour: $p(200) = \$6$, so $p = 3$ cents.
Fifth hour: $p(100) = \$6$, so $p = 6$ cents.

5.2 The profit figures corresponding to a price of $5/hundred are as shown in the last column of the table below, where we see that the profit-maximizing output (which here means the loss-minimizing output) is 0 bottles/day. Note that the company actually loses $40/day at that output level. But it would lose even more if it produced any other amount. If the company expects conditions to remain unchanged, it will want to go out of the bottle business as soon as its equipment lease expires. *(LO3)*

Q (bottles/day)	Total revenue ($/day)	Total labor cost ($/day)	Total cost ($/day)	Profit ($/day)
0	0	0	40	−40
100	5	10	50	−45
200	10	20	60	−50
300	15	40	80	−65
400	20	70	110	−90
500	25	110	150	−125
600	30	160	200	−170
700	35	220	260	−225

5.3 The profit figures corresponding to a price of $25/hundred are as shown in the last column of the table below, where we see that the profit-maximizing output (which here means the loss-minimizing output) is 300 bottles/day. Note that the company actually loses $5/day at that output level. But as long as it remains committed to its daily lease payment of $40, it would lose even more if it produced any other amount. If the company expects conditions to remain unchanged, it will want to go out of the bottle business as soon as its equipment lease expires. *(LO3)*

Q (bottles/day)	Total revenue ($/day)	Total labor cost ($/day)	Total cost ($/day)	Profit ($/day)
0	0	0	40	−40
100	25	10	50	−25
200	50	20	60	−10
300	75	40	80	−5
400	100	70	110	−10
500	125	110	150	−25
600	150	160	200	−50
700	175	220	260	−85

5.4 The fact that each of the city's 60,000 residents is willing to pay 0.00005 cent for each bottle removed means that the collective benefit of each bottle removed is (60,000)(0.00005) = 3 cents. So the city should set the redemption price at 3 cents, and from the supply curve we see that 15,000 bottles per day will be recycled at that price. *(LO3)*

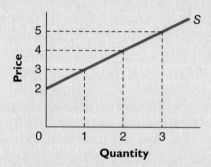

5.5 For the supply curve below, $Q = 1$ when $P = 3$, so elasticity of supply = $(P/Q) \times (1/\text{slope}) = (3) \times (1) = 3$. *(LO5)*

Efficiency, Exchange, and the Invisible Hand in Action

The market for ethnic cuisine in Ithaca, New York, offered few choices in the early 1970s: The city had one Japanese, two Greek, four Italian, and three Chinese restaurants. Today, more than 40 years later and with essentially the same population, Ithaca has one Sri Lankan, two Indian, one French, one Spanish, six Thai, two Korean, two Vietnamese, four Mexican, three Greek, seven Italian, two Caribbean, two Japanese, and nine Chinese restaurants. In some of the city's other markets, however, the range of available choices has narrowed. For example, several companies provided telephone answering service in 1972, but only one does so today.

Rare indeed is the marketplace in which the identities of the buyers and sellers remain static for extended periods. New businesses enter; established ones leave. There are more body-piercing studios in Ithaca now and fewer watch-repair shops; more marketing consultants and fewer intercity bus companies; and more appliances in stainless steel or black finishes, fewer in avocado or coppertone.

Driving these changes is the business owner's quest for profit. Businesses migrate to industries and locations in which profit opportunities abound and desert those whose prospects appear bleak. In perhaps the most widely quoted passage from his landmark treatise, *The Wealth of Nations,* Adam Smith wrote,

> It is not from the benevolence of the butcher, the brewer, or the baker that we expect our dinner, but from their regard of their own interest. We address ourselves not to their humanity, but to their self-love, and never talk to them of our necessities, but of their advantage.

Smith went on to argue that although the entrepreneur "intends only his own gain," he is "led by an invisible hand to promote an end which was no part of his intention." As Smith saw it, even though self-interest is the prime mover of economic activity, the end result is an allocation of goods and services that serves society's collective interests remarkably well. If producers are offering "too much" of one product and "not enough" of another, profit opportunities stimulate entrepreneurs into action. All the while, the system exerts relentless pressure on producers to hold the price of

LEARNING OBJECTIVES

After reading this chapter, you should be able to:

LO1 Define and explain the differences between accounting profit, economic profit, and normal profit.

LO2 Interpret why the quest for economic profit drives resource allocation and motivates firms to enter some industries and leave others.

LO3 Explain why economic profit, unlike economic rent, tends toward zero in the long run.

LO4 Identify conditions under which a market equilibrium may not be socially efficient.

LO5 Explain why no opportunities for gain remain open to individuals when a market is in equilibrium.

LO6 Explain how an economy's total economic surplus is affected by policies that prevent markets from reaching equilibrium.

Why do most American cities now have more tattoo parlors and fewer watch-repair shops than in 1972?

each good close to its cost of production, and indeed to reduce that cost in any ways possible. The invisible hand, in short, is about all the good things that can happen when people pursue their own interests in the marketplace.

Our task in this chapter is to gain deeper insight into the nature of the forces that guide the invisible hand. What exactly does "profit" mean? How is it measured, and how does the quest for it serve society's ends? And if competition holds price close to the cost of production, why do so many entrepreneurs become fabulously wealthy? We will also discuss cases in which misunderstanding of Smith's theory results in costly errors, both in everyday decision making and in the realm of government policy.

THE CENTRAL ROLE OF ECONOMIC PROFIT

The economic theory of business behavior is built on the assumption that the firm's goal is to maximize its profit. So we must be clear at the outset about what, exactly, profit means.

Three Types of Profit

The economist's understanding of profit is different from the accountant's, and the distinction between the two is important to understanding how the invisible hand works. Accountants define the annual profit of a business as the difference between the revenue it takes in and its **explicit costs** for the year, which are the actual payments the firm makes to its factors of production and other suppliers. Profit thus defined is called **accounting profit**.

explicit costs the actual payments a firm makes to its factors of production and other suppliers

accounting profit the difference between a firm's total revenue and its explicit costs

implicit costs the opportunity costs of the resources supplied by the firm's owners

economic profit (or excess profit) the difference between a firm's total revenue and the sum of its explicit and implicit costs

Accounting profit = total revenue − explicit costs.

Accounting profit is the most familiar profit concept in everyday discourse. It is the one that companies use, for example, when they provide statements about their profits in press releases or annual reports.[1]

Economists, by contrast, define profit as the difference between the firm's total revenue and not just its explicit costs, but also its **implicit costs**, which are the opportunity costs of all the resources supplied by the firm's owners. Profit thus defined is called **economic profit**, or **excess profit**.

Economic profit = total revenue − explicit costs − implicit costs.

To illustrate the difference between accounting profit and economic profit, consider a firm with $400,000 in total annual revenue whose only explicit costs are workers' salaries, totaling $250,000 per year. The owners of this firm have supplied machines and other capital equipment with a total resale value of $1 million. This firm's accounting profit then is $150,000, or the difference between its total revenue of $400,000 per year and its explicit costs of $250,000 per year.

To calculate the firm's economic profit, we must first calculate the opportunity cost of the resources supplied by the firm's owners. Suppose the current annual interest rate on

---

[1]For simplicity, this discussion ignores any costs associated with depreciation of the firm's capital equipment. Because the buildings and machines owned by a firm tend to wear out over time, the government allows the firm to consider a fraction of their value each year as a current cost of doing business. For example, a firm that employs a $1,000 machine with a 10-year life span might be allowed to record $100 as a current cost of doing business each year.

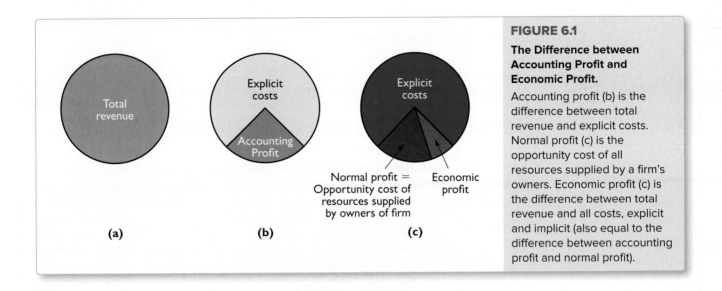

savings accounts is 10 percent. Had owners not invested in capital equipment, they could have earned an additional $100,000 per year interest by depositing their $1 million in a savings account. So the firm's economic profit is $400,000-per-year − $250,000 per year − $100,000 per year = $50,000 per year.

Note that this economic profit is smaller than the accounting profit by exactly the amount of the firm's implicit costs—the $100,000-per-year opportunity cost of the resources supplied by the firm's owners. This difference between a business's accounting profit and its economic profit is called its **normal profit**. Normal profit is simply the opportunity cost of the resources supplied to a business by its owners.

Figure 6.1 illustrates the difference between accounting and economic profit. Figure 6.1(a) represents a firm's total revenue, while (b) and (c) show how this revenue is apportioned among the various cost and profit categories.

normal profit the opportunity cost of the resources supplied by a firm's owners, equal to accounting profit minus economic profit

"All I know, Harrison, is that I've been on the board forty years and have yet to see an excess profit."

The following examples illustrate why the distinction between accounting and economic profit is so important.

EXAMPLE 6.1 **Accounting versus Economic Profit, Part 1**

Should Pudge Buffet stay in the farming business?

Pudge Buffet is a corn farmer who lives near Lincoln, Nebraska. His payments for land and equipment rental and for other supplies come to $10,000 per year. The only input he supplies is his own labor, and he considers farming just as attractive as his only other employment opportunity, managing a retail store at a salary of $11,000 per year. Apart from the matter of pay, Pudge is indifferent between farming and being a manager. Corn sells for a constant price per bushel in an international market too large to be affected by changes in one farmer's corn production. Pudge's revenue from corn sales is $22,000 per year. What is his accounting profit? His economic profit? His normal profit? Should he remain a corn farmer?

As shown in Table 6.1, Pudge's accounting profit is $12,000 per year, the difference between his $22,000 annual revenue and his $10,000 yearly payment for land, equipment, and supplies. His economic profit is that amount less the opportunity cost of his labor. Since the latter is the $11,000 per year he could have earned as a store manager, he is making an economic profit of $1,000 per year. Finally, his normal profit is the $11,000 opportunity cost of the only resource he supplies, namely, his labor. Since Pudge likes the two jobs equally well, he will be better off by $1,000 per year if he remains in farming.

TABLE 6.1
Revenue, Cost, and Profit Summary

Total revenue ($/year)	Explicit costs ($/year)	Implicit costs ($/year)	Accounting profit (= total revenue − explicit costs) ($/year)	Economic profit (= total revenue − explicit costs − implicit costs) ($/year)	Normal profit (= implicit costs) ($/year)
22,000	10,000	11,000	12,000	1,000	11,000

CONCEPT CHECK 6.1

In Example 6.1, how will Pudge's economic profit change if his annual revenue from corn production is not $22,000, but $20,000? Should he continue to farm?

economic loss an economic profit that is less than zero

When revenue falls from $22,000 to $20,000, Pudge has an economic profit of −$1,000 per year. A negative economic profit is also called an **economic loss**. If Pudge expects to sustain an economic loss indefinitely, his best bet would be to abandon farming in favor of managing a retail store.

You might think that if Pudge could just save enough money to buy his own land and equipment, his best option would be to remain a farmer. But as the following example illustrates, that impression is based on a failure to perceive the difference between accounting profit and economic profit.

EXAMPLE 6.2   **Accounting versus Economic Profit, Part 2**

Does owning one's own land make a difference?

Let's build on Example 6.1. Suppose Pudge's Uncle Warren, who owns the farmland Pudge has been renting, dies and leaves Pudge that parcel of land. If the land could be rented to some other farmer for $6,000 per year, should Pudge remain in farming?

As shown in Table 6.2, if Pudge continues to farm his own land, his accounting profit will be $16,000 per year, or $6,000 more than in Concept Check 6.1. But his economic profit will still be the same as before—that is, −$1,000 per year—because Pudge must deduct the $6,000 per year opportunity cost of farming his own land, even though he no longer must make an explicit payment to his uncle for it. The normal profit from owning and operating his farm will be $17,000 per year—the opportunity cost of the land and labor he provides. But since Pudge earns an accounting profit of only $16,000, he will again do better to abandon farming for the managerial job.

TABLE 6.2
Revenue, Cost, and Profit Summary

Total revenue ($/year)	Explicit costs ($/year)	Implicit costs ($/year)	Accounting profit (= total revenue − explicit costs) ($/year)	Economic profit (= total revenue − explicit costs − implicit costs) ($/year)	Normal profit (= implicit costs) ($/year)
20,000	4,000	17,000	16,000	−1,000	17,000

Pudge obviously would be wealthier as an owner than he was as a renter. But the question of whether to remain a farmer is answered the same way whether Pudge rents his farmland or owns it. He should stay in farming only if that is the option that yields the highest economic profit.

RECAP ↑

THE CENTRAL ROLE OF ECONOMIC PROFIT

A firm's accounting profit is the difference between its revenue and the sum of all explicit costs it incurs. Economic profit is the difference between the firm's revenue and *all* costs it incurs—both explicit and implicit. Normal profit is the opportunity cost of the resources supplied by the owners of the firm. When a firm's accounting profit is exactly equal to the opportunity cost of the inputs supplied by the firm's owners, the firm's economic profit is zero. For a firm to remain in business in the long run, it must earn an economic profit greater than or equal to zero.

THE INVISIBLE HAND THEORY

Two Functions of Price

rationing function of price changes in prices distribute scarce goods to those consumers who value them most highly

allocative function of price changes in prices direct resources away from overcrowded markets and toward markets that are underserved

invisible hand theory Adam Smith's theory that the actions of independent, self-interested buyers and sellers will often result in the most efficient allocation of resources

In the free enterprise system, market prices serve two important and distinct functions. The first, the **rationing function of price**, is to distribute scarce goods among potential claimants, ensuring that those who get them are the ones who value them most. Thus, if three people want the only antique clock for sale at an auction, the clock goes home with the person who bids the most for it. The second function, the **allocative function of price**, is to direct productive resources to different sectors of the economy. Resources leave markets in which price cannot cover the cost of production and enter those in which price exceeds the cost of production.

Both the allocative and rationing functions of price underlie Adam Smith's celebrated theory of the **invisible hand** of the market. Recall that Smith thought the market system often channels the selfish interests of individual buyers and sellers so as to promote the greatest good for society. The carrot of economic profit and the stick of economic loss, he argued, were often the only forces necessary to ensure that existing supplies in any market would be allocated efficiently and that resources would be allocated across markets to produce the most efficient possible mix of goods and services.

Responses to Profits and Losses

To get a feel for how the invisible hand works, we begin by looking at how firms respond to economic profits and losses. If a firm is to remain in business in the long run, it must cover all its costs, both explicit and implicit. A firm's normal profit is just a cost of doing business. Thus, the owner of a firm that earns no more than a normal profit has managed only to recover the opportunity cost of the resources invested in the firm. By contrast, the owner of a firm that makes a positive economic profit earns more than the opportunity cost of the invested resources; she earns a normal profit and then some.

Naturally, everyone would be delighted to earn more than a normal profit, and no one wants to earn less. The result is that those markets in which firms are earning an economic profit tend to attract additional resources, whereas markets in which firms are experiencing economic losses tend to lose resources.

The following example examines how the forces of the invisible hand would respond if not just Pudge Buffet but also all other farmers in Lincoln, Nebraska, were experiencing economic losses.

EXAMPLE 6.3 **The Invisible Hand Theory in Action**

What would happen if all farmers in Lincoln earned less than a normal profit?

Suppose the conditions confronting Pudge Buffet in the example summarized in Table 6.2 are essentially the same as those confronting all other farmers in Lincoln, Nebraska—that is, all earn less than a normal profit. What economic changes will result?

If all farmers in Lincoln are earning a negative economic profit, some farmers will begin switching to other activities. As they abandon farming, however, the market price for farmland—and hence its opportunity cost—will begin to fall. It will continue to fall until farmers in Lincoln can once again earn a normal profit. Specifically, the price of land will fall until the yearly rental for a farm like Pudge's is only $5,000, for at that rent the accounting profit of someone who farmed his own land would be $16,000 per year, exactly the same as his normal profit. His economic profit would be zero.

EXAMPLE 6.4   Incentive to Change Behavior

What would happen if all farmers earn more than a normal profit?

Suppose corn growers farm 80 acres of their own land, which sells for $1,000 per acre. Each farm's revenue from corn sales is $20,000 per year. Equipment and other supplies cost $4,000 per year, and the current annual interest rate on savings accounts is 5 percent. Farmers can earn $11,000 per year in alternative jobs that they like equally well as farming. What is normal economic profit for these farmers? How much accounting profit will they earn? How much economic profit? Is their economic situation stable? If not, how is it likely to change?

As shown in Table 6.3, accounting profit—the difference between the $20,000 annual revenue and the $4,000 annual expense for equipment and supplies—is $16,000 per year, as in the example just discussed. Normal profit is the opportunity cost of the farmer's time and land—$11,000 for his time and $4,000 for his land (since had he sold the land for $80,000 and put the money in the bank at 5 percent interest, he would have earned $4,000 per year in interest)—for a total of $15,000. Accounting profit thus exceeds normal profit by $1,000 per year, which means that farmers are earning an economic profit of $1,000 per year.

TABLE 6.3
Revenue, Cost, and Profit Summary

Total revenue ($/year)	Explicit costs ($/year)	Implicit costs ($/year)	Accounting profit (= total revenue − explicit costs) ($/year)	Economic profit (= total revenue − explicit costs − implicit costs) ($/year)	Normal profit (= implicit costs) ($/year)
20,000	4,000	15,000	16,000	1,000	15,000

To see whether this situation is stable, we must ask whether people have an incentive to change their behavior. Consider the situation from the perspective of a manager who is earning $11,000 per year. To switch to farming, he would need to borrow $80,000 to buy land, which would mean interest payments of $4,000 per year. With $20,000 per year in revenue from corn sales and $4,000 per year in expenses for supplies and equipment, in addition to $4,000 per year in interest payments, the manager would earn an accounting profit of $12,000 per year. And since that amount is $1,000 per year more than the opportunity cost of the manager's time, he will want to switch to farming. Indeed, *all* managers will want to switch to farming. At current land prices, there is cash on the table in farming.

Yet any situation with cash on the table is inherently unstable. There is only so much farmland to go around, so as demand for it increases, its price will begin to rise. The price will keep rising until there is no longer any incentive for managers to switch to farming.

How much must the price of land rise to eliminate the incentive to switch? If 80 acres of land sold for $100,000 (that is, if land sold for $1,250 per acre), the interest on the money borrowed to buy a farm would be $5,000 per year, an amount that would make workers indifferent between farming and being a manager. But if land sells for anything less than $1,250 per acre, there will be excess demand for farmland.

FIGURE 6.2

The Effect of Positive Economic Profit on Entry.

A market in which firms earn a positive economic profit will attract new firms from other markets. The resulting increase in supply will lead to a reduction in market price.

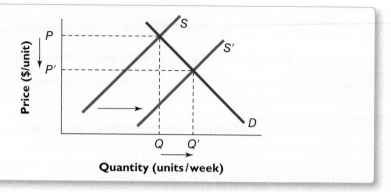

The Effect of Market Forces on Economic Profit

A firm's normal profit is just like any other cost of doing business. Thus the owner of a firm that earns no more than a normal profit has managed only to recover the opportunity cost of the resources invested in the firm. By contrast, the owner of a firm that makes a positive economic profit earns more than the opportunity cost of the invested resources; she earns a normal profit and then some. Naturally, everyone would be delighted to earn more than a normal profit, and no one wants to earn less. The result is that those markets in which firms are earning an economic profit tend to attract additional resources, whereas markets in which firms are experiencing economic losses tend to lose resources.

In Example 6.4, we assumed that the price of corn was set in a world market too large to be influenced by the amount of corn produced in any one locality. More generally, however, we need to consider the effects of supply shifts on price.

Consider first the effect of an influx of resources in a market in which firms are currently earning an economic profit. As new firms enter the market, the supply curve will shift to the right, causing a reduction in the price of the product (see Figure 6.2).

If firms continue to earn a positive economic profit at the new, lower price, P', additional firms will enter, causing the market price to fall still further. The process will continue until economic profit is driven down to zero—that is, until price is just sufficient to cover all costs, including a normal profit.

Now consider the effect of resources moving out of a market in which businesses are currently experiencing an economic loss. As firms leave, the market supply curve shifts to the left, causing the price of the product to rise, as shown in Figure 6.3. Firms will continue to exit until price rises to cover all resource costs—including the opportunity cost of the resources that owners have invested in their firms. The economic loss firms have been sustaining will be eliminated.

FIGURE 6.3

The Effect of Economic Losses on Market Exit.

Firms tend to leave a market when they experience an economic loss. The result is a leftward shift in the supply curve and a corresponding increase in price. Firms will continue to leave the market until the price rises enough to cover all costs, including the opportunity cost of resources supplied by a firm's owners.

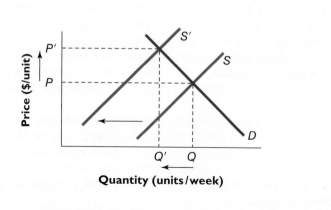

The net result of these resource movements is that in the long run all firms will tend to earn zero economic profit. Their *goal* is not to earn zero profit. Rather, the zero-profit tendency is a consequence of the dynamics of their entry into and exit from the market. That's because when people confront an opportunity for gain, they are almost always quick to exploit it.

The Importance of Free Entry and Exit

The allocative function of price cannot operate unless firms can enter new markets and leave existing ones at will. If new firms could not enter a market in which existing firms were making a large economic profit, economic profit would not tend to fall to zero over time, and price would not tend to gravitate toward the marginal cost of production.

Forces that inhibit firms from entering new markets are called **barriers to entry**. In the book publishing market, for example, the publisher of a book enjoys copyright protection granted by the government. Copyright law forbids other publishers from producing and selling their own editions of protected works. This barrier allows the price of a popular book to remain significantly above its cost of production for an extended period, all the while generating an economic profit for its publisher. (A copyright provides no *guarantee* of a profit, and indeed most new books actually generate an economic loss for their publishers.)

barrier to entry any force that prevents firms from entering a new market

Barriers to entry may result from practical as well as legal constraints. Some economists, for example, have argued that the compelling advantages of product compatibility have created barriers to entry in the computer software market. Since more than 85 percent of new desktop and laptop computers come with Microsoft's Windows software already installed, rival companies have difficulty selling other operating systems that may prevent users from exchanging files with friends and colleagues. This fact, more than any other, explains Microsoft's spectacular profit history. But the share of computers equipped with Windows has been steadily falling, leading many economists to predict that Microsoft's profits will follow a similar trajectory.

No less important than the freedom to enter a market is the freedom to leave. When the airline industry was regulated by the federal government, air carriers were often required to serve specific markets, even though they were losing money in them. When firms discover that a market, once entered, is difficult or impossible to leave, they become reluctant to enter new markets. Barriers to exit thus become barriers to entry. Without reasonably free entry and exit, then, the implications of Adam Smith's invisible hand theory cannot be expected to hold.

All things considered, producers enjoy a high degree of freedom of entry in most U.S. markets. Because free entry is one of the defining characteristics of perfectly competitive markets, unless otherwise stated, we'll assume its existence.

The Invisible Hand in Action

To help develop your intuition about how the invisible hand works, we will examine how it helps us gain insight into patterns we observe in a wide variety of different contexts. In each case, the key idea we want you to focus on is that opportunities for private gain seldom remain unexploited for very long. Perhaps more than any other, this idea encapsulates the essence of that distinctive mindset known as "thinking like an economist."

The Invisible Hand at the Supermarket and on the Freeway

As the following example illustrates, it is not just opportunities to earn economic profits that are likely to disappear quickly, but also any other opportunities to achieve unusually desirable outcomes.

The Economic Naturalist 6.1

Why do supermarket checkout lines all tend to be roughly the same length?

Pay careful attention the next few times you go grocery shopping and you'll notice that the lines at all the checkout stations tend to be roughly the same length. Suppose you saw one line that was significantly shorter than the others as you wheeled your cart toward the checkout area. Which line would you choose? The shorter one, of course; because most shoppers would do the same, the short line seldom remains shorter for long.

Why do you seldom see one supermarket checkout line that is substantially shorter than all the others?

CONCEPT CHECK 6.2

Use the same reasoning employed in The Economic Naturalist 6.1 to explain why all lanes on a crowded, multilane freeway move at about the same speed.

The Invisible Hand and Cost-Saving Innovations

When economists speak of perfectly competitive firms, they have in mind businesses whose contribution to total market output is too small to have a perceptible impact on market price. As explained earlier, such firms are often called price takers: They take the market price of their product as given and then produce that quantity of output for which marginal cost equals that price.

This characterization of the competitive firm gives the impression that the firm is essentially a passive actor in the marketplace. Yet for most firms, that is anything but the case. As the next example illustrates, even those firms that cannot hope to influence the market prices of their products have very powerful incentives to develop and introduce cost-saving innovations.

EXAMPLE 6.5	The Impact of Cost-Saving Innovations on Economic Profit

How do cost-saving innovations affect economic profit in the short run? In the long run?

Forty merchant marine companies operate supertankers that carry oil from the Middle East to the United States. The cost per trip, including a normal profit, is $500,000. An engineer at one of these companies develops a more efficient propeller design that results in fuel savings of $20,000 per trip. How will this innovation affect the company's accounting and economic profits? Will these changes persist in the long run?

In the short run, the reduction in a single firm's costs will have no impact on the market price of transoceanic shipping services. The firm with the more efficient propeller will thus earn an economic profit of $20,000 per trip (since its total revenue will be the same as before, while its total cost will now be $20,000 per trip lower). As other firms learn about the new design, however, they will begin to adopt it, causing their individual supply curves to shift downward (since the marginal cost per trip at these firms will drop by $20,000). The shift in these individual supply curves will cause the market supply curve to shift, which in turn will result in a lower market price for shipping and a decline in economic profit at the firm where the innovation originated. When all firms have adopted the new, efficient design, the long-run supply curve for the industry will have shifted downward by $20,000 per trip and each company will again be earning only a normal profit. At that point, any firm that did *not* adopt the new propeller design would suffer an economic loss of $20,000 per trip.

The incentive to come up with cost-saving innovations in order to reap economic profit is one of the most powerful forces on the economic landscape. Its beauty, in terms of the invisible hand theory, is that competition among firms ensures that the resulting cost savings will be passed along to consumers in the long run.

> **RECAP ↑**
>
> **THE INVISIBLE HAND THEORY**
>
> In market economies, the allocative and rationing functions of prices guide resources to their most highly valued uses. Prices influence how much of each type of good gets produced (the allocative function). Firms enter industries in which prices are sufficiently high to sustain an economic profit and leave those in which low prices result in an economic loss. Prices also direct existing supplies of goods to the buyers who value them most (the rationing function).
>
> Industries in which firms earn a positive economic profit tend to attract new firms, shifting industry supply to the right. Firms tend to leave industries in which they sustain an economic loss, shifting supply curves to the left. In each case, the supply movements continue until economic profit reaches zero. In long-run equilibrium, the value of the last unit produced to buyers is equal to its marginal cost of production, leaving no possibility for additional mutually beneficial transactions.

ECONOMIC RENT VERSUS ECONOMIC PROFIT

Microsoft cofounder Bill Gates is one of the wealthiest people on the planet, largely because the problem of compatibility prevents rival suppliers from competing effectively in the many software markets dominated by his company. Yet numerous people have become fabulously rich even in markets with no conspicuous barriers to entry. If market forces push economic profit toward zero, how can that happen?

economic rent that part of the payment for a factor of production that exceeds the owner's reservation price, the price below which the owner would not supply the factor

The answer to this question hinges on the distinction between economic profit and **economic rent**. Most people think of rent as the payment they make to a landlord or the supplier of a dorm refrigerator, but the term *economic rent* has a different meaning. Economic rent is that portion of the payment for an input that is above the supplier's reservation price for that input. Suppose, for example, that a landowner's reservation price for an acre of land is $100 per year. That is, suppose he would be willing to lease it to a farmer as long as he received an annual payment of at least $100, but for less than that amount he would rather leave it fallow. If a farmer gives him an annual payment not of $100 but of $1,000, the landowner's economic rent from that payment will be $900 per year.

Economic profit is like economic rent in that it, too, may be seen as the difference between what someone is paid (the business owner's total revenue) and her reservation price for remaining in business (the sum of all her costs, explicit and implicit). But whereas competition pushes economic profit toward zero, it has no such effect on the economic rent for inputs that cannot be replicated easily. For example, although the lease payments for land may remain substantially above the landowner's reservation price, year in and year out, new land cannot come onto the market to reduce or eliminate the economic rent through competition. There is, after all, only so much land to be had.

As the following example illustrates, economic rent can accrue to people as well as land.

EXAMPLE 6.6   **Economic Rent**

How much economic rent will a talented chef get?

A community has 100 restaurants, 99 of which employ chefs of normal ability at a salary of $30,000 per year, the same as the amount they could earn in other occupations that are equally attractive to them. But the 100th restaurant has an unusually talented chef. Because of her reputation, diners are willing to pay 50 percent more for the meals she cooks than for those prepared by ordinary chefs. Owners of the 99 restaurants with ordinary chefs each collect $300,000 per year in revenue, which is just enough to ensure that each earns exactly a normal profit. If the talented chef's opportunities outside the restaurant industry are the same as those of ordinary chefs, how much will she be paid by her employer at equilibrium? How much of her pay will be economic rent? How much economic profit will her employer earn?

Because diners are willing to pay 50 percent more for meals cooked by the talented chef, the owner who hires her will take in total receipts not of $300,000 per year but of $450,000. In the long run, competition should ensure that the talented chef's total pay each year will be $180,000 per year, the sum of the $30,000 that ordinary chefs get and the $150,000 in extra revenues for which she is solely responsible. Since the talented chef's reservation price is the amount she could earn outside the restaurant industry—by assumption, $30,000 per year, the same as for ordinary chefs—her economic rent is $150,000 per year. The economic profit of the owner who hires her will be exactly zero.

Since the talented chef's opportunities outside the restaurant industry are no better than an ordinary chef's, why is it necessary to pay the talented chef so much? Suppose her employer were to pay her only $60,000, which they both would consider a generous salary since it is twice what ordinary chefs earn. The employer would then earn an economic profit of $120,000 per year since his annual revenue would be $150,000 more than that of ordinary restaurants, but his costs would be only $30,000 more.

But this economic profit would create an opportunity for the owner of some other restaurant to bid the talented chef away. For example, if the owner of a competing restaurant were to hire the talented chef at a salary of $70,000, the chef would be $10,000 per year better off and the rival owner would earn an economic profit of $110,000 per year, rather than his current economic profit of zero. Furthermore, if the talented chef is the sole reason that a restaurant earns a positive economic profit, the bidding for that chef should continue as long as any economic profit remains. Some other owner will pay her $80,000, still another $90,000, and so on. Equilibrium will be reached only when the talented chef's salary has been bid up to the point that no further economic profit remains—in our example, at an annual paycheck of $180,000.

This bidding process assumes, of course, that the reason for the chef's superior performance is that she possesses some personal talent that cannot be copied. If instead it were the result of, say, training at a culinary institute in France, then her privileged position would erode over time, as other chefs sought similar training.

RECAP ↑

ECONOMIC RENT VERSUS ECONOMIC PROFIT

Economic rent is the amount by which the payment to a factor of production exceeds the supplier's reservation price. Unlike economic profit, which is driven toward zero by competition, economic rent may persist for extended periods, especially in the case of factors with special talents that cannot easily be duplicated.

THE DISTINCTION BETWEEN AN EQUILIBRIUM AND A SOCIAL OPTIMUM

When a market reaches equilibrium, no further opportunities for gain are available to individuals. One implication is that the market prices of resources that people own will eventually reflect their economic value. (As we will see in later chapters, the same cannot be said of resources that are not owned by anyone, such as fish in international waters.)

Note carefully, however, that these observations don't imply that there are *never* any valuable opportunities to exploit. For example, the story is told of two economists on their way to lunch when they spot what appears to be a $100 bill lying on the sidewalk. When the younger economist stoops to pick up the bill, his older colleague restrains him, saying, "That can't be a $100 bill." "Why not?" asks the younger colleague. "If it were, someone would have picked it up by now," the older economist replies.

The tendency for people to be quick to exploit profit opportunities doesn't mean that there *never* are any unexploited opportunities, but that there are none when the market is *in equilibrium*. Occasionally a $100 bill does lie on the sidewalk, and the person who first spots it and picks it up gains a windfall. Likewise, when a company's earnings prospects improve, *somebody* must be the first to recognize the opportunity, and that person can make a lot of money by purchasing the stock quickly.

Still, the observation that good opportunities tend to be snatched up quickly is important. It tells us, in effect, that there are only three ways to earn a big payoff: to work especially hard; to have some unusual skill, talent, or training; or simply to be lucky. The person who finds a big bill on the sidewalk is lucky, as are many of the investors whose stocks perform better than average. Other investors whose stocks do well achieve their gains through hard work or special talent. For example, the legendary investor Warren Buffett, whose portfolio has grown in value at almost three times the stock market average for the last 40 years, spends long hours studying annual financial reports and has a remarkably keen eye for the telling detail. Thousands of others work just as hard yet fail to beat the market averages.

It is important to stress, however, that a market being in equilibrium implies only that no additional opportunities are available *to individuals*. It does not imply that the resulting allocation is necessarily best from the point of view of society as a whole.

KEY TERMS

accounting profit
allocative function of price
barrier to entry
economic loss

economic profit (or excess profit)
economic rent
efficient (or Pareto efficient)
explicit costs

implicit costs
invisible hand theory
normal profit
rationing function of price

REVIEW QUESTIONS

1. How can a business owner who earns $10 million per year from his business credibly claim to earn zero economic profit? *(LO1)*

2. Why do most cities in the United States now have more radios but fewer radio repair shops than they did in 1960? *(LO2)*

3. Why do market forces drive economic profit but not economic rent toward zero? *(LO3)*

4. Why do economists emphasize efficiency as an important goal of public policy? *(LO4, LO5)*

5. You are a senator considering how to vote on a policy that would increase the economic surplus of workers by $100 million per year but reduce the economic surplus of retirees by $1 million per year. What additional measure might you combine with the policy to ensure that the overall result is a better outcome for everyone? *(LO6)*

PROBLEMS

connect

1. A perfectly competitive firm is observed to make zero economic profit. This implies that its: *(LO1)*
   a. Total revenue is equal to the sum of all its explicit and implicit costs.
   b. Marginal revenue is equal to its marginal cost.
   c. Average revenue is equal to its marginal cost.
   d. Average total cost is equal to its marginal cost.
   e. None of the above is correct.

2. True or false: Explain why the following statements are true or false: *(LO1–LO5)*
   a. The economic maxim "There's no cash on the table" means that there are never any unexploited economic opportunities.
   b. Firms in competitive environments make no accounting profit when the market is in long-run equilibrium.
   c. Firms that can introduce cost-saving innovations can make an economic profit in the short run.

3. John Jones owns and manages a café in Collegetown whose annual revenue is $5,000. Annual expenses are as follows: *(LO1, LO2)*

Labor	$2,000
Food and drink	500
Electricity	100
Vehicle lease	150
Rent	500
Interest on loan for equipment	1,000

   a. Calculate John's annual accounting profit.
   b. John could earn $1,000 per year as a recycler of aluminum cans. However, he prefers to run the café. In fact, he would be willing to pay up to $275 per year to run the café rather than to recycle. Is the café making an economic profit? Should John stay in the café business? Explain.

4. Refer to Problem 3. *(LO2, LO3)*
   a. Suppose the café's revenues and expenses remain the same, but recyclers' earnings rise to $1,100 per year. Is the café still making an economic profit? Explain.
   b. Suppose John had not had to get a $10,000 loan at an annual interest rate of 10 percent to buy equipment, but instead had invested $10,000 of his own money in equipment. How would your answers to 3a and 3b change?
   c. If John can earn $1,000 a year as a recycler, and he likes recycling just as well as running the café, how much additional revenue would the café have to collect each year to earn a normal profit?

5. Explain carefully why, in the absence of a patent, a technical innovation invented and pioneered in one tofu factory will cause the supply curve for the entire tofu industry to shift to the right. What will finally halt the rightward shift? *(LO2)*

6. The city of New Orleans has 200 advertising companies, 199 of which employ designers of normal ability at a salary of $100,000 a year. Paying this salary, each

of the 199 firms makes a normal profit on $500,000 in revenue. However, the 200th company employs Janus Jacobs, an unusually talented designer. This company collects $1,000,000 in revenues because of Jacobs's talent. *(LO3)*

a. How much will Jacobs earn? What proportion of her annual salary will be economic rent?

b. Why won't the advertising company for which Jacobs works be able to earn an economic profit?

7. Unskilled workers in a poor cotton-growing region must choose between working in a factory for $6,000 a year and being a tenant cotton farmer. One farmer can work a 120-acre farm, which rents for $10,000 a year. Such farms yield $20,000 worth of cotton each year. The total nonlabor cost of producing and marketing the cotton is $4,000 a year. A local politician whose motto is "working people come first" has promised that if he is elected, his administration will fund a fertilizer, irrigation, and marketing scheme that will triple cotton yields on tenant farms at no charge to tenant farmers. *(LO3)*

a. If the market price of cotton would be unaffected by this policy and no new jobs would be created in the cotton-growing industry, how would the project affect the incomes of tenant farmers in the short run? In the long run?

b. Who would reap the benefit of the scheme in the long run? How much would they gain each year?

8. The town of Wells has 50 restaurants, 49 of which employ chefs of average ability, who earn $200 per week, which is the usual market price for a chef. Paying this salary, each of these 49 restaurants makes normal profit and collects $1,000 per week in total revenue. The 50th restaurant employs an unusually talented chef, and collects $1,500 per week in total revenue because consumers are willing to pay more for the meals he cooks. This chef's weekly salary will be: *(LO3)*

a. $500 per week.
b. $200 per week.
c. $700 per week.
d. $1,500 per week.
e. None of the above.

9. Arguing that many senior citizens have difficulty paying their electric bills, regulators have ordered an electric utility company to charge seniors half the rate charged to other customers for each kilowatt-hour of power they use. The normal rates closely mirror the cost of providing power. *(LO6)*

a. What effect will this have on the seniors' decisions about whether to leave their porch lights on all night?

b. What effect will the new regulation have on total economic surplus?

10. In the preceding problem, how might regulators have tried to address their policy concern in a more efficient way? *(LO6)*

ANSWERS TO CONCEPT CHECKS

6.1 As shown in the table below, Pudge's accounting profit is now $10,000, the difference between his $20,000 annual revenue and his $10,000-per-year payment for land, equipment, and supplies. His economic profit is that amount minus the opportunity cost of his labor—again, the $11,000 per year he could have earned as a store manager. So Pudge is now earning a negative economic profit, −$1,000 per year. As before, his normal profit is the $11,000-per-year opportunity cost of his labor. Although an accountant would say Pudge is making an annual profit of $10,000, that amount is less than a normal profit for his activity. An economist would therefore say that he is making an economic loss of $1,000 per year. Since Pudge likes the two jobs equally well, he will be better off by $1,000 per year if he leaves farming to become a manager. *(LO1)*

Total revenue ($/year)	Explicit costs ($/year)	Implicit costs ($/year)	Accounting profit (= total revenue − explicit costs) ($/year)	Economic profit (= total revenue − explicit costs − implicit costs) ($/year)	Normal profit (= implicit costs) ($/year)
20,000	10,000	11,000	10,000	−1,000	11,000

6.2 If each lane did not move at about the same pace, any driver in a slower lane could reduce his travel time by simply switching to a faster one. People will exploit these opportunities until each lane moves at about the same pace. *(LO2)*

6.3 At a price of 50 cents per gallon, there is excess demand of 4,000 gallons per day. Suppose a seller produces an extra gallon of milk (marginal cost = 50 cents) and sells it to the buyer who values it most (reservation price = $2.50) for $1.50. Both buyer and seller will gain additional economic surplus of $1, and no other buyers or sellers will be hurt by the transaction. *(LO5)*

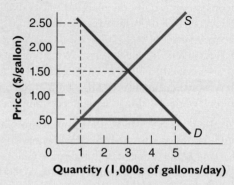

7

Monopoly, Oligopoly, and Monopolistic Competition

Some years ago, schoolchildren around the country became obsessed with the game of Magic: The Gathering. To play, you need a deck of Magic Cards, available only from the creators of the game. But unlike ordinary playing cards, which can be bought in most stores for only a dollar or two, a deck of Magic Cards sells for upward of $20. And since Magic Cards cost no more to manufacture than ordinary playing cards, their producer earns an enormous economic profit.

In a perfectly competitive market, entrepreneurs would see this economic profit as cash on the table. It would entice them to offer Magic Cards at slightly lower prices so that eventually the cards would sell for roughly their cost of production, just as ordinary playing cards do. But Magic Cards have been on the market for years now, and that hasn't happened. The reason is that the cards are copyrighted, which means the government has granted the creators of the game an exclusive license to sell them.

The holder of a copyright is an example of an *imperfectly competitive firm,* or **price setter**, that is, a firm with at least some latitude to set its own price. The competitive firm, by contrast, is a price taker, a firm with no influence over the price of its product.

Our focus in this chapter will be on the ways in which markets served by imperfectly competitive firms differ from those served by perfectly competitive firms. One salient difference is the imperfectly competitive firm's ability, under certain circumstances, to charge more than its cost of production. But if the producer of Magic Cards could charge any price it wished, why does it charge only $20? Why not $100, or even $1,000? We'll see that even though such a company may be the only seller of its product, its pricing freedom is far from absolute. We'll also see how some imperfectly competitive firms manage to earn an economic profit, even in the long run, and even without government protections like copyright. And we'll explore why Adam Smith's invisible hand is less in evidence in a world served by imperfectly competitive firms.

TABLE 7.1
Costs for Two Video Game Publishers (a)

	Nintendo	Sony Computer Entertainment
Annual production	1,000,000	1,200,000
Fixed cost	$200,000	$200,000
Variable cost	$800,000	$960,000
Total cost	$1,000,000	$1,160,000
Average total cost per game	$1.00	$0.97

In the next example, note how the picture changes when fixed cost looms large relative to marginal cost.

EXAMPLE 7.2   **Economies of Scale—Large Fixed Cost**

Two video game publishers, Nintendo and Sony Computer Entertainment, each have fixed costs of $10,000,000 and marginal costs of $0.20 per video game. If Nintendo produces 1 million units per year and Sony produces 1.2 million, how much lower will Sony's average total cost be?

The relevant cost categories for the two firms are now summarized in Table 7.2. The bottom row shows that Sony enjoys a $1.67 average total cost advantage over Nintendo, substantially larger than in the previous example.

If the video games the two firms produce are essentially similar, the fact that Sony can charge significantly lower prices and still cover its costs should enable it to attract customers away from Nintendo. As more and more of the market goes to Sony, its cost advantage will become self-reinforcing. Table 7.3 shows how a shift of 500,000 units from Nintendo to Sony would cause Nintendo's average total cost to rise to $20.20 per unit, while Sony's average total cost would fall to $6.08 per unit. The fact that a firm cannot long survive at such a severe disadvantage explains why the video game market is served now by only a small number of firms.

TABLE 7.2
Costs for Two Video Game Publishers (b)

	Nintendo	Sony Computer Entertainment
Annual production	1,000,000	1,200,000
Fixed cost	$10,000,000	$10,000,000
Variable cost	$200,000	$240,000
Total cost	$10,200,000	$10,240,000
Average total cost per game	$10.20	$8.53

TABLE 7.3
Costs for Two Video Game Publishers (c)

	Nintendo	Sony Computer Entertainment
Annual production	500,000	1,700,000
Fixed cost	$10,000,000	$10,000,000
Variable cost	$100,000	$340,000
Total cost	$10,100,000	$10,340,000
Average total cost per game	$20.20	$6.08

CONCEPT CHECK 7.1

How big will Sony's unit cost advantage be if it sells 2,000,000 units per year, while Nintendo sells only 200,000?

An important worldwide economic trend during recent decades is that an increasing share of the value embodied in the goods and services we buy stems from fixed investment in research and development. For example, in 1984 some 80 percent of the cost of a computer was in its hardware (which has relatively high marginal cost); the remaining 20 percent was in its software. But by 1990 those proportions were reversed. Fixed cost now accounts for about 85 percent of total costs in the computer software industry, whose products are included in a growing share of ordinary manufactured goods.

The Economic Naturalist 7.1

Why does Intel sell the overwhelming majority of all microprocessors used in personal computers?

The fixed investment required to produce a new leading-edge microprocessor such as the Intel Pentium chip currently runs upward of $2 billion. But once the chip has been designed and the manufacturing facility built, the marginal cost of producing each chip is only pennies. This cost pattern explains why Intel currently sells more than 80 percent of all microprocessors.

As fixed cost becomes more and more important, the perfectly competitive pattern of many small firms, each producing only a small share of its industry's total output, becomes less common. For this reason, we must develop a clear sense of how the behavior of firms with market power differs from that of the perfectly competitive firm.

Roz Chast/The New Yorker Collection/ © The Cartoon Bank

> **RECAP** ↑
>
> **ECONOMIES OF SCALE AND THE IMPORTANCE OF START-UP COSTS**
>
> Research, design, engineering, and other fixed costs account for an increasingly large share of all costs required to bring products successfully to market. For products with large fixed costs, marginal cost is lower, often substantially, than average total cost, and average total cost declines, often sharply, as output grows. This cost pattern explains why many industries are dominated by either a single firm or a small number of firms.

PROFIT MAXIMIZATION FOR THE MONOPOLIST

Regardless of whether a firm is a price taker or a price setter, economists assume that its basic goal is to maximize its profit. In both cases, the firm expands output as long as the benefit of doing so exceeds the cost. Further, the calculation of marginal cost is also the same for the monopolist as for the perfectly competitive firm.

The profit-maximizing decision for a monopolist differs from that of a perfectly competitive firm when we look at the benefits of expanding output. For both the perfectly competitive firm and the monopolist, the marginal benefit of expanding output is the additional revenue the firm will receive if it sells one additional unit of output. In both cases, this marginal benefit is called the firm's **marginal revenue**. For the perfectly competitive firm, marginal revenue is exactly equal to the market price of the product. If that price is $6, for example, then the marginal benefit of selling an extra unit is exactly $6.

marginal revenue the change in a firm's total revenue that results from a one-unit change in output

Marginal Revenue for the Monopolist

The situation is different for a monopolist. *To a monopolist, the marginal benefit of selling an additional unit is strictly less than the market price.* As the following discussion will make clear, the reason is that while the perfectly competitive firm can sell as many

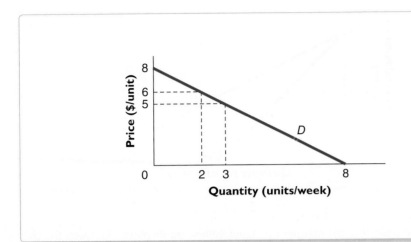

FIGURE 7.3

The Monopolist's Benefit from Selling an Additional Unit.
The monopolist shown receives $12 per week in total revenue by selling 2 units per week at a price of $6 each. This monopolist could earn $15 per week by selling 3 units per week at a price of $5 each. In that case, the benefit from selling the third unit would be $15 − $12 = $3, less than its selling price of $5.

units as it wishes at the market price, the monopolist can sell an additional unit only if it cuts the price—and it must do so not just for the additional unit but for the units it is currently selling.

Suppose, for example, that a monopolist with the demand curve shown in Figure 7.3 is currently selling 2 units of output at a price of $6 per unit. What would be its marginal revenue from selling an additional unit?

This monopolist's total revenue from the sale of 2 units per week is ($6 per unit) (2 units per week) = $12 per week. Its total revenue from the sale of 3 units per week would be $15 per week. The difference—$3 per week—is the marginal revenue from the sale of the third unit each week. Note that this amount is not only smaller than the original price ($6) but smaller than the new price ($5) as well.

CONCEPT CHECK 7.2

Calculate marginal revenue for the monopolist in Figure 7.3 as it expands output from 3 to 4 units per week, and then from 4 to 5 units per week.

For the monopolist whose demand curve is shown in Figure 7.3, a sequence of increases in output—from 2 to 3, from 3 to 4, and from 4 to 5—will yield marginal revenue of $3, $1, and −$1, respectively. We display these results in tabular form in Table 7.4.

TABLE 7.4
Marginal Revenue for a Monopolist ($ per unit)

Quantity	Marginal revenue
2	
	3
3	
	1
4	
	− 1
5	

FIGURE 7.4

Marginal Revenue in Graphical Form.

Because a monopolist must cut price to sell an extra unit, not only for the extra unit sold but also for all existing units, marginal revenue from the sale of the extra unit is less than its selling price.

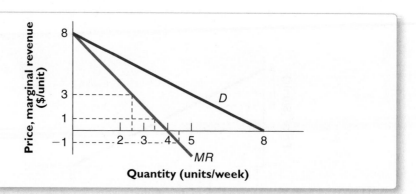

Note in the table that the marginal revenue values are displayed between the two quantity figures to which they correspond. For example, when the firm expanded its output from 2 units per week to 3, its marginal revenue was $3 per unit. Strictly speaking, this marginal revenue corresponds to neither quantity but to the movement between those quantities, hence its placement in the table. Likewise, in moving from 3 to 4 units per week, the firm earned marginal revenue of $1 per unit, so that figure is placed midway between the quantities of 3 and 4, and so on.

To graph marginal revenue as a function of quantity, we would plot the marginal revenue for the movement from 2 to 3 units of output per week ($3) at a quantity value of 2.5, because 2.5 lies midway between 2 and 3. Similarly, we would plot the marginal revenue for the movement from 3 to 4 units per week ($1) at a quantity of 3.5 units per week, and the marginal revenue for the movement from 4 to 5 units per week ($-$1$) at a quantity of 4.5. The resulting marginal revenue curve, *MR,* is shown in Figure 7.4.

More generally, consider a monopolist with a straight-line demand curve whose vertical intercept is a and whose horizontal intercept is Q_0, as shown in Figure 7.5. This monopolist's marginal revenue curve also will have a vertical intercept of a, and it will be twice as steep as the demand curve. Thus, its horizontal intercept will be not Q_0, but $Q_0/2$, as shown in Figure 7.5.

Marginal revenue curves also can be expressed algebraically. If the formula for the monopolist's demand curve is $P = a - bQ$, then the formula for its marginal revenue curve will be $MR = a - 2bQ$. If you have had calculus, this relationship is easy to derive,[2] but even without calculus you can verify it by working through a few numerical examples. First, translate the formula for the demand curve into a diagram, and then

FIGURE 7.5

The Marginal Revenue Curve for a Monopolist with a Straight-Line Demand Curve.

For a monopolist with the demand curve shown, the corresponding marginal revenue curve has the same vertical intercept as the demand curve, and a horizontal intercept only half as large as that of the demand curve.

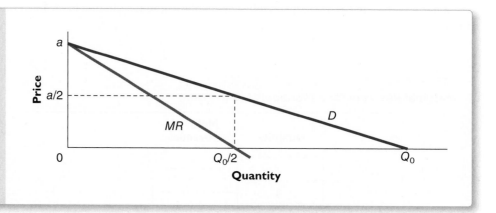

[2]For those who have had an introductory course in calculus, marginal revenue can be expressed as the derivative of total revenue with respect to output. If $P = a - bQ$, then total revenue will be given by $TR = PQ = aQ - bQ_2$, which means that $MR = dTR/dQ = a - 2bQ$.

construct the corresponding marginal revenue curve graphically. Reading from the graph, write the formula for that marginal revenue curve.

The Monopolist's Profit-Maximizing Decision Rule

Having derived the monopolist's marginal revenue curve, we are now in a position to describe how the monopolist chooses the output level that maximizes profit. As in the case of the perfectly competitive firm, the Cost-Benefit Principle says that the monopolist should continue to expand output as long as the gain from doing so exceeds the cost. At the current level of output, the benefit from expanding output is the marginal revenue value that corresponds to that output level. The cost of expanding output is the marginal cost at that level of output. Whenever marginal revenue exceeds marginal cost, the firm should expand. Conversely, whenever marginal revenue falls short of marginal cost, the firm should reduce its output. *Profit is maximized at the level of output for which marginal revenue precisely equals marginal cost.*

   When the monopolist's profit-maximizing rule is stated in this way, we can see that the perfectly competitive firm's rule is actually a special case of the monopolist's rule. When the perfectly competitive firm expands output by one unit, its marginal revenue exactly equals the product's market price (because the perfectly competitive firm can expand sales by a unit without having to cut the price of existing units). So when the perfectly competitive firm equates price with marginal cost, it is also equating marginal revenue with marginal cost. *Thus, the only significant difference between the two cases concerns the calculation of marginal revenue.*

EXAMPLE 7.3   Marginal Revenue

What is the monopolist's profit-maximizing output level?

Consider a monopolist with the demand and marginal cost curves shown in Figure 7.6. If this firm is currently producing 12 units per week, should it expand or contract production? What is the profit-maximizing level of output?

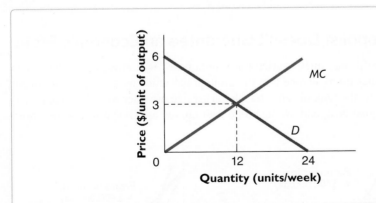

FIGURE 7.6

The Demand and Marginal Cost Curves for a Monopolist.

At the current output level of 12 units per week, price equals marginal cost. Since the monopolist's price is always greater than marginal revenue, marginal revenue must be less than marginal cost, which means this monopolist should produce less.

   In Figure 7.7, we begin by constructing the marginal revenue curve that corresponds to the monopolist's demand curve. It has the same vertical intercept as the demand curve, and its horizontal intercept is half as large. Note that the monopolist's marginal revenue at 12 units per week is zero, which is clearly less than its marginal cost of $3 per unit. This monopolist will therefore earn a higher profit by contracting production until marginal revenue equals marginal cost, which occurs at an output level of 8 units per week. At this profit-maximizing output level, the firm will charge $4 per unit, the price that corresponds to 8 units per week on the demand curve.

FIGURE 7.7

The Monopolist's Profit-Maximizing Output Level.

This monopolist maximizes profit by selling 8 units per week, the output level at which marginal revenue equals marginal cost. The profit-maximizing price is $4 per unit, the price that corresponds to the profit-maximizing quantity on the demand curve.

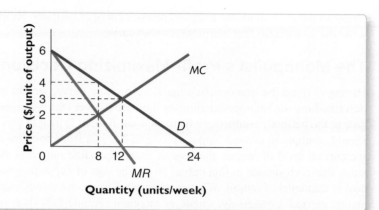

CONCEPT CHECK 7.3

For the monopolist with the demand and marginal cost curves shown, find the profit-maximizing price and level of output.

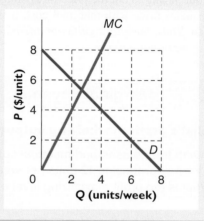

Being a Monopolist Doesn't Guarantee an Economic Profit

The fact that the profit-maximizing price for a monopolist will always be greater than marginal cost provides no assurance that the monopolist will earn an economic profit. Consider, for example, the long-distance telephone service provider whose demand, marginal revenue, marginal cost, and average total cost curves are shown in Figure 7.8(a).

FIGURE 7.8

Even a Monopolist May Suffer an Economic Loss.

The monopolist in (a) maximizes its profit by selling 20 million minutes per day of calls but suffers an economic loss of $400,000 per day in the process. Because the profit-maximizing price of the monopolist in (b) exceeds *ATC*, this monopolist earns an economic profit.

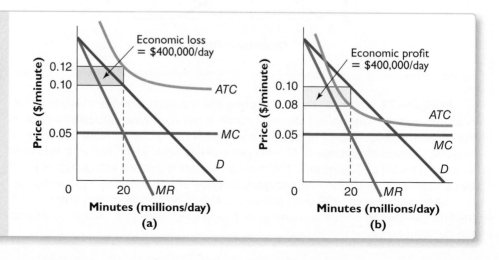

This monopolist maximizes its daily profit by selling 20 million minutes per day of calls at a price of $0.10 per minute. At that quantity, $MR = MC$, yet price is $0.02 per minute less than the company's average total cost of $0.12 per minute. As a result, the company sustains an economic loss of $0.02 per minute on all calls provided, or a total loss of ($0.02 per minute)(20,000,000 minutes per day) = $400,000 per day.

Recall that profit is the difference between a firm's total revenue ($P \times Q$) and its total cost. And because total cost is equal to average total cost times quantity ($ATC \times Q$), the firm's profit is equal to $P \times Q - ATC \times Q = (P - ATC) \times Q$. This observation suggests a convenient way to express profit graphically, as in Figure 7.8. When ATC is greater than P, as in Figure 7.8(a), the firm earns an economic loss, shown by the pink shaded rectangle. When P is greater than ATC, as in Figure 7.8(b), it earns an economic profit, shown by the blue shaded rectangle.

The monopolist in Figure 7.8(a) suffered a loss because its profit-maximizing price was lower than its ATC. If the monopolist's profit-maximizing price exceeds its average total cost, however, the company will, of course, earn an economic profit. Consider, for example, the long-distance provider shown in Figure 7.8(b). This firm has the same demand, marginal revenue, and marginal cost curves as the firm shown in Figure 7.8(a). But because the firm in (b) has lower fixed costs, its ATC curve is lower at every level of output than the ATC curve in (a). At the profit-maximizing price of $0.10 per minute, the firm in Figure 7.8(b) earns an economic profit of $0.02 per minute, for a total economic profit of $400,000 per day.

> **RECAP** ↑
>
> **PROFIT MAXIMIZATION FOR THE MONOPOLIST**
>
> Both the perfectly competitive firm and the monopolist maximize profit by choosing the output level at which marginal revenue equals marginal cost. But whereas marginal revenue equals the market price for the perfectly competitive firm, it is always less than the market price for the monopolist. A monopolist will earn an economic profit only if price exceeds average total cost at the profit-maximizing level of output.

WHY THE INVISIBLE HAND BREAKS DOWN UNDER MONOPOLY

In our discussion of equilibrium in perfectly competitive markets in the chapter *Efficiency, Exchange, and the Invisible Hand in Action*, we saw conditions under which the self-serving pursuits of consumers and firms were consistent with the broader interests of society as a whole. Let's explore whether the same conclusion holds true for the case of imperfectly competitive firms.

Consider the monopolist in Figures 7.6 and 7.7. Is this firm's profit-maximizing output level efficient from society's point of view? For any given level of output, the corresponding price on the demand curve indicates the amount buyers would be willing to pay for an additional unit of output. When the monopolist is producing 8 units per week, the marginal benefit to society of an additional unit of output is thus $4 (see Figure 7.7). And since the marginal cost of an additional unit at that output level is only $2 (again, see Figure 7.7), society would gain a net benefit of $2 per unit if the monopolist were to expand production by one unit above the profit-maximizing level. Because this economic surplus is not realized, the profit-maximizing monopolist is socially inefficient.

Recall that the existence of inefficiency means that the economic pie is smaller than it might be. If that is so, why doesn't the monopolist simply expand production? The answer is that the monopolist would gladly do so, if only there were some way to maintain the price of existing units and cut the price of only the extra units. As a practical matter, however, that is not always possible.

Now, let's look at this situation from a different angle. For the market served by this monopolist, what *is* the socially efficient level of output?

At any output level, the cost to society of an additional unit of output is the same as the cost to the monopolist, namely, the amount shown on the monopolist's marginal cost curve. The marginal benefit *to society* (not to the monopolist) of an extra unit of output is simply the amount people are willing to pay for it, which is the amount shown on the monopolist's demand curve. To achieve social efficiency, the monopolist should expand production until the marginal benefit to society equals the marginal cost, which in this case occurs at a level of 12 units per week. (Again, see Figure 7.7.) Social efficiency is thus achieved at the output level at which the market demand curve intersects the monopolist's marginal cost curve.

For a monopolist, profit maximization occurs when marginal cost equals marginal revenue. Since the monopolist's marginal revenue is always less than price, the monopolist's profit-maximizing output level is always below the socially efficient level. Under perfect competition, by contrast, profit maximization occurs when marginal cost equals the market price—the same criterion that must be satisfied for social efficiency. This difference explains why the invisible hand of the market is less evident in monopoly markets than in perfectly competitive markets.

If perfect competition is socially efficient and monopoly is not, why isn't monopoly against the law? Congress has, in fact, tried to limit the extent of monopoly through antitrust laws. But even the most enthusiastic proponents of those laws recognize the limited usefulness of the legislative approach since the alternatives to monopoly often entail problems of their own.

Suppose, for example, that a monopoly results from a patent that prevents all but one firm from manufacturing some highly valued product. Would society be better off without patents? Probably not, because eliminating such protection would discourage innovation. Virtually all successful industrial nations grant some form of patent protection, which gives firms a chance to recover the research and development costs without which new products would seldom reach the market.

Or suppose that the market in question is a natural monopoly—one that, because of economies of scale, is most cheaply served by a single firm. Would society do better to require this market to be served by many small firms, each with significantly higher average costs of production? Such a requirement would merely replace one form of inefficiency with another.

In short, we live in an imperfect world. Monopoly is socially inefficient, and that, needless to say, is bad. But the alternatives to monopoly aren't perfect either.

RECAP ↑

WHY THE INVISIBLE HAND BREAKS DOWN UNDER MONOPOLY

The monopolist maximizes profit at the output level for which marginal revenue equals marginal cost. Because its profit-maximizing price exceeds marginal revenue, and hence also marginal cost, the benefit to society of the last unit produced (the market price) must be greater than the cost of the last unit produced (the marginal cost). So the output level for an industry served by a profit-maximizing monopolist is smaller than the socially optimal level of output.

USING DISCOUNTS TO EXPAND THE MARKET

The source of inefficiency in monopoly markets is the fact that the benefit to the monopolist of expanding output is less than the corresponding benefit to society. From the monopolist's point of view, the price reduction the firm must grant existing buyers to expand output is a loss. But from the point of view of those buyers, each dollar of price reduction is a gain—one dollar more in their pockets.

Note the tension in this situation, which is similar to the tension that exists in all other situations in which the economic pie is smaller than it might otherwise be. When the economic pie grows larger, everyone can have a larger slice. To say that monopoly is inefficient means that steps could be taken to make some people better off without harming others. If people have a healthy regard for their own self-interest, why doesn't someone take those steps? Why, for example, doesn't the monopolist from the earlier examples sell 8 units of output at a price of $4, and then once those buyers are out the door, cut the price for more price-sensitive buyers?

Price Discrimination Defined

Sometimes the monopolist does precisely that. Charging different buyers different prices for the same good or service is a practice known as **price discrimination**. Examples of price discrimination include senior citizens' and children's discounts on movie tickets, supersaver discounts on air travel, and rebate coupons on retail merchandise.

　　Attempts at price discrimination seem to work effectively in some markets, but not in others. Buyers are not stupid, after all; if the monopolist periodically offered a 50 percent discount on the $8 list price, those who were paying $8 might anticipate the next price cut and postpone their purchases to take advantage of it. In some markets, however, buyers may not know, or simply may not take the trouble to find out, how the price they pay compares to the prices paid by other buyers. Alternatively, the monopolist may be in a position to prevent some groups from buying at the discount prices made available to others. In such cases, the monopolist can price-discriminate effectively.

price discrimination the practice of charging different buyers different prices for essentially the same good or service

The Economic Naturalist 7.2

Why do many movie theaters offer discount tickets to students?

Whenever a firm offers a discount, the goal is to target that discount to buyers who would not purchase the product without it. People with low incomes generally have lower reservation prices for movie tickets than people with high incomes. Because students generally have lower disposable incomes than working adults, theater owners can expand their audiences by charging lower prices to students than to adults. Student discounts are one practical way of doing so. Offering student discounts also entails no risk of some people buying the product at a low price and then reselling it to others at a higher price.

Why do students pay lower ticket prices at many movie theaters?

How Price Discrimination Affects Output

In the following examples, we will see how the ability to price-discriminate affects the monopolist's profit-maximizing level of output. First we will consider a baseline case in which the monopolist must charge the same price to every buyer.

EXAMPLE 7.4	Profit Maximization and Opportunity Cost

How many manuscripts should Carla edit?

Carla supplements her income as a teaching assistant by editing term papers for undergraduates. There are eight students per week for whom she might edit, each with a reservation price as given in the following table.

Student	Reservation price
A	$40
B	38
C	36
D	34
E	32
F	30
G	28
H	26

Carla is a profit maximizer. If the opportunity cost of her time to edit each paper is $29 and she must charge the same price to each student, how many papers should she edit? How much economic profit will she make? How much accounting profit?

Table 7.5 summarizes Carla's total and marginal revenue at various output levels. To generate the amounts in the total revenue column, we simply multiplied the corresponding reservation price by the number of students whose reservation prices were at least that high. For example, to edit 4 papers per week (for students *A, B, C,* and *D*), Carla must charge a price no higher than *D*'s reservation price ($34). So her total revenue when she edits 4 papers per week is (4)($34) = $136 per week. Carla should keep expanding the number of students she serves as long as her marginal revenue exceeds the opportunity cost of her time. Marginal

TABLE 7.5
Total and Marginal Revenue from Editing

Student	Reservation price ($ per paper)	Total revenue ($ per week)	Marginal revenue ($ per paper)
A	40	40	40
B	38	76	36
C	36	108	32
D	34	136	28
E	32	160	24
F	30	180	20
G	28	196	16
H	26	208	12

revenue, or the difference in total revenue that results from adding another student, is shown in the last column of Table 7.5.

Note that if Carla were editing 2 papers per week, her marginal revenue from editing a third paper would be $32. Since that amount exceeds her $29 opportunity cost, she should take on the third paper. But since the marginal revenue of taking on a fourth paper would be only $28, Carla should stop at 3 papers per week. The total opportunity cost of the time required to edit the 3 papers is (3)($29) = $87, so Carla's economic profit is $108 − $87 = $21 per week. Since Carla incurs no explicit costs, her accounting profit will be $108 per week.

EXAMPLE 7.5   Social Efficiency

What is the socially efficient number of papers for Carla to edit?

Again, suppose that Carla's opportunity cost of editing is $29 per paper and that she could edit as many as 8 papers per week for students whose reservation prices are again as listed in the following table.

Student	Reservation price
A	$40
B	38
C	36
D	34
E	32
F	30
G	28
H	26

What is the socially efficient number of papers for Carla to edit? If she must charge the same price to each student, what will her economic and accounting profits be if she edits the socially efficient number of papers?

Students A to F are willing to pay more than Carla's opportunity cost, so serving these students is socially efficient. But students G and H are unwilling to pay at least $29 for Carla's services. The socially efficient outcome, therefore, is for Carla to edit 6 papers per week. To attract that number, she must charge a price no higher than $30 per paper. Her total revenue will be (6)($30) = $180 per week, slightly more than her total opportunity cost of (6)($29) = $174 per week. Her economic profit will thus be only $6 per week. Again, because Carla incurs no explicit costs, her accounting profit will be the same as her total revenue, $180 per week.

EXAMPLE 7.6   Price Discrimination

If Carla can price-discriminate, how many papers should she edit?

Suppose Carla is a shrewd judge of human nature. After a moment's conversation with a student, she can discern that student's reservation price. The reservation prices of her potential customers are again as given in the following table. If Carla confronts the same market as before, but can charge students their respective reservation prices, how many papers should she edit, and how much economic and accounting profit will she make?

Student	Reservation price
A	$40
B	38
C	36
D	34
E	32
F	30
G	28
H	26

Carla will edit papers for students A to F and charge each exactly his or her reservation price. Because students G and H have reservation prices below $29, Carla will not edit their papers. Carla's total revenue will be $40 + $38 + $36 + $34 + $32 + $30 = $210 per week, which is also her accounting profit. Her total opportunity cost of editing 6 papers is (6)($29) = $174 per week, so her economic profit will be $210 − $174 = $36 per week, $30 per week more than when she edited six papers but was constrained to charge each customer the same price.

perfectly discriminating monopolist a firm that charges each buyer exactly his or her reservation price

A monopolist who can charge each buyer exactly his or her reservation price is called a **perfectly discriminating monopolist**. Notice that, when Carla was discriminating among customers in this way, her profit-maximizing level of output was exactly the same as the socially efficient level of output: 6 papers per week. With a perfectly discriminating monopoly, there is no loss of efficiency. All buyers who are willing to pay a price high enough to cover marginal cost will be served.

Note that although total economic surplus is maximized by a perfectly discriminating monopolist, consumers would have little reason to celebrate if they found themselves dealing with such a firm. After all, consumer surplus is exactly zero for the perfectly discriminating monopolist. In this instance, total economic surplus and producer surplus are one and the same.

In practice, of course, perfect price discrimination can never occur because no seller knows each and every buyer's precise reservation price. But even if some sellers did know, practical difficulties would stand in the way of their charging a separate price to each buyer. For example, in many markets the seller could not prevent buyers who bought at low prices from reselling to other buyers at higher prices, capturing some of the seller's business in the process. Despite these difficulties, price discrimination is widespread. But it is generally *imperfect price discrimination,* that is, price discrimination in which at least some buyers are charged less than their reservation prices.

The Hurdle Method of Price Discrimination

The profit-maximizing seller's goal is to charge each buyer the highest price that buyer is willing to pay. Two primary obstacles prevent sellers from achieving this goal. First, sellers don't know exactly how much each buyer is willing to pay. And second, they need some means of excluding those who are willing to pay a high price from buying at a low price. These are formidable problems, which no seller can hope to solve completely.

hurdle method of price discrimination the practice by which a seller offers a discount to all buyers who overcome some obstacle

One common method by which sellers achieve a crude solution to both problems is to require buyers to overcome some obstacle to be eligible for a discount price. This method is called the **hurdle method of price discrimination**. For example, the seller might sell a product at a standard list price and offer a rebate to any buyer who takes the trouble to mail in a rebate coupon.

The hurdle method solves both of the seller's problems, provided that buyers with low reservation prices are more willing than others to jump the hurdle. Because a decision to jump the hurdle must satisfy the Cost-Benefit Principle, such a link seems to exist. As noted earlier, buyers with low incomes are more likely than others to have low reservation prices (at least in the case of normal goods). Because of the low opportunity cost of their time, they are more likely than others to take the trouble to send in rebate coupons. Rebate coupons thus target a discount toward those buyers whose reservation prices are low and who therefore might not buy the product otherwise.

A **perfect hurdle** is one that separates buyers precisely according to their reservation prices, and in the process imposes no cost on those who jump the hurdle. With a perfect hurdle, the highest reservation price among buyers who jump the hurdle will be lower than the lowest reservation price among buyers who choose not to jump the hurdle. In practice, perfect hurdles do not exist. Some buyers will always jump the hurdle, even though their reservation prices are high. And hurdles will always exclude at least some buyers with low reservation prices. Even so, many commonly used hurdles do a remarkably good job of targeting discounts to buyers with low reservation prices. In the example that follows, we will assume for convenience that the seller is using a perfect hurdle.

perfect hurdle a threshold that completely segregates buyers whose reservation prices lie above it from others whose reservation prices lie below it, imposing no cost on those who jump the hurdle

EXAMPLE 7.7   Perfect Hurdle

How much should Carla charge for editing if she uses a perfect hurdle?

Suppose Carla again has the opportunity to edit as many as 8 papers per week for the students whose reservation prices are as given in the following table. This time she can offer a rebate coupon that gives a discount to any student who takes the trouble to mail it back to her. Suppose further that students whose reservation prices are at least $36 never mail in the rebate coupons, while those whose reservation prices are below $36 always do so.

Student	Reservation price
A	$40
B	38
C	36
D	34
E	32
F	30
G	28
H	26

If Carla's opportunity cost of editing each paper is again $29, what should her list price be, and what amount should she offer as a rebate? Will her economic profit be larger or smaller than when she lacked the discount option?

The rebate coupon allows Carla to divide her original market into two submarkets in which she can charge two different prices. The first submarket consists of students A, B, and C, whose reservation prices are at least $36 and who therefore will not bother to mail in a rebate coupon. The second submarket consists of students D through H, whose lower reservation prices indicate a willingness to use rebate coupons.

In each submarket, Carla must charge the same price to every buyer, just like an ordinary monopolist. She should therefore keep expanding output in each submarket as long as marginal revenue in that market exceeds her marginal cost. The relevant data for the two submarkets are displayed in Table 7.6.

TABLE 7.6

Price Discrimination with a Perfect Hurdle

Student	Reservation price ($ per paper)	Total revenue ($ per week)	Marginal revenue ($ per paper)
List Price Submarket			
A	40	40	40
B	38	76	36
C	36	108	32
Discount Price Submarket			
D	34	34	34
E	32	64	30
F	30	90	26
G	28	112	22
H	26	130	18

On the basis of the entries in the marginal revenue column for the list price submarket, we see that Carla should serve all three students *(A, B,* and *C)* since marginal revenue for each exceeds $29. Her profit-maximizing price in the list price submarket is $36, the highest price she can charge in that market and still sell her services to students *A, B,* and *C.* For the discount price submarket, marginal revenue exceeds $29 only for the first two students *(D* and *E).* So the profit-maximizing price in this submarket is $32, the highest price Carla can charge and still sell her services to *D* and *E.* (A discount price of $32 means that students who mail in the coupon will receive a rebate of $4 on the $36 list price.)

Note that the rebate offer enables Carla to serve a total of five students per week, compared to only three without the offer. Carla's combined total revenue for the two markets is (3)($36) + 2($32) = $172 per week. Since her opportunity cost is $29 per paper, or a total of (5)($29) = $145 per week, her economic profit is $172 per week − $145 per week = $27 per week, $6 more than when she edited three papers and did not offer the rebate.

CONCEPT CHECK 7.4

In Example 7.7, how much should Carla charge in each submarket if she knows that only those students whose reservation prices are below $34 will use rebate coupons?

Is Price Discrimination a Bad Thing?

We are so conditioned to think of discrimination as bad that we may be tempted to conclude that price discrimination must run counter to the public interest. In the example above, however, both consumer surplus and producer surplus were actually enhanced by the monopolist's use of the hurdle method of price discrimination. To show this, let's compare consumer and producer surpluses when Carla employs the hurdle method to the corresponding values when she charges the same price to all buyers.

When Carla had to charge the same price to every customer, she edited only the papers of students *A, B,* and *C,* each of whom paid a price of $36. We can tell at a glance that the total surplus must be larger under the hurdle method because not only are students *A, B,* and *C* served at the same price ($36), but also students *D* and *E* are now served at a price of $32.

To confirm this intuition, we can calculate the exact amount of the surplus. For any student who hires Carla to edit her paper, consumer surplus is the difference between her reservation price and the price actually paid. In both the single price and discount price examples, student *A*'s consumer surplus is thus $40 − $36 = $4; student *B*'s consumer surplus is $38 − $36 = $2; and student *C*'s consumer surplus is $36 − $36 = 0. Total consumer surplus in the list price submarket is thus $4 + $2 = $6 per week, which is the same as total consumer surplus in the original situation. But now the discount price submarket generates additional consumer surplus. Specifically, student *D* receives $2 per week of consumer surplus since this student's reservation price of $34 is $2 more than the discount price of $32. So total consumer surplus is now $6 + $2 = $8 per week, or $2 per week more than before.

Carla's producer surplus also increases under the hurdle method. For each paper she edits, her producer surplus is the price she charges minus her reservation price ($29). In the single-price case, Carla's surplus was (3)($36 − $29) = $21 per week. When she offers a rebate coupon, she earns the same producer surplus as before from students *A, B,* and *C* and an additional (2)($32 − $29) = $6 per week from students *D* and *E*. Total producer surplus with the discount is thus $21 + $6 = $27 per week. Adding that amount to the total consumer surplus of $8 per week, we get a total economic surplus of $35 per week with the rebate coupons, $8 per week more than without the rebate.

Note, however, that even with the rebate, the final outcome is not socially efficient because Carla does not serve student *F,* even though this student's reservation price of $30 exceeds her opportunity cost of $29. But though the hurdle method is not perfectly efficient, it is still more efficient than charging a single price to all buyers.

Examples of Price Discrimination

Once you grasp the principle behind the hurdle method of price discrimination, you will begin to see examples of it all around you. Next time you visit a grocery, hardware, or appliance store, for instance, notice how many different product promotions include cash rebates. Temporary sales are another illustration of the hurdle method. Most of the time, stores sell most of their merchandise at the "regular" price but periodically offer special sales at a significant discount. The hurdle in this instance is taking the trouble to find out when and where the sales occur and then going to the store during that period. This technique works because buyers who care most about price (mainly, those with low reservation prices) are more likely to monitor advertisements carefully and buy only during sale periods.

To give another example, book publishers typically launch a new book in hardcover at a price from $20 to $30, and a year later they bring out a paperback edition priced between $5 and $15. In this instance, the hurdle involves having to wait the extra year and accepting a slight reduction in the quality of the finished product. People who are strongly concerned about price end up waiting for the paperback edition, while those with high reservation prices usually spring for the hardback.

Or take the example of automobile producers, who typically offer several different models with different trim and accessories. Although GM's actual cost of producing a Cadillac may be only $2,000 more than its cost of producing a Chevrolet, the Cadillac's selling price may be $10,000 to $15,000 higher than the Chevrolet's. Buyers with low reservation prices purchase the Chevrolet, while those with high reservation prices are more likely to choose the Cadillac.

Commercial air carriers have perfected the hurdle method to an extent matched by almost no other seller. Their supersaver fares are often less than half their regular coach fares. To be eligible for these discounts, travelers must purchase their tickets 7 to 21 days in advance and their journey must include a Saturday night stayover. Vacation travelers can more easily satisfy these restrictions than business travelers, whose schedules often change at the last moment and whose trips seldom involve Saturday stayovers. And—no surprise—the business traveler's reservation price tends to be much higher than the vacation traveler's.

Many sellers employ not just one hurdle but several by offering deeper discounts to buyers who jump successively more difficult hurdles. For example, movie producers release their major films to first-run theaters at premium prices, and then several months later to neighborhood theaters at a few dollars less. Still later they make the films available on pay-per-view cable channels, then release them on DVD, and finally permit them to be shown on network television. Each successive hurdle involves waiting a little longer, and in the case of the televised versions, accepting lower quality. These hurdles are remarkably effective in segregating moviegoers according to their reservation prices.

Recall that the efficiency loss from single-price monopoly occurs because to the monopolist, the benefit of expanding output is smaller than the benefit to society as a whole. The hurdle method of price discrimination reduces this loss by giving the monopolist a practical means of cutting prices for price-sensitive buyers only. In general, the more finely the monopolist can partition a market using the hurdle method, the smaller the efficiency loss. Hurdles are not perfect, however, and some degree of efficiency will inevitably be lost.

The Economic Naturalist 7.3

Why might an appliance retailer instruct its clerks to hammer dents into the sides of its stoves and refrigerators?

The Sears "Scratch 'n' Dent Sale" is another example of how retailers use quality differentials to segregate buyers according to their reservation prices. Many Sears stores hold an annual sale in which they display appliances with minor scratches and blemishes in the parking lot at deep discounts. People who don't care much about price are unlikely to turn out for these events, but those with very low reservation prices often get up early to be first in line. Indeed, these sales have proven so popular that it might even be in a retailer's interest to put dents in some of its sale items deliberately.

Would a profit-maximizing appliance retailer ever deliberately damage its own merchandise?

portraits of small children. George, who owns and runs TotsPoses, expects to encounter an average of eight customers per day, each with a reservation price shown in the following table. *(LO4, LO5)*

Customer	Reservation price ($ per photo)
1	50
2	46
3	42
4	38
5	34
6	30
7	26
8	22

a. If the total cost of each photo portrait is $12, how much should George charge if he must charge a single price to all customers? At this price, how many portraits will George produce each day? How much economic profit will he earn?
b. How much consumer surplus is generated each day at this price?
c. What is the socially efficient number of portraits?
d. George is very experienced in the business and knows the reservation price of each of his customers. If he is allowed to charge any price he likes to any consumer, how many portraits will he produce each day? How much economic profit will he earn? (Assume the cost of each photo portrait is still $12.)
e. In this case, how much consumer surplus is generated each day?

8. Refer back to Problem 7 and answer the following questions. *(LO4, LO6)*
a. Suppose George is permitted to charge two prices. He knows that customers with a reservation price above $30 never bother with coupons, whereas those with a reservation price of $30 or less always use them. At what level should George set the list price of a portrait? At what level should he set the discount price? How many photo portraits will he sell at each price?

b. In this case, what is George's economic profit and how much consumer surplus is generated each day?

9. Beth is a second-grader who sells lemonade on a street corner in your neighborhood. Each cup of lemonade costs Beth 20 cents to produce; she has no fixed costs. The reservation prices for the 10 people who walk by Beth's lemonade stand each day are listed in the following table.

Person	Reservation price
1	$1.00
2	$0.90
3	$0.80
4	$0.70
5	$0.60
6	$0.50
7	$0.40
8	$0.30
9	$0.20
10	$0.10

Beth knows the distribution of reservation prices (that is, she knows that one person is willing to pay $1, another $0.90, and so on), but she does not know any specific individual's reservation price. *(LO4, LO6)*
a. Calculate the marginal revenue of selling an additional cup of lemonade. (Start by figuring out the price Beth would charge if she produced only one cup of lemonade, and calculate the total revenue; then find the price Beth would charge if she sold two cups of lemonade; and so on.)
b. What is Beth's profit-maximizing price?
c. At that price, what are Beth's economic profit and total consumer surplus?
d. What price should Beth charge if she wants to maximize total economic surplus?
e. Now suppose Beth can tell the reservation price of each person. What price would she charge each person if she wanted to maximize profit? Compare her profit to the total surplus calculated in 9d.

ANSWERS TO CONCEPT CHECKS

7.1 The relevant cost figures are shown in the following table, which shows that Sony's unit-cost advantage is now $50.20 − $5.20 = $45.00. *(LO3)*

	Nintendo	Sony Computer Entertainment
Annual production	200,000	2,000,000
Fixed cost	$10,000,000	$10,000,000
Variable cost	$40,000	$400,000
Total cost	$10,040,000	$10,400,000
Average total cost per game	$50.20	$5.20

7.2 When the monopolist expands from 3 to 4 units per week, total revenue rises from $15 to $16 per week, which means that the marginal revenue from the sale of the fourth unit is only $1 per week. When the monopolist expands from 4 to 5 units per week, total revenue drops from $16 to $15 per week, which means that the marginal revenue from the sale of the fifth unit is actually negative, or −$1 per week. *(LO4)*

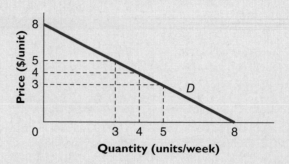

7.3 The profit-maximizing price and quantity are $P^* = \$6$/unit and $Q^* = 2$ units/week. *(LO4)*

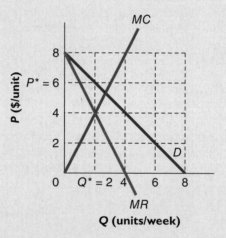

7.4 As the marginal revenue column in the following table shows, Carla should again serve students *A, B,* and *C* in the list price submarket (at a price of $36) and only student *E* in the discount submarket (at a price of $32). *(LO6)*

Student	Reservation price ($ per paper)	Total revenue ($ per week)	Marginal revenue ($ per paper)
List Price Submarket			
A	40	40	40
B	38	76	36
C	36	108	32
D	34	136	28
Discount Price Submarket			
E	32	32	32
F	30	60	28
G	28	84	24
H	26	104	20

8

Games and Strategic Behavior

LEARNING OBJECTIVES

After reading this chapter, you should be able to:

LO1 Describe the three basic elements of a game, how the possible payoffs are summarized, and the effects of dominant and dominated strategy choices.

LO2 Identify and explain the prisoner's dilemma and how it applies to real-world situations.

LO3 Explain games in which the timing of players' choices matters.

LO4 Discuss strategies that enable players to solve commitment problems through material or psychological incentives.

At a Christmas Eve dinner party in 1997, actor Robert DeNiro pulled singer Tony Bennett aside for a moment. "Hey, Tony—there's a film I want you in," DeNiro said. He was referring to the project that became the 1999 Warner Brothers hit comedy *Analyze This,* in which the troubled head of a crime family, played by DeNiro, seeks the counsel of a psychotherapist, played by Billy Crystal. In the script, both the mob boss and his therapist are big fans of Bennett's music.

Bennett heard nothing further about the project for almost a year. Then his son and financial manager, Danny Bennett, got a phone call from Warner Brothers, in which the studio offered Tony $15,000 to sing "Got the World on a String" in the movie's final scene. As Danny described the conversation, " . . . they made a fatal mistake. They told me they had already shot the film. So I'm like: 'Hey, they shot the whole film around Tony being the end gag and they're offering me $15,000?'"[1]

Warner Brothers wound up paying $200,000 for Bennett's performance.

In business negotiations, as in life, timing can be everything. If executives at Warner Brothers had thought the problem through carefully, they would have negotiated with Bennett *before* shooting the movie. At that point, Bennett would have realized that the script could be rewritten if he asked too high a fee. By waiting, studio executives left themselves with no attractive option other than to pay Bennett's price.

The payoff to many actions depends not only on the actions themselves, but also on when they are taken and how they relate to actions taken by others. In previous chapters, economic decision makers confronted an environment that was essentially fixed. This chapter will focus on cases in which people must consider the effect of their behavior on others. For example, an imperfectly competitive firm will want to weigh the likely responses of rivals when deciding whether to cut prices or to increase its advertising budget. Interdependencies of this sort are the rule rather than the exception in economic and social life. To make sense of the world we live in, then, we must take these interdependencies into account.

Our focus previously was on the pure monopolist. In this chapter, we will explore how a few simple principles from the theory of games can help us better understand the

[1]As quoted by Geraldine Fabrikant, "Talking Money with Tony Bennett," *The New York Times,* May 2, 1999, Money & Business, p. 1.

behavior of oligopolists and monopolistic competitors—the two types of imperfectly competitive firms for which strategic interdependencies are most important. Along the way, we also will see how the same principles enable us to answer a variety of interesting questions drawn from everyday social interaction.

USING GAME THEORY TO ANALYZE STRATEGIC DECISIONS

In chess, tennis, or any other game, the payoff to a given move depends on what your opponent does in response. In choosing your move, therefore, you must anticipate your opponent's responses, how you might respond, and what further moves your own response might elicit. Economists and other behavioral scientists have devised the theory of games to analyze situations in which the payoffs to different actors depend on the actions their opponents take.

The Three Elements of a Game

basic elements of a game the players, the strategies available to each player, and the payoffs each player receives for each possible combination of strategies

A game has three **basic elements**: the players, the list of possible actions (or strategies) available to each player, and the payoffs the players receive for each possible combination of strategies. We will use a series of examples to illustrate how these elements combine to form the basis of a theory of behavior.

The first example focuses on an important strategic decision confronting two oligopolists who produce an undifferentiated product and must decide how much to spend on advertising.

EXAMPLE 8.1   **The Cost of Advertising**

Should United Airlines spend more money on advertising?

Suppose that United Airlines and American Airlines are the only air carriers that serve the Chicago–St. Louis market. Each currently earns an economic profit of $6,000 per flight on this route. If United increases its advertising spending in this market by $1,000 per flight, and American spends no more on advertising than it does now, United's profit will rise to $8,000 per flight and American's will fall to $2,000. If both spend $1,000 more on advertising, each will earn an economic profit of $5,500 per flight. These payoffs are symmetric, so that if United spends the same amount on advertising while American increases its spending by $1,000, United's economic profit will fall to $2,000 per flight and American's will rise to $8,000. The payoff structure is also common knowledge—that is, each company knows what the relevant payoffs will be for both parties under each of the possible combinations of choices. If each must decide independently whether to increase spending on advertising, what should United do?

Think of this situation as a game. What are its three elements? The players are the two airlines. Each airline must choose one of two strategies: to raise ad spending by $1,000 or leave it the same. The payoffs are the economic profits that correspond to the four possible scenarios resulting from their choices. One way to summarize the relevant information about this game is to display the players, strategies, and payoffs in the form of a simple table called a **payoff matrix** (see Table 8.1).

payoff matrix a table that describes the payoffs in a game for each possible combination of strategies

Confronted with the payoff matrix in Table 8.1, what should United Airlines do? The essence of strategic thinking is to begin by looking at the situation from the other party's point of view. Suppose United assumes that American will raise its spending on advertising (the left column in Table 8.1). In that case, United's best bet would be to follow suit (the top row in Table 8.1). Why is the top row United's best response when American chooses the left column? United's economic profits, given in the upper-left cell of Table 8.1, will be $5,500, compared to only $2,000 if it keeps spending the same (see the lower-left cell).

TABLE 8.1
The Payoff Matrix for an Advertising Game

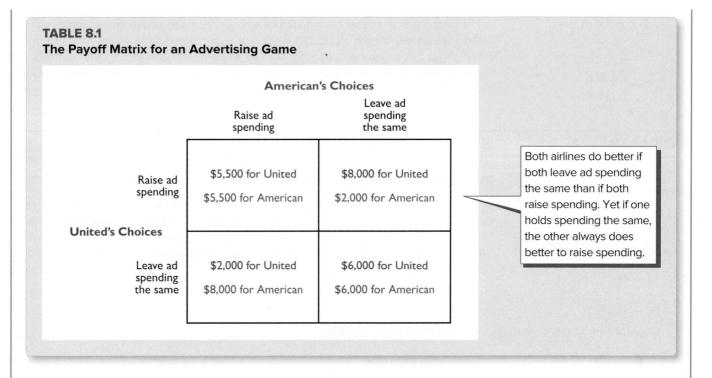

American's Choices

	Raise ad spending	Leave ad spending the same
Raise ad spending	$5,500 for United $5,500 for American	$8,000 for United $2,000 for American
Leave ad spending the same	$2,000 for United $8,000 for American	$6,000 for United $6,000 for American

United's Choices

Both airlines do better if both leave ad spending the same than if both raise spending. Yet if one holds spending the same, the other always does better to raise spending.

Alternatively, suppose United assumes that American will keep ad spending the same (that is, that American will choose the right column in Table 8.1). In that case, United would still do better to increase spending because it would earn $8,000 (the upper-right cell), compared to only $6,000 if it keeps spending the same (the lower-right cell). In this particular game, no matter which strategy American chooses, United will earn a higher economic profit by increasing its spending on advertising. And since this game is perfectly symmetric, a similar conclusion holds for American: No matter which strategy United chooses, American will do better by increasing its spending on ads.

When one player has a strategy that yields a higher payoff no matter which choice the other player makes, that player is said to have a **dominant strategy**. Not all games involve dominant strategies, but both players in this game have one, and that is to increase spending on ads. For both players, to leave ad spending the same is a **dominated strategy**—one that leads to a lower payoff than an alternative choice, regardless of the other player's choice.

Notice, however, that when each player chooses the dominant strategy, the resulting payoffs are smaller than if each had left spending unchanged. When United and American increase their spending on ads, each earns only $5,500 in economic profits, compared to the $6,000 each would have earned without the increase.

dominant strategy one that yields a higher payoff no matter what the other players in a game choose

dominated strategy any other strategy available to a player who has a dominant strategy

Nash Equilibrium

A game is said to be in equilibrium if each player's strategy is the best he or she can choose, given the other players' choices. This definition of equilibrium is sometimes called a **Nash equilibrium**, after the mathematician John Nash, who developed the concept in the early 1950s. Nash was awarded the Nobel Prize in Economics in 1994 for his contributions to game theory.[2] When a game is in equilibrium, no player has any incentive to deviate from his current strategy.

Nash equilibrium any combination of strategy choices in which each player's choice is his or her best choice, given the other players' choices

[2]Nash's life was also the subject of the Academy Award–winning film *A Beautiful Mind*.

If each player in a game has a dominant strategy, as in the advertising example, equilibrium occurs when each player follows that strategy. But even in games in which not every player has a dominant strategy, we can often identify an equilibrium outcome. Consider, for instance, the following variation on the advertising game as illustrated in Example 8.2.

EXAMPLE 8.2 **Nash Equilibrium**

Should American Airlines spend more money on advertising?

Suppose United Airlines and American Airlines are the only carriers that serve the Chicago–St. Louis market. Their payoff matrix for advertising decisions is shown in Table 8.2. Does United have a dominant strategy? Does American? If each firm does the best it can, given the incentives facing the other, what will be the outcome of this game?

TABLE 8.2
Equilibrium When One Player Lacks a Dominant Strategy

American's Choices

	Raise ad spending	Leave ad spending the same
United's Choices Raise ad spending	$3,000 for United / $4,000 for American	$8,000 for United / $3,000 for American
Leave ad spending the same	$4,000 for United / $5,000 for American	$5,000 for United / $2,000 for American

In this game, United lacks a dominant strategy, but American's dominant strategy is to raise its ad spending. Because United can predict that American will choose the left column, United will do best to leave its ad spending the same. Equilibrium occurs in the lower-left cell.

In this game, no matter what United does, American will do better to raise its ad spending, so raising the advertising budget is a dominant strategy for American. United, however, does not have a dominant strategy. If American raises its spending, United will do better to leave its spending unchanged; if American does not raise spending, however, United will do better to spend more. Even though United does not have a dominant strategy, we can examine the players' incentives to predict what is likely to happen in this game. United's managers are assumed to know what the payoff matrix is, so they can predict that American will spend more on ads since that is American's dominant strategy. Thus the best strategy for United, given the prediction that American will spend more on ads, is to keep its own spending unchanged. If both players do the best they can, taking account of the incentives each faces, this game will end in the lower-left cell of the payoff matrix: American will raise its spending on ads and United will not.

Note that the choices corresponding to the lower-left cell in Table 8.2 satisfy the definition of a Nash equilibrium. If United found itself in that cell, its alternative would be to raise its ad spending, a move that would reduce its payoff from $4,000 to $3,000. So United has no incentive to abandon the lower-left cell. Similarly, if American found itself in the lower-left cell of Table 8.2, its alternative would be to leave ad spending the same, a move that would reduce its payoff from $5,000 to $2,000. So American also has no incentive to abandon the lower-left cell. The lower-left cell of Table 8.2 is a Nash equilibrium—a combination of strategies for which each player's choice is the best available option, given the choice made by the other player.

CONCEPT CHECK 8.1

What should United and American do if their payoff matrix is modified as follows?

		American	
		Raise ad spending	Leave spending the same
United	Raise ad spending	$3,000 for United $8,000 for American	$4,000 for United $5,000 for American
	Leave spending the same	$8,000 for United $4,000 for American	$5,000 for United $2,000 for American

RECAP ↑

USING GAME THEORY TO ANALYZE STRATEGIC DECISIONS

The three elements of any game are the players, the list of strategies from which they can choose, and the payoffs to each combination of strategies. This information can be summarized in a payoff matrix.

Equilibrium in a game occurs when each player's strategy choice yields the highest payoff available, given the strategies chosen by other players. Such a combination of strategies is called a Nash equilibrium.

THE PRISONER'S DILEMMA

The first advertising example we discussed above belongs to an important class of games called the **prisoner's dilemma**. In the prisoner's dilemma, when each player chooses his dominant strategy, the result is unattractive to the group of players as a whole.

prisoner's dilemma a game in which each player has a dominant strategy, and when each plays it, the resulting payoffs are smaller than if each had played a dominated strategy

The Original Prisoner's Dilemma

The next example recounts the original scenario from which the prisoner's dilemma drew its name.

EXAMPLE 8.3   **Prisoner's Dilemma**

Should the prisoners confess?

Two prisoners, Horace and Jasper, are being held in separate cells for a serious crime that they did in fact commit. The prosecutor, however, has only enough hard evidence to convict them of a minor offense, for which the penalty is a year in jail. Each prisoner is told that if one confesses while the other remains silent, the confessor will be cleared of the crime, and the other will spend 20 years in prison. If both confess, they will get an intermediate sentence of five years. These payoffs are summarized in Table 8.3. The two prisoners are not allowed to communicate with one another. Do they have a dominant strategy? If so, what is it?

TABLE 8.3
The Payoff Matrix for a Prisoner's Dilemma

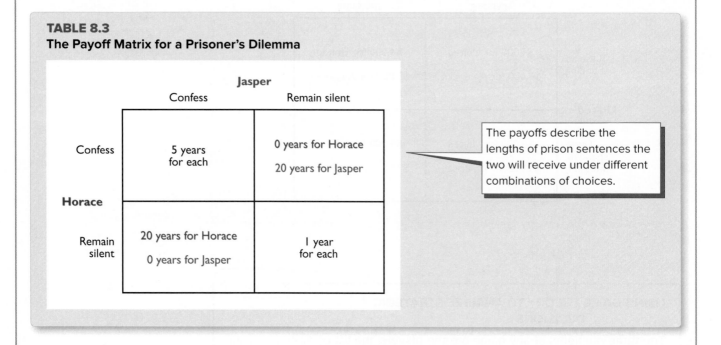

The payoffs describe the lengths of prison sentences the two will receive under different combinations of choices.

In this game, the dominant strategy for each prisoner is to confess. No matter what Jasper does, Horace will get a lighter sentence by speaking out. If Jasper confesses, Horace will get five years (upper-left cell) instead of 20 (lower-left cell). If Jasper remains silent, Horace will go free (upper-right cell) instead of spending a year in jail (lower-right cell). Because the payoffs are perfectly symmetric, Jasper will also do better to confess, no matter what Horace does. The difficulty is that when each follows his dominant strategy and confesses, both will do worse than if each had shown restraint. When both confess, they each get five years (upper-left cell), instead of the one year they would have gotten by remaining silent (lower-right cell). Hence the name of this game, the prisoner's dilemma.

CONCEPT CHECK 8.2

GM and Chrysler must both decide whether to invest in a new process. Games 1 and 2 below show how their profits depend on the decisions they might make. Which of these games is a prisoner's dilemma?

Game 1

Chrysler

		Don't invest	Invest
GM	Don't invest	10 for each	4 for GM 12 for Chrysler
	Invest	12 for GM 4 for Chrysler	5 for each

Game 2

Chrysler

		Don't invest	Invest
GM	Don't invest	4 for GM 12 for Chrysler	5 for each
	Invest	10 for each	12 for GM 4 for Chrysler

The prisoner's dilemma is one of the most powerful metaphors in all of human behavioral science. Countless social and economic interactions have payoff structures analogous to the one confronted by the two prisoners. Some of those interactions occur between only two players, as in the examples just discussed; many others involve larger groups. Games of the latter sort are called *multiplayer prisoner's dilemmas*. But regardless of the number of players involved, the common thread is one of conflict between the narrow self-interest of individuals and the broader interests of larger communities.

The Economics of Cartels

A **cartel** is any coalition of firms that conspires to restrict production for the purpose of earning an economic profit. As we will see in the next example, the problem confronting oligopolists who are trying to form a cartel is a classic illustration of the prisoner's dilemma.

> **cartel** a coalition of firms that agree to restrict output for the purpose of earning an economic profit

The Economic Naturalist 8.1

Why are cartel agreements notoriously unstable?

Consider a market for bottled water served by two oligopolists, Aquapure and Mountain Spring. Each firm can draw water free of charge from a mineral spring located on its own land. Customers supply their own bottles. Rather than compete with one another, the two firms decide to join together by selling water at the price a profit-maximizing pure monopolist would charge. Under their agreement (which constitutes a cartel), each firm would produce and sell half the quantity of water demanded by the market at the monopoly price (see Figure 8.1). The agreement is not legally enforceable, however, which means that each firm has the option of charging less than the agreed price. If one firm sells

FIGURE 8.1

The Market Demand for Mineral Water.

Faced with the demand curve shown, a monopolist with zero marginal cost would produce 1,000 bottles per day (the quantity at which marginal revenue equals zero) and sell them at a price of $1.00 per bottle.

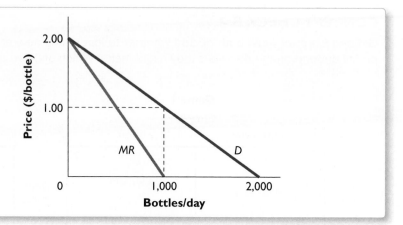

water for less than the other firm, it will capture the entire quantity demanded by the market at the lower price.

Why is this agreement likely to collapse?

Since the marginal cost of mineral water is zero, the profit-maximizing quantity for a monopolist with the demand curve shown in Figure 8.1 is 1,000 bottles per day, the quantity for which marginal revenue equals marginal cost. At that quantity, the monopoly price is $1 per bottle. If the firms abide by their agreement, each will sell half the market total, or 500 bottles per day, at a price of $1 per bottle, for an economic profit of $500 per day.

But suppose Aquapure reduced its price to 90 cents per bottle. By underselling Mountain Spring, it would capture the entire quantity demanded by the market, which, as shown in Figure 8.2, is 1,100 bottles per day. Aquapure's economic profit would rise from $500 per day to ($0.90 per bottle)(1,100 bottles per day) = $990 per day—almost twice as much as before. In the process, Mountain Spring's economic profit would fall from $500 per day to zero. Rather than see its economic profit disappear, Mountain Spring would match Aquapure's price cut, recapturing its original 50 percent share of the market. But when each firm charges $0.90 per bottle and sells 550 bottles per day, each earns an economic profit of ($0.90 per bottle)(550 bottles per day) = $495 per day, or $5 less per day than before.

FIGURE 8.2

The Temptation to Violate a Cartel Agreement.

By cutting its price from $1 per bottle to 90 cents per bottle, Aquapure can sell the entire market quantity demanded at that price, 1,100 bottles per day, rather than half the monopoly quantity of 1,000 bottles per day.

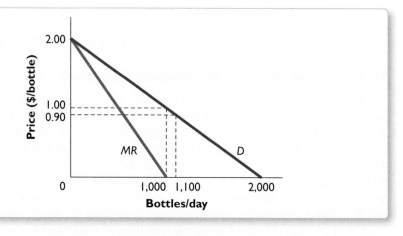

Why is it so difficult for companies to enforce agreements against price cutting?

Suppose we view the cartel agreement as an economic game in which the two available strategies are to sell for $1 per bottle or to sell for $0.90 per bottle. The payoffs are the economic profits that result from these strategies. Table 8.4 shows the payoff matrix for this game. Each firm's dominant strategy is to sell at the lower price, yet in following that strategy, each earns a lower profit than if each had sold at the higher price.

TABLE 8.4
The Payoff Matrix for a Cartel Agreement

	Mountain Spring	
	Charge $1/bottle	Charge $0.90/bottle
Aquapure Charge $1/bottle	$500/day for each	$0 for Aquapure $990/day for Mt. Spring
Charge $0.90/bottle	$990/day for Aquapure $0 for Mt. Spring	$495/day for each

The dominant strategy for each firm is to charge $0.90 per bottle, or 10 cents per bottle less than called for by the cartel agreement. Hence the notorious instability of cartel agreements.

The game does not end with both firms charging $0.90 per bottle. Each firm knows that if it cuts the price a little further, it can recapture the entire market, and in the process earn a substantially higher economic profit. At every step, the rival firm will match any price cut, until the price falls all the way to the marginal cost—in this example, zero.

Cartel agreements confront participants with the economic incentives inherent in the prisoner's dilemma, which explains why such agreements have historically been so unstable. Usually a cartel involves not just two firms, but several, an arrangement that can make retaliation against price cutters extremely difficult. In many cases, discovering which parties have broken the agreement is difficult. For example, the Organization of Petroleum Exporting Countries (OPEC), a cartel of oil producers formed in the 1970s to restrict oil production, has no practical way to prevent member countries from secretly pumping oil offshore in the dead of night.

Tit-for-Tat and the Repeated Prisoner's Dilemma

When all players cooperate in a prisoner's dilemma, each gets a higher payoff than when all defect. So people who confront prisoner's dilemmas will be on the lookout for ways to create incentives for mutual cooperation. What they need is some way to penalize players who defect. When players interact with one another only once, this turns out to be difficult. But when they expect to interact repeatedly, new possibilities emerge.

A **repeated prisoner's dilemma** is a standard prisoner's dilemma that confronts the same players not just once but many times. Experimental research on repeated prisoner's dilemmas in the 1960s identified a simple strategy that proves remarkably effective at limiting defection. The strategy is called **tit-for-tat**, and here is how it works: The first time you interact with someone, you cooperate. In each subsequent interaction, you simply do what that person did in the previous interaction. Thus, if your partner defected on your first interaction, you would then defect on your next interaction with her. If she then cooperates, your move next time will be to cooperate as well.

On the basis of elaborate computer simulations, University of Michigan political scientist Robert Axelrod showed that tit-for-tat was a remarkably effective strategy, even when pitted against a host of ingenious counterstrategies that had been designed for the explicit purpose of trying to exploit it. The success of tit-for-tat requires a reasonably stable set of players, each of whom can remember what other players have done in previous interactions. It also requires that players have a significant stake in what happens in the future, for it is the fear of retaliation that deters people from defecting.

Since rival firms in the same industry interact with one another repeatedly, it might seem that the tit-for-tat strategy would ensure widespread collusion to raise prices. And yet, as noted earlier, cartel agreements are notoriously unsuccessful. One difficulty is that tit-for-tat's effectiveness depends on there being only two players in the game. In competitive and monopolistically competitive industries, there are generally many firms, and even in oligopolies there are often several. When there are more than two firms and one defects now, how do the cooperators selectively punish the defector later? By cutting price? That will penalize everyone, not just the defector. Even if there are only two firms in an industry, these firms realize that other firms may enter their industry. So the would-be cartel members have to worry not only about each other, but also about the entire list of firms that might decide to compete with them. Each firm may see this as a hopeless task and decide to defect now, hoping to reap at least some economic profit in the short run. What seems clear, in any event, is that the practical problems involved in implementing tit-for-tat have made it difficult to hold cartel agreements together for long.

repeated prisoner's dilemma a standard prisoner's dilemma that confronts the same players repeatedly

tit-for-tat a strategy for the repeated prisoner's dilemma in which players cooperate on the first move and then mimic their partner's last move on each successive move

The Economic Naturalist 8.2

How did Congress unwittingly solve the television advertising dilemma confronting cigarette producers?

In 1970, Congress enacted a law making cigarette advertising on television illegal after January 1, 1971. As evidenced by the steadily declining proportion of Americans who smoke, this law seems to have achieved its stated purpose of protecting citizens against a proven health hazard. But the law also had an unintended effect, which was to increase the economic profit of cigarette makers, at least in the short run. In the year before the law's passage, manufacturers spent more than $300 million on advertising—about $60 million more than they spent during the year after the law was enacted. Much of the saving in advertising expenditures in 1971 was reflected in higher cigarette profits at year-end. But if eliminating television advertising made companies more profitable, why didn't the manufacturers eliminate the ads on their own?

When an imperfectly competitive firm advertises its product, its demand curve shifts rightward, for two reasons. First, people who have never used that type of product learn about it, and some buy it. Second, people who consume a different brand of the product may switch brands. The first effect boosts sales industrywide; the second merely redistributes existing sales among brands.

Although advertising produces both effects in the cigarette industry, its primary effect is brand switching. Thus, the decision of whether to advertise confronts the individual firm with a prisoner's dilemma. Table 8.5 shows the payoffs facing a pair of cigarette producers trying to decide whether to advertise. If both firms advertise on TV (upper-left cell), each earns a profit of only $10 million per year, compared to a profit of $20 million per year for each if neither advertises (lower-right cell). Clearly, both will benefit if neither advertises.

Yet note the powerful incentive that confronts each firm. RJR sees that if Philip Morris doesn't advertise, RJR can earn higher profits by advertising ($35 million per year) than by not advertising ($20 million per year). RJR also sees that if Philip

Why were cigarette manufacturers happy when Congress made it illegal for them to advertise on television?

TABLE 8.5
Cigarette Advertising as a Prisoner's Dilemma

	Philip Morris — Advertise on TV	Philip Morris — Don't advertise on TV
RJR — Advertise on TV	$10 million/yr for each	$35 million/yr for RJR; $5 million/yr for Philip Morris
RJR — Don't advertise on TV	$5 million/yr for RJR; $35 million/yr for Philip Morris	$20 million/yr for each

In many industries, the primary effect of advertising is to encourage consumers to switch brands. In such industries, the dominant strategy is to advertise heavily (upper-left cell), even though firms as a group would do better by not advertising (lower-right cell).

Morris does advertise, RJR will again earn more by advertising ($10 million per year) than by not advertising ($5 million per year). Thus, RJR's dominant strategy is to advertise. And because the payoffs are symmetric, Philip Morris's dominant strategy is also to advertise. So when each firm behaves rationally from its own point of view, the two together do worse than if they had both shown restraint. The congressional ad ban forced cigarette manufacturers to do what they could not have accomplished on their own.

As the following example makes clear, understanding the prisoner's dilemma can help the economic naturalist to make sense of human behavior not only in the world of business, but also in other domains of life as well.

The Economic Naturalist 8.3

Why do people shout at parties?

Whenever large numbers of people gather for conversation in a closed space, the ambient noise level rises sharply. After attending such gatherings, people often complain of sore throats and hoarse voices. If everyone spoke at a normal volume at parties, the overall noise level would be lower, and people would hear just as well. So why do people shout?

Why do people often have to shout to be heard at parties?

The problem involves the difference between individual incentives and group incentives. Suppose everyone starts by speaking at a normal level. But because of the crowded conditions, conversation partners have difficulty hearing one another, even when no one is shouting. The natural solution, from the point of the individual, is to simply raise one's voice a bit. But that is also the natural solution for everyone else. And when everyone speaks more loudly, the ambient noise level rises so that no one hears any better than before.

No matter what others do, the individual will do better by speaking more loudly. Doing so is a dominant strategy for everyone, in fact. Yet when everyone follows the dominant strategy, the result is worse (no one can hear well) than if everyone had continued to speak normally. While shouting is wasteful, individuals acting alone have no better option. If anyone were to speak softly while others shout, that person wouldn't be heard. No one wants to go home with raw vocal cords, but people apparently prefer that cost to the alternative of not being heard at all.

RECAP ↑

THE PRISONER'S DILEMMA

The prisoner's dilemma is a game in which each player has a dominant strategy, and in which the payoff to each player when each chooses that strategy is smaller than if each had chosen a dominated strategy. Incentives analogous to those found in the prisoner's dilemma help to explain a broad range of behavior in business and everyday life—among them excessive spending on advertising, cartel instability, and shouting at parties. The tit-for-tat strategy can help sustain cooperation in two-player repeated prisoner's dilemmas but tends to be ineffective in multiplayer repeated prisoner's dilemmas.

GAMES IN WHICH TIMING MATTERS

In the games discussed so far, players were assumed to choose their strategies simultaneously, and which player moved first didn't matter. For example, in the prisoner's dilemma, self-interested players would follow their dominant strategies even if they knew in advance what strategies their opponents had chosen. But in other situations, such as the negotiations between Warner Brothers and Tony Bennett described at the beginning of this chapter, timing is of the essence.

We begin with an example of a game whose outcome cannot be predicted if both players move simultaneously, but whose outcome is clear if one player has the opportunity to move before the other.

EXAMPLE 8.4   The Importance of Timing

Should Dodge build a hybrid Viper?

The Dodge Viper and the Chevrolet Corvette compete for a limited pool of domestic sports car enthusiasts. Each company knows that the other is considering whether to bring out a hybrid version of its car. If both companies bring out hybrids, each will earn $60 million in profit. If neither brings out a hybrid, each company will earn $50 million. If Chevrolet introduces a hybrid and Dodge does not, Chevrolet will earn $80 million and Dodge will earn $70 million. If Dodge brings out a hybrid and Chevrolet does not, Dodge will earn $80 million and Chevrolet will earn $70 million. Does either firm have a dominant strategy in this situation? What will happen in this game if Dodge gets to choose first, with Chevrolet choosing after having seen Dodge's choice?

When both companies must make their decisions simultaneously, the payoff matrix for the example looks like Table 8.6

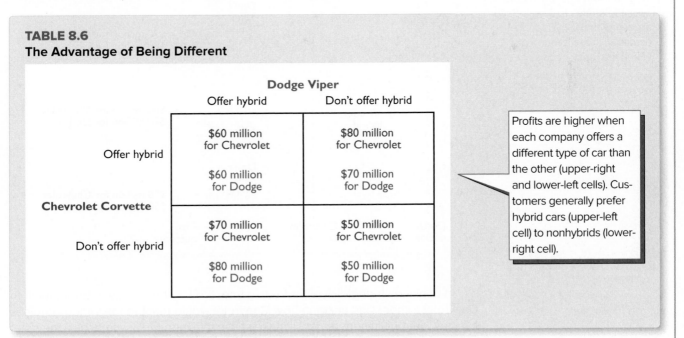

TABLE 8.6
The Advantage of Being Different

	Dodge Viper	
	Offer hybrid	Don't offer hybrid
Chevrolet Corvette Offer hybrid	$60 million for Chevrolet / $60 million for Dodge	$80 million for Chevrolet / $70 million for Dodge
Don't offer hybrid	$70 million for Chevrolet / $80 million for Dodge	$50 million for Chevrolet / $50 million for Dodge

Profits are higher when each company offers a different type of car than the other (upper-right and lower-left cells). Customers generally prefer hybrid cars (upper-left cell) to nonhybrids (lower-right cell).

The logic of the profit figures in Table 8.6 is that although consumers generally like the idea of a hybrid sports car (hence the higher profits when both companies bring out hybrids than when neither does), the companies will have to compete more heavily with one another if both offer the same type of car (and hence the lower profits when both offer the same type of car than when each offers a different type).

decision tree (or game tree) a diagram that describes the possible moves in a game in sequence and lists the payoffs that correspond to each possible combination of moves

In the payoff matrix in Table 8.6, neither company has a dominant strategy. The best outcome for Dodge is to offer a hybrid Viper while Chevrolet does not offer a hybrid Corvette (lower-left cell). The best outcome for Chevrolet is to offer a hybrid Corvette while Dodge does not offer a hybrid Viper (upper-right cell). Both the lower-left and upper-right cells are Nash equilibria of this game because if the companies found themselves in either of these cells, neither would unilaterally want to change its position. Thus, in the upper-right cell, Chevrolet wouldn't want to change (that cell is, after all, the best possible outcome for Chevrolet), and neither would Dodge (since switching to a hybrid would reduce its profit from $70 million to $60 million). But without being told more, we simply cannot predict where the two companies will end up.

If one side can move before the other, however, the incentives for action become instantly clearer. For games in which timing matters, a **decision tree**, or **game tree**, is a more useful way of representing the payoffs than a traditional payoff matrix. This type of diagram describes the possible moves in the sequence in which they may occur, and lists the final payoffs for each possible combination of moves.

If Dodge has the first move, the decision tree for the game is shown in Figure 8.3. At *A,* Dodge begins the game by deciding whether to offer a hybrid. If it chooses to offer one, Chevrolet must then make its own choice at *B*. If Dodge does not offer a hybrid, Chevrolet will make its choice at *C*. In either case, once Chevrolet makes its choice, the game is over.

FIGURE 8.3

Decision Tree for Hybrid Example.

This decision tree shows the possible moves and payoffs for the game in the hybrid example, in the sequence in which they may occur.

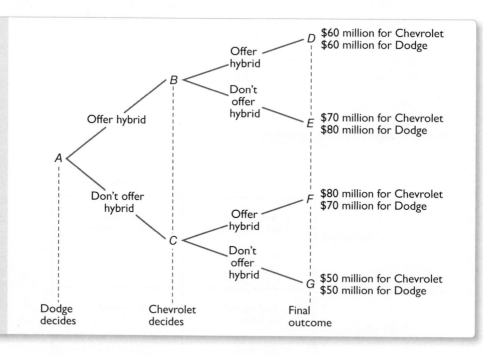

In thinking strategically about this game, the key for Dodge is to put itself in Chevrolet's shoes and imagine how Chevrolet would react to the various choices it might confront. In general, it will make sense for Dodge to assume that Chevrolet will respond in a self-interested way—that is, by choosing the available option that offers the highest profit for Chevrolet. Dodge knows that if it chooses to offer a hybrid, Chevy's best option at *B* will be not to offer a hybrid (since Chevy's profit is $10 million higher at *E* than at *D*). Dodge also knows that if it chooses not to offer a hybrid, Chevy's best option at *C* will be to offer one (since Chevy's profit is $30 million higher at *F* than at *G*). Dodge thus knows that if it offers a hybrid, it will end up at *E,* where it will earn $80 million, whereas if it does not offer a hybrid, it will end up at *F*, where it will earn only $70 million. So when Dodge has the first move in this game, its best strategy is to offer a hybrid. And Chevrolet then follows by choosing not to offer one.

Credible Threats and Promises

Could Chevrolet have deterred Dodge from offering a hybrid by threatening to offer a hybrid of its own, no matter what Dodge did? The problem with this strategy is such a threat would not have been credible. In the language of game theory, a **credible threat** is one that will be in the threatener's interest to carry out when the time comes to act. People are likely to be skeptical of any threat if they know there will be no incentive to follow through when the time comes. The problem here is that Dodge knows that it would not be in Chevrolet's interest to carry out its threat in the event that Dodge offered a hybrid. After all, once Dodge has already offered the hybrid, Chevy's best option is to offer a nonhybrid.

credible threat a threat to take an action that is in the threatener's interest to carry out

The concept of a credible threat figured prominently in the negotiations between Warner Brothers' managers and Tony Bennett over the matter of Mr. Bennett's fee for performing in *Analyze This*. Once most of the film had been shot, managers knew they couldn't threaten credibly to refuse Mr. Bennett's salary demand because at that point adapting the film to another singer would have been extremely costly. In contrast, a similar threat made before production of the movie had begun would have been credible.

Just as in some games credible threats are impossible to make, in others **credible promises** are impossible. A credible promise is one that is in the interests of the promiser to keep when the time comes to act. In the following example, both players suffer because of the inability to make a credible promise.

credible promise a promise to take an action that is in the promiser's interest to keep

EXAMPLE 8.5   A Credible Promise

Should the business owner open a remote office?

The owner of a thriving business wants to start up an office in a distant city. If she hires someone to manage the new office, she can afford to pay a weekly salary of $1,000—a premium of $500 over what the manager would otherwise be able to earn—and still earn a weekly economic profit of $1,000 for herself. The owner's concern is that she will not be able to monitor the manager's behavior. The owner knows that by managing the remote office dishonestly, the manager can boost his take-home pay to $1,500 while causing the owner an economic loss of $500 per week. If the owner believes that all managers are selfish income maximizers, will she open the new office?

The decision tree for the remote-office game is shown in Figure 8.4. At *A*, the managerial candidate promises to manage honestly, which brings the owner to *B*, where she must decide whether to open the new office. If she opens it, they reach *C*, where the manager must decide whether to manage honestly. If the manager's only goal is to make as much money as he can, he will manage dishonestly (bottom branch at *C*) since that way he will earn $500 more than by managing honestly (top branch at *C*).

So if the owner opens the new office, she will end up with an economic loss of $500. If she had not opened the office (bottom branch at *B*), she would have realized an economic profit of zero. Since zero is better than −$500, the owner will choose not to open the remote office. In the end, the opportunity cost of the manager's inability to make a credible promise is $1,500: the manager's forgone $500 salary premium and the owner's forgone $1,000 return.

FIGURE 8.4

Decision Tree for the Remote-Office Game.

The best outcome is for the manager to open the office at B and for the manager to manage the office honestly at C. But if the manager is purely self-interested and the owner knows it, this path will not be an equilibrium outcome.

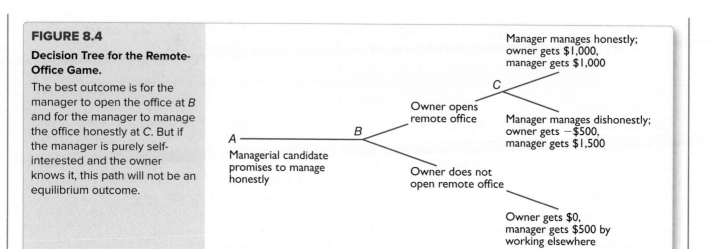

Managerial candidate promises to manage honestly

Owner opens remote office

Owner does not open remote office

Manager manages honestly; owner gets $1,000, manager gets $1,000

Manager manages dishonestly; owner gets −$500, manager gets $1,500

Owner gets $0, manager gets $500 by working elsewhere

CONCEPT CHECK 8.3

Smith and Jones are playing a game in which Smith has the first move at *A* in the decision tree shown below. Once Smith has chosen either the top or bottom branch at *A*, Jones, who can see what Smith has chosen, must choose the top or bottom branch at *B* or *C*. If the payoffs at the end of each branch are as shown, what is the equilibrium outcome of this game? If before Smith chose, Jones could make a credible commitment to choose either the top or bottom branch when his turn came, what would he do?

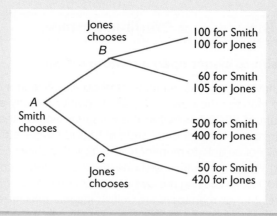

Jones chooses B
100 for Smith
100 for Jones

60 for Smith
105 for Jones

A
Smith chooses

500 for Smith
400 for Jones

C
Jones chooses
50 for Smith
420 for Jones

Monopolistic Competition When Location Matters

In many sequential games, the player who gets to move first enjoys a strategic advantage. That was the case, for instance, in the decision of whether to produce a hybrid sports car in Example 8.4. In that example, the first mover did better because he was able to exploit the knowledge that both firms do better if each one's product is different from the other's rather than similar to it. But that won't always be true. When the feature that differentiates one seller's product from another's is temporal or spatial location, the firm with the last move in a game sometimes enjoys the upper hand, as The Economic Naturalist 8.4 illustrates.

The Economic Naturalist 8.4

Why do we often see convenience stores located on adjacent street corners?

In many cities, it is common to see convenience stores located in clusters, followed by long stretches with no stores at all. If the stores were more spread out, almost all consumers would enjoy a shorter walk to the nearest convenience store. Why do stores tend to cluster in this fashion?

In Figure 8.5, suppose that when the convenience store located at A first opened, it was the closest store for the 1,200 shoppers who live in identical apartment houses evenly distributed along the road between A and the freeway one mile to the east.[3] Those who live to the east of the freeway shop elsewhere because they cannot cross the freeway. Those who live to the west of the store at A shop either at A or at some other store still further to the west, whichever is closer. In this setting, why might a profit-maximizing entrepreneur planning to open a new store between A and the freeway choose to locate at B rather than at some intermediate location such as C?

It turns out that a store located at C would in fact minimize the distance that shoppers living between A and the freeway would have to walk to reach the nearest store. If there were a store at C, no shopper on this stretch of road would have to walk more than ⅓ of a mile to reach the nearest store. The 800 people who live between point D (which is halfway between A and C) and the freeway would shop at C, while the 400 who live between D and A would shop at A.

Despite the fact that C is the most attractive location for a new store from the perspective of consumers, it is not the most advantageous for the store's owner. The reason is that the owner's profit depends on how many people choose to shop at his store, not on how far they have to walk to get there. Given that consumers shop

Why do retail merchants tend to locate in clusters?

at the store closest to where they live, the best option from the entrepreneur's perspective is to locate his store at B, on the street corner just east of A. That way, his store will be closer to all 1,200 people who live between A and the

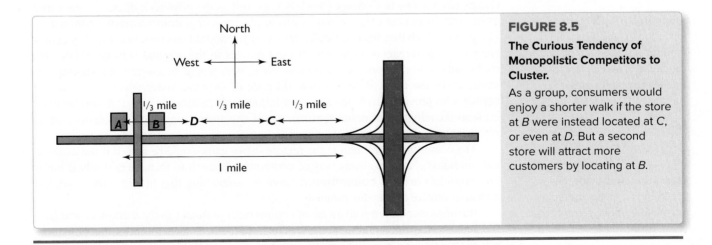

FIGURE 8.5

The Curious Tendency of Monopolistic Competitors to Cluster.

As a group, consumers would enjoy a shorter walk if the store at B were instead located at C, or even at D. But a second store will attract more customers by locating at B.

[3]"Evenly distributed" means that the number of shoppers who live on any segment of the road between A and the freeway is exactly proportional to the length of that segment. For example, the number who live along a segment one-tenth of a mile in length would be 1/10 × 1,200 = 120.

freeway. It is this logic that helps explain the clustering of convenience stores, gas stations, and other monopolistically competitive firms whose most important differentiating feature is geographic location.

The insight that helped answer the question posed in The Economic Naturalist 8.4 is due to the economist Harold Hotelling.[4] Hotelling employed this insight to explain why two hot dog vendors on a stretch of beach almost invariably locate next to one another midway between the endpoints of the beach.

For many oligopolistic or monopolistically competitive firms, an important dimension of product differentiation is location in time rather than in physical space. The timing of flight departures for different airlines in the New York–Los Angeles market is one example. The timing of film showings by different local movie theaters is another. In these cases, too, we often see product clustering. Thus, in the New York–Los Angeles market, both United and American have flights throughout the afternoon departing exactly on the hour. And in many local movie markets, the first evening showing starts at 7:15 p.m. in dozens of different theaters.

In other examples, the differentiating features that matter most might be said to describe the product's location in a more abstract "product space." With soft drinks, for example, we might array different products according to their degrees of sweetness or carbonation. Here, too, it is common to see rival products that lie very close to one another such as Coca-Cola and Pepsi. Clustering occurs in these cases for the reasons analogous to those discussed by Hotelling in his classic paper.

> **RECAP ↑**
>
> **GAMES IN WHICH TIMING MATTERS**
>
> The outcomes in many games depend on the timing of each player's move. For such games, the payoffs are best summarized by a decision tree rather than a payoff matrix. Sometimes the second mover does best to offer a product that differs markedly from existing products. Other times the second mover does best to mimic existing products closely.

COMMITMENT PROBLEMS

commitment problem a situation in which people cannot achieve their goals because of an inability to make credible threats or promises

Games like the one in Concept Check 8.3, as well as the prisoner's dilemma, the cartel game, and the remote-office game, confront players with a **commitment problem**—a situation in which they have difficulty achieving the desired outcome because they cannot make credible threats or promises. If both players in the original prisoner's dilemma could make a binding promise to remain silent, both would be assured of a shorter sentence, hence the logic of the underworld code of *Omerta,* under which the family of anyone who provides evidence against a fellow mob member is killed. A similar logic explains the adoption of military-arms-control agreements, in which opponents sign an enforceable pledge to curtail weapons spending.

commitment device a way of changing incentives so as to make otherwise empty threats or promises credible

The commitment problem in the remote-office game could be solved if the managerial candidate could find some way of committing himself to manage honestly if hired. The candidate needs a **commitment device**—something that provides the candidate with an incentive to keep his promise.

Business owners are well aware of commitment problems in the workplace and have adopted a variety of commitment devices to solve them. Consider, for example, the problem confronting the owner of a restaurant. She wants her table staff to provide good service so that customers will enjoy their meals and come back in the future. Since good service is valuable to her, she would be willing to pay waiters extra for it. For their part,

[4]Harold Hotelling, "Stability and Competition," *Economic Journal* 39, no. 1 (1929), pp. 41–57.

waiters would be willing to provide good service in return for the extra pay. The problem is that the owner cannot always monitor whether the waiters do provide good service. Her concern is that having been paid extra for it, the waiters may slack off when she isn't looking. Unless the owner can find some way to solve this problem, she will not pay extra, the waiters will not provide good service, and she, they, and the diners will suffer. A better outcome for all concerned would be for the waiters to find some way to commit themselves to good service.

Restaurateurs in many countries have tried to solve this commitment problem by encouraging diners to leave tips at the end of their meals. The attraction of this solution is that the diner is *always* in a good position to monitor service quality. The diner should be happy to reward good service with a generous tip since doing so will help to ensure good service in the future. And the waiter has a strong incentive to provide good service because he knows that the size of his tip may depend on it.

The various commitment devices just discussed—the underworld code of *Omerta*, military-arms-control agreements, the tip for the waiter—all work because they change the incentives facing the decision makers. But as the next example illustrates, changing incentives in precisely the desired way is not always practical.

EXAMPLE 8.6   **Changing Incentives**

Will Sylvester leave a tip when dining on the road?

Sylvester has just finished a $100 steak dinner at a restaurant that is 500 miles from where he lives. The waiter provided good service. If Sylvester cares only about himself, will he leave a tip?

Once the waiter has provided good service, there is no way for him to take it back if the diner fails to leave a tip. In restaurants patronized by local diners, failure to tip is not a problem because the waiter can simply provide poor service the next time a nontipper comes in. But the waiter lacks that leverage with out-of-town diners. Having already received good service, Sylvester must choose between paying $100 and paying $115 for his meal. If he is an essentially selfish person, the former choice may be a compelling one.

Will leaving a tip at an out-of-town restaurant affect the quality of service you receive?

CONCEPT CHECK 8.4

A traveler dines at a restaurant far from home. Both he and the waiter who serves him are rational and self-interested in the narrow sense. The waiter must first choose between providing good service and bad service, whereupon the diner must choose whether or not to leave a tip. The payoffs for their interaction are as summarized on the accompanying game tree on the next page. What is the most the diner would be willing to pay for the right to make a binding commitment (visible to the waiter) to leave a tip at the end of the meal in the event of having received good service?

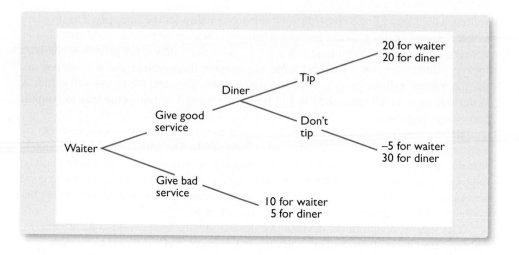

Solving Commitment Problems with Psychological Incentives

In all the games we have discussed so far, players were assumed to care only about obtaining the best possible outcome for themselves. Thus, each player's goal was to get the highest monetary payoff, the shortest jail sentence, the best chance to be heard, and so on. The irony, in most of these games, is that players do not attain the best outcomes. Better outcomes can sometimes be achieved by altering the material incentives selfish players face, but not always.

If altering the relevant material incentives is not possible, commitment problems can sometimes be solved by altering people's psychological incentives. As the next example illustrates, in a society in which people are strongly conditioned to develop moral sentiments—feelings of guilt when they harm others, feelings of sympathy for their trading partners, feelings of outrage when they are treated unjustly—commitment problems arise less often than in more narrowly self-interested societies.

EXAMPLE 8.7   **The Impact of Moral Sentiments**

In a moral society, will the business owner open a remote office?

Consider again the owner of the thriving business who is trying to decide whether to open an office in a distant city. Suppose the society in which she lives is one in which all citizens have been strongly conditioned to behave honestly. Will she open the remote office?

Suppose, for instance, that the managerial candidate would suffer guilt pangs if he embezzled money from the owner. Most people would be reluctant to assign a monetary value to guilty feelings. But for the sake of discussion, let's suppose that those feelings are so unpleasant that the manager would be willing to pay at least $10,000 to avoid them. On this assumption, the manager's payoff if he manages dishonestly will be not $1,500, but $1,500 − $10,000 = −$8,500. The new decision tree is shown in Figure 8.6.

In this case, the best choice for the owner at B will be to open the remote office because she knows that at C the manager's best choice will be to manage honestly. The irony, of course, is that the honest manager in this example ends up richer than the selfish manager in the previous example, who earned only a normal salary.

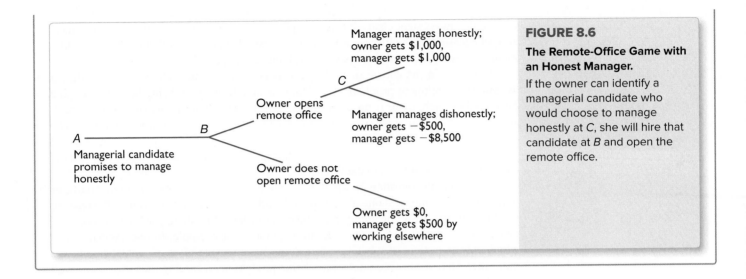

FIGURE 8.6

The Remote-Office Game with an Honest Manager.

If the owner can identify a managerial candidate who would choose to manage honestly at *C*, she will hire that candidate at *B* and open the remote office.

Are People Fundamentally Selfish?

As Example 8.7 suggests, the assumption that people are self-interested in the narrow sense of the term does not always capture the full range of motives that govern choice in strategic settings. Think, for example, about the last time you had a meal at an out-of-town restaurant. Did you leave a tip? If so, your behavior was quite normal. Researchers have found that tipping rates in restaurants patronized mostly by out-of-town diners are essentially the same as in restaurants patronized mostly by local diners.

Indeed, there are many exceptions to the outcomes predicted on the basis of the assumption that people are self-interested in the most narrow sense of the term. People who have been treated unjustly often seek revenge even at ruinous cost to themselves. Every day, people walk away from profitable transactions whose terms they believe to be "unfair." In these and countless other ways, people do not seem to be pursuing self-interest narrowly defined. And if motives beyond narrow self-interest are significant, we must take them into account in attempting to predict and explain human behavior.

Preferences as Solutions to Commitment Problems

Economists tend to view preferences as ends in themselves. Taking them as given, they calculate what actions will best serve those preferences. This approach to the study of behavior is widely used by other social scientists, and by game theorists, military strategists, philosophers, and others. In its standard form, it assumes purely self-interested preferences for present and future consumption goods of various sorts, leisure pursuits, and so on. Concerns about fairness, guilt, honor, sympathy, and the like typically play no role.

Yet such concerns clearly affect the choices people make in strategic interactions. Sympathy for one's trading partner can make a businessperson trustworthy even when material incentives favor cheating. A sense of justice can prompt a person to incur the costs of retaliation, even when incurring those costs will not undo the original injury.

Preferences can clearly shape behavior in these ways; however, this alone does not solve commitment problems. The solution to such problems requires not only that a person *have* certain preferences, but also that others have some way of *discerning* them. Unless the business owner can identify the trustworthy employee, that employee cannot land a job whose pay is predicated on trust. And unless the predator can identify a potential victim whose character will motivate retaliation, that person is likely to become a victim.

From among those with whom we might engage in ventures requiring trust, can we identify reliable partners? If people could make *perfectly* accurate character judgments, they could always steer clear of dishonest persons. That people continue to be victimized at least occasionally by dishonest persons suggests that perfectly reliable character judgments are either impossible to make or prohibitively expensive.

Vigilance in the choice of trading partners is an essential element in solving (or avoiding) commitment problems, for if there is an advantage in being honest and being perceived as such, there is an even greater advantage in only *appearing* to be honest. After all, a liar who appears trustworthy will have better opportunities than one who glances about furtively, sweats profusely, and has difficulty making eye contact. Indeed, he will have the same opportunities as an honest person but will get higher payoffs because he will exploit them to the fullest.

In the end, the question of whether people can make reasonably accurate character judgments is an empirical one. Experimental studies have shown that even on the basis of brief encounters involving strangers, subjects are adept at predicting who will cooperate and who will defect in prisoner's dilemma games. For example, in one experiment in which only 26 percent of subjects defected, the accuracy rate of predicted defections was more than 56 percent. One might expect that predictions regarding those we know well would be even more accurate.

Do you know someone who would return an envelope containing $1,000 in cash to you if you lost it at a crowded concert? If so, then you accept the claim that personal character can help people to solve commitment problems. As long as honest individuals can identify at least some others who are honest, and can interact selectively with them, honest individuals can prosper in a competitive environment.

RECAP ↑

COMMITMENT PROBLEMS AND THE EFFECTS OF PSYCHOLOGICAL INCENTIVES

The inability to make credible threats and promises prevents people from achieving desired outcomes. Games with this property are said to confront players with commitment problems. Such problems can sometimes be solved by employing commitment devices—ways of changing incentives to facilitate making credible threats or promises.

Most applications of the theory of games assume that players are self-interested in the narrow sense of the term. In practice, however, many choices—such as leaving tips in out-of-town restaurants—appear inconsistent with this assumption.

The fact that people seem driven by a more complex range of motives makes behavior more difficult to predict, but also creates new ways of solving commitment problems. Psychological incentives often can serve as commitment devices when changing players' material incentives is impractical. For example, people who are able to identify honest trading partners, and interact selectively with them, are able to solve commitment problems that arise from lack of trust.

SUMMARY

- Economists use the theory of games to analyze situations in which the payoffs of one's actions depend on the actions taken by others. Games have three basic elements: the players; the list of possible actions, or strategies, from which each player can choose; and the payoffs the players receive for those strategies. The payoff matrix is the most useful way to summarize this information in games in which the timing of the players' moves is not decisive. In games in which timing matters, a decision tree provides a much more useful summary of the information. (*LO1, LO3*)

- Equilibrium in a game occurs when each player's strategy choice yields the highest payoff available, given the strategies chosen by the other. *(LO1)*

- A dominant strategy is one that yields a higher payoff regardless of the strategy chosen by the other player. In some games such as the prisoner's dilemma, each player has a dominant strategy. Equilibrium occurs in such games when each player chooses his or her dominant strategy. In other games, not all players have a dominant strategy. *(LO1, LO2)*

- Equilibrium outcomes are often unattractive from the perspective of players as a group. The prisoner's dilemma has this feature because it is each prisoner's dominant strategy to confess, yet each spends more time in jail if both confess than if both remain silent. The incentive structure of this game helps explain such disparate social dilemmas as excessive advertising, military arms races, and failure to reap the potential benefits of interactions requiring trust. *(LO2, LO3)*

- Individuals often can resolve these dilemmas if they can make binding commitments to behave in certain ways. Some commitments—such as those involved in military-arms-control agreements—are achieved by altering the material incentives confronting the players. Other commitments can be achieved by relying on psychological incentives to counteract material payoffs. Moral sentiments such as guilt, sympathy, and a sense of justice often foster better outcomes than can be achieved by narrowly self-interested players. For this type of commitment to work, the relevant moral sentiments must be discernible by one's potential trading partners. *(LO4)*

KEY TERMS

basic elements of a game
cartel
commitment device
commitment problem
credible promise

credible threat
decision tree
dominant strategy
dominated strategy
game tree

Nash equilibrium
payoff matrix
prisoner's dilemma
repeated prisoner's dilemma
tit-for-tat

REVIEW QUESTIONS

1. Identify the three basic elements of a game. *(LO1)*

2. How is your incentive to defect in a prisoner's dilemma altered if you learn that you will play the game not just once but rather indefinitely many times with the same partner? *(LO2)*

3. Explain why a military arms race is an example of a prisoner's dilemma. *(LO2, LO3)*

4. Why did Warner Brothers make a mistake by waiting until the filming of *Analyze This* was almost finished before negotiating with Tony Bennett to perform in the final scene? *(LO3)*

5. Suppose General Motors is trying to hire a small firm to manufacture the door handles for Pontiac sedans. The task requires an investment in expensive capital equipment that cannot be used for any other purpose. Why might the president of the small firm refuse to undertake this venture without a long-term contract fixing the price of the door handles? *(LO3)*

6. Describe the commitment problem that narrowly self-interested diners and waiters would confront at restaurants located on interstate highways. Given that in such restaurants tipping does seem to ensure reasonably good service, do you think people are always selfish in the narrowest sense? *(LO4)*

PROBLEMS
connect

1. Consider the following game, called matching pennies, which you are playing with a friend. Each of you has a penny hidden in your hand, facing either heads up or tails up (you know which way the one in your hand is facing). On the count of "three," you simultaneously show your pennies to each other. If the face-up side of your coin matches the face-up side of your friend's coin, you get to keep the two pennies. If the faces do not match, your friend gets to keep the pennies. *(LO1)*
   a. Who are the players in this game? What are each player's strategies? Construct a payoff matrix for the game.

b. Is there a dominant strategy? If so, what?

c. Is there an equilibrium? If so, what?

2. In studying for his economics final, Sam is concerned about only two things: his grade and the amount of time he spends studying. A good grade will give him a benefit of 20; an average grade, a benefit of 5; and a poor grade, a benefit of 0. By studying a lot, Sam will incur a cost of 10; by studying a little, a cost of 6. Moreover, if Sam studies a lot and all other students study a little, he will get a good grade and they will get poor ones. But if they study a lot and he studies a little, they will get good grades and he will get a poor one. Finally, if he and all other students study the same amount of time, everyone will get average grades. Other students share Sam's preferences regarding grades and study time. *(LO2)*

a. Model this situation as a two-person prisoner's dilemma in which the strategies are to study a little and to study a lot, and the players are Sam and all other students. Include the payoffs in the matrix.

b. What is the equilibrium outcome in this game? From the students' perspective, is it the best outcome?

3. Blackadder and Baldrick are rational, self-interested criminals imprisoned in separate cells in a dark medieval dungeon. They face the prisoner's dilemma displayed in the matrix.

Blackadder

	Confess	Deny
Confess	5 years for each	0 for Baldrick / 20 years for Blackadder
Deny	20 years for Baldrick / 0 for Blackadder	1 year for each

(Baldrick rows on left)

Assume that Blackadder is willing to pay $1,000 for each year by which he can reduce his sentence below 20 years. A corrupt jailer tells Blackadder that before he decides whether to confess or deny the crime, she can tell him Baldrick's decision. How much is this information worth to Blackadder? *(LO2)*

4. Newfoundland's fishing industry has recently declined sharply due to overfishing, even though fishing companies were supposedly bound by a quota agreement. If all fishermen had abided by the agreement, yields could have been maintained at high levels. *(LO2)*

a. Model this situation as a prisoner's dilemma in which the players are Company A and Company B and the strategies are to keep the quota and break the quota. Include appropriate payoffs in the matrix. Explain why overfishing is inevitable in the absence of effective enforcement of the quota agreement.

b. Provide another environmental example of a prisoner's dilemma.

c. In many potential prisoner's dilemmas, a way out of the dilemma for a would-be cooperator is to make reliable character judgments about the trustworthiness of potential partners. Explain why this solution is not available in many situations involving degradation of the environment.

5. Two airplane manufacturers are considering the production of a new product, a 150-passenger jet. Both are deciding whether to enter the market and produce the new planes. The payoff matrix is as follows (payoff values are in millions of dollars):

Airbus

	Produce	Don't produce
Produce	−5 for each	100 for Boeing / 0 for Airbus
Don't produce	0 for Boeing / 100 for Airbus	0 for each

(Boeing rows on left)

The implication of these payoffs is that the market demand is large enough to support only one manufacturer. If both firms enter, both will sustain a loss. *(LO2)*

a. Identify two possible equilibrium outcomes in this game.

b. Consider the effect of a subsidy. Suppose the European Union decides to subsidize the European producer, Airbus, with a check for $25 million if it enters the market. Revise the payoff matrix to account for this subsidy. What is the new equilibrium outcome?

c. Compare the two outcomes (pre- and post-subsidy). What qualitative effect does the subsidy have?

6. Jill and Jack both have two pails that can be used to carry water down from a hill. Each makes only one trip down the hill, and each pail of water can be sold for $5. Carrying the pails of water down requires considerable effort. Both Jill and Jack would be willing to pay $2 each to avoid carrying one pail down the hill, and an

additional $3 to avoid carrying a second pail down the hill. *(LO2)*

a. Given market prices, how many pails of water will each child fetch from the top of the hill?

b. Jill and Jack's parents are worried that the two children don't cooperate enough with one another. Suppose they make Jill and Jack share equally their revenues from selling the water. Given that both are self-interested, construct the payoff matrix for the decisions Jill and Jack face regarding the number of pails of water each should carry. What is the equilibrium outcome?

7. The owner of a thriving business wants to open a new office in a distant city. If he can hire someone who will manage the new office honestly, he can afford to pay that person a weekly salary of $2,000 ($1,000 more than the manager would be able to earn elsewhere) and still earn an economic profit of $800. The owner's concern is that he will not be able to monitor the manager's behavior and that the manager would therefore be in a position to embezzle money from the business. The owner knows that if the remote office is managed dishonestly, the manager can earn $3,100, which results in an economic loss of $600 per week. *(LO3)*

a. If the owner believes that all managers are narrowly self-interested income maximizers, will he open the new office?

b. Suppose the owner knows that a managerial candidate is a devoutly religious person who condemns dishonest behavior, and who would be willing to pay up to $15,000 to avoid the guilt she would feel if she were dishonest. Will the owner open the remote office?

8. Consider the following "dating game," which has two players, A and B, and two strategies, to buy a movie ticket or a baseball ticket. The payoffs, given in points, are as shown in the matrix below. Note that the highest payoffs occur when both A and B attend the same event.

	B Buy movie ticket	Buy baseball ticket
A Buy movie ticket	2 for A / 3 for B	0 for A / 0 for B
Buy baseball ticket	1 for A / 1 for B	3 for A / 2 for B

Assume that players A and B buy their tickets separately and simultaneously. Each must decide what to do knowing the available choices and payoffs but not what the other has actually chosen. Each player believes the other to be rational and self-interested. *(LO1, LO2, LO3)*

a. Does either player have a dominant strategy?

b. How many potential equilibria are there? (*Hint:* To see whether a given combination of strategies is an equilibrium, ask whether either player could get a higher payoff by changing his or her strategy.)

c. Is this game a prisoner's dilemma? Explain.

d. Suppose player A gets to buy his or her ticket first. Player B does not observe A's choice but knows that A chose first. Player A knows that player B knows he or she chose first. What is the equilibrium outcome?

e. Suppose the situation is similar to part d, except that player B chooses first. What is the equilibrium outcome?

9. Consider the following game. Harry has four quarters. He can offer Sally from one to four of them. If she accepts his offer, she keeps the quarters Harry offered her and Harry keeps the others. If Sally declines Harry's offer, they both get nothing ($0). They play the game only once, and each cares only about the amount of money he or she ends up with. *(LO1, LO3)*

a. Who are the players? What are each player's strategies? Construct a decision tree for this game.

b. Given their goal, what is the optimal choice for each player?

10. Imagine yourself sitting in your car in a campus parking lot that is currently full, waiting for someone to pull out so that you can park your car. Somebody pulls out, but at the same moment a driver who has just arrived overtakes you in an obvious attempt to park in the vacated spot before you can. Suppose this driver would be willing to pay up to $10 to park in that spot and up to $30 to avoid getting into an argument with you. (That is, the benefit of parking is $10 and the cost of an argument is $30.) At the same time he guesses, accurately, that you too would be willing to pay up to $30 to avoid a confrontation and up to $10 to park in the vacant spot. *(LO3, LO4)*

a. Model this situation as a two-stage decision tree in which his bid to take the space is the opening move and your strategies are (1) to protest and (2) not to protest. If you protest (initiate an argument), the rules of the game specify that he has to let you take the space. Show the payoffs at the end of each branch of the tree.

b. What is the equilibrium outcome?

c. What would be the advantage of being able to communicate credibly to the other driver that your *failure* to protest would be a significant psychological cost to you?

ANSWERS TO CONCEPT CHECKS

8.1 No matter what American does, United will do better to leave ad spending the same. No matter what United does, American will do better to raise ad spending. So each player will play its dominant strategy: American will raise its ad spending and United will leave its ad spending the same. *(LO1)*

American's Choice

United's Choice	Raise ad spending	Leave ad spending the same
Raise ad spending	United gets $3,000 American gets $8,000	United gets $4,000 American gets $5,000
Leave ad spending the same	United gets $8,000 American gets $4,000	United gets $5,000 American gets $2,000

8.2 In game 1, no matter what Chrysler does, GM will do better to invest, and no matter what GM does, Chrysler will do better to invest. Each has a dominant strategy, but in following it, each does worse than if it had not invested. So game 1 is a prisoner's dilemma. In game 2, no matter what Chrysler does, GM again will do better to invest; but no matter what GM does, Chrysler will do better *not* to invest. Each has a dominant strategy, and in following it, each gets a payoff of 10—5 more than if each had played its dominated strategy. So game 2 is not a prisoner's dilemma. *(LO2)*

8.3 Smith assumes that Jones will choose the branch that maximizes his payoff, which is the bottom branch at either *B* or *C*. So Jones will choose the bottom branch when his turn comes, no matter what Smith chooses. Since Smith will do better (60) on the bottom branch at *B* than on the bottom branch at *C* (50), Smith will choose the top branch at *A*. So equilibrium in this game is for Smith to choose the top branch at *A* and Jones to choose the bottom branch at *B*. Smith gets 60 and Jones gets 105. *(LO3)*

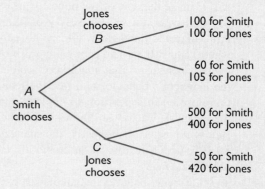

If Jones could make a credible commitment to choose the top branch no matter what, both would do better. Smith would choose the bottom branch at *A* and Jones would choose the top branch at *C,* giving Smith 500 and Jones 400.

8.4 The equilibrium of this game in the absence of a commitment to tip is that the waiter will give bad service because if he provides good service, he knows that the diner's best option will be not to tip, which leaves the waiter worse off than if he had provided good service. Since the diner gets an outcome of 20 if he can commit to leaving a tip (15 more than he would get in the absence of such a commitment), he would be willing to pay up to 15 for the right to commit. *(LO3)*

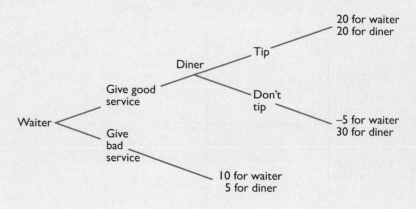

Externalities and Property Rights

9

LEARNING OBJECTIVES

After reading this chapter, you should be able to:

LO1 Define negative and positive externalities and analyze their effect on resource allocation.

LO2 Explain and discuss the Coase theorem.

LO3 Explain how the effects of externalities can be remedied and why the optimal amount of an externality is almost never zero.

LO4 Illustrate the tragedy of the commons, and show how private ownership is a way of preventing it.

LO5 Define positional externalities and their effects and show how they can be remedied.

A droll television ad for a British brand of pipe tobacco opens with a distinguished-looking gentleman sitting quietly on a park bench, smoking his pipe and reading a book of poetry. Before him lies a pond, unrippled except for a mother duck swimming peacefully with her ducklings. Suddenly a raucous group of teenage boys bursts onto the scene with a remote-controlled toy warship. Yelling and laughing, they launch their boat and maneuver it in aggressive pursuit of the terrified ducks.

Interrupted of his relaxation, the gentleman looks up from his book and draws calmly on his pipe as he surveys the scene before him. He then reaches into his bag, pulls out a remote control of his own, and begins manipulating the joystick. The scene shifts underwater, where a miniature submarine rises from the depths of the pond. Once the boys' boat is in the sub's sights, the gentleman pushes a button on his remote control. Seconds later, the boat is blown to smithereens by a torpedo. The scene fades to a close-up of the tobacco company's label.

EXTERNAL COSTS AND BENEFITS

External costs and **external benefits—externalities**, for short—are activities that generate costs or benefits that accrue to people not directly involved in those activities. These effects are generally unintended. From the pipe smoker's point of view, the noise generated by the marauding boys was an external cost. Had others been disturbed by the boys' rowdiness, they may well have regarded the pipe smoker's retaliatory gesture as an external benefit.

This chapter focuses on how externalities affect the allocation of resources. Adam Smith's theory of the invisible hand applies to an ideal marketplace in which externalities do not exist. In such situations, Smith argued, the self-interested actions of individuals would lead to socially efficient outcomes. We will see that when the parties affected by externalities can easily negotiate with one another, the invisible hand will still produce an efficient outcome.

But in many cases, such as the scene depicted in the tobacco ad, negotiation is impractical. In those cases, the self-serving actions of individuals will not lead to efficient

externality an external cost or benefit of an activity

outcomes. The need to deal with externalities is one of the most important rationales for the existence of government along with a variety of other forms of collective action.

How Externalities Affect Resource Allocation

The following examples illustrate the ways in which externalities distort the allocation of resources.

EXAMPLE 9.1   Positive Externalities

external benefit (or positive externality) a benefit of an activity received by people other than those who pursue the activity

Does the honeybee keeper face the right incentives? (Part I)

Phoebe earns her living as a keeper of honeybees. Her neighbors on all sides grow apples. Because bees pollinate apple trees as they forage for nectar, the more hives Phoebe keeps, the larger the harvests will be in the surrounding orchards. If Phoebe takes only her own costs and benefits into account in deciding how many hives to keep, will she keep the socially optimal number of hives?

Phoebe's hives constitute an external benefit, or a positive externality, for the orchard owners. If she takes only her own personal costs and benefits into account, she will add hives only until the added revenue she gets from the last hive just equals the cost of adding it. But since the orchard owners also benefit from additional hives, the total benefit of adding another hive at that point will be greater than its cost. Phoebe, then, will keep too few hives.

As we will discuss later in the chapter, problems like the one in Example 9.1 have several possible solutions. One is for orchard owners to pay beekeepers for keeping additional hives. But such solutions often require complex negotiations between the affected parties. For the moment, we assume that such negotiations are not practical.

EXAMPLE 9.2   Negative Externalities

external cost (or negative externality) a cost of an activity that falls on people other than those who pursue the activity

Does the honeybee keeper face the right incentives? (Part 2)

As in Example 9.1, Phoebe earns her living as a keeper of honeybees. But now her neighbors are not apple growers but an elementary school and a nursing home. The more hives Phoebe keeps, the more students and nursing home residents will be stung by bees. If Phoebe takes only her own costs and benefits into account in deciding how many hives to keep, will she keep the socially optimal number of hives?

For the students and nursing home residents, Phoebe's hives constitute an external cost, or a negative externality. If she considers only her own costs and benefits in deciding how many hives to keep, she will continue to add hives until the added revenue from the last hive is just enough to cover its cost. But since Phoebe's neighbors also incur costs when she adds a hive, the benefit of the last hive at that point will be smaller than its cost. Phoebe, in other words, will keep too many hives.

Every activity involves costs and benefits. When all the relevant costs and benefits of an activity accrue directly to the person who carries it out—that is, when the activity generates no externalities—the level of the activity that is best for the individual will be best for society as a whole. But when an activity generates externalities, be they positive or negative, individual self-interest does not produce the best allocation of resources. Individuals who consider only their own costs and benefits will tend to engage too much in activities that generate negative externalities and too little in activities that generate positive externalities. When an activity generates both positive and negative externalities, private and social interests will coincide only in the unlikely event that the opposing effects offset one another exactly.

The Coase Theorem

To say that a situation is inefficient means that it can be rearranged in a way that would make at least some people better off without harming others. Such situations, we have seen, are a source of creative tension. The existence of inefficiency, after all, means that there is cash on the table, which usually triggers a race to see who can capture it. For example, we saw that because monopoly pricing results in an inefficiently low output level, the potential for gain gave monopolists an incentive to make discounts available to price-sensitive buyers. As the next examples illustrate, the inefficiencies that result from externalities create similar incentives for remedial action.

EXAMPLE 9.3   **Inefficiencies That Result from Externalities**

Will Abercrombie dump toxins in the river? (Part I)

Abercrombie's factory produces a toxic waste by-product. If Abercrombie dumps it in the river, he causes damage to Fitch, a fisherman located downstream. The toxins are short-lived and cause no damage to anyone other than Fitch. At a cost, Abercrombie can filter out the toxins, in which case Fitch will suffer no damage at all. The relevant gains and losses for the two individuals are listed in Table 9.1.

TABLE 9.1
Costs and Benefits of Eliminating Toxic Waste (Part I)

	With filter	Without filter
Gains to Abercrombie	$100/day	$130/day
Gains to Fitch	$100/day	$50/day

If the law does not penalize Abercrombie for dumping toxins in the river, and if Abercrombie and Fitch cannot communicate with one another, will Abercrombie operate with or without a filter? Is that choice socially efficient?

Abercrombie has an incentive to operate without a filter since he earns $30 per day more than if he operates with a filter. But the outcome when he does so is socially inefficient. Thus, when Abercrombie operates without a filter, the total daily gain to both parties is only $130 + $50 = $180, compared to $100 + $100 = $200 if Abercrombie had operated with a filter. The daily cost of the filter to Abercrombie is only $130 − $100 = $30, which is smaller than its daily benefit to Fitch of $100 − $50 = $50. The fact that Abercrombie does not install the filter implies a squandered daily surplus of $20.

EXAMPLE 9.4	Negotiating Efficient Solutions to Externalities

Will Abercrombie dump toxins in the river? (Part 2)

Suppose the costs and benefits of using the filter are as in the previous example except that Abercrombie and Fitch can now communicate with one another at no cost. Even though the law does not require him to do so, will Abercrombie use a filter?

This time, Abercrombie will use a filter. Recall that when the economic pie grows larger, everyone can have a larger slice. Because use of a filter would result in the largest possible economic surplus, it would enable both Abercrombie and Fitch to have a larger net gain than before. Fitch thus has an incentive to *pay* Abercrombie to use a filter. Suppose, for instance, that Fitch offers Abercrombie $40 per day to compensate him for operating with a filter. Both Abercrombie and Fitch will then be exactly $10 per day better off than before, for a total daily net gain of $20.

CONCEPT CHECK 9.1

In Example 9.4, what is the largest whole-dollar amount by which Fitch could compensate Abercrombie for operating with a filter and still be better off than before?

Coase theorem if at no cost people can negotiate the purchase and sale of the right to perform activities that cause externalities, they can always arrive at efficient solutions to the problems caused by externalities

Ronald Coase, a professor at the University of Chicago Law School, was the first to see clearly that if people can negotiate with one another at no cost over the right to perform activities that cause externalities, they will always arrive at an efficient solution. This insight, which is often called the **Coase theorem**, is a profoundly important idea, for which Coase (rhymes with "dose") was awarded the 1991 Nobel Prize in Economics.

Why, you might ask, should Fitch pay Abercrombie to filter out toxins that would not be there in the first place if not for Abercrombie's factory? The rhetorical force of this question is undeniable. Yet Coase points out that externalities are reciprocal in nature. The toxins do harm Fitch, to be sure, but preventing Abercrombie from emitting them would penalize Abercrombie, by exactly $30 per day. Why should Fitch necessarily have the right to harm Abercrombie? Indeed, as the next example illustrates, even if Fitch had that right, he would exercise it only if filtering the toxins proved the most efficient outcome.

EXAMPLE 9.5	Social Efficiency

Will Abercrombie dump toxins in the river? (Part 3)

Suppose the law says that Abercrombie may *not* dump toxins in the river unless he has Fitch's permission. If the relevant costs and benefits of filtering the toxins are as shown in Table 9.2, and if Abercrombie and Fitch can negotiate with one another at no cost, will Abercrombie filter the toxins?

Note that this time the most efficient outcome is for Abercrombie to operate without a filter, for the total daily surplus in that case will be $220 as compared to only $200 with a filter. Under the law, however, Fitch has the right to insist that Abercrombie use a filter. We might expect him to exercise that right since his own gain would rise from $70 to $100 per day if he did so. But because this outcome would be socially inefficient, we know that each party can do better.

Suppose, for example, that Abercrombie gives Fitch $40 per day in return for Fitch's permission to operate without a filter. Each would then have a net daily gain

TABLE 9.2
Costs and Benefits of Eliminating Toxic Waste (Part 3)

	With filter	Without filter
Gains to Abercrombie	$100/day	$150/day
Gains to Fitch	$100/day	$70/day

of $110, which is $10 better for each of them than if Fitch had insisted that Abercrombie use a filter. Abercrombie's pollution harms Fitch, sure enough. But failure to allow the pollution would have caused even greater harm to Abercrombie.

The Coase theorem tells us that regardless of whether the law holds polluters liable for damages, the affected parties will achieve efficient solutions to externalities if they can negotiate costlessly with one another. Note carefully that this does not imply that affected parties will be indifferent about whether the law holds polluters responsible for damages. If polluters are liable, they will end up with lower incomes and those who are injured by pollutants will end up with higher incomes than if the law does not hold polluters liable—even though the same efficient production methods are adopted in each case. When polluters are held liable, they must remove the pollution at their own expense. When they are not held liable, those who are injured by pollution must pay polluters to cut back.

Externalities are hardly rare and isolated occurrences. On the contrary, finding examples of actions that are altogether free of them is difficult. And because externalities can distort the allocation of resources, it is important to recognize them and deal intelligently with them. Consider the following example of an externality that arises because of shared living arrangements.

EXAMPLE 9.6   Cost-Benefit Principle—Shared Living Expenses

Will Ann and Betty share an apartment?

Ann and Betty can live together in a two-bedroom apartment for $600 per month, or separately in 2 one-bedroom apartments, each for $400 per month. If the rent paid were the same for both alternatives, the two women would be indifferent between living together or separately, except for one problem: Ann talks constantly on the telephone. Ann would pay up to $250 per month for this privilege. Betty, for her part, would pay up to $150 per month to have better access to the phone. If the two cannot install a second phone line, should they live together or separately?

Ann and Betty should live together only if the benefit of doing so exceeds the cost. The benefit of living together is the reduction in their rent. Since 2 one-bedroom apartments would cost a total of $800 per month, compared to $600 for a two-bedroom unit, their benefit from living together is $200 per month. Their cost of living together is the least costly accommodation they can make to Ann's objectionable telephone habits. Since Ann would be willing to pay up to $250 per month to avoid changing her behavior, the $200 rent saving is too small to persuade her to change. But Betty is willing to put up with Ann's behavior for a compensation payment of only $150 per month. Since that amount is smaller than the total saving in rent, the least costly solution to the problem is for Betty to live with Ann and simply put up with her behavior.

Table 9.3 summarizes the relevant costs and benefits of this shared living arrangement. The Cost-Benefit Principle tells us that Ann and Betty should live together if and only if the benefit of living together exceeds the cost. The cost of the shared living arrangement is not the sum of all possible costs but the least costly accommodation to the problem (or problems) of shared living. Since the $200 per month saving in rent exceeds the least costly accommodation to the phone problem, Ann and Betty can reap a total gain in economic surplus of $50 per month by sharing their living quarters.

TABLE 9.3
The Gain in Surplus from Shared Living Arrangements

Benefits of Shared Living		
Total cost of separate apartments	**Total cost of shared apartment**	**Rent savings from sharing**
(2)($400/month) $800/month	$600/month	$200/month

Costs of Shared Living			
Problem	**Ann's cost of solving problem**	**Betty's cost of solving problem**	**Least costly solution to the problem**
Ann's phone usage	Curtailed phone usage: $250/month	Tolerate phone usage: $150/month	Betty tolerates Ann's phone usage: $150/month

Gain in Surplus from Shared Living				
Rent savings ($200/month)	−	Least costly accommodation to shared living problems ($150/month)	=	Gain in surplus: ($50/month)

Some people might conclude that Ann and Betty should not live together because if the two share the rent equally, Betty will end up paying $300 per month—which when added to the $150 cost of putting up with Ann's phone behavior comes to $50 more than the cost of living alone. As persuasive as that argument may sound, however, it is mistaken. The source of the error, as the following example illustrates, is the assumption that the two must share the rent equally.

EXAMPLE 9.7   **Cost-Benefit Principle—Paying Unequal Rent Amounts**

What is the highest rent Betty would be willing to pay for the two-bedroom apartment?

In Example 9.6, Betty's alternative is to live alone, which would mean paying $400 per month, her reservation price for a living arrangement with no phone problem. Since the most she would be willing to pay to avoid the phone problem is $150 per month, the highest monthly rent she would be willing to pay for the shared apartment is $400 − $150 = $250. If she pays that amount, Ann will have to pay the difference, namely, $350 per month, which is clearly a better alternative for Ann than paying $400 to live alone.

EXAMPLE 9.8   Cost-Benefit Principle—Splitting Economic Surplus

How much should Ann and Betty pay if they agree to split their economic surplus equally?

As we saw in Table 9.3, the total rent saving from the shared apartment is $200, and since the least costly solution to the phone problem is $150, the monthly gain in economic surplus is $50. We know from Example 9.7 that Ann's reservation price for living together is $400 per month and Betty's is $250. So if the two women want to split the $50 monthly surplus equally, each should pay $25 less than her reservation price. Ann's monthly rent will thus be $375 and Betty's, $225. The result is that each is $25 per month better off than if she had lived alone.

CONCEPT CHECK 9.2

As in Examples 9.6 and 9.7, Ann and Betty can live together in a two-bedroom apartment for $600 per month or separately in 2 one-bedroom apartments, each for $400 per month. Ann would pay up to $250 per month rather than moderate her telephone habits, and Betty would pay up to $150 per month to achieve reasonable access to the telephone. Now, suppose Betty would also be willing to pay up to $60 per month to avoid the loss of privacy that comes with shared living space. Should the two women live together?

Remedies for Externalities

Laws and Regulations

We have seen that efficient solutions to externalities can be found whenever the affected parties can negotiate with one another at no cost. But negotiation is not always practical. A motorist with a noisy muffler imposes costs on others, yet they cannot flag him down and offer him a compensation payment to fix his muffler. In recognition of this difficulty, most governments simply require that cars have working mufflers. Indeed, the explicit or implicit purpose of a large share—perhaps the lion's share—of laws is to solve problems caused by externalities. The goal of such laws is to help people achieve the solutions they might have reached had they been able to negotiate with one another.

When negotiation is costless, the task of adjustment generally falls on the party who can accomplish it at the lowest cost. For instance, in our examples, Betty put up with Ann's annoying phone habits because doing so was less costly than asking Ann to change her habits. Many municipal noise ordinances also place the burden of adjustment on those who can accomplish it at the lowest cost. Consider, for example, the restrictions on loud party music, which often take effect at a later hour on weekends than on weekdays. This pattern reflects both the fact that the gains from loud music tend to be larger on weekends and the fact that such music is more likely to disturb people on weekdays. By setting the noise curfew at different hours on different days of the week, the law places the burden on partygoers during the week and on sleepers during the weekend. Similar logic explains why noise ordinances allow motorists to honk their horns in most neighborhoods, but not in the immediate vicinity of a hospital.

The list of laws and regulations that may be fruitfully viewed as solutions to externalities is a long one. When a motorist drives his car at high speed, he endangers not just his own life and property, but also the lives and property of others. Speed limits, no-passing zones, right-of-way rules, and a host of other traffic laws may be seen as reasoned attempts to limit the harm one party inflicts on another. Many jurisdictions even have laws requiring that motorists install snow tires on their cars by the first of

November. These laws promote not just safety, but also the smooth flow of traffic: if one motorist can't get up a snow-covered hill, he delays not only himself, but also the motorists behind him.

Similar reasoning helps us understand the logic of zoning laws that restrict the kinds of activities that take place in various parts of cities. Because many residents place a high value on living in an uncongested neighborhood, some cities have enacted zoning laws specifying minimum lot sizes. In places like Manhattan, where a shortage of land encourages developers to build very large and tall buildings, zoning laws limit both a building's height and the proportion of a lot it may occupy. Such restrictions recognize that the taller a building is, and the greater the proportion of its lot that it occupies, the more it blocks sunlight from reaching surrounding properties. The desire to control external costs also helps to explain why many cities establish separate zones for business and residential activity. Even within business districts, many cities limit certain kinds of commercial activity. For example, in an effort to revitalize the Times Square neighborhood, New York City enacted a zoning law banning adult bookstores and pornographic movie theaters from the area.

Limitations on the discharge of pollutants into the environment are perhaps the clearest examples of laws aimed at solving problems caused by externalities. The details of these laws reflect the principle of placing the burden of adjustment on those who can accomplish it at least cost. The discharge of toxic wastes into rivers, for example, tends to be most strictly regulated on those waterways whose commercial fishing or recreational uses are most highly valued. On other waterways, the burden of adjustment is likely to fall more heavily on fishermen, recreational boaters, and swimmers. Similarly, air-quality regulations tend to be strictest in the most heavily populated regions of the country, where the marginal benefit of pollution reduction is the greatest.

The following examples suggest additional ways in which Coase's insights about how societies deal with externalities provide rich fodder for the economic naturalist.

The Economic Naturalist 9.1

Why does the U.S. Constitution protect the right of free speech?

What is the purpose of free speech laws?

The First Amendment's protection of free speech and the pattern of exceptions to that protection are another illustration of how legal remedies are used to solve the problems caused by externalities. The First Amendment acknowledges the decisive value of open communication, as well as the practical difficulty of identifying and regulating acts of speech that cause more harm than good. Yet there are some important exceptions. The Supreme Court has ruled, for instance, that the First Amendment does not allow someone to yell "fire" in a crowded theater if there is no fire, nor does it allow someone to advocate the violent overthrow of the government. In those instances, the external benefits of free speech are far too small to justify the external costs.

The Economic Naturalist 9.2

Why does the government subsidize private property owners to plant trees on their hillsides?

Societies use laws not only to discourage activities that generate negative externalities, but also to encourage activities that generate positive externalities. The planting of trees on hillsides, for example, benefits not just the landowner, but also his neighbors by limiting the danger of flooding. In recognition of this fact, many jurisdictions subsidize the planting of trees. Similarly, Congress budgets millions of dollars each year in support of basic research—an implicit acknowledgment of the positive externalities associated with the generation of new knowledge.

Why does the government subsidize scientific research?

The Optimal Amount of Negative Externalities Is Not Zero

Curbing pollution and other negative externalities entails both costs and benefits. As we saw in the chapter *Perfectly Competitive Supply,* when we analyzed how many cans should be recycled, the best policy is to curtail pollution until the cost of further abatement just equals the marginal benefit. In general, the marginal cost of abatement rises with the amount of pollution eliminated, since polluters use the cheapest cleanup methods first and then turn to more expensive ones. And the law of diminishing marginal utility suggests that beyond some point, the marginal benefit of pollution reduction tends to fall as more pollution is removed. As a result, the marginal cost and marginal benefit curves almost always intersect at less than the maximum amount of pollution reduction.

The intersection of the two curves marks the socially optimal level of pollution reduction. If pollution is curtailed by any less than that amount, society will gain more than it will lose by pushing the cleanup effort a little further. But if regulators push beyond the point at which the marginal cost and benefit curves intersect, society will incur costs that exceed the benefits. The existence of a socially optimal level of pollution reduction implies the existence of a socially optimal level of pollution, and that level will almost always be greater than zero.

Because people have been conditioned to think of pollution as bad, many cringe when they hear the phrase "socially optimal level of pollution." How can any positive level of pollution be socially optimal? *But to speak of a socially optimal level of pollution is not the same as saying that pollution is good.* It is merely to recognize that society has an interest in cleaning up the environment, but only up to a certain point. The underlying idea is no different from the idea of an optimal level of dirt in an apartment. After all, even if you spent the whole day, every day, vacuuming your apartment, there would be *some* dirt left in it. And because you have better things to do than vacuum all day, you probably tolerate substantially more than the minimal amount of dirt. A dirty apartment is not good, nor is pollution in the air you breathe. But in both cases, the cleanup effort should be expanded only until the marginal benefit equals the marginal cost.

Compensatory Taxes and Subsidies

As noted, when transaction costs prohibit negotiation among affected parties, negative externalities lead to excessive output levels because activities that produce negative externalities are misleadingly attractive to those who engage in them. One solution to this problem, proposed by the British economist A. C. Pigou, is to make such activities less attractive by taxing them.

Although many critics insist that taxes always reduce economic efficiency, here we have an example of a tax that actually makes the economy *more* efficient. The tax has that effect because it forces producers to take explicit account of the fact that each additional unit of output they produce imposes an external cost on the rest of society.

Similar reasoning suggests that a subsidy to producers can serve to counteract misallocations that result from positive externalities. The subsidy makes the economy more efficient because it induces producers to take account of a relevant benefit that they otherwise would have ignored.

RECAP ↑

EXTERNAL COSTS AND BENEFITS

Externalities occur when the costs or benefits of an activity accrue to people other than those directly involved in the activity. The Coase theorem says that when affected parties can negotiate with one another without cost, activities will be pursued at efficient levels, even in the presence of positive or negative externalities. But when negotiation is prohibitively costly, inefficient behavior generally results. Activities that generate negative externalities are pursued to excess, while those that generate positive externalities are pursued too little. Laws and regulations, including taxes and subsidies, are often adopted in an effort to alter inefficient behavior that results from externalities.

PROPERTY RIGHTS AND THE TRAGEDY OF THE COMMONS

People who grow up in industrialized nations tend to take the institution of private property for granted. Our intuitive sense is that people have the right to own any property they acquire by lawful means and to do with that property as they see fit. In reality, however, property laws are considerably more complex in terms of the rights they confer and the obligations they impose.

The Problem of Unpriced Resources

To understand the laws that govern the use of property, let's begin by asking why societies created the institution of private property in the first place. The following examples, which show what happens to property that nobody owns, suggest an answer.

EXAMPLE 9.9 **Individual Income**

How many steers will villagers send onto the commons?

A village has five residents, each of whom has accumulated savings of $100. Each villager can use the money to buy a government bond that pays 13 percent interest per year or to buy a year-old steer, send it onto the commons to graze, and sell it after 1 year. The price the villager will get for the 2-year-old steer depends on the amount of weight it gains while grazing on the commons, which in turn depends on the number of steers sent onto the commons, as shown in Table 9.4.

TABLE 9.4
The Relationship between Herd Size and Steer Price

Number of steers on the commons	Price per 2-year-old steer ($)	Income per steer ($/year)
1	126	26
2	119	19
3	116	16
4	113	13
5	111	11

The price of a 2-year-old steer declines with the number of steers grazing on the commons because the more steers, the less grass available to each. The villagers make their investment decisions one at a time, and the results are public. If each villager decides how to invest individually, how many steers will be sent onto the commons, and what will be the village's total income?

If a villager buys a $100 government bond, he will earn $13 of interest income at the end of 1 year. Thus, he should send a steer onto the commons if and only if that steer will command a price of at least $113 as a 2-year-old. When each villager chooses in this self-interested way, we can expect four villagers to send a steer onto the commons. (Actually, the fourth villager would be indifferent between investing in a steer or buying a bond since he would earn $13 either way. For the sake of discussion, we'll assume that in the case of a tie, people choose to be cattle owners.) The fifth villager, seeing that he would earn only $11 by sending a fifth steer onto the commons, will choose instead to buy a government bond. As a result of these decisions, the total village income will be $65 per year—$13 for the one bondholder and 4($13) = $52 for the four cattle owners.

Has Adam Smith's invisible hand produced the most efficient allocation of these villagers' resources? We can tell at a glance that it has not since their total village income is only $65—precisely the same as it would have been had the possibility of cattle raising not existed. The source of the difficulty will become evident in the following example.

EXAMPLE 9.10   Maximizing Total Group Income

What is the socially optimal number of steers to send onto the commons?

Suppose the five villagers in the previous example confront the same investment opportunities as before, except that this time they are free to make their decisions as a group rather than individually. How many steers will they send onto the commons, and what will be their total village income?

This time the villagers' goal is to maximize the income received by the group as a whole. When decisions are made from this perspective, the criterion is to send a steer onto the commons only if its marginal contribution to village income is at least $13, the amount that could be earned from a government bond. As the entries in the last column of Table 9.5 indicate, the first steer clearly meets this criterion since it contributes $26 to total village income. But the second steer does not. Sending that steer onto the commons raises the village's income from cattle raising from $26 to $38, a gain of just $12. The $100 required to buy the second steer would thus have been better invested in a government bond. Worse, the collective return from sending a third steer is only $10; from a fourth, only $4; and from a fifth, only $3.

TABLE 9.5
Marginal Income and the Socially Optimal Herd Size

Number of steers on the commons	Price per 2-year-old steer ($)	Income per steer ($/year)	Total village income ($/year)	Marginal income ($/year)
				26
1	126	26	26	
				12
2	119	19	38	
				10
3	116	16	48	
				4
4	113	13	52	
				3
5	111	11	55	

In sum, when investment decisions are made with the goal of maximizing total village income, the best choice is to buy four government bonds and send only a single steer onto the commons. The resulting village income will be $78: $26 from sending the single steer and $52 from the four government bonds. That amount is $13 more than the total income that resulted when villagers made their investment decisions individually. Once again, the reward from moving from an inefficient allocation to an efficient one is that the economic pie grows larger. And when the pie grows larger, everyone can get a larger slice. For instance, if the villagers agree to pool their income and share it equally, each will get $15.60, or $2.60 more than before.

CONCEPT CHECK 9.3

How would your answers to Examples 9.9 and 9.10 change if the interest rate was 11 percent per year rather than 13 percent?

Why do the villagers in Examples 9.9 and 9.10 do better when they make their investment decisions collectively? The answer is that when individuals decide alone, they ignore the fact that sending another steer onto the commons will cause existing steers to gain less weight. Their failure to consider this effect makes the return from sending another steer seem misleadingly high to them.

The grazing land on the commons is a valuable economic resource. When no one owns it, no one has any incentive to take the opportunity cost of using it into account. And when that happens, people will tend to use it until its marginal benefit is zero. This problem, and others similar to it, is known as the **tragedy of the commons**. The essential cause of the tragedy of the commons is the fact that one person's use of commonly held property imposes an external cost on others by making the property less valuable. Each individual villager behaves rationally by sending an additional steer onto the commons, yet the overall outcome falls far short of the attainable ideal.

tragedy of the commons the tendency for a resource that has no price to be used until its marginal benefit falls to zero

The Effect of Private Ownership

As the following example illustrates, one solution to the tragedy of the commons is to place the village grazing land under private ownership.

EXAMPLE 9.11   Private Ownership

How much will the right to control the village commons sell for?

Suppose the five villagers face the same investment opportunities as before, except that this time they decide to auction off the right to use the commons to the highest bidder. Assuming that villagers can borrow as well as lend at an annual interest rate of 13 percent, what price will the right to use the commons fetch? How will the owner of that property right use it, and what will be the resulting village income?

To answer these questions, simply ask yourself what you would do if you had complete control over how the grazing land were used. As we saw earlier, the most profitable way to use this land is to send only a single steer to graze on it. If you do so, you will earn a total of $26 per year. Since the opportunity cost of the $100 you spent on the single yearling steer is the $13 in interest you could have earned from a bond, your economic profit from sending a single steer onto the commons will be $13 per year, provided you can use the land for free. But you cannot; to finance your purchase of the property right, you must borrow money (since you used your $100 savings to buy a year-old steer).

What is the most you would be willing to pay for the right to use the commons? Since its use generates an income of $26 per year, or $13 more than the opportunity cost of your investment in the steer, the most you would pay is $100 (because that amount used to purchase a bond that pays 13 percent interest would also generate income of $13 per year). If the land were sold at auction, $100 is precisely the amount you would have to pay. Your annual earnings from the land would be exactly enough to pay the $13 interest on your loan and cover the opportunity cost of not having put your savings into a bond.

Note that when the right to use the land is auctioned to the highest bidder, the village achieves a more efficient allocation of its resources because the owner has a strong incentive to take the opportunity cost of more intensive grazing fully into account. Total village income in this case will again be $78. If the annual interest on the $100 proceeds from selling the land rights is shared equally among the five villagers, each will again have an annual investment income of $15.60.

The logic of economic surplus maximization helps to explain why the most economically successful nations have all been ones with well-developed private property laws. Property that belongs to everyone belongs, in effect, to no one. Not only is its potential economic value never fully realized; it usually ends up being of no value at all.

Bear in mind, however, that in most countries the owners of private property are not free to do *precisely* as they wish with it. For example, local zoning laws may give the owner of a residential building lot the right to build a three-story house but not a six-story house. Here, too, the logic of economic surplus maximization applies, for a fully informed and rational legislature would define property rights so as to create the largest possible total economic surplus. In practice, of course, such ideal legislatures never really exist. Yet the essence of politics is the cutting of deals that make people better off. If a legislator could propose a change in the property laws that would enlarge the total economic surplus, she could also propose a scheme that would give each of her constituents a larger slice, thus enhancing her chances for reelection.

As an economic naturalist, challenge yourself to use this framework when thinking about the various restrictions you encounter in private property laws: zoning laws that constrain what you can build and what types of activities you can conduct on your land; traffic laws that constrain what you can do with your car; employment and environmental laws that constrain how you can operate your business. Your understanding of these and countless other laws will be enhanced by the insight that everyone can gain when the private property laws are defined so as to create the largest total economic surplus.

When Private Ownership Is Impractical

Do not be misled into thinking that the law provides an *ideal* resolution of all problems associated with externalities and the tragedy of the commons. Defining and enforcing efficient property rights entail costs, after all, and sometimes, as in the following examples, the costs outweigh the gains.

The Economic Naturalist 9.3

Why do blackberries in public parks get picked too soon?

Wild blackberries grow profusely at the edge of a wooded area in a crowded city park. The blackberries will taste best if left to ripen fully, but they still taste reasonably good if picked and eaten a few days early. Will the blackberries be left to ripen fully?

Obviously, the costs of defining and enforcing the property rights to blackberries growing in a public park are larger than the potential gains, so the blackberries will remain common property. That means that whoever picks them first gets them. Even though everyone would benefit if people waited until the berries were fully ripe, everyone knows that those who wait are likely to end up with no berries at all. And that means that the berries will be eaten too soon.

Why does fruit that grows in public places get picked too soon?

The Economic Naturalist 9.4

Why are shared milkshakes consumed too quickly?

Sara and Susan are identical twins who have been given a chocolate milkshake to share. If each has a straw and each knows that the other is self-interested, will the twins consume the milkshake at an optimal rate?

Because drinking a milkshake too quickly chills the taste buds, the twins will enjoy their shake more if they drink it slowly. Yet each knows that the other will drink any part of the milkshake she doesn't finish herself. The result is that each will consume the shake at a faster rate than she would if she had half a shake all to herself.

Why are shared milkshakes drunk too quickly?

Here are some further examples in which the tragedy of the commons is not easily solved by defining private ownership rights.

Harvesting Timber on Remote Public Land On remote public lands, enforcing restrictions against cutting down trees may be impractical. Each tree cutter knows that a tree that is not harvested this year will be bigger, and hence more valuable, next year. But he also knows that if he doesn't cut the tree down this year, someone else might do so. In contrast, private companies that grow trees on their own land have no incentive to harvest timber prematurely and a strong incentive to prevent outsiders from doing so.

Harvesting Whales in International Waters Each individual whaler knows that harvesting an extra whale reduces the breeding population, and hence the size of the future whale population. But the whaler also knows that any whale that is not harvested today may be taken by some other whaler. The solution would be to define and enforce property rights to whales. But the oceans are vast, and the behavior of whalers is hard to monitor. And even if their behavior could be monitored, the concept of national sovereignty would make the international enforcement of property rights problematic.

More generally, the animal species that are most severely threatened with extinction tend to be those that are economically valuable to humans but that are not privately owned by anyone. This is the situation confronting whales as well as elephants. Contrast this with the situation confronting chickens, which are also economically valuable to humans but which, unlike whales, are governed by traditional laws of private property. This difference explains why no one worries that Colonel Sanders might threaten the extinction of chickens.

Controlling Multinational Environmental Pollution Each individual polluter may know that if he and all others pollute, the damage to the environment will be greater than the cost of not polluting. But if the environment is common property into which all are free to dump, each has a powerful incentive to pollute. Enforcing laws and regulations that limit the discharge of pollution may be practical if all polluters live under the jurisdiction of a single government. But if polluters come from many different countries, solutions are much more difficult to implement. Thus, the Mediterranean Sea has long suffered serious pollution since none of the many nations that border it has an economic incentive to consider the effects of its discharges on other countries.

As the world's population continues to grow, the absence of an effective system of international property rights will become an economic problem of increasing significance.

> **RECAP ↑**
>
> **PROPERTY RIGHTS AND THE TRAGEDY OF THE COMMONS**
>
> When a valuable resource has a price of zero, people will continue to exploit it as long as its marginal benefit remains positive. The tragedy of the commons describes situations in which valuable resources are squandered because users are not charged for them. In many cases, an efficient remedy is to define and enforce rights to the use of valuable property. But this solution is difficult to implement for resources such as the oceans and the atmosphere because no single government has the authority to enforce property rights for these resources.

POSITIONAL EXTERNALITIES

Former tennis champion Steffi Graf received more than $1.6 million in tournament winnings in 1992; her endorsement and exhibition earnings totaled several times that amount. By any reasonable measure, the quality of her play was outstanding, yet she consistently lost to archrival Monica Seles. But in April of 1993, Seles was stabbed in the back by a deranged fan and forced to withdraw from the tour. In the ensuing months, Graf's tournament winnings accumulated at almost double her 1992 pace, despite little change in the quality of her play.

Payoffs That Depend on Relative Performance

In professional tennis and a host of other competitive situations, the rewards people receive typically depend not only on how they perform in absolute terms but also on how they perform relative to their closest rivals. In these situations, competitors have an incentive to take actions that will increase their odds of winning. For example, tennis players can increase their chances of winning by hiring personal fitness trainers and sports psychologists to travel with them on the tour. Yet the simple mathematics of competition tells us that the sum of all individual payoffs from such investments will be larger than the collective payoff. In any tennis match, for example, each contestant will get a sizable payoff from money spent on fitness trainers and sports psychologists, yet each match will have exactly one winner and one loser, no matter how much players spend. The overall gain to tennis spectators is likely to be small, and the overall gain to players as a group must be zero. To the extent that each contestant's payoff depends on his or her relative performance, then, the incentive to undertake such investments will be excessive, from a collective point of view.

Consider the following example.

The Economic Naturalist 9.5

Why do football players take anabolic steroids?

The offensive linemen of many National Football League teams currently average more than 330 pounds. In the 1970s, by contrast, offensive linemen in the league averaged barely 280 pounds, and the all-decade linemen of the 1940s averaged only 229 pounds. One reason that today's players are so much heavier is that players' salaries have escalated sharply over the last two decades, which has intensified competition for the positions. Size and strength are the two cardinal virtues of an offensive lineman, and other things being equal, the job will go to the larger and stronger of two rivals.

Size and strength, in turn, can be enhanced by the consumption of anabolic steroids. But if all players consume these substances, the rank ordering of players by size and strength—and hence the question of who lands the jobs—will be largely unaffected. And since the consumption of anabolic steroids entails potentially serious long-term health consequences, as a group football players are clearly worse off if they consume these drugs. So why do football players take steroids?

The problem here is that contestants for starting berths on the offensive line confront a prisoner's dilemma, like the ones analyzed in the *Games and Strategic Behavior* chapter. Consider two closely matched rivals—Smith and Jones—who are competing for a single position. If neither takes steroids, each has a 50 percent chance of winning the job and a starting salary of $1 million per year. If both take steroids, each again has a 50 percent chance of winning the job. But if one takes steroids and the other doesn't, the first is sure to win the job. The loser ends up selling insurance for $60,000 per year. Neither likes the fact that the drugs may have adverse health consequences, but each would be willing to take that risk in return for a shot at the big salary. Given these choices, the two competitors face a payoff matrix like the one shown in Table 9.6.

Why do so many football players take steroids?

TABLE 9.6
Payoff Matrix for Steroid Consumption

		Jones	
		Don't take steroids	Take steroids
Smith	Don't take steroids	Second best for each	Best for Jones Worst for Smith
	Take steroids	Best for Smith Worst for Jones	Third best for each

---

Clearly, the dominant strategy for both Smith and Jones is to take steroids. Yet when they do, each gets only the third-best outcome, whereas they could have gotten the second-best outcome by not taking the drugs—hence the attraction of rules that forbid the consumption of anabolic steroids.

Positional Arms Races and Positional Arms Control Agreements

The steroid problem is an example of a **positional externality**. Whenever the payoffs to one contestant depend at least in part on how he or she performs relative to a rival, any step that improves one side's relative position must necessarily worsen the other's. The

positional externality occurs when an increase in one person's performance reduces the expected reward of another's in situations in which reward depends on relative performance

positional arms race a series of mutually offsetting investments in performance enhancement that is stimulated by a positional externality

positional arms control agreement an agreement in which contestants attempt to limit mutually offsetting investments in performance enhancement

shouting-at-parties example discussed in the chapter *Games and Strategic Behavior* is another instance of a positional externality. Just as the invisible hand of the market is weakened by the presence of standard externalities, it is also weakened by positional externalities.

We have seen that positional externalities often lead contestants to engage in an escalating series of mutually offsetting investments in performance enhancement. We call such spending patterns **positional arms races**.

Because positional arms races produce inefficient outcomes, people have an incentive to curtail them. Steps taken to reduce positional arms races such as blue laws and rules against anabolic steroids may therefore be thought of as **positional arms control agreements**.

Once you become aware of positional arms races, you will begin to see them almost everywhere. You can hone your skills as an economic naturalist by asking these questions about every competitive situation you observe: What form do the investments in performance enhancement take? What steps have contestants taken to limit these investments? Sometimes positional arms control agreements are achieved by the imposition of formal rules or by the signing of legal contracts. Some examples of this type of agreement follow.

Campaign Spending Limits In the United States, presidential candidates routinely spend more than $100 million on advertising. Yet if both candidates double their spending on ads, each one's odds of winning will remain essentially the same. Recognition of this pattern led Congress to adopt strict spending limits for presidential candidates. (That those regulations have proved difficult to enforce does not call into question the logic behind the legislation.)

Roster Limits Major League Baseball permits franchises to have only 25 players on the roster during the regular season. The National Football League sets its roster limit at 53; the National Basketball Association at 12. Why these limits? In their absence, any team could increase its chance of winning by simply adding players. Inevitably, other teams would follow suit. On the plausible assumption that, beyond some point, larger rosters do not add much to the entertainment value for fans, roster limits are a sensible way to deliver sports entertainment at a more reasonable cost.

Arbitration Agreements In the business world, contracting parties often sign a binding agreement that commits them to arbitration in the event of a dispute. By doing so, they sacrifice the option of pursuing their interests as fully as they might wish to later, but they also insulate themselves from costly legal battles. Other parties in the legal system may sometimes take steps to limit spending on litigation. For example, a federal judge in South Dakota announced—presumably to the approval of litigants—that he would read only the first 15 pages of any brief submitted to his court.

Mandatory Starting Dates for Kindergarten A child who is a year or so older than most of her kindergarten classmates is likely to perform better, in relative terms, than if she had entered school with children her own age. And since most parents are aware that admission to prestigious universities and eligibility for top jobs upon graduation depend largely on *relative* academic performance, many are tempted to keep their children out of kindergarten a year longer than necessary. Yet there is no social advantage in holding *all* children back an extra year since their relative performance would essentially be unaffected. In most jurisdictions, therefore, the law requires children who reach their fifth birthday before December 1 of a given year to start kindergarten the same year.

Social Norms as Positional Arms Control Agreements

In some cases, social norms may take the place of formal agreements to curtail positional arms races. Some familiar examples follow.

Nerd Norms Some students care more—in the short run, at least—about the grades they get than how much they actually learn. When such students are graded on the curve—that is, on the basis of their performance relative to other students—a positional arms race ensues because if all students were to double the amount of time they studied, the distribution of grades would remain essentially the same. Students who find themselves in this situation are often quick to embrace "nerd norms," which brand as social misfits those who "study too hard."

Fashion Norms Social norms regarding dress and fashion often change quickly because of positional competitions. Consider, for instance, the person who wishes to be on the cutting edge of fashion. In some American social circles during the 1950s, that goal could be accomplished by having pierced ears. But as more and more people adopted the practice, it ceased to communicate avant-garde status. At the same time, those who wanted to make a conservative fashion statement gradually became freer to have their ears pierced.

Is being on fashion's cutting edge more valuable now than in the 1950s?

For a period during the 1960s and 1970s, one could be on fashion's cutting edge by wearing two earrings in one earlobe. But by the 1990s multiple ear piercings had lost much of their social significance, the threshold of cutting-edge status having been raised to upward of a dozen piercings of each ear, or a smaller number of piercings of the nose, eyebrows, or other body parts. A similar escalation has taken place in the number, size, and placement of tattoos.

The increase in the required number of tattoos or body piercings has not changed the value of avant-garde fashion status to those who desire it. Being on the outer limits of fashion has much the same meaning now as it once did. To the extent that there are costs associated with body piercings, tattoos, and other steps required to achieve avant-garde status, the current fashions are wasteful compared to earlier ones. In this sense, the erosion of social norms against tattoos and body piercings has produced a social loss. Of course, the costs associated with this loss are small in most cases. Yet since each body piercing entails a small risk of infection, the costs will continue to rise with the number of piercings. And once those costs reach a certain threshold, support may mobilize on behalf of social norms that discourage body mutilation.

Norms of Taste Similar cycles occur with respect to behaviors considered to be in bad taste. In the 1950s, for example, prevailing norms prevented major national magazines from accepting ads that featured nude photographs. Naturally, advertisers had a powerful incentive to chip away at such norms in an effort to capture the reader's limited attention. And indeed, taboos against nude photographs have eroded in the same way as taboos against body mutilation.

Consider, for instance, the evolution of perfume ads. First came the nude silhouette; then, increasingly well-lighted and detailed nude photographs; and more recently, photographs of what appear to be group sex acts. Each innovation achieved just the desired effect: capturing the reader's instant and rapt attention. Inevitably, however, other advertisers followed suit, causing a shift in our sense of what is considered attention-grabbing. Photographs that once would have shocked readers now often draw little more than a bored glance.

Opinions differ, of course, about whether this change is an improvement. Many believe that the earlier, stricter norms were ill-advised, the legacy of a more prudish and repressive era. Yet even people who take that view are likely to believe that *some* kinds of photographic material ought not to be used in magazine advertisements. Obviously, what is acceptable will differ from person to person, and each person's threshold of discomfort will depend in part on current standards. But as advertisers continue to break new ground in their struggle to capture attention, the point may come when people begin to mobilize in favor of stricter standards of "public decency." Such a campaign would provide yet another case of a positional arms control agreement.

Norms against Vanity Cosmetic and reconstructive surgery has produced dramatic benefits for many people, enabling badly disfigured accident victims to recover a normal appearance. It also has eliminated the extreme self-consciousness felt by people born with strikingly unusual features. Such surgery, however, is by no means confined to the conspicuously disfigured. Increasingly, "normal" people are seeking surgical improvements to their appearance. Some 2 million cosmetic "procedures" were done in

"We're looking for the kind of bad taste that will grab—but not appall."

1991—six times the number just a decade earlier[1]—and demand has continued to grow steadily in the years since. Once a carefully guarded secret, these procedures are now offered as prizes in southern California charity raffles.

In individual cases, cosmetic surgery may be just as beneficial as reconstructive surgery is for accident victims. Buoyed by the confidence of having a straight nose or a wrinkle-free complexion, patients sometimes go on to achieve much more than they ever thought possible. But the growing use of cosmetic surgery also has had an unintended side effect: It has altered the standards of normal appearance. A nose that once would have seemed only slightly larger than average may now seem jarringly big. The same person who once would have looked like an average 55-year-old may now look nearly 70. And someone who once would have tolerated slightly thinning hair or an average amount of cellulite may now feel compelled to undergo hair transplantation or liposuction. Because such procedures shift people's frame of reference, their payoffs to individuals are misleadingly large. From a social perspective, therefore, reliance on them is likely to be excessive.

Legal sanctions against cosmetic surgery are difficult to imagine. But some communities have embraced powerful social norms against cosmetic surgery, heaping scorn and ridicule on the consumers of face-lifts and tummy tucks. In individual cases, such norms may seem cruel. Yet without them, many more people might feel compelled to bear the risk and expense of cosmetic surgery.

> **RECAP ↑**
>
> **POSITIONAL EXTERNALITIES**
>
> Positional externalities occur when an increase in one person's performance reduces the expected reward of another person in situations in which reward depends on relative performance. Positional arms races are a series of mutually offsetting investments in performance enhancement that are stimulated by a positional externality. Positional arms control agreements are sometimes enacted in an attempt to limit positional arms races. In some cases, social norms can act as positional arms control agreements.

[1]*The Economist,* January 11, 1992, p. 25.

SUMMARY

- Externalities are the costs and benefits of activities that accrue to people who are not directly involved in those activities. When all parties affected by externalities can negotiate with one another at no cost, the invisible hand of the market will produce an efficient allocation of resources. According to the Coase theorem, the allocation of resources is efficient in such cases because the parties affected by externalities can compensate others for taking remedial action. *(LO1, LO2)*

- Negotiation over externalities is often impractical, however. In these cases, the self-serving actions of individuals typically will not lead to an efficient outcome. The attempt to forge solutions to the problems caused by externalities is one of the most important rationales for collective action. Sometimes collective action takes the form of laws and government regulations that alter the incentives facing those who generate, or are affected by, externalities. Such remedies work best when they place the burden of accommodation on the parties who can accomplish it at the lowest cost. Traffic laws, zoning laws, environmental protection laws, and free speech laws are examples. *(LO3)*

- Curbing pollution and other negative externalities entails costs as well as benefits. The optimal amount of pollution reduction is the amount for which the marginal benefit of further reduction just equals the marginal cost. In general, this formula implies that the socially optimal level of pollution, or of any other negative externality, is greater than zero. *(LO3)*

- When grazing land and other valuable resources are owned in common, no one has an incentive to take into account the opportunity cost of using those resources. This problem is known as the tragedy of the commons. Defining and enforcing private rights governing the use of valuable resources is often an effective solution to the tragedy of the commons. Not surprisingly, most economically successful nations have well-developed institutions of private property. Property that belongs to everyone belongs, in effect, to no one. Not only is its potential economic value never fully realized; it usually ends up having no value at all. *(LO4)*

- The difficulty of enforcing property rights in certain situations explains a variety of inefficient outcomes such as the excessive harvest of whales in international waters and the premature harvest of timber on remote public lands. The excessive pollution of seas that are bordered by many countries also results from a lack of enforceable property rights. *(LO4)*

- Situations in which people's rewards depend on how well they perform in relation to their rivals give rise to positional externalities. In these situations, any step that improves one side's relative position necessarily worsens the other's. Positional externalities tend to spawn positional arms races—escalating patterns of mutually offsetting investments in performance enhancement. Collective measures to curb positional arms races are known as positional arms control agreements. These collective actions may take the form of formal regulations or rules such as rules against anabolic steroids in sports, campaign spending limits, and binding arbitration agreements. Informal social norms can also curtail positional arms races. *(LO5)*

KEY TERMS

Coase theorem
external benefit
external cost
externality

negative externality
positional arms control
 agreement
positional arms race

positional externality
positive externality
tragedy of the commons

REVIEW QUESTIONS

1. If Congress could declare any activity that imposes external costs on others illegal, would such legislation be advisable? *(LO2)*

2. What incentive problem explains why the freeways in cities like Los Angeles suffer from excessive congestion? *(LO3)*

3. Why does the Great Salt Lake, which is located wholly within the state of Utah, suffer lower levels of pollution than Lake Erie, which is bordered by several states and Canada? *(LO3)*

4. How would you explain to a friend why the optimal amount of freeway congestion is not zero? *(LO3)*

5. Explain why the wearing of high-heeled shoes might be viewed as the result of a positional externality. *(LO5)*

PROBLEMS   connect

1. For each good listed below, discuss whether the good is likely to entail either an external cost or an external benefit. In addition, discuss whether the private market is likely to provide more or less than the socially optimal quantity of the good. *(LO1)*
   a. Vaccinations
   b. Cigarettes
   c. Antibiotics

2. Suppose the law says that Jones may *not* emit smoke from his factory unless he gets permission from Smith, who lives downwind. The relevant costs and benefits of filtering the smoke from Jones's production process are as shown in the following table. If Jones and Smith can negotiate with one another at no cost, will Jones emit smoke? *(LO2)*

	Jones emits smoke	Jones does not emit smoke
Surplus for Jones	$200	$160
Surplus for Smith	$400	$420

3. John and Karl can live together in a two-bedroom apartment for $500 per month, or each can rent a single-bedroom apartment for $350 per month. Aside from the rent, the two would be indifferent between living together and living separately, except for one problem: John leaves dirty dishes in the sink every night. Karl would be willing to pay up to $175 per month to avoid John's dirty dishes. John, for his part, would be willing to pay up to $225 to be able to continue his sloppiness.
   a. Should John and Karl live together? If they do, will there be dirty dishes in the sink? Explain. *(LO2)*
   b. If John would be willing to pay up to $30 per month to avoid giving up his privacy by sharing quarters with Karl, should John and Karl live together? *(LO2)*

4. Barton and Statler are neighbors in an apartment complex in downtown Manhattan. Barton is a concert pianist, and Statler is a poet working on an epic poem. Barton rehearses his concert pieces on the baby grand piano in his front room, which is directly above Statler's study. The following matrix shows the monthly payoffs to Barton and Statler when Barton's front room is and is not soundproofed. The soundproofing will be effective only if it is installed in Barton's apartment. *(LO2)*

	Soundproofed	Not soundproofed
Gains to Barton	$100/month	$150/month
Gains to Statler	$120/month	$80/month

   a. If Barton has the legal right to make any amount of noise he wants and he and Statler can negotiate with one another at no cost, will Barton install and maintain soundproofing? Explain. Is his choice socially efficient?
   b. If Statler has the legal right to peace and quiet and can negotiate with Barton at no cost, will Barton install and maintain soundproofing? Explain. Is his choice socially efficient?
   c. Does the attainment of an efficient outcome depend on whether Barton has the legal right to make noise, or Statler the legal right to peace and quiet?

5. Refer to Problem 4. Barton decides to buy a full-sized grand piano. The new payoff matrix is as follows: *(LO2)*

	Soundproofed	Not soundproofed
Gains to Barton	$100/month	$150/month
Gains to Statler	$120/month	$60/month

   a. If Statler has the legal right to peace and quiet and Barton and Statler can negotiate at no cost, will Barton install and maintain soundproofing? Explain. Is this outcome socially efficient?
   b. Suppose that Barton has the legal right to make as much noise as he likes and that negotiating an agreement with Barton costs $15 per month. Will Barton install and maintain soundproofing? Explain. Is this outcome socially efficient?
   c. Suppose Statler has the legal right to peace and quiet, and it costs $15 per month for Statler and Barton to negotiate any agreement. (Compensation for noise damage can be paid without incurring negotiation cost.) Will Barton install and maintain soundproofing? Is this outcome socially efficient?
   d. Why does the attainment of a socially efficient outcome now depend on whether Barton has the legal right to make noise?

6. Determine whether the following statements are true or false, and briefly explain why: *(LO3)*
   a. A given total emission reduction in a polluting industry will be achieved at the lowest possible total cost when the cost of the last unit of pollution curbed is equal for each firm in the industry.
   b. In an attempt to lower their costs of production, firms sometimes succeed merely in shifting costs to outsiders.

7.* A village has six residents, each of whom has accumulated savings of $100. Each villager can use this money either to buy a government bond that pays 15 percent interest per year or to buy a year-old llama, send it onto the commons to graze, and sell it after 1 year. The price the villager gets for the 2-year-old llama depends on the quality of the fleece it grows while grazing on the commons. That in turn depends on the animal's access to grazing, which depends on the number of llamas sent to the commons, as shown in the following table:

Number of llamas on the commons	Price per 2-year-old llama ($)
1	122
2	118
3	116
4	114
5	112
6	109

The villagers make their investment decisions one after another, and their decisions are public. *(LO4)*

a. If each villager decides individually how to invest, how many llamas will be sent onto the commons, and what will be the resulting net village income?

b. What is the socially optimal number of llamas for this village? Why is that different from the actual number? What would net village income be if the socially optimal number of llamas were sent onto the commons?

c. The village committee votes to auction the right to graze llamas on the commons to the highest bidder. Assuming villagers can both borrow and lend at 15 percent annual interest, how much will the right sell for at auction? How will the new owner use the right, and what will be the resulting village income?

8. Suppose that Lance and Jan are the two top cyclists in the world. Both are scheduled to compete in an upcoming cycling competition in which the winner will receive $100,000 in prize money while the rest of the competitors receive nothing. Both cyclists are very talented, but they can increase their chances of winning by doping (i.e., taking performance-enhancing drugs). The cost to each of doping is $25,000 (this includes not just the cost of the drugs, but also both the health costs and the expected damage to their reputations if they are caught). Each has a 50 percent chance of winning the race either if both of them dope or if neither of them dopes. On the other hand, if only one of them dopes, then the one who dopes will win the race for sure. *(LO5)*

a. Discuss whether this situation involves a positional externality.

b. Write down the expected payoff matrix for this game, assuming that both Lance and Jan make their decisions simultaneously.

c. Will the outcome of this game be socially optimal? Explain.

*Problems marked with an asterisk (*) are more difficult.

ANSWERS TO CONCEPT CHECKS

9.1 Since Fitch gains $50 per day when Abercrombie operates with a filter, he could pay Abercrombie as much as $49 per day and still come out ahead. *(LO2)*

9.2 If the two were to live together, the most efficient way to resolve the telephone problem would be as before, for Betty to give up reasonable access to the phone. But on top of that cost, which is $150, Betty would also bear a $60 cost from the loss of her privacy. The total cost of their living together would thus be $210 per month. Since that amount is greater than the $200 saving in rent, the two should live separately. *(LO2)*

9.3 The income figures from the different levels of investment in cattle would remain as before, as shown in the table. What is different is the opportunity cost of investing in each steer, which is now $11 per year instead of $13. The last column of the table shows that the socially optimal number of steers is now 2 instead of 1. And if individuals still favor holding cattle, all other things being equal, they will now send 5 steers onto the commons instead of 4, as shown in the middle column. *(LO4)*

Number of steers on the commons	Price per 2-year-old steer ($)	Income per steer ($/year)	Total village income ($/year)	Marginal income ($/year)
				26
1	126	26	26	
				12
2	119	19	38	
				10
3	116	16	48	
				4
4	113	13	52	
				3
5	111	11	55	

Using Economics to Make Better Policy Choices

In 1979, in the wake of the second major oil supply interruption in a decade, officials in the Carter administration met to discuss policies for reducing the risks to domestic security inherent in U.S. dependence on foreign oil. The proposal they ultimately put forward was a gasoline tax of 50 cents per gallon. Anticipating objections that the tax would impose an unacceptable hardship on the poor, policymakers proposed to return the revenues from the tax to the citizenry by reducing the payroll tax—the tax on wages that supports the Social Security system.

Proponents of the gasoline tax argued that in addition to reducing the nation's dependence on foreign oil, the tax would reduce air pollution and ease highway congestion. But critics ridiculed the proposal, charging that if the revenues from the tax were returned to the people, the quantity of gasoline demanded would remain essentially the same. Their argument tipped the debate, and officials never managed to implement the proposal.

Whatever the ultimate merits of the administration's proposal, there was no merit at all in the argument the critics used to attack it. True, the proposed tax rebate meant that people *could* have bought just as much gasoline as before the tax. Yet the tax would have given them a powerful incentive not to do so. Consumers can change their behavior to escape the effects of a steep rise in the after-tax price of gasoline—by switching to cars with smaller, more fuel-efficient engines; forming car pools; and so on. Such changes free up money to spend on other goods and services, which become relatively more attractive because they are not taxed.

No society can hope to formulate and implement intelligent economic policies unless its citizens and leaders share an understanding of basic economic principles. Our aim in this chapter is to explore how careful application of these principles can help us design policies that both expand the economic pie and make everyone's slice larger. We will explore the economics of health care delivery, environmental regulation, and public health and safety regulation. The unifying thread running through these issues is the problem of scarcity. In each case, we will explore how the Cost-Benefit Principle can help to resolve the resulting trade-offs.

10

LEARNING OBJECTIVES

After reading this chapter, you should be able to:

LO1 Describe how the Cost-Benefit Principle applies even to choices involving health.

LO2 Explain why health care costs have been rising so rapidly.

LO3 Compare and contrast the ways in which taxes and tradable permits can be used to reduce pollution.

LO4 Assess the economic pros and cons of the various methods used to reduce poverty in the United States.

THE ECONOMICS OF HEALTH CARE

Political leaders are often reluctant to discuss expenditures on public health programs in cost-benefit terms. But because we live in a world of scarcity, we cannot escape the fact that spending more on health means spending less on other things of value.

Illnesses, like accidents, are costly to prevent. The socially optimal expenditure on a health measure that reduces a specific illness is that amount for which the marginal benefit to society of the measure exactly equals its marginal cost. For example, in deciding how much to spend on vaccinating against measles, a rational public health policy would expand the proportion of the population vaccinated until the marginal cost of an additional vaccination was exactly equal to the marginal value of the illnesses thus prevented.

As we explain in the following section, however, the decision of whether to become vaccinated looks very different from each individual's perspective.

The Case for Mandatory Immunization Laws

Being vaccinated against a childhood illness entails a small but potentially serious risk. The vaccine against pertussis (whooping cough), for example, is believed to cause some form of permanent brain damage in one out of every 110,000 children vaccinated. Contracting the disease itself also poses serious health risks, and in an environment in which infections were sufficiently likely to occur, individuals would have a compelling reason to bear the risk of being vaccinated in order to reduce the even larger risk from infection. The problem is that in an environment in which most children were vaccinated, infection rates would be low, making the risk of vaccination loom relatively large in the eyes of individual families.

The ideal situation from the perspective of any individual family would be to remain unvaccinated in an environment in which all other families were vaccinated. But as more and more families decided to forgo vaccination, infection rates would mount. Eventually the vaccination rate would stabilize at the point at which the additional risk to the individual family of becoming vaccinated would be exactly equal to the risk from remaining unvaccinated. But this calculation ignores the fact that a decision to remain unvaccinated poses risk not just to the individual decision maker, but also to others who have decided to become vaccinated (since no vaccine affords 100 percent protection against infection).

Relegating the vaccination decision to individuals thus results in a suboptimally low vaccination rate because individual decision makers fail to take adequate account of the cost that their becoming infected will impose on others. It is for this reason that most states require vaccinations against specific childhood illnesses. Proof of immunization against diphtheria, measles, poliomyelitis, and rubella, for example, is now universally required for entry into American public schools. Most states also require immunization against tetanus (49 states), pertussis (44 states), mumps (43 states), and hepatitis B (26 states).

Even these laws, however, allow parents to apply for exemptions on religious or philosophical grounds. Communities vary in the extent to which parents avail themselves of these exemptions. In Colorado, for instance, Boulder County heads the list of parents who opt to exempt their children from taking the pertussis vaccine (with an exemption rate of 8.4 percent, more than four times the rate statewide). Not surprisingly, the incidence of whooping cough is much higher in Boulder (34.7 cases per year per 100,000 people) than in the state as a whole (9.4 cases per year per 100,000 people).[1]

EXPLAINING RISING HEALTH CARE COSTS

In the United States, real health care expenditures per capita have grown more rapidly than real income per capita for as long as the relevant data have been available. As a share of national income, health care costs have risen from only 4 percent in 1940 to roughly 17 percent today. Part of this increase is the result of costly new health care technologies and procedures. Diagnostic tests have grown more expensive and sophisticated, and

[1] Colorado Department of Public Health and Environment, www.cdphe.state.co.us.

procedures like coronary bypass surgery and organ transplantation have grown far more common. Yet a great deal of medical expenditure inflation has nothing to do with these high-tech developments. Rather, it is the result of fundamental changes in the way we pay for medical services.

The most important change has been the emergence of the so-called third-party payment system. Earlier in the twentieth century, many people insured themselves against catastrophic illness but purchased routine medical care out of their own pockets, just as they did food, clothing, and other consumer goods. Starting after World War II, and increasingly since the mid-1960s, people have come to depend on insurance for even routine medical services. Some of this insurance is provided privately by employers, some by the government. In the latter category, Medicaid covers the medical expenses of the poor and Medicare, those of the elderly and disabled.

The spread of medical insurance, especially government-financed medical insurance, owes much to the belief that an inability to pay should not prevent people from receiving medical care they need. Indeed, medical insurance has surely done much to shelter people from financial hardship. The difficulty is that in its most common form, it also has spawned literally hundreds of billions of dollars of waste each year.

To understand the nature of this waste, we must recognize that although medical services differ from other services in many ways, they are in one fundamental respect the same: The cost-benefit test is the only sensible criterion for deciding which services ought to be performed. The fact that a medical procedure has *some* benefit does not, by itself, imply that the procedure should be performed. Rather, it should be performed only if its marginal benefit, broadly construed, exceeds its marginal cost.

The costs of medical procedures are relatively easy to measure, using the same methods applied to other goods and services. But the usual measure of the benefit of a good or service, a person's willingness to pay, may not be acceptable in the case of many medical services. For example, most of us would not conclude that a lifesaving appendectomy that costs $2,000 is unjustified merely because one person who needs it can afford to pay only $1,000. When someone lacks the resources to pay for what most of us would consider an essential medical service, society has at least some responsibility to help. Hence the proliferation of government-sponsored medical insurance.

Many other medical expenditures are not as pressing as an emergency appendectomy, however. Following such surgery, for example, the patient requires a period of recuperation in the hospital. How long should that period last—2 days? 5? 10? The Cost-Benefit Principle is critically important to thinking intelligently about such questions. But as Example 10.1 illustrates, the third-party payment system has virtually eliminated cost-benefit thinking from the medical domain.

EXAMPLE 10.1   The Impact of a Third-Party Payment System on Cost-Benefit Thinking

How long should David stay in the hospital?

To eliminate recurrent sore throats, David plans to have his tonsils removed. His surgeon tells him that the average hospital stay after this procedure is two days (some people stay only one day, while others stay three, four, or even five days). Hospital rooms cost $300 per day. If David's demand curve for days in the hospital is as shown in Figure 10.1, how many days will he stay if he must pay for his hospital room himself? How many days will he stay if his medical insurance fully covers the cost of his hospital room?

If David must pay for his hospital room himself, his best option will be to stay for just one day. But if the cost of his hospital room is completely covered by insurance, the marginal cost *to him* will be zero. In that case, he will stay for three days.

FIGURE 10.1

The Demand for Hospital Care.

The demand curve for postoperative hospital care is downward-sloping, just like any other demand curve. At higher prices, people choose shorter hospital stays, not because there is no benefit to a longer stay, but because they prefer to spend their money in other ways.

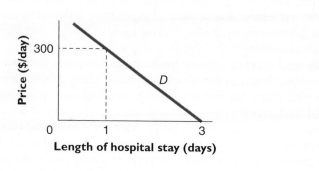

CONCEPT CHECK 10.1

In Example 10.1, how long would David choose to stay in the hospital if his health insurance covered 50 percent of the cost of his hospital room?

Should we be concerned that people choose longer hospital stays when their expenses are fully insured? The Cost-Benefit Principle tells us that a hospital stay should be extended another day only if the benefit of doing so would be at least as great as the cost of the resources required to extend the stay. But when hospital costs are fully covered by insurance, the decision maker sees a marginal cost of zero, when in fact the marginal cost is several hundred dollars. According to the Cost-Benefit Principle, then, full insurance coverage leads to wastefully long hospital stays. That is not to say that the additional days in the hospital do no good at all. Rather, their benefit, as measured by the decision maker's willingness to pay for them, is less than their cost ($300 per day).

Designing a Solution

The amount of waste caused by full insurance coverage depends on the price elasticity of demand for medical services—the more elastic the demand, the greater the waste. Proponents of full coverage believe that the demand for medical services is almost completely inelastic with respect to price and that the resulting waste is therefore negligible. Critics of full coverage argue that the demand for medical services is actually quite sensitive to price and that the resulting waste is significant.

Who is right? One way to determine this is to examine whether people who lack full insurance coverage spend significantly less than those who have it. The economist W. G. Manning and several co-authors did so by performing an experiment in which they assigned subjects randomly to one of two different kinds of medical insurance policy.[2] The first group of subjects received **first-dollar coverage**, meaning that 100 percent of their medical expenses was covered by insurance. The second group got "$1,000-deductible" coverage, meaning that only expenses beyond the first $1,000 a year were covered. (For example, someone with $1,200 of medical bills would receive $1,200 from his insurance company if he belonged to the first group, but only $200 if he belonged to the second.) In effect, since most people incur less than $1,000 a year in medical expenses, most subjects in the second group effectively paid full price for their medical services, while subjects in the first group paid nothing. Manning and his colleagues found that *people with $1,000-deductible policies spent between 40 and 50 percent less on health care than subjects with first-dollar coverage. More important, there were no measurable differences in health outcomes between the two groups.*

Taken at face value, the results of the Manning study suggest that a large share of the inflation in medical expenditures since World War II has been caused by growth in first-dollar medical insurance. The problem with first-dollar coverage is that it completely ignores people's incentives. Why not simply abandon first-dollar coverage in favor of high

first-dollar insurance coverage insurance that pays all expenses generated by the insured activity

[2]W. G. Manning, J. P. Newhouse, E. B. Keeler, A. Liebowitz, and M. S. Marquis, "Health Insurance and the Demand for Medical Care," *American Economic Review* 77 (June 1987), pp. 251–77.

deductibles? People would still be protected against financial catastrophe but would have a strong incentive to avoid medical services whose benefit does not exceed their cost.

Some would say that Medicaid and Medicare should not carry high deductibles because the resulting out-of-pocket payments would impose too great a burden on poor families. But as in other instances in which concern for the poor is offered in defense of an inefficient policy, an alternative can be designed that is better for rich and poor alike. For example, all health insurance could be written to include high deductibles, and the poor could be given an annual stipend to defray the initial medical expenses not covered by insurance. At year's end, any unspent stipend would be theirs to keep. Here again, concern for the well-being of the poor is no reason for not adopting the most efficient policy. Again, when the economic pie grows larger, it is possible for everyone to have a larger slice.

The HMO Revolution

During the 1990s, the high cost of conventional health insurance led many people to switch to **health maintenance organizations (HMOs)**. An HMO is a group of physicians that provides its patients with medical services in return for a fixed annual fee. As The Economic Naturalist 10.1 illustrates, the incentive to provide any given medical service is weaker under the standard HMO contract than under conventional health insurance.

health maintenance organization (HMO) a group of physicians that provides health services to individuals and families for a fixed annual fee

The Economic Naturalist 10.1

Why is a patient with a sore knee more likely to receive an MRI exam if he has conventional health insurance than if he belongs to a health maintenance organization?

When a patient visits his physician complaining of a sore knee, the physician has several options. After hearing the patient describe his symptoms and examining the knee manually, the physician may prescribe anti-inflammatory drugs and advise the patient to abstain from vigorous physical activity for a period; or she may advise the patient to undergo a magnetic resonance imaging (MRI) exam, a costly diagnostic procedure that generates images of the inner workings of the injured joint. The physician in an HMO receives no additional revenue if she orders the MRI because all services are covered by the patient's fixed annual fee. Under conventional health insurance, in contrast, the physician will be reimbursed at a fixed rate, usually well above her marginal cost, for each additional service performed.

"Well, Bob, it looks like a paper cut, but just to be sure let's do lots of tests."

Robert Mankoff/The New Yorker Collection/© The Cartoon Bank

In many instances, the most prudent course of treatment is unambiguous, and in such cases physicians will make the same recommendation despite this striking difference in incentives. But in many other cases, it may not be obvious which decision is best. And in these cases, HMO physicians are less likely to order expensive tests.

People who switch to HMOs pay less for their health plans than those who stick with conventional health insurance since the HMO contract provides a strong incentive for doctors not to prescribe nonessential services. Many people fear, however, that the very same incentive may sometimes result in their not receiving valuable care. These concerns have led to proposed legislation granting patients rights of appeal when they are denied care by an HMO.

The Problem with Health Care Provision through Private Insurance

It is troubling, but perhaps not surprising, that access to medical care is extremely limited in many of the world's poorest nations. After all, citizens of those nations lack enough income to buy adequate food, shelter, and many other basic goods and services. What is surprising, however, is that despite the movement to less expensive HMO plans, almost 50 million Americans still had no health coverage of any kind when President Barack Obama took office in 2009. Politicians in both parties agreed that something had to be done. But why were so many without health coverage in the first place?

The answer to that question is rooted in the fact that the United States was almost alone among the world's nations in its reliance on unregulated private insurance markets to orchestrate the delivery of health care to its citizens. This approach was essentially a historical accident, a consequence of the fact that many labor unions managed to negotiate employer-provided health insurance as part of their compensation packages during the rapidly growing economy of the immediate post–World War II years. Under government policy, employer expenditures for health insurance were nontaxable. Employer-provided insurance was thus much cheaper for employees than private insurance purchased individually with income on which they had already been taxed. That incentive induced nonunion employers to join their union counterparts in offering employer-provided health insurance. And as long as health care spending was a fairly small share of total income, coverage was broad and the system functioned reasonably well.

An important policy detail was that eligibility for the tax exemption was conditional on insurance being made available to all employees irrespective of preexisting medical conditions. Given the high cost of treating individuals with chronic medical problems, private insurance companies are generally reluctant to issue policies to people with serious health problems. But by covering large groups of employees, only a small percentage of whom would be likely to have serious health problems during any year, insurance companies could issue these policies without taking unacceptable risks. Indeed, the large new employer-provided insurance market was sufficiently lucrative that most insurance companies were eager to participate in it.

Yet unregulated private insurance markets are a deeply flawed mechanism for providing access to health care, and no other industrial nation relies on unregulated markets for this purpose. The tax exemption, coupled with the requirement of group coverage, has enabled participants on both sides of the insurance market to sidestep the problem that undermines private insurance markets.

Economists call it the adverse-selection problem. It arises in individual insurance markets because individuals generally know much more about their own health status than the companies that sell insurance. To remain in business, a private insurance company must collect enough in premiums to cover the cost of the medical treatments it covers. If its rates are based on the expected medical expenses of a person with average health status, its policy will seem like a bargain to potential customers who know themselves to be in bad health. At the same time, its policies will seem overpriced to those who know themselves to be in excellent health.

The upshot is that a disproportionate share of the customers it attracts will have below-average health status, which means its initial premiums will be too low to cover its costs. To stay in business, it will have to raise its rates. But then potential customers in good health will find its policies even less attractive. A downward spiral often ensues, with the end result that insurance becomes unaffordable for most people.

Although the employer-provided group insurance approach helped keep the adverse-selection problem at bay for many years, this approach began to unravel as medical costs continued to rise relative to all other goods and services. With health insurance premiums taking a bigger and bigger bite out of workers' paychecks and heightened competition forcing companies to look for new ways to cut costs, some began offering higher wages in lieu of employer-provided health coverage. Younger, healthier workers—for whom medical expenses are normally small—found these offers increasingly tempting.

Parents who didn't buy health insurance for their families were once viewed as irresponsible, but this stigma lost some of its sting as the number of uninsured grew. As more and more people took jobs without health coverage, going without insurance became more socially acceptable. Making matters worse was the changing composition of the pool of the insured. As more healthy families took jobs without coverage, those left tended to be sicker and more costly to treat, forcing premiums to rise still more rapidly. In short, our health insurance system was caught in a long-term death spiral.

The Affordable Care Act of 2010

Passed by Congress and signed into law by President Obama in March 2010, the Affordable Care Act was the government's first serious attempt to halt that death spiral. It contained three main provisions, each one of which was essential for reform to succeed. First, it required insurance companies to offer coverage to everyone on roughly equal terms, irrespective of preexisting medical conditions. Without this provision, the economic imperative of every private insurance company would have been to take every step possible to deny coverage to anyone expected to incur significant medical expenses. Any insurance system that couldn't cover those who most need care would clearly be unacceptable.

Because insurance companies cannot cover their costs if they insure only the least healthy people, it was also necessary for the Affordable Care Act to include a mandate requiring everyone to buy health insurance. Without such a mandate, healthy individuals would face strong incentives to go without health insurance until they got sick, since they would then be able to buy affordable insurance from companies that were forbidden to charge high rates based on preexisting conditions.

The third major feature of the Affordable Care Act was to provide for subsidies to low-income families. You can't require people to buy insurance if they can't afford it. With health care costs already high and rapidly rising, it was essential to include some provision to ease the burden on those who are unable to pay.

The act contained numerous other provisions, many of which were designed to reduce the growth rate of health care costs by requiring more streamlined medical record keeping and supporting research on the questions of which treatments were most effective.

But the essence of the act lies in its three main provisions—nondiscrimination on the basis of preexisting conditions, the mandate, and subsidies for low-income families. Without all three of these provisions, the health insurance industry's death spiral would have surely continued.

RECAP ↑

THE ECONOMICS OF HEALTH CARE DELIVERY

The rapid escalation in medical expenditures since World War II is attributable in large part to the spread of first-dollar insurance coverage, which encourages people to behave as if medical services were free of charge. Total economic surplus would be larger if we switched to insurance coverage with high deductibles because such policies provide an incentive to use only those services whose benefit exceeds their cost.

The switch to HMOs addresses this problem because the standard HMO contract provides a strong incentive for physicians not to prescribe nonessential services. Some voice concern, however, that HMO contracts may lead physicians to withhold services that satisfy the cost-benefit test.

Mounting insurance premiums have caused many people in good health to do without health coverage, resulting in higher premiums for those who remain insured. The Affordable Care Act of 2010 was enacted in an attempt to remedy market failures that exist in attempts to provide health care access through unregulated private insurance contracts. The act's three key provisions are that (1) insurance be made available to all at rates independent of preexisting conditions; (2) everyone be required to purchase such insurance; and (3) low-income people receive subsidies to help meet this mandate.

USING PRICE INCENTIVES IN ENVIRONMENTAL REGULATION

As discussed earlier, goods whose production generates negative externalities, such as atmospheric pollution, tend to be overproduced whenever negotiation among private parties is costly. Suppose we decide, as a society, that the best attainable outcome would be to have half as much pollution as would occur under completely unregulated conditions. In that case, how should the cleanup effort be distributed among those firms that currently discharge pollution into the environment?

The most efficient—and hence best—distribution of effort is the one for which each polluter's marginal cost of abatement is exactly the same. To see why, imagine that under current arrangements, the cost to one firm of removing a ton of pollution from the air is larger than the cost to another firm. Society could then achieve the same total reduction in pollution at lower cost by having the first firm discharge 1 ton more into the air and the second firm 1 ton less.

Unfortunately, government regulators seldom have detailed information on how the cost of reducing pollution varies from one firm to another. Many pollution laws therefore require all polluters simply to cut back their emissions by the same proportion or to meet the same absolute emissions standards. If different polluters have different marginal costs of pollution abatement, however, these approaches will not be efficient.

Taxing Pollution

Fortunately, alternative policies can distribute the cleanup more efficiently, even if the government lacks detailed information about how much it costs different firms to curtail pollution. One method is to tax pollution and allow firms to decide for themselves how much pollution to emit. The following example illustrates the logic of this approach.

EXAMPLE 10.2   **Taxing Pollution**

What is the least costly way to cut pollution by half?

Two firms, Sludge Oil and Northwest Lumber, have access to five production processes, each of which has a different cost and produces a different amount of pollution. The daily costs of the processes and the number of tons of smoke emitted are as shown in Table 10.1. Pollution is currently unregulated, and negotiation between the firms and those who are harmed by pollution is impossible, which means that each firm uses process A, the least costly of the five. Each firm emits 4 tons of pollution per day, for a total of 8 tons of pollution per day.

TABLE 10.1

Costs and Emissions for Different Production Processes

Process (smoke)	A (4 tons/day)	B (3 tons/day)	C (2 tons/day)	D (1 ton/day)	E (0 tons/day)
Cost to Sludge Oil ($/day)	100	200	600	1,300	2,300
Cost to Northwest Lumber ($/day)	300	320	380	480	700

The government is considering two options for reducing total emissions by half. One is to require each firm to curtail its emissions by half. The other is to set a tax of $T per ton of smoke emitted each day. How large must T be to curtail emissions by half? What would be the total cost to society under each alternative?

If each firm is required to cut pollution by half, each must switch from process A to process C. The result will be 2 tons per day of pollution for each firm. The cost of the switch for Sludge Oil will be $600 per day − $100 per day = $500 per day. The cost to Northwest Lumber will be $380 per day − $300 per day = $80 per day, for a total cost of $580 per day.

Consider now how each firm would react to a tax of $T per ton of pollution. If a firm can cut pollution by 1 ton per day, it will save $T per day in tax payments. Whenever the cost of cutting a ton of pollution is less than $T, then, each firm has an incentive to switch to a cleaner process. For example, if the tax were set at $40 per ton, Sludge Oil would stick with process A because switching to process B would cost $100 per day extra but would save only $40 per day in taxes. Northwest Lumber, however, would switch to process B because the $40 saving in taxes would be more than enough to cover the $20 cost of switching.

The problem is that a $40-per-day tax on each ton of pollution results in a reduction of only 1 ton per day, 3 short of the 4-ton target. Suppose instead that the government imposed a tax of $101 per ton. Sludge Oil would then adopt process B because the $100 extra daily cost of doing so would be less than the $101 saved in taxes. Northwest Lumber would adopt process D because, for every process up to and including C, the cost of switching to the next process would be less than the resulting tax saving.

Overall, then, a tax of $101 per ton would result in the desired pollution reduction of 4 tons per day. The total cost of the reduction would be only $280 per day ($100 per day for Sludge Oil and $180 per day for Northwest Lumber), or $300 per day less than when each firm was required to cut its pollution by half. (The taxes paid by the firms do not constitute a cost of pollution reduction because the money can be used to reduce whatever taxes would otherwise need to be levied on citizens.)

CONCEPT CHECK 10.2

In Example 10.2, if the tax were $61 per ton of pollution emitted each day, which production processes would the two firms adopt?

The advantage of the tax approach is that it concentrates pollution reduction in the hands of the firms that can accomplish it at least cost. Requiring each firm to cut emissions by the same proportion ignores the fact that some firms can reduce pollution much more cheaply than others. Note that under the tax approach, the cost of the last ton of smoke removed is the same for each firm, so the efficiency condition is satisfied.

One problem with the tax approach is that unless the government has detailed knowledge about each firm's cost of reducing pollution, it cannot know how high to set the pollution tax. A tax that is too low will result in too much pollution, while a tax that is too high will result in too little. Of course, the government could start by setting a low tax rate and gradually increase the rate until pollution is reduced to the target level. But because firms often incur substantial sunk costs when they switch from one process to another, that approach might be even more wasteful than requiring all firms to cut their emissions by the same proportion.

Auctioning Pollution Permits

Another alternative is to establish a target level for pollution and then auction off permits to emit that level. The virtues of this approach are illustrated in the following example.

EXAMPLE 10.3   Pollution Permits

How much will pollution permits sell for?

Two firms, Sludge Oil and Northwest Lumber, again have access to the production processes described earlier (which are reproduced in Table 10.2). The government's goal is to cut the current level of pollution, 8 tons per day, by half. To do so, the government auctions off four permits, each of which entitles the bearer to emit 1 ton of smoke per day. No smoke may be emitted without a permit. What price will the pollution permits fetch at auction, how many permits will each firm buy, and what will be the total cost of the resulting pollution reduction?

TABLE 10.2
Costs and Emissions for Different Production Processes

Process (smoke)	A (4 tons/day)	B (3 tons/day)	C (2 tons/day)	D (1 ton/day)	E (0 tons/day)
Cost to Sludge Oil ($/day)	100	200	600	1,300	2,300
Cost to Northwest Lumber ($/day)	300	320	380	480	700

If Sludge Oil has no permits, it must use process *E,* which costs $2,300 per day to operate. If it had one permit, it could use process *D,* which would save it $1,000 per day. Thus, the most Sludge Oil would be willing to pay for a single 1-ton pollution permit is $1,000 per day. With a second permit, Sludge Oil could switch to process *C* and save another $700 per day; with a third permit, it could switch to process *B* and save another $400; and with a fourth permit, it could switch to process *A* and save another $100. Using similar reasoning, we can see that Northwest Lumber would pay up to $220 for one permit, up to $100 for a second, up to $60 for a third, and up to $20 for a fourth.

Suppose the government starts the auction at a price of $90. Sludge Oil will then demand four permits and Northwest Lumber will demand two, for a total demand of six permits. Since the government wishes to sell only four permits, it will keep raising the price until the two firms together demand a total of only four permits. Once the price reaches $101, Sludge Oil will demand three permits and Northwest Lumber will demand only one, for a total quantity demanded of four permits. Compared to the unregulated alternative, in which each firm used process *A*, the daily cost of the auction solution is $280: Sludge Oil spends $100 switching from process *A* to process *B,* and Northwest Lumber spends $180 switching from *A* to *D.* This total is $300 less than the cost of requiring each firm to reduce its emissions by half. (Again, the permit fees paid by the firms do not constitute a cost of cleanup because the money can be used to reduce taxes that would otherwise have to be collected.)

The auction method has the same virtue as the tax method: It concentrates pollution reduction in the hands of those firms that can accomplish it at the lowest cost. But the auction method has other attractive features that the tax approach does not. First, it does not induce firms to commit themselves to costly investments that they will have to abandon if the cleanup falls short of the target level. And second, it allows private citizens a direct voice in determining where the emission level will be set. For example, any group that believes the pollution target is too lenient could raise money to buy permits at auction. By keeping those permits locked away in a safe, the group could ensure that they will not be used to emit pollution.

Several decades ago, when economists first proposed the auctioning of pollution permits, reactions of outrage were widely reported in the press. Most of those reactions amounted to the charge that the proposal would "permit rich firms to pollute to their hearts' content." Such an assertion betrays a total misunderstanding of the forces that generate pollution. Firms pollute not because they *want* to pollute but because dirty production processes are cheaper than clean ones. Society's only real interest is in keeping the total amount of pollution from becoming excessive, not in *who* actually does the polluting. And in any event, the firms that do most of the polluting under an auction system will not be rich firms, but those for whom pollution reduction is most costly.

Economists have argued patiently against these misinformed objections to the auction system, and their efforts have finally borne fruit. The sale of pollution permits is now common in several parts of the United States, and there is growing interest in the approach in other countries.

Climate Change and Carbon Taxes

Growing concentrations of carbon dioxide (CO_2) in the atmosphere are widely believed to be a principal contributor to global warming. Concerns about the consequences of climate change have led to proposals to tax CO_2 emissions or require marketable permits for them. Critics of these proposals emphasize that forecasts involving climate change are highly uncertain, a fact they view as arguing against taking action. But uncertainty is a two-edged sword. Climate researchers themselves readily concede that estimates based on their models are extremely uncertain.

But that means that although the actual outcome might be much better than their median forecast, it might also be significantly worse. Organizers of the 2009 climate conference in Copenhagen sought to limit global warming to 3.6°F by the end of the twenty-first century. But even an increase that small would cause deadly harm, and the most respected climate change models estimate that there is essentially no chance that average temperature will rise by less than that amount if we take no action.

According to recent estimates from the Integrated Global Systems Model at the Massachusetts Institute of Technology, the median forecast is for a climb of 9°F by century's end, in the absence of effective countermeasures.[3] The same model estimates a 10 percent chance of temperature rising by more than 12°F. If that happened, the permafrost would melt, freeing vast quantities of methane into the atmosphere. Methane is 50 times more potent a greenhouse gas than CO_2. Thus, according to the MIT model, we face a roughly 1 in 10 chance of global warming sufficient to extinguish much of life on Earth.

Again, forecasts from climate models are highly uncertain. Things might not be as bad as predicted. But they could also be much worse. Should we take action? To respond to that question, we must ask, how much would it cost? The answer, as it turns out, is astonishingly little.

The Intergovernmental Panel on Climate Change estimated that a tax of $80 per ton on carbon emissions would be needed by 2030 to achieve climate stability by 2100.[4] A tax that high would raise the price of gasoline by about 70 cents a gallon. This figure was determined, however, before the arrival of the more pessimistic MIT estimates. And in the years since the MIT study was published, estimates have grown still more pessimistic. So let's assume a tax of $300 a ton, just to be safe. Under such a tax, the prices of goods would rise in proportion to their carbon footprints—in the case of gasoline, for example, by roughly $3 a gallon. As American motorists saw in 2008, a sudden price increase of that magnitude could indeed be painful. But if phased in gradually, it would cause much less harm.

Facing steadily increasing fuel prices, for example, manufacturers would scramble to develop more efficient vehicles. Many Europeans now pay $4 a gallon more for gas than Americans do. But precisely because of that fact, European automakers have pioneered development of many of the world's most fuel-efficient cars. Europeans actually spend less on gas than Americans do, yet seem no less happy with their rides.

If a family traded in its aging Ford Bronco (15 mpg) for a Ford Focus wagon (32 mpg), it would spend less on gas than before, even if it drove just as much. The tax could be phased in slowly, to give people time to adjust. People would also move closer to work, form car pools, choose less distant vacation destinations, and so on. Some of the revenue from the tax could be used to send checks to low-income families to ease the burden of higher gas prices. Portions of it could help pay down debt and rebuild crumbling infrastructure, or reduce other taxes.

In 2009 the U.S. House of Representatives actually passed an energy bill that included a comprehensive carbon cap and trade system, the functional equivalent of a carbon tax. But seasoned congressional observers say there's virtually no chance that meaningful climate legislation could win passage in the U.S. Senate anytime soon. Viewed within the economist's cost-benefit framework, this reluctance to take remedial action constitutes a mystery of the highest order.

RECAP ↑

USING PRICE INCENTIVES IN ENVIRONMENTAL REGULATION

An efficient program for reducing pollution is one for which the marginal cost of abatement is the same for all polluters. Taxing pollution has this desirable property, as does the auction of pollution permits. The auction method has the advantage that regulators can achieve a desired abatement target without having detailed knowledge of the abatement technologies available to polluters.

Climate scientists warn that increasing atmospheric concentrations of greenhouse gases threatens to cause catastrophic global warming. That risk could be averted by imposition of a carbon tax or equivalent carbon permit system.

---

[3]See A. P. Sokolov, P. H. Stone, C. E. Forest, et al., "Probabilistic Forecast for 21st Century Climate Based on Uncertainties in Emissions (without Policy) and Climate Parameters," MIT Joint Program on the Science and Policy of Global Change, Report No. 169, January 2009, http://globalchange.mit.edu/files/document/MITJP-SPGC_Rpt169.pdf.

[4]"Climate Change Policy and CO_2 Emissions from Passenger Vehicles," Congressional Budget Office, October 6, 2008, www.cbo.gov/ftpdocs/98xx/doc9830/10-06-ClimateChange_Brief.pdf.

METHODS OF INCOME REDISTRIBUTION

The challenge is to find ways to raise the living standard of low-income people, without at the same time undermining their incentive to work, and without using scarce resources to subsidize those who are not poor. Of course, some people simply cannot work, or cannot find work that pays enough to live on. In a world of perfect information, the government could make generous cash payments to those people, and withhold support from those who can fend for themselves. In practice, however, the two groups are often hard to distinguish from each other. And so we must choose among imperfect alternative measures.

Welfare Payments and In-Kind Transfers

Cash transfers and in-kind transfers are at the forefront of antipoverty efforts around the globe. **In-kind transfers** are direct transfers of goods or services to low-income individuals or families, such as food stamps, public housing, subsidized school lunches, and Medicaid.

From the mid-1960s until 1996, the most important federal program of cash transfers was Aid to Families with Dependent Children (AFDC), which in most cases provided cash payments to poor single-parent households. Critics of this program charged that the program ignored people's incentives. AFDC created incentives that undermined family stability because a poor mother was ineligible for AFDC payments in many states if her husband or other able-bodied adult male lived with her and her children. This provision confronted many long-term unemployed fathers with an agonizing choice. They could leave their families, making them eligible for public assistance; or they could remain, making them ineligible. Even many who deeply loved their families understandably chose to leave.

Concern about work incentives led Congress to pass the **Personal Responsibility Act** in 1996, abolishing the federal government's commitment to provide cash assistance to low-income families. The new law requires the federal government to make lump-sum cash grants to the states, which are then free to spend the funds on AFDC benefits or other income-support programs of their own design. For each welfare recipient, the new law also sets a five-year lifetime limit on receipt of benefits under the AFDC program.

Supporters of the Personal Responsibility Act argue that it has reduced the nation's welfare rolls substantially and that it will encourage greater self-reliance over the long run. Skeptics fear that denial of benefits may eventually impose severe hardships on poor children if overall economic conditions deteriorate even temporarily. Debate continues about the extent to which the observed rise in homelessness and malnutrition among the nation's poorest families during the economic downturns of 2001 and 2008 was attributable to the Personal Responsibility Act. What is clear, however, is that abolition of a direct federal role in the nation's antipoverty effort does not eliminate the need to discover efficient ways of providing assistance to people in need.

in-kind transfer a payment made not in the form of cash, but in the form of a good or service

Personal Responsibility Act the 1996 federal law that transferred responsibility for welfare programs from the federal level to the state level and placed a five-year lifetime limit on payment of AFDC benefits to any given recipient

Means-Tested Benefit Programs

Many welfare programs, including AFDC, are **means-tested**, which means that the more income a family has, the smaller the benefits it receives under these programs. The purpose of means testing is to avoid paying benefits to those who don't really need them. But because of the way welfare programs are administered, means testing often has a pernicious effect on work incentives.

Consider, for example, an unemployed participant in four welfare programs: food stamps, rent stamps, energy stamps, and day care stamps. Each program gives him $100 worth of stamps per week, which he is then free to spend on food, rent, energy, and day care. If he gets a job, his benefits in each program are reduced by 50 cents for each dollar he earns. Thus, if he accepts a job that pays $50 per week, he will lose $25 in weekly benefits from each of the four welfare programs, for a total benefit reduction of $100 per week. Taking the job thus leaves him $50 per week worse off than before. Low-income persons need no formal training in economics to realize that seeking gainful employment does not pay under these circumstances.

means-tested a benefit program whose benefit level declines as the recipient earns additional income

What is more, means-tested programs of cash and in-kind transfers are extremely costly to administer. If the government were to eliminate all existing welfare and social service agencies that are involved in these programs, the resulting savings would be enough to lift every poor person out of poverty. One proposal to do precisely this is the negative income tax.

The Negative Income Tax

negative income tax (NIT) a system under which the government would grant every citizen a cash payment each year, financed by an additional tax on earned income

Under the **negative income tax (NIT)**, every man, woman, and child—rich or poor—would receive a substantial income tax credit, say $4,500 per year. A person who earns no income would receive this credit in cash. People who earn income would receive the same initial credit, and their income would continue to be taxed at some rate less than 100 percent.

The negative income tax would do much less than current programs to weaken work incentives because, unlike current programs, it would ensure that someone who earned an extra dollar would keep at least a portion of it. And because the program would be administered by the existing Internal Revenue Service, administrative costs would be far lower than under the current welfare system.

Despite these advantages, however, the negative income tax is by no means a perfect solution to the income-transfer problem. Although the incentive problem under the program would be less severe than under current welfare programs, it would remain a serious difficulty. To see why, note that if the negative income tax were the *sole* means of insulating people against poverty, the payment to people with no earned income would need to be at least as large as the government's official **poverty threshold**.

poverty threshold the level of income below which the federal government classifies a family as poor

The poverty threshold is the annual income level below which a family is officially classified as "poor" by the government. The threshold is based on government estimates of the cost of the so-called economy food plan, the least costly of four nutritionally adequate food plans designed by the Department of Agriculture. The department's 1955 Household Food Consumption Survey found that families of three or more people spent approximately one-third of their after-tax income on food, so the government pegs the poverty threshold at three times the cost of the economy food plan. In 2014, that threshold was approximately $23,850 for a family of four.

For a family of four living in a city, $23,850 a year is scarcely enough to make ends meet. But suppose a group of, say, eight families were to pool their negative tax payments and move to the mountains of northern New Mexico. With a total of more than $190,000 per year to spend, plus the fruits of their efforts at gardening and animal husbandry, such a group could live very nicely indeed.

Once a small number of experimental groups demonstrated the feasibility of quitting their jobs and living well on the negative income tax, others would surely follow suit. Two practical difficulties would ensue. First, as more and more people left their jobs to live at government expense, the program would eventually become prohibitively costly. And second, the political cost of the program would almost surely force supporters to abandon it long before that point. Reports of people living lives of leisure at taxpayers' expense would be sure to appear on the nightly news. People who worked hard at their jobs all day long would wonder why their tax dollars were being used to support those who were capable of holding paying jobs, yet chose not to work. If the resulting political backlash did not completely eliminate the negative income tax program, it would force policymakers to cut back the payment so that members of rural communes could no longer afford to live comfortably. And that would mean the payment would no longer support an urban family. This difficulty has led policymakers to focus on other ways to increase the incomes of the working poor.

Minimum Wages

The United States and many other industrialized countries have sought to ease the burden of low-wage workers by enacting minimum wage legislation—laws that prohibit employers from paying workers less than a specified hourly wage. The federal minimum wage in the United States is currently set at $7.25 per hour, as of July 2009.

At one point, economists were almost unanimous in their opposition to minimum wage laws, arguing that those laws reduce total economic surplus, as do other regulations that prevent markets from reaching equilibrium. In recent years, however, some economists have softened their opposition to minimum wage laws, citing studies that have failed to show significant reductions in employment following increases in minimum wage levels. These studies may well imply that as a group, low-income workers are better off with minimum wage laws than without them. But as we saw previously, any policy that prevents a market from reaching equilibrium causes a reduction in total economic surplus—which means society ought to be able to find a more effective policy for helping low-wage workers.

The Earned-Income Tax Credit

One such policy is the **earned-income tax credit (EITC)**, which gives low-wage workers a credit on their federal income tax each year. The EITC was enacted into law in 1975, and in the years since has drawn praise from both liberals and conservatives. The program is essentially a wage subsidy in the form of a credit against the amount a family owes in federal income taxes. For example, a family of four with total earned income of $15,000 in 2014 would have received an annual tax credit of approximately $5,500 under this program. That is, the program would have reduced the annual federal income tax payment of this family by roughly that amount. Families who earned more would have received a smaller tax credit, with no credit at all for families of four earning more than $54,000. Families whose tax credit exceeds the amount of tax owed actually receive a check from the government for the difference. The EITC is thus essentially the same as a negative income tax, except that eligibility for the program is confined to people who work.

Like both the negative income tax and the minimum wage, the EITC puts extra income into the hands of workers who are employed at low wage levels. But unlike the minimum wage, the earned-income tax credit creates no incentive for employers to lay off low-wage workers.

earned-income tax credit (EITC) a policy under which low-income workers receive credits on their federal income tax

Public Employment for the Poor

The main shortcoming of the EITC is that it does nothing for the unemployed poor. The negative income tax lacks that shortcoming but may substantially weaken work incentives. There is yet another method of transferring income to the poor that avoids both shortcomings. Government-sponsored jobs could pay wages to the unemployed poor for useful work. With public service employment, the specter of people living lives of leisure at public expense simply does not arise.

But public service employment has difficulties of its own. Evidence shows that if government jobs pay the same wages as private jobs, many people will leave their private jobs in favor of government jobs, apparently because they view government jobs as being more secure. Such a migration would make public service employment extremely expensive. Other worrisome possibilities are that such jobs might involve make-work tasks, and that they would prompt an expansion in government bureaucracy.

Acting alone, government-sponsored jobs for the poor, the EITC, or the negative income tax cannot solve the income-transfer problem. But a combination of these programs might do so.

A Combination of Methods

Consider a negative income tax whose cash grant is far too small for anyone to live on, but that is supplemented if necessary by a public service job at below minimum wage. Keeping the wage in public service jobs well below the minimum wage would eliminate the risk of a large-scale exodus from private jobs. And while living well on either the negative income tax or the public service wage would be impossible, the two programs together could lift people out of poverty (see Figure 10.2).

To prevent an expansion of the bureaucracy, the government could solicit bids from private management companies to oversee the public service employment program. The fear that this program would inevitably become a make-work project is allayed by evidence that unskilled workers can, with proper supervision, perform many valuable tasks that would not otherwise be performed in the private sector. They can, for example, do landscaping and

Can unskilled workers perform useful public service jobs?

FIGURE 10.2

Income by Source in a Combination NIT–Jobs Program.

Together, a small negative income tax and a public job at below minimum wage would provide a family enough income to escape poverty, without weakening work incentives significantly.

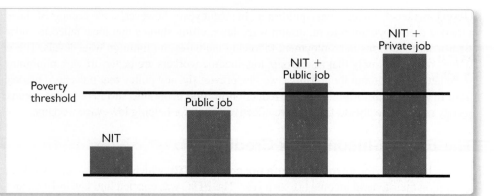

maintenance in public parks; provide transportation for the elderly and those with disabilities; fill potholes in city streets and replace burned-out street lamps; transplant seedlings in erosion control projects; remove graffiti from public places and paint government buildings; recycle newspapers and containers; staff day care centers; and so on.

This combination of a small negative income tax payment and public service employment at a subminimum wage would not be cheap. But the direct costs of existing welfare programs are also large, and the indirect costs, in the form of perverse work incentives and misguided attempts to control prices, are even larger. In economic terms, dealing intelligently with the income-transfer problem may in fact prove relatively inexpensive, once society recognizes the enormous opportunity cost of failing to deal intelligently with it.

RECAP ↑

METHODS OF INCOME REDISTRIBUTION

Minimum wage laws reduce total economic surplus by contracting employment. The earned-income tax credit boosts the incomes of the working poor without that drawback, but neither policy provides benefits for those who are not employed.

Other instruments in the battle against poverty include in-kind transfers such as food stamps, subsidized school lunches, Medicaid, and public housing as well as cash transfers such as Aid to Families with Dependent Children. Because benefits under most of these programs are means-tested, beneficiaries often experience a net decline in income when they accept paid employment.

SUMMARY

- Our aim in this chapter has been to apply basic microeconomic principles to a variety of government policy questions. These principles help to show how different methods of paying for health care affect the efficiency with which medical services are delivered. In the case of health care, the gains from marginal cost pricing can often be achieved through insurance policies with large deductibles. *(LO1, LO2)*

- An understanding of the forces that give rise to environmental pollution can help to identify those policy mea-

sures that will achieve a desired reduction in pollution at the lowest possible cost. Both the taxing of pollution and the sale of transferable pollution rights promote this goal. Each distributes the cost of the environmental cleanup effort so that the marginal cost of pollution abatement is the same for all polluters. *(LO3)*

- Policies and programs for reducing poverty include minimum wage laws, the earned-income tax credit, food stamps, subsidized school lunches, Medicaid, public housing, and Aid to Families with Dependent Children. Of these, all but the earned-income tax credit fail to maximize total economic surplus, either by interfering with work incentives or by preventing markets from reaching equilibrium. *(LO4)*

• The negative income tax works much like the earned-income tax credit, except that it includes those who are

not employed. A combination of a small negative income tax and access to public service jobs at subminimum wages could ensure adequate living standards for the poor without significantly undermining work incentives. *(LO4)*

KEY TERMS

earned-income tax credit (EITC)
first-dollar insurance coverage
health maintenance organization (HMO)

in-kind transfer
means-tested
negative income tax (NIT)

Personal Responsibility Act
poverty threshold

REVIEW QUESTIONS

1. Why is vaccination against many childhood illnesses a legal requirement for entry into public schools? *(LO1)*

2. Why is first-dollar health care coverage inefficient? *(LO2)*

3. Why do economists believe that pollution taxes and effluent permits are a more efficient way to curb

pollution than laws mandating across-the-board cutbacks? *(LO3)*

4. Why is a negative income tax, by itself, unlikely to be successful policy for maintaining the living standards of the poor? *(LO4)*

PROBLEMS

connect

1. In the event he requires an appendectomy, David's demand for hospital accommodations is as shown in the diagram below. David's current insurance policy fully covers the cost of hospital stays. The marginal cost of providing a hospital room is $150 per day. *(LO2)*

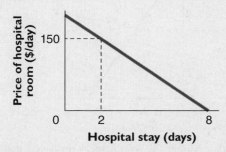

a. If David's only illness this year results in an appendectomy, how many days will he choose to stay in the hospital?

b. How many days would David have chosen to stay in the hospital if his insurance covered only the cost of

hospital stays that exceed $1,000 per illness? Explain why that choice would have failed to satisfy the cost-benefit test.

2. Dave's willingness to pay for hospital recovery time following his upcoming appendectomy is $300 for the first day, $200 for the second, $100 for the third, $50 for the fourth, and nothing for days beyond four. *(LO2)*

a. If Dave is uninsured and the cost of providing a hospital room is $250 per day, how many days will he stay in the hospital following his operation?

b. How many days would he stay if his insurance covered half the cost of each hospital day?

c. Describe a change in the terms of his insurance policy that would benefit both Dave and his insurer.

3. Two firms, Sludge Oil and Northwest Lumber, have access to five production processes, each one of which has a different cost and gives off a different amount of pollution. The daily costs of the processes and the corresponding number of tons of smoke emitted are as shown in the following table: *(LO3)*

Process (smoke)	A (4 tons/day)	B (3 tons/day)	C (2 tons/day)	D (1 ton/day)	E (0 tons/day)
Cost to Sludge Oil ($/day)	50	70	120	200	500
Cost to Northwest Lumber ($/day)	100	180	500	1,000	2,000

a. If pollution is unregulated, which process will each firm use, and what will be the total daily smoke emission?

b. The City Council wants to curb smoke emissions by 50 percent. To accomplish this, it requires each firm to curb its emissions by 50 percent. What will be the increase in total cost to society due to this policy?

c. The City Council again wants to curb emissions by half. This time, it sets a tax of $T per day on each ton of smoke emitted. How large will T have to be to effect the desired reduction? What is the total cost to society of this policy?

4. Refer to Problem 3. Instead of taxing pollution, the city council decides to auction off four permits, each of which entitles the bearer to emit 1 ton of smoke per day. No smoke may be emitted without a permit. Suppose the government conducts the auction by starting at $1 and asking how many permits each firm wants to buy at that price. If the total is more than four, it then raises the price by $1 and asks again, and so on, until the total quantity of demanded permits falls to four.

How much will each permit sell for in this auction? How many permits will each firm buy? What will be the total cost to society of this reduction in pollution? *(LO3)*

5. A senator has argued that we should not spend hundreds of billions of dollars to reduce greenhouse gas emissions because we are not even sure that such emissions will lead to costly changes in the Earth's climate. Comment critically on this argument. *(LO3)*

6.* Suppose employers and workers are risk-neutral, and Congress is about to enact the $12-per-hour minimum wage. Congressional staff economists have urged legislators to consider adopting an earned-income tax credit instead. Suppose neither workers nor employers would support that proposal unless the expected value of each party's economic surplus would be at least as great as under the minimum wage. Describe an earned-income tax credit (and a tax that would raise enough money to pay for it) that would receive unanimous support from both workers and employers. *(LO4)*

*Denotes more difficult problem.

ANSWERS TO CONCEPT CHECKS

10.1 With 50 percent coverage, David would have to pay $150 for each additional day in the hospital, so he would choose to stay for two days. *(LO2)*

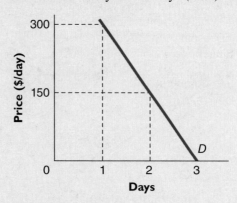

10.2 With a tax of $61 per ton each day, Sludge Oil would adopt process *A* and Northwest Lumber would adopt process *C*. *(LO3)*

Process (smoke)	A (4 tons/day)	B (3 tons/day)	C (2 tons/day)	D (1 ton/day)	E (0 tons/day)
Cost to Sludge Oil ($/day)	100	200	600	1,300	2,300
Cost to Northwest Lumber ($/day)	300	320	380	480	700

11

International Trade and Trade Policy

LEARNING OBJECTIVES

After reading this chapter, you should be able to:

LO1 Explain and apply the concept of comparative advantage and explain how it differs from absolute advantage.

LO2 Explain how price of tradable goods is set in a closed economy or an open economy and how quantity demanded and quantity supplied affect the quantities of imports or exports.

LO3 Illustrate why free trade is often politically controversial, even though it promises to increase total income.

On April 13, 1861, Southern troops fired on Fort Sumter in Charleston harbor, initiating the American Civil War. Less than a week later, on April 19, President Lincoln proclaimed a naval blockade of the South. Code-named the Anaconda Plan (after the snake that squeezes its prey to death), the blockade required the Union navy to patrol the Southern coastline, stopping and boarding ships that were attempting to land or depart. The object of the blockade was to prevent the Confederacy from shipping cotton to Europe, where it could be traded for military equipment, clothing, foodstuffs, and other supplies.

Historians are divided on the effectiveness of the Union blockade in choking off Confederate trade. In the early years of the war, the North had too few ships to cover the 3,600-mile Southern coastline, so "running" the blockade was not difficult. But in the latter part of the war the number of Union ships enforcing the blockade increased from about 90 to more than 600, and sailing ships were replaced with faster, more lethal ironclad vessels. Still, private blockade runners—like the fictitious Rhett Butler in Margaret Mitchell's *Gone with the Wind*—attempted to elude the Union navy in small, fast ships. Because the price of raw cotton in Great Britain was between 10 and 20 times what it was in the Confederacy (a differential that indicated disruption in the normal flow of trade), blockade runners enjoyed huge profits when they were successful. But despite their efforts, by 1864 the Southern war effort was seriously hampered by a lack of military equipment and supplies, at least in part as a result of the blockade.

The use of a naval blockade as a weapon of war highlights a paradox in contemporary attitudes toward trade between nations. Presumably, an attempt by a foreign power to blockade U.S. ports would today be considered a hostile act that would elicit a strong response from the U.S. government. Yet one often hears politicians and others arguing that trade with other nations is harmful to the United States and should be restricted—in effect, that the United States should blockade its own ports! For example, politicians from both the Republican and Democratic parties often complain about China's exports to the U.S. Some of these politicians propose taking action against the Chinese government because, they claim, it engages in unfair policies that cause Chinese products to sell in the U.S. for prices that are too *cheap*. So is trade a good thing or not? And if it is, why does it sometimes face determined opposition?

He appreciated the economic benefits of trade.

This chapter addresses international trade and its effects on the broader economy. We will begin by introducing the idea of *comparative advantage*. We will show that everyone can enjoy more goods and services if nations specialize in those products in which they have a comparative advantage, and then trade freely among themselves. Furthermore, if trade is unrestricted, market forces will ensure that countries produce those goods in which they have a comparative advantage.

Having shown the potential benefits of trade, we will turn next to the reasons for opposition to trade. Although opening the economy to trade *can* in our model increase economic welfare overall, some groups—such as workers in industries that face competition from foreign producers—may in reality be made worse off. The fact that open trade may hurt some groups creates political pressure to enact measures restricting trade, such as taxes on imported goods (called tariffs) and limits on imports (called quotas). We will analyze the effects of these trade restrictions, along with other ways of responding to concerns about affected industries and workers. From an economic point of view, providing direct assistance to those who are hurt by increased trade is preferable to blocking or restricting trade. But economists also understand that it may be rational for some groups to oppose trade, if these groups expect to be hurt by trade and believe that direct assistance to them will not arrive or will not be effective—for example, because the government will fail to pass and implement effective assistance programs in the future.

COMPARATIVE ADVANTAGE AS A BASIS FOR TRADE

One of the most important insights of modern economics is that when two people (or two nations) have different opportunity costs of producing different goods and services, they can always increase the total value of available goods and services by trading with one another. Recall from the *Thinking Like an Economist* chapter that the opportunity cost of spending more time (or other resources) on any one activity is having less time (or other resources) available to spend on others. To illustrate this insight, we will start with an example.

EXAMPLE 11.1 | **Scarcity Principle**

Should Joe Jamail prepare his own will?

Should Joe Jamail write his own will?

Joe Jamail, known in the legal profession as "The King of Torts," is the most renowned trial lawyer in American history. And at number 269 on the Forbes list of the 400 richest Americans, he is also one of the wealthiest, with net assets totaling more than $1.5 billion.

But although Jamail devotes virtually all of his working hours to high-profile litigation, he is also competent to perform a much broader range of legal services. Suppose, for example, that he could prepare his own will in two hours, only half as long as it would take any other attorney. Does that mean that Jamail should prepare his own will?

On the strength of his talent as a litigator, Jamail earns many millions of dollars a year, which means that the opportunity cost of any time he spends preparing his will would be several thousand dollars per hour. Attorneys who specialize in property law typically earn far less than that amount. Jamail would have little difficulty engaging a competent property lawyer who could prepare his will for him for less than $800. So even though Jamail's considerable skills would enable him to perform this task more quickly than another attorney, it would not be in his interest to prepare his own will.

In Example 11.1, economists would say that Jamail has an **absolute advantage** at preparing his will but a **comparative advantage** at trial work. He has an absolute advantage at preparing his will because he can perform that task in less time than a property lawyer could. Even so, the property lawyer has a comparative advantage at preparing wills because her opportunity cost of performing that task is lower than Jamail's.

Example 11.1 made the implicit assumption that Jamail would have been equally happy to spend an hour preparing his will or preparing for a trial. But suppose he was tired of trial preparation and felt it might be enjoyable to refresh his knowledge of property law. Preparing his own will might then have made perfect sense! But unless he expected to gain extra satisfaction from performing that task, he'd almost certainly do better to hire a property lawyer. The property lawyer would also benefit, or else she wouldn't have offered to prepare wills for the stated price.

In summary, this example demonstrates that by specializing in the activities at which they have comparative advantage (i.e., in the activities with lowest opportunity cost), Jamail and another lawyer could both gain. Indeed, the gains made possible from specialization based on comparative advantage constitute the rationale for market exchange. They explain why each person does not devote 10 percent of his or her time to producing cars, 5 percent to growing food, 25 percent to building housing, 0.0001 percent to performing brain surgery, and so on. By concentrating on those tasks at which we are relatively most productive, together we can produce vastly more than if we all tried to be self-sufficient. (In addition, our relative productivity in those activities we concentrate on can itself increase, for example, through specialized training and experience—in turn further increasing our comparative advantage in those activities.) The next example illustrates more concretely how these productivity gains come about.

absolute advantage one person has an absolute advantage over another if he or she takes fewer hours to perform a task than the other person

comparative advantage one person has a comparative advantage over another if his or her opportunity cost of performing a task is lower than the other person's opportunity cost

EXAMPLE 11.2   Comparative Advantage

Should Mary update her own web page?

Consider a small community in which Mary is the only professional bicycle mechanic and Paula is the only professional HTML programmer. Mary also happens to be an even better HTML programmer than Paula. If the amount of time each of them takes to perform these tasks is as shown in Table 11.1, and if each regards the two tasks as equally pleasant (or unpleasant), does the fact that Mary can program faster than Paula imply that Mary should update her own web page?

The entries in the table show that Mary has an absolute advantage over Paula in both activities. While Mary, the mechanic, needs only 20 minutes to update a web page, Paula, the programmer, needs 30 minutes. Mary's advantage over Paula is even greater when the task is fixing bikes: She can complete a repair in only 10 minutes, compared to Paula's 30 minutes.

TABLE 11.1
Productivity Information for Paula and Mary

	Time to update a web page	Time to complete a bicycle repair
Mary	20 minutes	10 minutes
Paula	30 minutes	30 minutes

But the fact that Mary is a better programmer than Paula does *not* imply that Mary should update her own web page. As with the lawyer who litigates instead of preparing his own will, Paula has a comparative advantage over Mary at programming: She is *relatively* more productive at programming than Mary. Similarly, Mary has a comparative advantage in bicycle repair. (Remember that a person has a comparative advantage at a given task if his or her opportunity cost of performing that task is lower than another person's.)

What is Paula's opportunity cost of updating a web page? Since she takes 30 minutes to update each page—the same amount of time she takes to fix a bicycle—her opportunity cost of updating a web page is one bicycle repair. In other words, by taking the time to update a web page, Paula is effectively giving up the opportunity to do one bicycle repair. Mary, in contrast, can complete two bicycle repairs in the time she takes to update a single web page. For her, the opportunity cost of updating a web page is two bicycle repairs. Mary's opportunity cost of programming, measured in terms of bicycle repairs forgone, is twice as high as Paula's. Thus, Paula has a comparative advantage at programming.

The interesting and important implication of the opportunity cost comparison summarized in Table 11.2 is that the total number of bicycle repairs and web updates accomplished if Paula and Mary both spend part of their time at each activity will always be smaller than the number accomplished if each specializes in the activity in which she has a comparative advantage. Suppose, for example, that people in their community demand a total of 16 web page updates per day. If Mary spent half her time updating web pages and the other half repairing bicycles, an eight-hour workday would yield 12 web page updates and 24 bicycle repairs. To complete the remaining 4 updates, Paula would have to spend two hours programming, which would leave her six hours to repair bicycles. And since she takes 30 minutes to do each repair, she would have time to complete 12 of them. So when the two women try to be jacks-of-all-trades, they end up completing a total of 16 web page updates and 36 bicycle repairs.

TABLE 11.2
Opportunity Costs for Paula and Mary

	Opportunity cost of updating a web page	Opportunity cost of a bicycle repair
Mary	2 bicycle repairs	0.5 web page update
Paula	1 bicycle repair	1 web page update

Consider what would have happened had each woman specialized in her activity of comparative advantage. Paula could have updated 16 web pages on her own and Mary could have performed 48 bicycle repairs. Specialization would have created an additional 12 bicycle repairs out of thin air.

When computing the opportunity cost of one good in terms of another, we must pay close attention to the form in which the productivity information is presented. In Example 11.2, we were told how many minutes each person needed to perform each task. Alternatively, we might be told how many units of each task each person can perform in an hour. Work through the following concept check to see how to proceed when information is presented in this alternative format.

"We're a natural, Rachel. I handle intellectual property, and you're a content-provider."

CONCEPT CHECK 11.1

Should Meg update her own web page?

Consider a small community in which Meg is the only professional bicycle mechanic and Pat is the only professional HTML programmer. If their productivity rates at the two tasks are as shown in the table, and if each regards the two tasks as equally pleasant (or unpleasant), does the fact that Meg can program faster than Pat imply that Meg should update her own web page?

	Productivity in programming	Productivity in bicycle repair
Pat	2 web page updates per hour	1 repair per hour
Meg	3 web page updates per hour	3 repairs per hour

The insight that specialization and trade among individuals can yield impressive gains in productivity can be applied to nations. Factors such as climate, natural resources, technology, workers' skills and education, and culture provide countries with comparative advantages in the production of different goods and services. For example, the large number of leading research universities in the United States gives that nation a comparative advantage in the design of technologically sophisticated computer hardware and software. Likewise, the wide international use of the English language endows the United States with a comparative advantage in producing popular films and TV shows. Similarly, France's climate and topography, together with the accumulated knowledge of generations of vintners, provides that country a comparative advantage in producing fine wines, while Australia's huge expanses of arable land give that country a comparative advantage in producing grain.

We can all enjoy more goods and services when each country produces according to its comparative advantage, and then trades with other countries. So, while in reality

Climate and long experience give France a comparative advantage in producing fine wines.

software, films, TV shows, wine, and grain are all produced by each of the three countries (the U.S., France, and Australia), by concentrating on producing the specific products each country has comparative advantage at and then trading with the other countries, consumers in each of these countries can enjoy a greater variety and quantity of these products.

However, there is an important difference between applying the principle of comparative advantage to individuals and applying it to nations: that a nation as a whole—in the aggregate—enjoys more goods and services does not imply that *everyone* in the nation enjoys more goods and services. Rather, it is possible that within the nation, some individuals will gain from opening up to trade, while others will lose. So when we say that in the transition from a **closed economy**—one that does not trade with the rest of the world—to a more **open economy**—one that does trade with other economies—everybody *can* gain, we are not saying that everybody *will* gain. For everybody to gain, or be better off, the winners from trade will have to share a sufficient amount of their gains with the losers. In itself, opening up for trade does not guarantee that the gains will be shared. We return to these issues in the next section.

closed economy an economy that does not trade with the rest of the world

open economy an economy that trades with other countries

> *RECAP* ↑
>
> ### COMPARATIVE ADVANTAGE AS A BASIS OF TRADE
>
> Gains from exchange are possible if trading partners have comparative advantage in producing different goods and services. You have a comparative advantage in producing, say, web pages if your opportunity cost of producing a web page—measured in terms of other production opportunities forgone—is smaller than the corresponding opportunity costs of your trading partners. Maximum production is achieved if each person specializes in producing the good or service in which he or she has the lowest opportunity cost. This comparative advantage makes specialization worthwhile even if one trading partner is more productive than others, in absolute terms, in every activity.

A SUPPLY AND DEMAND PERSPECTIVE ON TRADE

In this section we will look more carefully at how international trade affects supply and demand in the markets for specific goods. We will see that when it is costly for workers and firms to change industries, opening to trade with other countries may create groups of winners and losers among producers even as it helps consumers.

Let's see how trade affects the markets for computers and coffee in a hypothetical economy that produces only these two goods. We will call this economy Costa Rica. Figure 11.1 shows the supply and demand for computers in that economy. As usual, the price is shown on the vertical axis and the quantity on the horizontal axis. For now, think of the price of computers as being measured in terms of coffee rather than in terms of dollars (in other words, we measure the price of computers *relative* to the price of the other good in the economy). As usual, the upward-sloping curve in Figure 11.1 is the supply curve of computers, in this case for computers produced in Costa Rica; and the downward-sloping curve is the demand curve for computers by Costa Rican residents. The supply curve for computers in Costa Rica reflects the opportunity cost of supplying computers. Specifically, at any level of computer production, the relative price at which Costa Rican firms are willing to supply an additional computer equals their opportunity cost of doing so. The demand curve, which tells us the number of computers Costa Ricans will purchase at each relative price, reflects the preferences and buying power of Costa Rican consumers.

If the Costa Rican economy is closed to international trade, then market equilibrium occurs where the domestic supply and demand curves intersect, at point E in Figure 11.1. The equilibrium price will be p and the equilibrium quantity, q.

If Costa Rica opens its market to trade, however, the relevant price for computers becomes the **world price** of computers, the price at which computers are traded internationally. The world price for computers is determined by the worldwide supply and

world price the price at which a good or service is traded on international markets

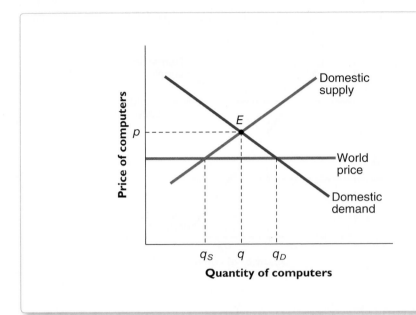

FIGURE 11.1

The Market for Computers in Costa Rica.

If Costa Rica is closed to international trade, the equilibrium price and quantity of computers are determined by the intersection of the domestic supply and demand curves at point E. But if Costa Rica is open to trade, the domestic price of computers must equal the world price. At that price, Costa Ricans will demand q_D computers, but domestic producers will supply only q_S computers. Thus $q_D - q_S$ computers must be imported from abroad.

demand for computers. If we assume that Costa Rica's computer market is too small to affect the world price for computers very much, the world price can be treated as fixed, and represented by a horizontal line in the figure. Figure 11.1 shows the world price for computers as being lower than Costa Rica's closed-economy price.

If Costa Ricans are free to buy and sell computers on the international market, then the price of computers in Costa Rica must be the same as the world price. (No one in Costa Rica will buy a computer at a price above the world price, and no one will sell one at a price below the world price.) Figure 11.1 shows that at the world price, Costa Rican consumers and firms demand q_D computers, but Costa Rican computer producers will supply only q_S computers. The difference between the two quantities, $q_D - q_S$, is the number of computers that Costa Rica must import from abroad. Figure 11.1 illustrates a general conclusion: *If the price of a good or service in a closed economy is greater than the world price, and that economy opens itself to trade, the economy will tend to become a net importer of that good or service.*

A different outcome occurs in Costa Rica's coffee market, shown in Figure 11.2. The price of coffee (measured relative to the price of computers) is shown on the vertical axis, and the quantity of coffee on the horizontal axis. The downward-sloping demand curve in the figure shows how much coffee Costa Rican consumers want to buy at each relative price, and the upward-sloping supply curve how much coffee Costa Rican producers are willing to supply at each relative price. If Costa Rica's economy is closed to trade with the rest of the world, then equilibrium in the market for coffee will occur at point E, where the domestic demand and supply curves intersect. The quantity produced will be q and the price p.

Now imagine that Costa Rica opens its coffee market to international trade. As in the case of computers, if free trade in coffee is permitted, then the prevailing price for coffee in Costa Rica must be the same as the world price. Unlike the case of computers, however, the world price of coffee as shown in Figure 11.2 is *higher* than the domestic equilibrium price. How do we know that the world price of coffee will be higher than the domestic price? Recall that the price of coffee is measured relative to the price of computers, and vice versa. If the price of computers relative to the price of coffee is higher in Costa Rica than in the world market, then the price of coffee relative to the price of computers must be lower, as each price is the reciprocal of the other. More generally, when two people or two countries trade with each other, neither can have a comparative advantage in *every* good and service. Thus, in an example with only two goods, if non-Costa Rican producers have a comparative advantage in computers, reflected in the lower cost of computers relative to coffee in the world market, then Costa Rican producers must

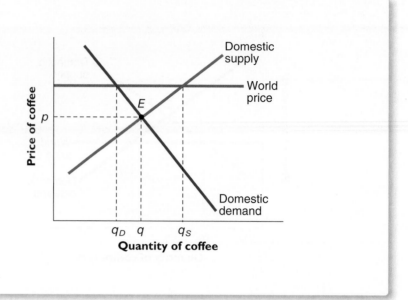

FIGURE 11.2

The Market for Coffee in Costa Rica.

With no international trade, the equilibrium price and quantity of coffee in Costa Rica are determined by the intersection of the domestic supply and demand curves (point *E*). But if the country opens to trade, the domestic price of coffee must equal the world price. At the higher world price, Costa Ricans will demand the quantity of coffee q_D, less than the amount supplied by Costa Rican producers, q_s. The excess coffee supplied by Costa Rican producers, $q_s - q_D$, is exported.

have a comparative advantage in coffee. By definition, this comparative advantage implies that the opportunity cost of coffee in terms of computers must be lower in Costa Rica than in the rest of the world.

Figure 11.2 shows that at the world price for coffee, Costa Rican producers are willing to supply q_s coffee, while Costa Rican consumers want to purchase a smaller amount, q_D. The difference between domestic production and domestic consumption, $q_s - q_D$, is exported to the world market. The general conclusion of Figure 11.2 is this: *If the price of a good or service in a closed economy is lower than the world price, and that economy opens itself to trade, the economy will tend to become a net exporter of that good or service.*

These examples illustrate how the market translates comparative advantage into mutually beneficial gains from trade. If trade is unrestricted, then countries with a comparative advantage in a particular good will profit by supplying that good to the world market and using the revenue earned to import goods in which they do not have a comparative advantage. Thus the workings of the free market automatically ensure that goods will be produced where the opportunity cost is lowest, leading to the highest possible consumption possibilities for the world as a whole.

Winners and Losers from Trade

If trade is so wonderful, why do politicians so often resist free trade and "globalization"? As mentioned above, the reason is that although free trade benefits the economy as a whole, specific groups may not benefit. If groups who are hurt by trade have sufficient political influence, they may be able to persuade politicians to enact policies that restrict the free flow of goods and services across borders.

The supply and demand analyses shown in Figures 11.1 and 11.2 are useful in clarifying who gains and who loses when an economy opens up to trade. Look first at Figure 11.1, which shows the market for computers in Costa Rica. When Costa Rica opens its computer market to international competition, Costa Rican consumers enjoy a larger quantity of computers at a lower price. Clearly, Costa Rican computer users benefit from the free trade in computers. In general, *domestic consumers of imported goods benefit from free trade.* However, Costa Rican computer producers will not be so happy about opening their market to international competition. The fall in computer prices to the international level implies that less efficient domestic producers will go out of business, and that those who remain will earn lower profits. Unemployment in the Costa Rican computer industry will rise and may persist over time, particularly if displaced computer workers cannot easily move to a new industry.[1] We see that, in general, *domestic producers of imported goods are hurt by free trade*.

Consumers are helped, and producers hurt, when imports increase. The opposite conclusions apply for an increase in exports (see Figure 11.2). In the example of Costa Rica, an opening of the coffee market raises the domestic price of coffee to the world price and creates the opportunity for Costa Rica to export coffee. Domestic producers of coffee benefit from the increased market (they can now sell coffee abroad as well as at home) and from the higher price of their product. In short, *domestic producers of exported goods benefit from free trade*. Costa Rican coffee drinkers will be less enthusiastic, however, since they now have to pay the higher world price of coffee, and can therefore consume less. *Thus domestic consumers of exported goods are hurt by free trade.*

Free trade is *efficient* in the sense that it increases the size of the pie available to the economy. Indeed, the efficiency of free trade is an application of the *equilibrium principle:* Markets in equilibrium leave no unexploited opportunities for individuals. Despite the efficiency of free trade, however, some groups may lose from trade, which generates political pressures to block or restrict trade. In the next section we will discuss the major types of policy used to restrict trade.

> *RECAP* ↑
>
> **A SUPPLY AND DEMAND PERSPECTIVE ON TRADE**
>
> - For a closed economy, the domestic supply and demand for a good or service determine the equilibrium price and quantity of that good or service.
> - In an open economy, the price of a good or service traded on international markets equals the world price. If the domestic quantity supplied at the world price exceeds the domestic quantity demanded, the difference will be exported to the world market. If the domestic quantity demanded at the world price exceeds the domestic quantity supplied, the difference will be imported.
> - Generally, if the price of a good or service in a closed economy is lower than the world price and the economy opens to trade, the country will become a net exporter of that good or service. If the closed-economy price is higher than the world price and the economy opens to trade, the country will tend to become a net importer of the good or service.
> - Consumers of imported goods and producers of exported goods benefit from trade, whereas consumers of exported goods and producers of imported goods are hurt by trade. If those groups that are hurt have sufficient political influence, they may persuade the government to enact barriers to trade.
>
> **TRADE WINNERS AND LOSERS**
>
> **Winners**
>
> - Consumers of imported goods
> - Producers of exported goods
>
> **Losers**
>
> - Consumers of exported goods
> - Producers of imported goods

[1] The wages paid to Costa Rican computer workers will also fall, reflecting the lower relative price of computers.

PROTECTIONIST POLICIES: TARIFFS AND QUOTAS

protectionism the view that free trade is injurious and should be restricted

tariff a tax imposed on an imported good

quota a legal limit on the quantity of a good that may be imported

The view that free trade is injurious and should be restricted is known as **protectionism**. Supporters of this view believe the government should attempt to "protect" domestic markets by raising legal barriers to imports. (Interestingly, protectionists rarely attempt to restrict exports, even though they hurt consumers of the exported good.) Two of the most common types of such barriers are tariffs and quotas. A **tariff** is a tax imposed on an imported good. A **quota** is a legal limit on the quantity of a good that may be imported.

Tariffs

The effects of tariffs and quotas can be explained using supply and demand diagrams. Suppose that Costa Rican computer makers, dismayed by the penetration of "their" market by imported computers, persuade their government to impose a tariff—that is, a tax—on every computer imported into the country. Computers produced in Costa Rica will be exempt from the tax. Figure 11.3 shows the likely effects of this tariff on the domestic Costa Rican computer market. The lower of the two horizontal lines in the figure indicates the world price of computers, not including the tariff. The higher of the two lines indicates the price Costa Rican consumers will actually pay for imported computers, including the tariff. We refer to the price of computers including the tariff as p_T. The vertical distance between the two lines equals the amount of the tariff that is imposed on each imported computer.

From the point of view of domestic Costa Rican producers and consumers, the imposition of the tariff has the same effects as an equivalent increase in the world price of computers. Because the price (including the tariff) of imported computers has risen, Costa Rican computer producers will be able to raise the price they charge for their computers to the world price plus tariff, p_T. Thus the price Costa Rican consumers must pay—whether their computers are imported or not—equals p_T, represented by the upper horizontal line in Figure 11.3.

The rise in the price of computers created by the tariff affects the quantities of computers supplied and the quantities demanded by Costa Ricans. Domestic computer producers, facing a higher price for computers, increase their production from q_S to q_S' (see Figure 11.3). Costa Rican consumers, also reacting to the higher price, reduce their computer purchases from q_D to q_D'. As a result, the number of imported computers—the difference between domestic purchases and domestic production—falls from $q_D - q_S$ to $q_D' - q_S'$.

FIGURE 11.3

The Market for Computers after the Imposition of an Import Tariff.

The imposition of a tariff on imported computers raises the price of computers in Costa Rica to the world price plus tariff, p_T, represented by the upper horizontal line. Domestic production of computers rises from q_S to q_S', domestic purchases of computers fall from q_D to q_D', and computer imports fall from $q_D - q_S$ to $q_D' - q_S'$. Costa Rican consumers are worse off and Costa Rican computer producers are better off. The Costa Rican government collects revenue from the tariff equal to the area of the pale blue rectangle.

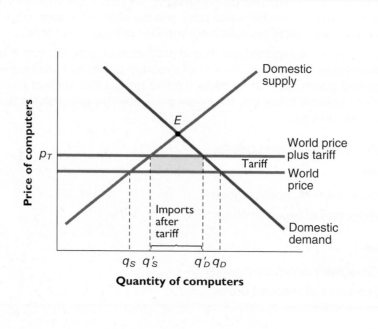

Who are the winners and the losers from the tariff, then? Relative to an environment with free trade and no tariff, the winners are the domestic computer producers, who sell more computers and receive a higher price for them. The clearest losers are Costa Rican consumers, who must now pay more for their computers. Another winner is the government, which collects revenue from the tariff. The blue area in Figure 11.3 shows the amount of revenue the government collects, equal to the quantity of computer imports after the imposition of the tariff, $q'_D - q'_S$, times the amount of the tariff.

EXAMPLE 11.3   A Tariff on Imported Computers

What are the effects of a tariff on trade?

Suppose that the Costa Rican market for computers is represented by Figure 11.4. Thus, if the Costa Rican economy is closed to trade, the equilibrium price for computers would be $2,000, and 2,000 computers would be bought and sold in the Costa Rican computer market every year (point *E*). Assuming that the world price of computers is $1,400, how would this market be affected by opening to trade, and how would it be affected by the imposition of a tariff of $400 per computer?

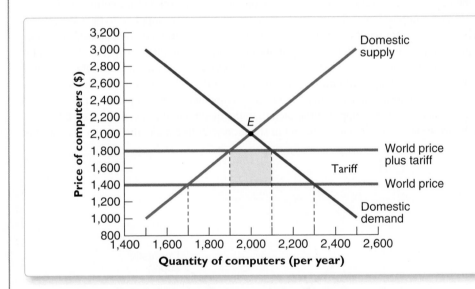

FIGURE 11.4

The Market for Computers in Costa Rica after the Imposition of an Import Tariff.

A tariff of $400 per computer raises the price of computers by $400 and reduces imports by 400 computers per year.

If the economy opens to trade, the domestic price of computers must equal the world price of $1,400. At this price, the domestic quantity demanded is 2,300 computers per year and the domestic quantity supplied is 1,700 computers per year. Imports equal the difference between the domestic quantities demanded and supplied, or 2,300 − 1,700 = 600 computers per year.

The imposition of a tariff of $400 per computer raises the price from $1,400 to $1,800. This price rise causes Costa Rican computer producers to increase their production from 1,700 to 1,900 computers per year, and it causes Costa Rican consumers to reduce their computer purchases from 2,300 to 2,100. As a result, the number of imported computers—the difference between domestic purchases and domestic production—falls from 600 to 200 (2,100 − 1,900).

Thus the tariff has raised the price of computers by $400 and reduced imports by 400 computers per year. The tariff revenue collected by the government is $400 per imported computer times 200 computers per year = $80,000 per year.

Quotas

An alternative to a tariff is a quota, or legal limit, on the number or value of foreign goods that can be imported. One means of enforcing a quota is to require importers to obtain a license or permit for each good they bring into the country. The government then distributes exactly the same number of permits as the number of goods that may be imported under the quota.

How does the imposition of a quota on, say, computers affect the domestic market for computers? Figure 11.5, which is similar to Figure 11.3, illustrates the effect of a quota on imported computers. As before, assume that at first there are no restrictions on trade. Consumers pay the world price for computers, and $q_D - q_S$ computers are imported. Now suppose once more that domestic computer producers complain to the government about competition from foreign computer makers, and the government agrees to act. However, this time, instead of a tariff, the government imposes a quota on the number of computers that can be imported. For comparability with the tariff analyzed in Figure 11.3, let's assume that the quota permits the same level of imports as entered the country under the tariff: specifically, $q_D' - q_S'$ computers. What effect does this ruling have on the domestic market for computers?

After the imposition of the quota, the quantity of computers supplied to the Costa Rican market is the production of domestic firms plus the $q_D' - q_S'$ imported computers allowed under the quota. Figure 11.5 shows the quantity of computers supplied inclusive of the quota. The total supply curve, labeled "Domestic supply plus quota," is the same as the domestic supply curve shifted $q_D' - q_S'$ units to the right. The domestic demand curve is the same as in Figure 11.3. Equilibrium in the domestic market for computers occurs at point F in Figure 11.5, at the intersection of the supply curve including the quota and the domestic demand curve. The figure shows that, relative to the initial situation with free trade, the quota (1) raises the

FIGURE 11.5

The Market for Computers after the Imposition of an Import Quota.

The figure shows the effects of the imposition of a quota that permits only $q_D' - q_S'$ computers to be imported. The total supply of computers to the domestic economy equals the domestic supply curve shifted to the right by $q_D' - q_S'$ units (the fixed amount of imports). Market equilibrium occurs at point F. The effects of the quota on the domestic market are identical to those of the tariff analyzed in Figure 11.3. The domestic price rises to p_T, domestic production of computers rises from q_S to q_S', domestic purchases of computers fall from q_D to q_D', and computer imports fall from $q_D - q_S$ to $q_D' - q_S'$. The quota differs from the tariff in that under a quota system the government collects no revenue.

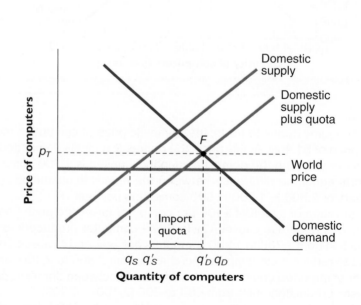

domestic price of computers above the world price, to the level marked p_T in Figure 11.5; (2) reduces domestic purchases of computers from q_D to q_D'; (3) increases domestic production of computers from q_S to q_S'; and (4) reduces imports to $q_D' - q_S'$, consistent with a quota. Like a tariff, the quota helps domestic producers by increasing their sales and the price they receive for their output, while hurting domestic consumers by forcing them to pay a higher price.

Interestingly, under our assumption that the quota is set to permit the same level of imports as the tariff, the effects on the domestic market of the tariff (Figure 11.3) and the quota (Figure 11.5) are not only similar: they are *equivalent.* Comparing Figures 11.3 and 11.5, you can see that the two policies have identical effects on the domestic price, domestic purchases, domestic production, and imports.

Although the market effects of a tariff and a quota are the same, there is one important difference between the two policies, which is that a tariff generates revenue for the government, whereas a quota does not. With a quota, the revenue that would have gone to the government goes instead to those firms that hold the import licenses. A holder of an import license can purchase a computer at the world price and resell it in the domestic market at price p_T, pocketing the difference. Thus with a tariff the government collects the difference between the world price and the domestic market price of the good; with a quota, private firms or individuals collect that difference. Why then would the government ever impose a quota rather than a tariff? One possibility is that the distribution of import licenses is a means of rewarding the government's political supporters. Sometimes, international political concerns may also play a role (see Economic Naturalist 11.1 for a possible example).

EXAMPLE 11.4   Effects of an Import Quota

What are the effects of an import quota on trade?

Suppose the supply of and demand for computers in Costa Rica, as well as the world price of computers, are as given in Figure 11.6, which is similar to Figure 11.4 from Example 11.3. Suppose that the government imposes a quota of 200 on the number of computers that can be imported. What effect would this have on the domestic market for computers (relative to the free-trade alternative)?

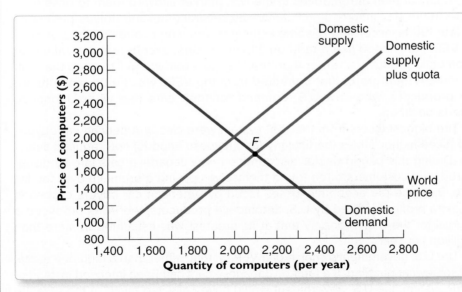

FIGURE 11.6

The Market for Computers in Costa Rica after the Imposition of an Import Quota

A quota of 200 computers per year raises the price of computers by $400 and reduces imports by 400 computers per year.

After the quota is imposed, the equilibrium in the domestic market occurs at point *F* in the figure. As the figure shows, relative to free trade, the domestic price increases to $1,800 per computer, domestic purchases of computers decrease to 2,100, domestic production of computers increases to 1,900, and imports decrease to 200 (the difference between the 2,100 computers demanded and the 1,900 computers domestically produced).

Note that the domestic price, domestic production, and domestic demand are the same in Examples 11.3 and 11.4. Thus, under the assumptions we made, the tariff and the quota have the same effects on the domestic market for computers. The only difference between the two policies is that with a quota, the government does not get the tariff revenue it got in Example 11.3. That revenue goes instead to the holders of import licenses, who can buy computers on the world market at $1,400 and sell them in the domestic market at $1,800.

The Economic Naturalist 11.1

Who benefited from and who was hurt by voluntary export restraints on Japanese automobiles in the 1980s?

After the oil price increases of the 1970s, American consumers began to buy small, fuel-efficient Japanese automobiles in large numbers. Reeling from the new foreign competition, U.S. automobile producers petitioned the U.S. government for assistance. In response, in May 1981 the U.S. government negotiated a system of so-called *voluntary export restraints,* or VERs, with Japan. Under the VER system, each Japanese auto producer would "voluntarily" restrict exports to the United States to an agreed-upon level. VER quotas were changed several times before the system was formally eliminated in 1994. Who benefited from, and who was hurt by, VERs on Japanese automobiles?

Several groups benefited from the VER system. As should be expected, U.S. auto producers saw increased sales and profits when their Japanese competition was reduced. But Japanese automobile producers also profited from the policy, despite the reduction in their U.S. sales. The restrictions on the supply of their automobiles to the U.S. market allowed them to raise their prices in the U.S. market significantly—by several thousand dollars per car by the late 1980s, according to some estimates. From an economic point of view, the VERs functioned like a tariff on Japanese cars, except that the Japanese automobile producers, rather than the U.S. government, got to keep the tariff revenue. A third group that benefited from the VERs was European automobile producers, who saw U.S. demand for their cars rise when Japanese imports declined.

The biggest losers from the VER system were clearly American car buyers, who faced higher prices (particularly for Japanese imports) and reduced selection. During this period dealer discounts on new Japanese cars largely disappeared, and customers often found themselves paying a premium over the list price. Because the economic losses faced by American car buyers exceeded the extra profits received by U.S. automobile producers, the VERs produced a net loss for the U.S. economy that at its greatest was estimated at more than $3 billion per year.

The U.S. government's choice of a VER system, rather than a tariff or a quota, was somewhat puzzling. If a tariff on Japanese cars had been imposed instead of a VER system, the U.S. government would have collected much of the revenue that went instead to Japanese auto producers. Alternatively, a quota system with import licenses given to U.S. car dealers would have captured some revenue for domestic car dealers rather than Japanese firms. The best explanation for why the U.S. government chose VERs is probably political. U.S. policymakers may have been concerned that the Japanese government would retaliate against U.S. trade restrictions by imposing its own restrictions on U.S. exports. By instituting a system

Who benefited from "voluntary" export restraints on Japanese cars?

that did minimal financial harm to—or even helped—Japanese auto producers, they may have hoped to avoid retaliation from the Japanese.[2]

Tariffs and quotas are not the only barriers to trade that governments erect. Importers may be subject to unnecessarily complex bureaucratic rules (so-called red tape barriers), and regulations of goods that are nominally intended to promote health and safety sometimes have the side effect, whether intentionally or unintentionally, of restricting trade. One example is European restrictions on imports of genetically modified foods. Although these regulations were motivated in part by concerns about the safety of such foods, they also help to protect Europe's politically powerful farmers from foreign competition.

The Inefficiency of Protectionism

Free trade is efficient because it allows countries to specialize in the production of goods and services in which they have the greatest comparative advantage. Conversely, protectionist policies that limit trade are inefficient—they reduce the total economic pie. Why, then, do governments adopt such policies? The reason is that tariffs and quotas benefit certain groups. Because those who benefit from these restrictions (such as firms facing import competition) are often better organized politically than those who lose from trade barriers (such as consumers in general), lawmakers are sometimes persuaded to enact the restrictions.

The fact that free trade is efficient suggests an alternative to trade restrictions, however. Because eliminating restrictions on trade increases the overall economic pie, in general the winners from free trade will be able to compensate the losers in such a way that everyone becomes better off. Government programs that assist and retrain workers displaced by import competition are an example of such compensation. Developing and improving such programs, and making them widely available, could help those who lose from trade. Spreading the benefits of free trade—or at least reducing its adverse effects on certain groups—reduces the incentives of those groups to inhibit free trade.

Although we have focused on the winners and losers from trade, not all opposition to free trade is motivated by economic interest. For example, many who oppose further opening to trade cite environmental concerns. Protecting the environment is an important and laudable goal, but restricting trade may not be the most effective means of achieving that goal. Restricting trade lowers world income, reducing the resources available to deal with environmental problems. (High levels of economic development are in fact associated with lower, not higher, amounts of pollution.) Furthermore, much of the income loss arising from barriers to trade is absorbed by poor nations trying to develop their economies. For this reason, leaders of developing countries are among the strongest advocates of free trade.

The Economic Naturalist 11.2

What is fast track authority?

In practice, trade agreements among countries are very complex. For example, agreements usually spell out in great detail the goods and services for which tariffs are being reduced or quotas are being expanded. Trade negotiators must also take into account barriers to trade other than explicit tariffs or quotas, such as rules that require a country's government to buy only from domestic suppliers. Because trade negotiations can be so complex, having each country's legislature vote on each item in a proposed trade agreement is not practical.

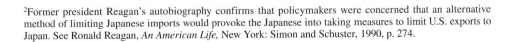

[2]Former president Reagan's autobiography confirms that policymakers were concerned that an alternative method of limiting Japanese imports would provoke the Japanese into taking measures to limit U.S. exports to Japan. See Ronald Reagan, *An American Life*, New York: Simon and Schuster, 1990, p. 274.

5. The demand and supply for automobiles in a certain country is given in the graph below. *(LO2, LO3)*

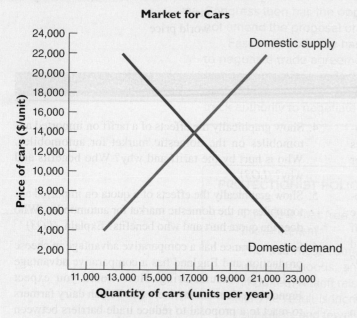

Market for Cars

a. Assuming that the economy is closed, find the equilibrium price and production of automobiles.

b. The economy opens to trade. The world price of automobiles is $8,000. Find the domestic quantities demanded and supplied and the quantity of imports or exports. Who will favor the opening of the automobile market to trade, and who will oppose it?

c. The government imposes a tariff of $2,000 per car. Find the effects on domestic quantities demanded and supplied.

d. As a result of the tariff, what will happen to the quantity of imports or exports, and what is the revenue raised by the tariff. Who will favor the imposition of the tariff, and who will oppose it?

6. Suppose the domestic demand and supply for automobiles is as given in Problem 5. *(LO2, LO3)*

a. The economy opens to trade. The world price of automobiles is $10,000. Find the domestic quantities demanded and supplied and the quantity of imports or exports.

b. Now assume that the government imposes a quota on automobile imports of 2,000 cars. What will happen to the quantity of imports or exports?

c. Who will favor the imposition of the quota, and who will oppose it?

7. You are the president of Islandia, a small island nation that enjoys a comparative advantage in tourism. Trade representatives from the United States, which enjoys a comparative advantage in manufactured goods, have proposed a free trade agreement between the two countries. Manufacturing workers have opposed the agreement, arguing that Islandia should maintain its steep tariff on American manufactured goods. In an election, the union representing these workers has more than enough votes to prevail over the union representing tourism workers. If you are determined to keep your job, how should you respond to the American proposal? *(LO3)*

ANSWERS TO CONCEPT CHECKS

11.1

	Productivity in programming	Productivity in bicycle repair
Pat	2 web page updates per hour	1 repair per hour
Meg	3 web page updates per hour	3 repairs per hour

The entries in the table tell us that Meg has an absolute advantage over Pat in both activities. While Meg, the mechanic, can update 3 web pages per hour, Pat, the programmer, can update only 2. Meg's absolute advantage over Pat is even greater in the task of fixing bikes—3 repairs per hour versus Pat's 1.

But as in the second example in this chapter, the fact that Meg is a better programmer than Pat does not imply that Meg should update her own web page. Meg's opportunity cost of updating a web page is 1 bicycle repair, whereas Pat must give up only half a repair to update a web page. Pat has a comparative advantage

over Meg at programming and Meg has a comparative advantage over Pat at bicycle repair. *(LO1)*

11.2 If the world price of computers is $1,200, domestic demand for computers is 2,400 computers. Domestic supply is 1,600 computers. The difference between the quantity demanded and the quantity supplied, 800 computers, is imported.

A tariff of $400 raises the domestic price of computers to $1,600. Now domestic demand is 2,200 and domestic supply is 1,800. The difference, 400 computers, equals imports. Revenue for the government is ($400/computer) (400 imported computers) = $160,000.

If the world price of computers is $1,800 and there is no tariff, domestic demand is 2,100; domestic supply is 1,900; and imports are 200. A tariff of $400 raises the world price to $2,200, which is greater than the domestic price when there is no trade ($2,000). No computers are imported in this case and no tariff revenue is raised. *(LO3)*

GLOSSARY

A

Absolute advantage. One person has an absolute advantage over another if he or she takes fewer hours to perform a task than the other person.

Accounting profit. The difference between a firm's total revenue and its explicit costs.

Allocative function of price. Changes in prices direct resources away from overcrowded markets and toward markets that are underserved.

American Recovery and Reinvestment Act. A combination of increased government spending and tax cuts in hopes of shortening the Great Recession.

Animal spirits. Emotions that shift supply and demand curves in ways that cause prices to depart from levels expected to prevail in the long run.

Austerity. Any combination of government spending reductions and tax increases implemented with the intention of reducing government budget deficits.

Average benefit. The total benefit of undertaking n units of an activity divided by n.

Average cost. The total cost of undertaking n units of an activity divided by n.

Average fixed cost. A firm's fixed cost divided by its level of output.

Average total cost (*ATC*). Total cost divided by total output.

B

Barrier to entry. Any force that prevents firms from entering a new market.

Basic elements of a game. The players, the strategies available to each player, and the payoffs each player receives for each possible combination of strategies.

Buyer's reservation price. The largest dollar amount the buyer would be willing to pay for a good.

Buyer's surplus. The difference between the buyer's reservation price and the price he or she actually pays.

C

Cartel. A coalition of firms that agree to restrict output for the purpose of earning an economic profit.

Cash on the table. Economic metaphor for unexploited gains from exchange.

Change in demand. A shift of the entire demand curve.

Change in the quantity demanded. A movement along the demand curve that occurs in response to a change in price.

Change in the quantity supplied. A movement along the supply curve that occurs in response to a change in price.

Change in supply. A shift of the entire supply curve.

Classical macroeconomic theorists. Early economic theorists who believed that economic downturns would generally reverse themselves quickly without policy intervention.

Closed economy. An economy that does not trade with the rest of the world.

Coase theorem. If at no cost people can negotiate the purchase and sale of the right to perform activities that cause externalities, they can always arrive at efficient solutions to the problems caused by externalities.

Commitment device. A way of changing incentives so as to make otherwise empty threats or promises credible.

Commitment problem. A situation in which people cannot achieve their goals because of an inability to make credible threats or promises.

Comparative advantage. One person has a comparative advantage over another if his or her opportunity cost of performing a task is lower than the other person's opportunity cost.

Complements. Two goods are complements in consumption if an increase in the price of one causes a leftward shift in the demand curve for the other (or if a decrease causes a rightward shift).

Constant (or **parameter**). A quantity that is fixed in value.

Constant returns to scale. A production process is said to have constant returns to scale if, when all inputs are changed by a given proportion, output changes by the same proportion.

Credible promise. A promise to take an action that is in the promiser's interest to keep.

Credible threat. A threat to take an action that is in the threatener's interest to carry out.

Cross-price elasticity of demand. The percentage by which quantity demanded of the first good changes in response to a 1 percent change in the price of the second.

D

Decision tree (or **game tree**). A diagram that describes the possible moves in a game in sequence and lists the payoffs that correspond to each possible combination of moves.

Demand curve. A schedule or graph showing the quantity of a good that buyers wish to buy at each price.

Dependent variable. A variable in an equation whose value is determined by the value taken by another variable in the equation.

Dominant strategy. One that yields a higher payoff no matter what the other players in a game choose.

Dominated strategy. Any other strategy available to a player who has a dominant strategy.

E

Earned-income tax credit (EITC). A policy under which low-income workers receive credits on their federal income tax.

Economic efficiency. *See* **Efficiency**.

Economic loss. An economic profit that is less than zero.

Economic profit (or **excess profit**). The difference between a firm's total revenue and the sum of its explicit and implicit costs.

Economic rent. That part of the payment for a factor of production that exceeds the owner's reservation price, the price below which the owner would not supply the factor.

Economic stimulus. Increased government spending or interest rate reductions undertaken to stimulate spending during economic downturns.

Economic surplus. The economic surplus from taking any action is the benefit of taking the action minus its cost.

Economics. The study of how people make choices under conditions of scarcity and of the results of those choices for society.

Economies of scale. *See* **Increasing Returns to Scale**.

Efficiency (or **economic efficiency**). Condition that occurs when all goods and services are produced and consumed at their respective socially optimal levels.

Efficient (or **Pareto efficient**). A situation is efficient if no change is possible that will help some people without harming others.

Elastic. The demand for a good is elastic with respect to price if its price elasticity of demand is greater than 1.

Equation. A mathematical expression that describes the relationship between two or more variables.

Equilibrium. A balanced or unchanging situation in which all forces at work within a system are canceled by others.

Equilibrium price and **equilibrium quantity.** The price and quantity of a good at the intersection of the supply and demand curves for the good.

Excess demand (or **shortage**). The amount by which quantity demanded exceeds quantity supplied when the price of the good lies below the equilibrium price.

Excess supply (or **surplus**). The amount by which quantity supplied exceeds quantity demanded when the price of the good exceeds the equilibrium price.

Explicit costs. The actual payments a firm makes to its factors of production and other suppliers.

External benefit (or **positive externality**). A benefit of an activity received by people other than those who pursue the activity.

External cost (or **negative externality**). A cost of an activity that falls on people other than those who pursue the activity.

Externality. An external cost or benefit of an activity.

F

Factor of production. An input used in the production of a good or service.

Financial crisis. A sharp decline in the prices of financial or other assets that forces borrowers to offer additional assets for sale, further depressing prices.

First-dollar insurance coverage. Insurance that pays all expenses generated by the insured activity.

Fixed cost. The sum of all payments made to the firm's fixed factors of production.

Fixed factor of production. An input whose quantity cannot be altered in the short run.

G

Game tree. *See* **Decision tree.**

H

Health maintenance organization (HMO). A group of physicians that provides health services to individuals and families for a fixed annual fee.

Hurdle method of price discrimination. The practice by which a seller offers a discount to all buyers who overcome some obstacle.

I

Imperfectly competitive firm (or **price setter**). A firm that has at least some control over the market price of its product.

Implicit costs. The opportunity costs of the resources supplied by the firm's owners.

In-kind transfer. A payment made not in the form of cash, but in the form of a good or service.

Income effect. The change in the quantity demanded of a good that results because a change in the price of a good changes the buyer's purchasing power.

Income elasticity of demand. The percentage by which a good's quantity demanded changes in response to a 1 percent change in income.

Increasing returns to scale (or **economies of scale**). A production process is said to have increasing returns to scale if, when all inputs are changed by a given proportion, output changes by more than that proportion.

Independent variable. A variable in an equation whose value determines the value taken by another variable in the equation.

Inelastic. The demand for a good is inelastic with respect to price if its price elasticity of demand is less than 1.

Inferior good. A good whose demand curve shifts leftward when the incomes of buyers increase and rightward when the incomes of buyers decrease.

Invisible hand theory. Adam Smith's theory that the actions of independent, self-interested buyers and sellers will often result in the most efficient allocation of resources.

L

Law of diminishing returns. A property of the relationship between the amount of a good or service produced and the amount of a variable factor required to produce it. The law says that when some factors of production are fixed, increased production of the good eventually requires ever larger increases in the variable factor.

Long run. A period of time of sufficient length that all the firm's factors of production are variable.

M

Macroeconomics. The study of the performance of national economies and the policies that governments use to try to improve that performance.

Marginal benefit. The increase in total benefit that results from carrying out one additional unit of the activity.

Marginal cost. The increase in total cost that results from carrying out one additional unit of the activity.

Marginal revenue. The change in a firm's total revenue that results from a one-unit change in output.

Market. The market for any good consists of all buyers or sellers of that good.

Market equilibrium. Occurs in a market when all buyers and sellers are satisfied with their respective quantities at the market price.

Market power. A firm's ability to raise the price of a good without losing all its sales.

Means-tested. A benefit program whose benefit level declines as the recipient earns additional income.

Microeconomics. The study of individual choice under scarcity and its implications for the behavior of prices and quantities in individual markets.

Monopolistic competition. An industry structure in which a large number of firms produce slightly differentiated products that are reasonably close substitutes for one another.

N

Nash equilibrium. Any combination of strategy choices in which each player's choice is his or her best choice, given the other players' choices.

Negative externality. *See* **External cost.**

Negative income tax (NIT). A system under which the government would grant every citizen a cash payment each year, financed by an additional tax on earned income.

Nominal price. The absolute price of a good in dollar terms.

Normal good. A good whose demand curve shifts rightward when the incomes of buyers increase and leftward when the incomes of buyers decrease.

Normal profit. The opportunity cost of the resources supplied by the firm's owners; Normal profit = Accounting profit − Economic profit.

Normative economic principle. One that says how people should behave.

O

Oligopoly. An industry structure in which a small number of large firms produce products that are either close or perfect substitutes.

Open economy. An economy that trades with other countries.

Opportunity cost. The opportunity cost of an activity is the value of what must be forgone to undertake the activity.

P

Payoff matrix. A table that describes the payoffs in a game for each possible combination of strategies.

Perfect hurdle. A threshold that completely segregates buyers whose reservation prices lie above it from others whose reservation prices lie below it, imposing no cost on those who jump the hurdle.

Perfectly competitive market. A market in which no individual supplier has significant influence on the market price of the product.

Perfectly discriminating monopolist. A firm that charges each buyer exactly his or her reservation price.

Perfectly elastic demand. The demand for a good is perfectly elastic with respect to price if its price elasticity of demand is infinite.

Perfectly elastic supply. Supply is perfectly elastic with respect to price if elasticity of supply is infinite.

Perfectly inelastic demand. The demand for a good is perfectly inelastic with respect to price if its price elasticity of demand is zero.

Perfectly inelastic supply. Supply is perfectly inelastic with respect to price if elasticity is zero.

Personal Responsibility Act. The 1996 federal law that transferred responsibility for welfare programs from the federal level to the state level and placed a five-year lifetime limit on payment of AFDC benefits to any given recipient.

Positional arms control agreement. An agreement in which contestants attempt to limit mutually offsetting investments in performance enhancement.

Positional arms race. A series of mutually offsetting investments in performance enhancement that is stimulated by a positional externality.

Positional externality. Occurs when an increase in one person's performance reduces the expected reward of another's in situations in which reward depends on relative performance.

Positive economic principle. One that predicts how people will behave.

Positive externality. *See* **External benefit.**

Poverty threshold. The level of income below which the federal government classifies a family as poor.

Price ceiling. A maximum allowable price, specified by law.

Price discrimination. The practice of charging different buyers different prices for essentially the same good or service.

Price elasticity of demand. The percentage change in the quantity demanded of a good or service that results from a 1 percent change in its price.

Price elasticity of supply. The percentage change in the quantity supplied that occurs in response to a 1 percent change in the price of a good or service.

Price setter. *See* **Imperfectly competitive firm.**

Price taker. A firm that has no influence over the price at which it sells its product.

Prisoner's dilemma. A game in which each player has a dominant strategy, and when each plays it, the resulting payoffs are smaller than if each had played a dominated strategy.

Profit. The total revenue a firm receives from the sale of its product minus all costs—explicit and implicit—incurred in producing it.

Profit-maximizing firm. A firm whose primary goal is to maximize the difference between its total revenues and total costs.

Protectionism. The view that free trade is injurious and should be restricted.

Pure monopoly. The only supplier of a unique product with no close substitutes.

Q

Quota. A legal limit on the quantity of a good that may be imported.

R

Rational person. Someone with well-defined goals who tries to fulfill those goals as best he or she can.

Rationing function of price. Changes in prices distribute scarce goods to those consumers who value them most highly.

Real price. The dollar price of a good relative to the average dollar price of all other goods and services.

Repeated prisoner's dilemma. A standard prisoner's dilemma that confronts the same players repeatedly.

Run. *See* **Slope.**

S

Says Law. The claim, attributed to the French classical macro-economist Jean Baptiste Say, that any aggregate value of a good produced necessarily creates an equal value of aggregate demand for those goods.

Seller's reservation price. The smallest dollar amount for which a seller would be willing to sell an additional unit, generally equal to marginal cost.

Seller's surplus. The difference between the price received by the seller and his or her reservation price.

Short run. A period of time sufficiently short that at least some of the firm's factors of production are fixed.

Shortage. *See* **Excess demand.**

Slope. In a straight line, the ratio of the vertical distance the straight line travels between any two points *(rise)* to the corresponding horizontal distance *(run)*.

Socially optimal quantity. The quantity of a good that results in the maximum possible economic surplus from producing and consuming the good.

Speculative bubble. Rapid growth in asset prices, usually caused by unrealistic expectations of further price growth.

Sticky downturns. The tendency of prices and wages to resist downward movements.

Substitutes. Two goods are substitutes in consumption if an increase in the price of one causes a rightward shift in the demand curve for the other (or if a decrease causes a leftward shift).

Substitution effect. The change in the quantity demanded of a good that results because buyers switch to or from substitutes when the price of the good changes.

Sunk cost. A cost that is beyond recovery at the moment a decision must be made.

Supply curve. A graph or schedule showing the quantity of a good that sellers wish to sell at each price.

Surplus. *See* **Excess supply.**

T

Tariff. A tax imposed on an imported good.

Tit-for-tat. A strategy for the repeated prisoner's dilemma in which players cooperate on the first move and then mimic their partner's last move on each successive move.

Total cost. The sum of all payments made to the firm's fixed and variable factors of production.

Total expenditure = Total revenue. The dollar amount consumers spend on a product ($P \times Q$) is equal to the dollar amount that sellers receive.

Total revenue. *See* **Total expenditure.**

Total surplus. The difference between the buyer's reservation price and the seller's reservation price.

Tragedy of the commons. The tendency for a resource that has no price to be used until its marginal benefit falls to zero.

Troubled Asset Relief Program (TARP). U.S. government purchase of assets and equity from financial institutions to strengthen its financial sector and to prevent large financial institutions from collapse.

U

Unit elastic. The demand for a good is unit elastic with respect to price if its price elasticity of demand is equal to 1.

V

Variable. A quantity that is free to take a range of different values.

Variable cost. The sum of all payments made to the firm's variable factors of production.

Variable factor of production. An input whose quantity can be altered in the short run.

Vertical intercept. In a straight line, the value taken by the dependent variable when the independent variable equals zero.

W

World price. The price at which a good or service is traded on international markets.

INDEX

Page numbers followed by n indicate material found in notes.

Market power
  defined, 157
  economies of scale, 157
  government licenses/franchises, 157
  network economies, 158
  patents and copyrights, 157
  sources of control over inputs, 157
Market supply curve, 103–105
Marshall, Alfred, 32–33
Mathematical models, 142
Means-tested benefit programs, 243–244
Medicaid, 233
Medicare, 233
Miami Heat, 121
Microeconomics, defined, 12
Microsoft Corporation, 106, 137, 138, 158
Microsoft Windows, 137
Midpoint formula, 90
Military-arms-control agreements, 198, 199
Minimum wage, 244–245
  effect on economic surplus, 244
Monopolist, 155
  demand curve, 163–164
  economic profit, 166–167
  marginal cost curve, 164, 165
  marginal revenue for, 162–164
  output level, 165–166
  perfectly discriminating, 172
  price discrimination by, 168–176
  profit maximization, 162–167
  profit-maximizing decision rule, 165–166
  socially inefficient, 167–168
  using discounts to expand market, 168–176
Monopolistic competition, 154–155
  when location matters, 196–198
Monopoly, 155
  antitrust laws and, 168
  breakdown of invisible hand, 167–168
  natural, 157
  pure, 154
Morton salt, 85
Movie industry, 176
Multinational environmental pollution, 222

N

Nash, John, 183
Nash equilibrium, 183–185
National Aeronautics and Space Administration
    (NASA), 9–10
National Basketball Association, 121, 225
National Football League, 223–224, 225
Natural monopoly, 157
Naval blockade, 249
Needs, 77
Negative externalities, 208
  optimal amount, 215
  taxes on, 216
Negative income tax, 244
Nerd norm, 225–226
Network economies, 158
New Deal, 67–68
New York City
  food supply, 29–30
  rental housing, 30
  rent control, 31, 32, 39–41
New York Times, 118

Nintendo, 159–162
Noise ordinances, 213
Nominal price, 79
Normal goods, 45–46
Normal profit, 131
  earnings less than, 134
  earnings more than, 135
Normative economic principle, 12
Norms, social, as positional arms control
    agreements, 225–227
Norms against vanity, 226–227
Norms of taste, 226
North Korea, 31

O

Obama, Barack, 236, 237
Oil supertankers, 140–141
Oligopolist, 155
Oligopoly, 155
  cartel agreements, 187–190
Omerta, 198
Open economy, 254
Opportunity cost
  comparative advantage and, 250–252
  defined, 4
  economic profit and, 136
  profit maximization and, 170–171
  of pursuing an occupation, 101
  supply curve and, 46–49
  theory of supply and, 102–103
Organization of Petroleum Exporting Countries
    (OPEC), 120, 190
Output
  chosen to maximize profit, 107–110
  effect of price discrimination, 170–172
  GDP as measure of, 228–299
  monopolist's decision rule, 165–166
  socially inefficient, 167–168

P

Parameter, 19
Pareto, Vilfredo, 143
Pareto efficiency, 143
Patents, 157, 168
Payoff matrix, 184
  for cartel agreements, 189
  defined, 182–183
  for prisoner's dilemma, 186–187
  for steroid consumption, 224
Payoffs depending on relative performance,
    223–224
Peer influence, demand and, 76–77
Pentagon attack, 120
Perfect hurdle, 173–174
Perfectly competitive firms, 140
  compared to imperfectly competitive
    firms, 156
  demand curves, 106, 156
  marginal benefit exceeds marginal cost, 110
  monopolist decision rule and, 165–166
  price equals marginal cost, 110–111
  prices, 106–107
  price takers, 105
  profit maximization, 105–106
  profit-maximizing output, 107–110

seller's supply role, 114–115
seller's supply rule, 110–111
short-run production, 106–107
shutdown decision, 111
supply curve, 113
Perfectly competitive markets, 105–106
Perfectly discriminating monopolist, 172
Perfectly elastic demand, 91
Perfectly elastic supply, 117
Perfectly inelastic demand, 91
Perfectly inelastic supply, 116
Personal Responsibility Act of 1996, 243
Pharmaceutical companies, 157
Philip Morris, 191–192
Picasso, Pablo, 32
Pigou, A. C., 216
Policy responses. *See* Government policies
Pollock, Jackson, 32
Pollution
  auctioning pollution permits, 240–241
  climate change and carbon tax, 241–242
  limiting discharge of, 214
  market equilibrium and, 54
  multinational, 222
  socially optimal level, 215
  taxes on, 238–240
  toxic waste, 209–212
Pollution permits, 240–241
Positional arms control agreements
  examples, 225–227
  as social norms, 225–227
Positional arms race, 224–225
Positional externalities
  arms control agreements, 225–227
  arms races, 224–225
  defined, 224
  payoffs depending on performance, 223–224
Positive economic principle, 12
Positive externalities, 208
  subsidized by government, 216–217
Poverty, rent control and, 40
Poverty threshold, 244
Preferences
  origin of, 76
  selfishness and, 201–202
  shifts in demand curve, 46
  as solution to commitment problem,
    201–202
  strategic role of, 200–202
Price(s). *See also* Equilibrium price
  above or below equilibrium, 145
  allocative function, 134
  buyer's reservation price, 33–34
  classical macroeconomic theory, 64
  confusion over determinants of, 34–35
  demand curve and, 33–34
  equal to marginal cost, 110–111
  input prices, 114
  in invisible hand theory, 134–137
  maximizing profit and change in, 108–109
  in perfectly competitive firms, 106–107
  rationing function, 134
  real vs. nominal, 79
  socially optimal, 52
  supply curve and, 34–35
  value to user and, 32
  wages and, 101